The Paradox of Democracy
in Latin America

The Paradox of Democracy in Latin America

Ten Country Studies of Division and Resilience

written and edited by

Katherine Isbester

with contributions from

Viviana Patroni, Lauren Phillips,
Roberta Rice, and Judith Teichman

UTP

University of Toronto Press

Library and Archives Canada Cataloguing in Publication

Isbester, Katherine, 1962–
    The paradox of democracy in Latin America : ten country studies of division and resilience / written and edited by Katherine Isbester ; with contributions from Viviana Patroni ... [et al.].

Includes bibliographical references and index.
Also issued in electronic formats.
ISBN 978-1-4426-0196-3 (bound).—ISBN 978-1-4426-0180-2 (pbk.)

    1. Democracy—Latin America.   2. Democracy—Latin America—Case studies.   3. Latin America—Politics and government.   4. Latin America—Politics and government—Case studies.   I. Patroni, Viviana, 1957–   II. Title.

JL966.I83 2010   321.8098   C2010-906033-4

We welcome comments and suggestions regarding any aspect of our publications—please feel free to contact us at news@utphighereducation.com or visit our Internet site at www.utphighereducation.com.

North America   *UK, Ireland, and continental Europe*
5201 Dufferin Street   NBN International
North York, Ontario,   Estover Road, Plymouth,
Canada, M3H 5T8   PL6 7PY, UK
                                             ORDERS PHONE: 44 (0) 1752 202301
2250 Military Road   ORDERS FAX: 44 (0) 1752 202333
Tonawanda, New York,   ORDERS E-MAIL: enquiries@nbninternational.com
USA, 14150

ORDERS PHONE: 1-800-565-9523
ORDERS FAX: 1-800-221-9985
ORDERS E-MAIL: utpbooks@utpress.utoronto.ca

The University of Toronto Press acknowledges the financial support for its publishing activities of the Government of Canada through the Canada Book Fund.

Printed in Canada

Mixed Sources
Product group from well-managed forests, controlled sources and recycled wood or fiber
FSC   www.fsc.org Cert no. SW-COC-000952
© 1996 Forest Stewardship Council

For Kees 't Hooft, like so much else, with love

CONTENTS

LIST OF TABLES

PREFACE

Latin America stretches from the US border south to Tierra del Fuego, near the Antarctic Circle. This vast expanse of land has alpine, temperate, desert, tropical, and subarctic climates. Rich in natural resources, Latin America has the potential to be a wealthy region. For example, Brazil has the world's largest environmental capital, the grasslands of Argentina have the potential to feed at least South America if not more of the world, and Bolivia has half the world's supply of lithium, a chemical necessary to make batteries. The population of Latin America is approximately 500 million scattered through 21 countries, speaking as their first tongue Spanish, Portuguese, English, French, Dutch, and the pre-Conquest Amerindian languages.[1] Half the population is either Brazilian or Mexican, with the population of the region growing at 1.7 per cent. Racially, the population includes black, Amerindian, and white, with most people being a mixture of the three. Although Latin America struggled to establish democracy throughout the twentieth century, the entire region has democratized and clean elections are now regularly held. Literacy in Latin America is at 90 per cent. As infant and maternal mortality in the region has declined, life expectancy has risen to 71 years. In the five years before the global credit crunch, the region averaged an annual economic growth rate of 5 per cent and an annual increase per capita of 3 per cent (PAHO 2007; Brea 2003; ECLAC 2008).

And yet, prosperity seems to slip between its fingers. Most countries remain mired in underdevelopment; the region as a whole has 34 per cent of its inhabitants living in poverty, with an additional 13 per cent living in extreme poverty. While levels of poverty have slowly declined in the past few years, the absolute number living in poverty has increased. Economic growth remains stubbornly low, and social indices of development are even lower. Chile, the best performing nation in Latin America on the human development index (HDI), is approximately on par with Poland and Latvia, two nations only recently emerging from Soviet rule. Despite Brazil's global leadership position, it scored lower than Albania on the same index, while Mexico (a member of NAFTA and the OECD) scored below Cuba and only slightly above Libya[2] (ECLAC 2009; UNDP 2008).

This paradox of Latin America's continued struggle for prosperity despite generous resources, both natural and demographic, has moved thinkers over the years to seek solutions, generally economic. Throughout the twentieth century, Latin America has served as a global guinea pig for political economics, most recently with the world's strictest neoliberal restructuring. The failure of neoliberalism to produce the prosperity its proponents promised has reopened inquiry into the nature of the state and civil society within a democracy, and the relationship between these factors and economic development. Given the ascendancy of democracy as an answer to economic underdevelopment, political instability, and unfriendly foreign relations, it is imperative that we take a long hard look at it, without ideology or hopeful yearnings.

I began this book with considerable optimism about the future of Latin America. Democracy has become the only system of power in Latin America, a substantial and delightful change from the time when I was a student. When I was in Guatemala in 1984, as they mopped up a scorched earth campaign against the indigenous peoples, I would not have believed that a mere decade later the ruling government and the guerrilla movement would start negotiating sweeping peace accords. You'd have to be hardhearted not to be moved by the enormous transition underway.

But as my research into democracy grew, I became increasingly ambivalent about the quality of Latin American democracies. On the one hand, the democracy there now is infinitely preferable to the autocracies that preceded it. Human rights violations have diminished substantially. Innovative practices to strengthen democracy's hold are evident in many Latin American nations. There is increasing agreement that poverty, exclusion, and inequality must be addressed. Civil society is becoming more robust and organized. Elected governments are reforming their states to improve the caliber of state institutions and democratic governance. These reforms are reflected in the generally improving happiness of Latin American citizens (Latinobarómetro 2008). The volume and depth of the reforms demonstrate the resiliency of Latin American democracies.

Nonetheless, in many countries democracy is fragile and, in some, it is regressing. The weakness in Latin America's democracies lies in the region's profound divisions. Latin America has the highest division of wealth in the world, the lowest levels of interpersonal trust in the world, and the highest percentage of the population of indigenous peoples with the lowest levels of political representation in the world. These and other inequalities profoundly undermine the ability of the region's democracies to function as they should. Socioeconomic inequalities hollow out the content of democracy's institutions, moral code, and procedures. This process is augmented by the organization of power, that is, presidentialism, the codification of neoliberalism, and malapportioned legislatures, among other issues. Together, inequality and poorly structured relations of power have produced a weak state and a minimal (electoral) democracy in many Latin American countries.

Without economic and social equality, a densely organized civil society, and a strong autonomous state able to act with capacity, Latin America's democracies have been unable to overcome their problems. This stifles economic prosperity. As a result, the populace of Latin America are voting in the Pink Tide governments that struggle with reform while being prone to populism and authoritarianism.

Examining Latin America through the lens of democracy grants a broad perspective on the issues confronting the region today. The first chapter of this book analyzes democracy as a complex system for dispersing power through state and civil society institutions, as well as being a system with an ethical content. Democracy's relationship with the economy, the state, and civil society is examined, as is the impact of globalization on the region. Although the first chapter is relevant to any democratic nation, I have generally used Latin Americanists as theorists and examples from Latin America to highlight aspects of the argument. The second chapter posits Latin America's struggle for democracy within a historical context before addressing its transition to the neoliberal democratic state. It suggests that Latin America's political history shows repeated attempts to establish democracy, and these efforts failed due to a weak captured state, and unresolved socioeconomic inequalities. The third chapter looks at elements of the Latin American democratic system and issues within Latin American societies that affect democratic governance. These issues range from the organization of the state to the rise of ethnicity. These three chapters put Latin America into a broad context, and permit general understandings of the complex interplay between political structures, the economy, and civil society in Latin America.

The ten country studies that follow focus on each nation's development. These case studies are beneficial as both an introduction to each country and as specific examples of the stresses and challenges of Latin America's democratization. The book concludes with a chapter comparing the results of the country chapters and integrating data about economic and political development. The final chapter suggests that some nations' political economies work rather well, although with some widely recognized weaknesses. These nations are Chile, Costa Rica, and Uruguay. Other nations are attempting to reform their polity to achieve deeper democracies and more productive economies within a neoliberal political economy. These countries include the giants of Latin America: Mexico, Argentina, and Brazil, as well as many of the Pink Tide nations. The two nations of Venezuela and Bolivia have embraced alternative forms of governance based on a radical redistribution of power. In comparison, Central America (with the exception of Costa Rica) has quietly eroded core democratic processes, norms, and institutions. The success of all these attempts at reform, regardless of their depth, will depend substantially on how well Latin American nations ride out the global economic crisis. If reforms are maintained despite contracting economies, then Latin America's neoliberal democracies will have been profoundly altered with stronger states, greater social welfare, and improved trust in democracy.

The Internet is useful because it can easily provide recent data about climate, size of cities, volume of exports, and social indices like literacy and mortality. It is also useful for timelines of presidents, parties, and major events. While the bibliography at the end of every chapter shows key authors and resources, there is also a list of some of the major electronic resources. Frequently, these websites list more resources. It is assumed that those who are interested in acquiring more information about these topics will consult both published analyses and electronic data. Simultaneous to the easily accessible data that the Internet offers, there is the narrowing of access to sources of guaranteed, high-quality information. Library access, academic journals, and CD-ROMs have become prohibitively expensive or difficult to obtain. As an independent scholar, I am very grateful to the British Library for bucking the latter trend and allowing everyone in. I would also like to thank my little local library, Clapham Library in London, for assisting me in some of my odder requests. I am also grateful to those academics who upload their conference papers onto the Web, and international institutions and think tanks who make the results of their research easily available online.

I have been blessed with generous-spirited and capable friends who kindly read drafts of this book. I would like to thank them for their contributions: Jackie Isbester, Jordi Díez, Lisa Mills, Hwajeong Kim, Paul Tomlin, Sarah Nelson, Melissa MacLean, and the three anonymous reviewers of the manuscript. I am grateful to my two editors, Greg Yantz and Michael Harrison, who seem as excited about this book as I am. I especially enjoyed the collegial exchanges between the contributors to this book and myself, and I would like to thank them for ensuring that this book has been a pleasure to work on. Finally, I would like to thank my husband, Kees 't Hooft, for his unwavering support for this project. Of course any errors that remain are wholly my own.

NOTES

1 In this book I do not include the island nations of the Caribbean, the unique nation of Panama, the ex-Dutch colony of Suriname, the ex-British colonies of Belize and Guyana, and the French protectorate of French Guiana in my analysis of democracy.
2 NAFTA is the North American Free Trade Agreement signed between Canada, the US, and Mexico. OECD is the Organization of Economic Cooperation and Development, which is predominantly for first world nations. ECLAC is the Economic Commission on Latin America and the Caribbean. 2009. *Social Panorama 2008*. UNDP is the United Nations Development Program. 2008. *Human Development Report*.

REFERENCES

Brea, Jorge A. 2003. "Population Dynamics in Latin America." *Population Bulletin* 58(1). June 10, 2010. www.prb.org/Publications/PopulationBulletins/2003/PopulationDynamicsLatinAmericaPDF318K.aspx.

Economic Commission on Latin America and the Caribbean (ECLAC). 2008. *Preliminary Overview of the Economies of Latin America and the Caribbean 2008*. June 10, 2010. www.eclac.org/cgi-bin/getProd.asp?xml=/publicaciones/xml/4/34844/P34844.xml&xsl=/de/tpl-i/p9f.xsl&base=/tpl/top-bottom.xslt.

——. 2009. *Social Panorama 2008*. June 10, 2010. www.eclac.org/cgi-bin/getProd. asp?xml=/publicaciones/xml/3/34733/P34733.xml&xsl=/dds/tpl-i/p9f.xsl&base=/tpl-i/top-bottom.xsl.

Latinobarómetro. 2008. June 10, 2010. www.latinobarómetro.org/docs/INFORME_LATINOBAROMETRO_2008.pdf.

Pan American Health Organization (PAHO). 2007. June 10, 2010. *Health in the Americas: Regional Report*. www.pahp.org/hia/homeing.html.

United Nations Development Program. 2008. *Human Development Report 2008*. June 10, 2010. hdr.undp.org/en/media/HDR_20072008_EN_Complete.pdf.

ONE
Democracy: A Complex Balance

KATHERINE ISBESTER

DEFINING DEMOCRACY

Democracy has become the most widely used system of government in the world, with 64 per cent of the countries in the world having an electoral democracy. This was not the case a generation ago, when a larger proportion of the world's nations were mired in dictatorships or sham democracies. In 1976, when Freedom House did its first analysis of democracy and freedoms in the world, 65 countries (41 per cent) were not free, 53 (34 per cent) were partly free, and only 40 (25 per cent) were free. By 2006, the number of not free countries had dropped to 45 (23 per cent), with corresponding increases in the number of partly free, 58 (30 per cent), and free, 89 (47 per cent) (Freedom House 2007).[1]

In Latin America, the number of free countries and democracies has risen impressively. In 1976, 5 countries in Latin America were not free, 13 were partly free, and 11 were free. By 2006, there were only 2 not free countries, 9 partly free, and 24 free. Only Cuba remains a one-party dictatorship. Even so, the Cuban government claims that its government is democratic. The prevalence of democratic states and the evocation of democratic language even among dictatorships have caused some to claim that democracy is now a universal value embraced by everyone, everywhere. A global survey shows that over 80 per cent of the world's population agrees with the statement that "democracy may have its problems but it is better than any other form of government" (quoted in Diamond 2008, 33).

There are nonetheless different understandings about what constitutes a democracy. In fact, there are at least 550 different types of democracies

(Schedler 1998, 92). At its simplest, a democracy means the rule of the majority, as opposed to rule by an individual (monarchy) or group (aristocracy). The assumption underlying majority rule is that it is a superior method of ruling compared to individualized rule. This is because majority rule grants a degree of freedom from arbitrary or individualized rule, and instead offers a commonly created rule. However, majority rule is not necessarily beneficial to all people in a society. Majority rule can degenerate into mob rule, which persecutes a minority or only addresses short-term needs. In order to distinguish the rule of the majority from mob rule, democracy can be thought of as "rule by the people, for the people." In other words, majority rule should benefit all people.

Democracy today is complex. Defining democracy as a majority rule that benefits all people is too simplistic to be useful. Rather, democracy is best understood as a system that disperses power through its institutions and procedures so that the domination of one person, group, or interest can be kept to a minimum. Domination, an unethical form of power, can be political, economic, or social in nature. Power, or domination, cannot be extinguished. Therefore, power must be dispersed throughout the system so that it is not embodied in any one individual or institution. A democratic system includes incentives so that people will voluntarily and collectively participate in the polity in a thoughtful and deliberative manner (Shapiro 2003, 3–5). Because everyone participates in shaping the political regime and its institutions, no one is able to overly impose his or her power on another. This definition of democracy admits that people individually or in groups are not to be trusted; however, collectively, people can create rules, institutions, and values that benefit everyone.

Deeply embedded in any definition or form of democracy is a moral code. Democracy is a system with an ethical content. It is a moral call for freedom, equality, and justice. Statements about good and bad, along with right and wrong, weave their way through any discussion of democracy. For example, domination is an unethical form of power because it robs people of their freedom. There is little discussion about whether that is true or not, or whether people really need their freedom. Democracy's moral code tends to consist of strongly held beliefs regularly evoked but rarely debated.

The ethical content of democracy is hard to quantify, install through a program, or chart as it progresses. Citizens' demands and the resulting policies that a democracy produces can include conflicting ethical results. Consequently, it is difficult to analyze a given democracy's moral content. As a result, the moral element of democracy tends to be underappreciated by analysts. Nonetheless, some thinkers have suggested that to understand democracy, it is better to reduce it to principles or values rather than to procedures, rights, and institutions. It is from principles that processes, constitutions, and political and civil rights emerge. However, stating those principles is difficult, and proving them to be correct even more so.

Creating a broad picture of democracy's moral content, O'Donnell (1999, 31) and Boron (1995) weave a third strand of virtue into democracy's traditional two threads of civil and political rights, so that a democracy would also have the moral element of being a good citizen participating in a good government. Virtue could include not only participation in government but also political skill, civic spirit, tolerance, integrity, and respect. Like Boron and O'Donnell, Sen also makes virtue essential to democracy (1999, 9). However, he clearly defines virtue, as well as showing how it affects democracy. According to Sen, democracy has three virtues: intrinsic, instrumental, and constructive. Participating in the political, economic, and social world has intrinsic value to human well-being. To be denied participation in the process of creating one's own reality is a serious deprivation. The second virtue is instrumental, the value of being heard and then organizing around expressed ideas. By allowing its citizens to fully participate in the polity, a democracy improves good governance and economic growth. As a result, democracy produces a good material life, which reinforces the democratic system. Finally, a democracy allows its citizens to learn from one another, creating values, setting priorities, and expressing needs. A democracy thus has the virtue of constructing its own ethical values. Democracy, then, is a form of development in the broadest meaning of the word.

The debate over the ethical content of democracy suggests that it needs to be an ongoing, never-completed process toward something meaningful, just, and virtuous. Since a democracy is made up of people, this means that citizenship must permit a meaningful engagement with the polity, an ongoing process of development both at an individual level and within a group. When a democratic state does not pursue moral ends (for example, abuses civil liberties, blocks participation, or denies its own values), the system falls into disrepute and democracy as a governing system can lose legitimacy. People then feel entitled to look at alternative mechanisms for government, such as authoritarianism.

Because the structure of the democratic system places such importance on protecting people from domination and promoting meaningful participation, many thinkers focus on this aspect of democracy. Democracy developed as a mechanism to control and constrain the state from impinging unnecessarily on an individual's freedom, while nonetheless ensuring that a strong government remained. This system of democracy has two basic components. The first is civil liberties. These liberties, or freedoms, are sometimes called the substance of a democracy, with the freedoms called substantive rights, civil rights, or civil liberties. While civil liberties are considered to be an end unto themselves, they are also a means to limit the power of the state. If citizens have maximum control over their own lives, the state is less able to be dictatorial, and furthermore lacks the moral basis to acquire more power. Similarly, people can only be given control if they are all equal to one another, otherwise one person would be able to exert power over another. So equality is implicit in civil liberties. Like freedom, equality is both a good in and of itself, in addition to being an integral part of liberalism's corrective restraint on government.[2]

Civil liberties belong to every citizen over a certain age, and they include:

♦ freedom of speech and press
♦ freedom of movement and assembly
♦ freedom of belief, creed, and religion
♦ freedom to vote and participate in the polity ("adult suffrage," or the "franchise")

Using concepts from human rights, the list of freedoms is expanding to include ethnic rights (freedom of cultural practices, which includes the use of different language and dress), freedom of sexual orientation, gender equality, and, most recently, environmental rights. Protecting group rights, such as those of women and minorities, has been a contentious issue within some democracies, because group rights contradict the idea of individually based civil liberties.

In a democracy, the powers of the state are limited to allow people to be free and equal. A democratic system of government is a self-restraining state. That is to say, the state itself has mechanisms so that no government, ruling party, or group of people (such as the social elite or the military) can impose itself upon the individual or the group. These mechanisms are called political rights, procedural rights, or democratic procedures, because they deal with the processes of a functioning democracy. They include:

♦ separation of powers (legislative, executive, judicial) with each branch being autonomous and with power equally balanced between them
♦ free, fair, contested and regular elections (i.e., accountability)
♦ mechanisms of representation, for example, political parties
♦ rule of law

For civil liberties and democratic procedures, power is dispersed between individuals and groups, processes and institutions. While it is theoretically neat and tidy to separate democracy's civil liberties from its democratic procedures, in reality the two interact and influence each other. Democratic procedures are affected by citizens who mobilize to support or oppose democracy's operations, by media scrutiny, or by non-political actors, such as religious leaders, who speak out. In turn, civil liberties can be hampered or strengthened by democracy's procedures, such as those undertaken by the judiciary. Rights are rarely static, even in established democracies. Instead, they expand and contract, depending on the wider context. There is no guaranteed path promising that once democratic rights are obtained, then inevitably civil rights will follow and from that come social rights, or vice versa.

Traditionally, a state that combines civil liberties and democratic procedures is called a liberal democracy. Not every democracy is a liberal one. For example, there can be civil liberties without democratic procedures. With the Internet granting access to cheaply made documentaries that can be easily burned onto DVDs or uploaded, suppressing freedom of speech has become increasingly difficult. This was most obvious during the protests against Iran's spring 2009 election. At best, it was unclear who had won, and by how much. Mass protests took place. Police brutality against protesters was filmed on mobile phones and sent around the world, strengthening the opposition movement. Regardless of how flawed democratic procedures actually were in Iran at that time, there was freedom of speech whether the state wanted it or not. Nonetheless, a liberal democracy remains our assumption of what constitutes a genuine democracy, as though it were an unacknowledged default setting. So, when a state is called "democratic," there is the assumption that it has the full array of civil liberties and democratic procedures. Furthermore, we assume it needs little else. As a later section of this chapter will show, the concept of liberal democracy is problematic because embedded within the theory is little economic analysis or recognition of the non-democratic sources of power residing within a democracy.

There are other ways of describing the rights and institutions that make up a liberal democracy. The term has fallen out of favor, and usually is replaced by Robert Dahl's eight criteria of what constitutes a democracy. These criteria are as follows: freedom to mobilize within civil society, freedom of speech, right to vote, right to run for office, right to a competitive election, right to alternative sources of information, free and fair elections, and accountable institutions (Dahl 1971). This is a useful checklist and it has been widely applied to both established democracies and newly democratized states. Like the concept of liberal democracy, with which Dahl's eight essential elements closely correspond, there is a noticeable absence of the powerful impact that money has on the functioning of a democracy. Dahl's later work recognized this shortcoming and has attempted to redress it. However, his early works have become so influential that they are now considered classics, and are quoted without reference to his later improvements on them.

Civil liberties and democratic procedures are the rules by which the state governs. They grant a degree of predictability and stability to the uncertainty and change inherent in democratic politics. In effect, these mechanisms shape the possible outcomes of policy choices, political conflict, and crises, whether those crises are economic downturns, social upheavals, natural disasters, or foreign interventions. For example, if a government passes legislation to fund a new program for targeted childcare, then the legislation can be shaped by the following democratic procedures: vigorous debate from opposition parties that highlight weaknesses in the legislation, which can prompt a rewrite; media support or criticism; civil society agitation for or against it; judicial oversight to ensure that the legislation is constitutional; and executive implementation, without which the legislation is automatically nullified. Thus, crafting legislation means that democracy is a negotiated process of compromise and accommodation.

Democracies are inherently competitive and confrontational. Competition is a means to check power and thereby control ambition and domination. In a democracy, political conflict is institutionalized through the democratic system so that it does not degrade into personal antagonism or go beyond legal boundaries. Conflict and change can only be negotiated through the vote or, to put it more poetically, through the tongue and not the gun. Generally, solutions to conflict are compromises, which tend to be messy and unsatisfying to everyone concerned. As a result, the conflict continues, producing another compromise, and so on. Consequentially, change in democracies tends to take place in small increments. Substantial change can be difficult to see except in the long term, which can be frustrating to those attempting to make their society a better one.

Conflict and compromise (or competition and accommodation) are opposite sides of the same coin of democratic politics. Managing conflict so that a compromise can be reached is considered the "art" of doing politics. This process is sometimes called deliberative democracy. The process can be unpleasant, even unscrupulous.

But by accommodating all voices, even to a limited degree, a democracy is inclusive, integrating all citizens into the polity. If voices are systematically excluded from the deliberative process, then these groups within society tend to become isolated from each other, debate becomes polarized, and compromises are harder to find. When deliberative democracy fails, the democratic process itself loses legitimacy. Without legitimacy, people feel entitled to protest government policies in non-democratic ways. For example, the disabled, a minority group, have successfully petitioned through political channels to have their needs recognized and included in the very organization of society, from the design of sidewalks and buildings to financial assistance. In comparison, animal rights activists have deployed a range of non-democratic means to achieve their ends, including harassing researchers and breaking and entering.

Uncertainty is built into this system. There is always the element of the unpredictable in democratic politics. It is often unclear how much political actors will get and how much they will lose from compromise solutions. Sure winners can watch their lead evaporate during an election year. The history of democracy is replete with unforeseen triumphs or surprisingly narrow losses, so no one knows for certain by how much or for how long anyone will win or lose. The unpredictable nature of democracy is offset by its generosity to the losing side. Losers don't really lose, they just win less. If an individual loses, his or her ideas might still influence the debate. The individual could continue to work in politics in a different area (for example, in think tanks or consulting firms, as political appointees, or within political parties), then compete and have the chance to win at another time. Both winners and losers are able to move into the top echelons of society and business. This reality is equally true of political parties, which might win seats in the governing body but perhaps not enough to rule with a majority, or of social movements, which might lobby unsuccessfully for a piece of public policy to be passed and yet are consulted in the policy-making process that results. Democracy is a system in which more people win than lose, and no one wins or loses absolutely. This system ensures that political actors continue to invest in it, rather than in an alternative organization of power, such as a dictatorship.

Despite the widespread acceptance of the ideas and institutions that underlie a democracy, the practice of it in the real world can and often does fall short. Democracy has been criticized for failing to meet its own ideal; that is, for failing to implement a system that offsets domination through dispersing power, promoting participation, and constructing values. Some supporters of democracy overlook or downplay the domination that is inherent within social and economic inequality. Economic inequality fosters social inequality, and vice versa. Social and economic inequality undermines political equality and democracy, because inequality weakens values such as trust, collective action, and cooperation, all of which are critical to a democracy. Furthermore, when the economic elite obtain undue rewards from their actions in the marketplace, then non-democratic access to positions of power and influence is more likely. As a result, non-democratic practices such as nepotism, bureaucratic patrimonialism, cronyism, and clientelism become institutionalized.

When social and economic inequality is endemic in a democracy, it is difficult to say that all people enjoy the same civil and political rights. In comparison, social, economic, and political equality tend to foster more equality overall and strengthen democracy. Alexis de Tocqueville's analysis of democracy concluded that it demands such a high amount of social and economic equality that a liberal democracy and equality are codependent.

While this truism that democracy and equality are codependent has been around for hundreds of years, widespread social and economic equality has proven elusive. Instead, many democracies around the world have evolved a system called "equality of opportunity," which consists of programs or a societal infrastructure that permit the disadvantaged to rise through society, while simultaneously ensuring that the rich do not have undue access to the corridors of power. These programs work in addition to laws criminalizing actions such as corruption, police or state brutality, and nepotism. Equality of opportunity systems differ from country to country, and they have changed over the decades as societies continue to transform. However, they generally include high-quality state education and healthcare, affordable housing and transportation, restrictions on funding for political parties and lobby groups, legislation protecting labor, minorities, and small businesses, along with redistributive taxes.

Democracy has also been accused of accepting a passive citizenry. Schumpeter (1942) criticized the workings of a democracy as more passive than its ideals or its structure would suggest. He described a democracy as being little more than an institutional arrangement of governing where citizenship is reduced to ticking a box once every few years. According to Schumpeter's argument, democracy is a form of consumerism, where leaders package themselves and their ideas using techniques from advertising to achieve broad appeal. The choice of the citizen, then, is made based on superficial criteria, using inadequate information and thought.

Using Schumpeter's analysis, it is possible to consider that democracy has been bureaucratized into political parties, think tanks, and lobby groups, and then further mediated by rules, state officials, and party ideologies. This bureaucratization separates citizens from the act of doing politics, preventing them from engaging with democracy on a day-to-day basis. As a result, citizens become accustomed to being separated from democratic procedures, and lack experience and knowledge of democracy. Citizens replicate these practices of a weak and bureaucratized democracy within their lives, and consider it acceptable, indeed, the only way to go through life.

With passive citizenry, it becomes easier to create or serve political, social, and economic needs that may not reflect the interests of most people. If a democracy permits the elite to have substantial—if covert—control over the political arena, then this group can ensure that its interests are protected, and even enhanced. This can be achieved democratically through constitutional reforms, through political parties in which members of the elite usually run as candidates for office, and through a political agenda tilted in the elite's favor. This ensures that the interests and needs of the majority are rarely, if ever, debated, much less become policy.

Unsurprisingly, people then become disillusioned with elections, because elections do not appear to alter the lives of most voters in a meaningful way. Apathy increases, party affiliation is weakened, and voting declines. These critiques of democracy have been persuasive in Latin America, where there is a high level of social and economic inequality, and hence a hollowing out of democracy's civil liberties and procedural rights. Some of those trying to strengthen democracy's presence have agitated for participatory democracy. At its simplest, it could include compulsory voting, a practice successfully enacted in some advanced democracies, like Australia. However, participatory democracy suggests that citizens need to be more actively engaged with democratic practices. Citizens need to shape and implement policies and budgets, replacing the professionals. Referendums on a wide range of issues from economic policy to moral questions would be prevalent. More radically, participatory democracy would entail an extension of democracy to the workplace, neighborhood, classroom, and domestic situation, including the parent–child relationship. From these experiences and skills, citizens would then be able to make better judgments about who is best qualified to lead the country representing a given political belief. Because democracy would be more than an election once every four years, and instead would involve ongoing citizen engagement at all levels of society, representatives of labor unions, community groups, and other civil society organizations might have a seat in the government to better present the full range of citizens' needs and opinions. This organization of government would be a different form of representation for citizens than most current democratic systems.

There is nothing inherent within the concept of participatory democracy to suggest that it would not offer the same civil and political freedoms as a liberal democracy. Indeed, in many countries, elements of participatory democracy coexist with representative democracy. Sometimes, however, political leaders who wish to justify the erosion of political and civil freedoms do so through embracing elements of participatory democracy, and claim that it is a different democratic system. Rather than expanding the experience of democracy throughout daily life, participatory democracy can replace representation. In order to assess whether or not a democracy is being strengthened or weakened by legislative reforms, it is necessary to understand the working components of a democracy.

DEMOCRACY'S COMPONENTS

Regardless of what kind of a democracy it is, the governing apparatus ties the functioning of the state to the lives of its citizenry, both at an individual level and through groups like political parties or civil society organizations. In other words, every democracy is not merely a means by which the state is organized into a political order, or a creed by which one lives; it is also a relationship between citizens and the governing regime.

There are three rather large components to any democracy. They are the state, civil society, and the economy. The kind of relationship that exists between a state and its citizenry determines the kind of democracy it is, and how viable it is.

THE STATE

In a democracy, the state is a broad political apparatus that negotiates the interests of competing groups, wages war or protects the populace from external or internal aggression, and promotes social welfare. It includes bureaucrats who shape policy, party representatives who actively create policy, and a variety of officials who carry out (or block) policy. These practices and players, the government, and its set of institutions are more or less coordinated by an executive authority (Skocpol 1979, 29). The state has an extractive power to obtain resources (e.g., taxation), a regulatory power, and a policing capacity to ensure its powers are enforced and its territory defended. The state has the monopoly on both internal and externally oriented violence, and that violence is both institutionalized and legitimate. The state is unique because it dominates society and government, while implementing and maintaining coherence between the other parts. So it is both integral to and yet more than democracy's operations alone.

How the democratic state functions has been much debated, with different theorists emphasizing or downplaying the various aspects of life that the state influences. Robert Dahl (1971) suggested that the state responds to mobilized groups within the populace, groups which can make ad hoc alliances with each other to achieve a common goal. It is not just one elite who runs the state and the economy, but rather a number of elites who compete with one another to obtain goods and services from the state. Thus, most governments by definition are minority governments because they are not elected with a popular base. Individuals and groups who want to change public policy need skills and resources to mobilize their constituencies. While the state may not necessarily have a bias in favor of the business class, it may appear that this is the case because the business class is well organized and has resources. Although a government can intend to reform the polity in favor of the poor, it can be difficult for such reforms to be carried through, since the poor lack the skills to override more sophisticated groupings within society. Dahl called this approach to democracy "polyarchy" (i.e., pluralism). Dahl did not consider polyarchy to be the ideal form of a democracy, but instead a realistic analysis of how a democracy actually functions.

Left-of-center theorists resist Dahl's idea that the state is a neutral arbiter, or an arena in which competing interests agitate for differing definitions of the common good. Instead, they emphasize the necessity of the state to maintain a thriving economy. The state is a complex series of mechanisms to facilitate profit extraction and capital accumulation. This includes supporting the business class, who generally correspond to the socioeconomic elite. So, while the state and the elected government may engage with day-to-day decision-making, it is the unelected elite who silently influence the decisions behind the scenes. This perspective suggests that the masses may vote, and they may have freedoms and democratic procedures, but their opinions are manipulated by the state to serve the needs of the elite. The state manifests society's economic, political, and social relations of power. It then replicates and legitimates that power relationship through its policies and institutions. The more powerful the elite, the more the state responds to it. When there is a conflict between the ruling elite and other citizens, it is surprisingly difficult for even reasonable reforms to be enacted. The classic example is labor's agitation for better working conditions. This group won concessions only by disrupting production (i.e., going on strike), thereby reducing capital accumulation. When labor was replaced with illegal workers or offshore production, the ability of the labor movement to obtain resources or influence public policy decreased. The less influence it had, the less it was able to counteract negative portrayals of organized labor. In effect, with the loss of its economic power and political influence, the labor movement also lost its societal legitimacy to organize.

If the state were to become bankrupt, then the marketplace's ability to accumulate capital would be interrupted. Therefore, the only time the state might overrule the elite is when the state's solvency is under threat, capitalism is in crisis, or the elite is divided about how to manage the state and the economy. Thus, the state has its own agenda, logic, and integrity distinct from a socioeconomic class (Miliband 1973).

Most theorists agree that if a state is to function efficiently and effectively, then it must have a degree of autonomy from citizens both individually and in a group, from all socioeconomic classes, and from ethnic or racial groupings. The ability of the state to act autonomously from groups in order to identify, develop, and implement solutions to problems is called state capacity. It means that agents of the state can intervene in non-state resources, activities, and connections to alter them and the relationships between them. Succinctly put, the state must be dominant. Tilly (2007, 17) makes a one-on-one correlation between democracy and state capacity. State capacity strengthens the regime in the eyes of its citizens because the ability of the state to competently identify problems and solutions for them, and then to efficiently implement those solutions, creates legitimacy and stability. When a state has legitimacy, it has a greater capacity to utilize force to suppress disruptions and protests, reform the state or social institutions, or pass unpopular legislation.

In comparison, if the state is captured or colonized by a particular group so that the state has no agenda of its own, then it is weakened, and its democratic institutions and procedures will not function effectively. These states are called weak states. Despite its name, a weak state can quite effectively debate, pass, and enact legislation. However, that legislation is always in the interests of the ruling elite, and may violate international agreements, domestic laws, and public demands. A weak state struggles to enforce its monopoly on violence, coordinate and integrate institutions necessary for governing, extract resources to fund itself, promote citizen participation and the creation of societal values, and act as the dominant centralizing power in society. In time, the state and democracy suffer a loss of legitimacy and support, and the state can be destabilized (Linz and Stepan 1978, 16–20).

For a democratic state to have capacity, it must have democratic institutions. Good state institutions are important to a democracy because they protect the state from being captured or unduly influenced by a minority group. Better institutions build state capacity. Institutions are the formal and informal frameworks governed by rules and informal conventions that shape human interactions and incentives (IMF 2005). Institutions direct and constrain opportunities and incentives for individual and group action. These actions then are processed and produce results, which reshape institutions. Institutions can be written down and organized, or not. Institutions can be as vague as a collection of broadly agreed-upon values, norms, attitudes, routines, and procedures. They exist in all aspects and parts of society. Marriage, for example, is an institution because it is rule-bound and regulated by the state; however, the institution of marriage is also profoundly shaped by history, political expediency, and changing social norms. Examples of state institutions are the judiciary, healthcare, the education system, and regulatory or monitoring bodies. Like the institution of marriage, state institutions are shaped by ideas, history, culture, neighboring institutions, per capita income, educational standards, and freedom of press. State institutions are essentially political in nature, and like much else in politics, respond to events by shifting resources, goals, and actors.

For these institutions to be effective, for a state to have autonomy and capacity, resources are necessary. Bureaucratic competence, efficient public management policy, regulation of the economy, extractive ability (i.e., taxation), and democratic processes cannot be adequately performed by a weak, underfinanced state. Schmitter (2005, 17) found that state capacity, or the resources necessary for state capacity, tend to increase with economic development so that wealthier nations tend to have stronger states. He found this to be especially true of democratic regimes. If the state, through economic mismanagement or through a deep cutting of its budget, loses its employees or even their loyalty, then the state's capacity to act is curtailed. Paradoxically, reforming the state to make it more efficient, or to reform economic structures, requires long-term investment in the state, even if the ultimate goal is the reduction of the state machinery itself.

In response to economic crises within liberalized economies (Mexico 1995, Asia 1997, Russia 1998, Brazil 1999, Argentina 2002, US 2008), there has been a renewed awareness of the role institutions play and a debate over how to improve them. North and Thomas (1973, 1990) argued that institutions shape economic development to a far greater degree than had been previously recognized. The first world became the first world and the third world remained the third because of the difference in the quality of institutions, rather than from the form of economic development or political organization. Research by Rodrik, Subramanian, and Trebbi (2002) draws a stronger correlation between economic growth and good institutions, than with open economies (free trade) or geography—although both free trade and geography can influence and improve institutions indirectly. It still remains unclear, however, whether stronger economic growth produces stronger institutions or vice versa. Quality institutions increase the productivity of physical capital, which then provides an incentive to invest. Furthermore, an excellent bureaucracy has institutionalized connections with pertinent groups within society but outside the state in order to negotiate policies and goals. Evans (1995) called this "embedded autonomy" where the bureaucracy is autonomous from social groups but nonetheless maintains permanent and deep ties to these groups, binding the state and society together. Such ties give the bureaucracy sources of intelligence and channels for implementation and feedback for public policy. They can build infant industries and a coherent, forward-looking entrepreneurial class. Quality institutions and state capacity can help the economy correct itself before it collapses. Although institutions reform themselves most readily in response to economic need, institutional reform tends to happen slowly (Chang 2007). In poorer countries, where the populace has low levels of human capital, quality institutions are especially important to economic growth and stability (Eicher, García-Peñalosa, and Teksoz 2006). The overwhelming importance of institutions to democracy and development was noted by Colombia's ex-president César Gaviria in a speech when he said, "When we look at all of Latin America, we have to recognize that the real problem is public institutions" (2007).

One of the counterintuitive concepts about the democratic state is that it must not be too effective, nor can it have too much capacity. If it does, then it can intervene too much in the lives of the citizens, with the potential to undermine civil liberties and democratic procedures. A democracy's legitimacy and its long-term viability depend on finding a balance between a strong state and its mechanisms for protecting the individual. Thus, the state in a democracy must be "self-restraining" (Schedler, Diamond, and Platter 1999). The self-restraining state assumes some ugly truths. The first is that elections are necessary but insufficient to achieve democracy. Power is opaque, and the state must continuously expose its own actions to public gaze, regardless of whether there is a demand for it or not. The state must force itself to be transparent. The second is that power corrupts, and there is a need to safeguard against this reality. It is insufficient to ask for high moral standards from individual political actors; instead, the self-restraining state must impose institutional oversight to ensure that the individual has high moral standards. In this light, humans are regarded as flawed beings working in a flawed system with imperfect information and imperfect transparency. Because of these assumptions, a self-restraining state supports institutions and policies over individuals.

A self-restraining state is accountable, and operates in a transparent and responsive manner. If a state acts transparently, then any wrongdoing or rule-breaking becomes apparent. If it is responsive and accountable, then the parties involved will be charged within a reasonable time frame. The mechanisms or processes that a state goes through to be accountable and transparent are part of the democratic process. For example, let's say an official within government takes kickbacks for influencing the awarding of government contracts. If the state is transparent, then this official's activities are uncovered and disciplinary action is taken against him or her. If an opposition party or the media can demonstrate that kickbacks are well-accepted practices, and can further demonstrate that the governing party has loosened regulations to facilitate the awarding of government contracts to friends, then the populace might hold the entire government accountable in the next election and vote them out. If, however, the state is not transparent, then either the official's wrongdoings never come to light, or they are buried and unknown. The state is not responsive because there is nothing to be responsive to, and there is no individual, policy, or party that is held accountable. When this is the case, the state is not merely corrupt, it is also no longer abiding by one of democracy's processes: the rule of law. Without the rule of law, political actors can stand beyond the reach of justice. State-wide corruption can lead to human rights violations, clientelism, cronyism, bureaucratic patrimonialism, and the arbitrary exercise of power.

There are three forms of accountability. The first is vertical accountability, where the people can vote out of power those above them in the power pyramid; that is, the president, political party, and elected representatives. The second, horizontal accountability is the capacity of state institutions to investigate, monitor, announce, and check abuses by other state institutions, public agencies, and branches of government. These state institutions include electoral and other commissions, a central bank, an ombudsman, constitutional and other courts, task forces, and auditing agencies. These oversight bodies need to have highly trained and specialized staff, and have ample resources, be autonomous from other state agencies, and be insulated from political pressure. It is paradoxical that in order to protect democracy the state needs elitist, highly trained professional agencies that operate outside democratic politics. Although vertical and horizontal accountability are interconnected and mutually supportive, there is little incentive for a government to encourage horizontal accountability, and many do not. It is inherently conflictive, and an activity from which no government benefits. The third form is social accountability. Citizens express their displeasure through strikes, demonstrations, and public opinion polls. These protests are fomented by civil society organizations and the media. Social accountability can highlight scandals exposing individuals, groups, or institutional failures; it brings issues to the fore such as human rights violations, lack of judicial autonomy or electoral irregularities; and it activates mechanisms for vertical or horizontal accountability. However, social accountability is not the strongest form of accountability, because it can focus on non-issues such as the actions of celebrities, can be manipulated by the wealthy, and is reliant on an independent media to create a common narrative to galvanize the masses (Peruzzotti and Smulovitz 2006).

So the state must be dominant and autonomous while acting with capacity in order for democracy to function well. To check the power and protect democracy from a state with capacity, power is dispersed through democratic procedures (vertical accountability), state institutions (horizontal accountability), and civil society (social accountability).

CIVIL SOCIETY

To state the obvious, a democracy needs to have citizens live and operate within civil society. At its simplest level, a citizen is an individual with the ability to participate in the polity. Democracy requires that citizens be more involved with politics than occasionally voting. A robust democracy needs citizens acting in an organized, dense, and engaged civil society. "The fundamental prerequisite of democracy is the existence of a healthy polity" (Garretón and Newton 2001, 4).

Civil society is the realm of organized social life that is voluntary, self-generating, and largely self-supporting, autonomous from the state, and bound by a legal order or set of shared rules. It is distinct from "society" in general in that it involves citizens acting collectively in the public sphere to express their interests, passions, and ideas, exchange information, achieve mutual goals, make demands on the state, and hold state officials account-able. Civil society is an intermediary entity, standing between the private sphere and the state. Thus, it excludes individual and family life, inward-looking group activities (e.g., entertainment and spirituality), profit-making enterprises, and the political efforts to take control of the state (Diamond 1999, 221).

In other words, citizenship is not merely political participation but a public, collective, deliberative participation voluntarily organized around private interests, from which political activity can emerge. Making too rigid a dichotomy between the state and civil society would be inaccurate because sometimes civil society activity works against the state, and sometimes it works with the state. This conception of civil society includes both individual and collective action, with a stronger emphasis on the role that the collective has on a democracy. Civil society can have patterns of interactions and associations, but is too vast and inchoate to be analytically grasped. Much of civil society flies below the radar and so analysts, the media, and public attention tend to focus on well-organized and well-resourced civil society organizations.

In effect, there are in every democracy two civil societies. One is small, democratic, official, recognized, and elite-dominated. The other is large and grassroots, and is more likely to be poorly organized, under-resourced, and undemocratic. Because the political aspect of civil society is mediated by the nature of the state, civil society changes from country to country, and within a nation. An engaged citizenry is sometimes referred to as social capital.[3]

Citizens, organizing through civil society organizations, create the values that underpin a functioning democracy. Civic participation forces democracy to fulfill its own promises of political rights and democratic processes. In so doing, political issues or social concerns are discussed and debated before becoming policy. The development of common expectations is expressed in public spaces, reinforced by political practices and insti-tutions. Civil society creates the values such as trust, tolerance, equality, and participation that underlie a democracy. In a cross-national study of democracies, Inglehart (1999) shows that these crucial values stem from subjective feelings of well-being, which in turn are influenced by religion, levels of economic development, and forms of social interaction. Feelings of well-being permit interpersonal trust and reduce conflict between citizens. With generalized trust between citizens, democratic norms can be established. High levels of trust, tolerance, and equality are linked to high levels of support for democracy, and vice versa (Itzigsohn 2006, 89). These values are sometimes called a nation's political culture.[4]

Tocqueville, commenting on the nascent democracy of the United States, noticed that civil society organizations forged bonds of trust, equality, and mutual dependency, which were then reflected in their political engagement, their elected representatives, and their demands from the government. Putnam, Leonardi, and Nanetti (1994) arrived at a similar conclusion, adding that networks within civil society increased its efficiency by facilitating coordinated actions, and granting disparate civil society organizations an aggregate power. His analysis suggested that the greater the civic participation, the better the democracy. The better the democracy, the more incentive people (including the disenfranchised) have to participate producing a virtuous spiral.

Countries with recent transitions from authoritarianism to democracy tend to have low levels of trust. Standards of living might not have improved, the polity is typically rife with informal institutions, and there are few shared rules, norms, or values. The state can block civil society from acting autonomously, thereby weakening the impetus to organize. People can erode civil liberties through authoritarian practices or through politicizing traditional family values. More subtly, economic crises, unchecked crime, and an irresponsible media can all inhibit civil society from organizing (Whitehead 2004). As a result, citizens have low levels of subjective well-being, and hence low levels of trust. To overcome this deficit of trust, Offe (1999) suggests that political institutions be impeccably transparent, truth-telling, and rule-abiding. Nonetheless, it is entirely possible to have a democracy with authoritarian practices, distrusted public institutions acting unfairly, and a weak civil society without trust, tolerance, and mutuality. Democracy then becomes a flawed and disrespected patina overlaying traditional norms of authoritarianism and hierarchy, distrust, and passivity.

Generally, when the state has capacity, is responsive, and has resources, then civil society and the state can work together to achieve mutually beneficial goals. Linkages between state and civil society help to inform each other of emerging demands and agendas, to design and implement policies, and to safeguard democratic procedures and civil liberties. There is the suggestion that a strong and active civil society can advance economic development even if democracy itself is weak.[5] Civil society organizations explicitly convened to change the political organization of power are called social movements or non-governmental organizations (NGOs). Social movements are civil society organizations or networks operating in broad or narrow alliances, sometimes including governmental actors, resources, and institutions both domestic and foreign. They can be member-supported organizations like unions, neighborhood groups, or professional associations with little contact between members, or any combination thereof. NGOs are generally professionally run, social movement organizations with explicit mandates and sources of funding from outside the government (i.e. externally financed).

When the state is repressive, civil society organizations can be purely antagonistic. In Latin America, social movements emerged under dictatorships because there were limited mechanisms for citizens to be heard. But social movements can also emerge under democracies for three reasons. First, they can emerge when democratic representations do not adequately express or engage with new civil society organizations, such as the women's movement. Second, social movements can emerge among the poor because they have no stake in the existing system, so they do not consider using political parties or democratic mechanisms. Third, social movements can be seen as a form of organizing parallel to democratic institutions, both of which are necessary to ensure citizens' voices are being heard. France, for example, has extremely powerful social movements.

Social movements and other civil society movements are important for democracy because they normalize democratic procedures. They generally insist on equality and freedom of speech. They are usually non-hierarchical and prefer participatory decision-making structures. Social movements are essential to disseminate information through their own networks and to the media, thereby creating new social norms. Social movements critique government policies and actions, and propose alternative solutions. These can be picked up by political parties, and reinserted back into the political process, possibly affecting public policy. Through these democratic practices, social movements help break down the traditional practices of clientelism, corruption, and authoritarianism, permitting democratic processes more scope. By mobilizing the community, citizens are empowered, and eventually lose their fear of becoming politically active. In the process, people learn the techniques of organizing, strategizing, and lobbying. Even if the social movement is unsuccessful, it might raise new questions, shift the political agenda, or sensitize the general public to an issue. Social movements help redefine the role of the state and its relationship with its citizens. "Social movements are battles to redefine citizenship, in effect, constructing a broader and more inclusionary meaning" (Stahler-Sholk 2007, 9).

In the literature on democracy, there is a constant evocation for a strong civil society to protect and strengthen democracy. One commentator said civil society is treated like chicken soup because, whatever ails the polity, a dosage of civil society will make it better (Levine 2008, 214). However, civil society organizations are constrained by a number of factors. First, social movements need to act against an anonymous modern state. They cannot act against a *caudillo* using clientelism or patronage with much success, because too many people owe the patron too much. If there is a modern state to organize against, it would be preferable if it were democratic. A repressive state tends to dismantle autonomous civil society organizations because they are inherently threatening. To continue to organize and agitate while living under a repressive regime requires enormous courage. So civil society organizations in a dictatorship are caught in a catch-22, where there is little point in organizing to democratize unless there already is a viable democracy in place. It is a measure of the tenacity of the human spirit that many people have protested against oppressive regimes in support of democracy despite this reality.

Second, social movements have no inherent moral content. They do not necessarily practice democracy, equality, or freedom. They are in favor of whatever the participants decide. Social movements can make strategic alliances with non-democratic parties to obtain non-democratic goals. The officials of the Nazi Party in Germany mobilized an effective social movement to assist them in becoming elected, and then in concentrating power around themselves. Therefore, when analyzing a civil society organization, its goals, operating practices, and ideology must be taken into consideration.

Third, social movements rarely mobilize to dismantle or reform democracy, but instead agitate for concrete goods or services. In politics, there is a tendency to get what you go for. So governments with weak democratic institutions practicing clientelism might well gain legitimacy by responding to the concrete demands from a social movement, which in the long run weakens democratic processes. A canny leader can take advantage of social movements by allowing them to smother legitimate but weak democratic processes and institutions, which in the long run benefits the leader. Conversely, by generating mass support for a project, a successful social movement can overwhelm a weak state if political parties and weak institutions cannot absorb the high levels of citizen participation. This can lead to mob rule, an unhealthy political development (Pearce 2004b, 105).

Finally, while it is lovely to envision poorer sectors of society mobilizing for improved goods and services, the reality is more problematic. Communication is integral to successful organization. This generally requires literacy, and the poor have higher levels of illiteracy than the rest of society. Money is needed for radio shows, advertisements, information pamphlets, meeting hall rentals, and staff. Without literacy and resources, the poor cannot organize extensively. Consequently, civil society organizations tend not to emerge organically from the poor, and social movements in poor societies tend to exclude the majority because the majority is poor. Social movements typically replicate existing power structures and are usually dominated by the middle class.

If the democratic procedures and the state are weak, and as a result unable to respond to the demands of the social movements, then there is little point in social movements targeting the state. Instead, activists can take advantage of the globalized nature of information and use non-governmental organizations (NGOs) to target international actors and the state. NGOs are replacing the work typically done by civil society organizations. These groups are a variety of civil society organization because they are set up by private individuals. But unlike most civil society organizations, NGOs are legally constituted to achieve a mandated goal, such as supplying bicycles to ease transport problems. NGOs generally obtain private financial support. Sometimes, a state will support an NGO to achieve a common goal. In theory (but not often in practice) the source of the funding will not affect the NGO's actions. NGOs can drive policy change and regime change. National NGOs can operate with either supportive foreign agencies or be part of an international non-governmental organization (INGO) sharing ideas, resources, and personnel. Many NGOs are run by professionals who are possibly from abroad and supported by foreign money. With the rise to dominance of NGOs, there is, for the first time, a degree of professionalization of civil society with foreigners on temporary contracts agitating for political change. This phenomenon calls into question the role of political representation and democratic mechanisms to address the questions and needs of the citizenry. Ultimately, civil society organizations and social movements need democratic processes and institutions as much as democracy needs them (Pearce 2004a, 502).

THE ECONOMY

While political processes, institutions, and civil society shape the relationship between citizens and the state, economic practices do as well. However, there is a debate among theorists over the role the economy plays in a democracy, and what organization of the economy has the most impact on democracy.

Logically, democracy seems to be more suitable to economic development than authoritarianism because of its flexibility and responsiveness, its openness to new ideas and innovations, and, its horizontal sharing of power. Democracies assume that all things are up for debate, including the idea of economic change and economic rights. This debate changes primary values over time to expand people's ability to participate in the workplace (among other things). Debate and the sharing of information within society allow for increased discussion over options and concerns, and thereby better, more informed decision-making. As a result, economic errors tend to be smaller and more easily corrected. The turnover of governments increases responsiveness to policy errors. Economic stability results. With stability and accessible information, there is investment and confidence in the market, transparency in market-workings, and efficient allocation of resources. Economic growth results. This growth offsets political instability. With democracy, the populace can use the sheer weight of its numbers to insist that the resources be directed toward improving state services and equality of opportunity, which boosts economic productivity. So there is a positive dynamic where democracy improves economic functioning which allows its roots to deepen, which in turn promotes economic development. This entwining of democratic structures and economic growth has been dubbed the "democracy advantage" (Halperin, Siegle, and Weinstein 2005).

This logic has been supported over the decades by theorists from both the left and the right. From the right, Nobel Prize–winning economists Milton Friedman (1962) and Friedrich von Hayek (1944) extolled the value of deregulating the market to create economic freedom as a necessary pre-condition to democracy because it allowed individuals to hold capital and thereby offset the power and control of government. With capital in the hands of individuals, new ideas could be presented and existing ideas critiqued. Government intervention, though well-meaning, frequently infringed on personal freedom and created inefficiencies in the market, lowering the ability of the economy to create wealth. Without wealth, people were not merely poorer but they were also less able to protect democracy. Friedman's ideal government would control monetary policy with a floating exchange rate, but otherwise would rarely intervene.

Both men emphasized the necessity to have competition as a system to control power and to check domination, suggesting that competition acting through the marketplace was the most effective mechanism for organizing society. Fearing that collusion masqueraded as a democratic consensus, Hayek in particular was very much against unionized labor and collective negotiation, state welfare or healthcare, or state investment in infrastructure, such as transportation. However, neither Hayek nor Friedman recognized unequal relationships of power which permit an elite class to distort the market in its favor, or any positive benefit from having a strong state.[6] Despite these failings, their ideas were highly influential within neoliberalism, the dominant economic ideology of recent decades.

Coming from a more critical perspective, William I. Robinson (1996) and C.B. MacPherson (1977) gave sophisticated explanations for why capitalism produces, indeed needs, democracy. They suggested that when capitalism emerged in Europe as a new form of accumulation; it needed a state to facilitate intra-elite competition, deregulation, trade networks, and non-vertical power relationships within the business class. The new state had to establish itself as an overarching whole for stability, continuity, legitimacy, and occasionally coercive behavior, should capitalism require it. Through creating a democracy with a minimal amount of civil liberties and democratic processes, the economic elite reconstituted its control through participating in a political system based on compromise, negotiation, and social consensus, rather than coercive authoritarianism. Because of the democracy advantage, these minimum democracies operated better than authoritarian regimes. Both Robinson and MacPherson felt that globalization, transnational corporations, and economic inequality limited the ability of new democracies to deepen democratic rights, and threatened existing democracies.

Despite its widespread popularity and intellectual support, the democracy advantage argument has a problem with history. As A.M. Rosenthal, a conservative American thinker, noted, "Capitalism has shown itself flexible enough to have worked for the security of rulers, and the profit of investors, under governments based on fascism, religious fundamentalism, slavery, internal terrorism, apartheid, absolute monarchy, militarism—the whole nasty menu of non-democratic regimes" (quoted in Lowi 2002, 44). In the Southern Cone countries of Latin America (Brazil, Paraguay, Uruguay, and Argentina), bureaucratic-authoritarian regimes were able to combine capitalist accumulation with dictatorships. Apparently, capitalism does not necessarily produce, protect, or even need democracy to function.

Przeworski, Alvarez, Cheibub, and Limongi (2000) supported Rosenthal's conclusions, drawn from the analysis of the histories of 135 countries. He found no correlation between the type of regime and the level of economic development. However, the research showed that countries with low levels of per capita GDP (less than $2,000 per annum in constant dollars) had little chance of sustaining democracy. It is not that the poor do not try to have a democracy, it is that the democracy has less chance of surviving. Costa Rica is a rare poor country that democratized in 1899 and has managed to maintain its democracy ever since. If income per capita is greater than $2,000, then democracy becomes a possibility, while the higher the per capita GDP, the greater the chance of democracy surviving. Once the country has a per capita income of $6,500, democracy is all but assured. Democracies in a high-income economy are very robust and survive all sorts of crises, be they economic downturns, political instability, or social upheaval. Przeworski, Alvarez, Cheibub and Limongi had a controversial caveat. If a dictatorship produces a high level of per capita GDP, then democracy has little chance of being established, and authoritarianism becomes robust. In other words, whichever political system produces wealth becomes established. China's transition to a wealthier, more capitalist economy without loosening its authoritarianism is an example. So countries democratize for reasons other than capitalism, and then the GDP supports or erodes that effort.

Recent debate on the relationship between the economy and democracy has focused on inequality and how that affects both aspects of society. First, there is the strong suggestion that high levels of economic inequality reduce economic growth overall. The unequal distribution of assets restricts the development of investment opportunities and markets for the rest of society. Because high economic inequality tends to coexist with high social inequality, poor people (who are the majority) lack the skills and resources to participate in the marketplace. A wide gap between the rich and the poor is linked to limited, unequal access to education, credit, land rights, legal rights, a fair judicial system, healthcare and sanitation, and public infrastructure such as electricity. Without these public goods, poor people are unable to contribute efficiently to economic growth (Sen 1992). Consequently, there is little incentive to participate in the marketplace and a decline in labor productivity. Instead, there is an increase in social tension and in predatory and criminal activities, which raises the transaction costs of doing business (Cornia 2004).

Second, what economic growth there is tends not to trickle down to the poor. In a 2005 World Bank study of countries with low economic inequality, each percentage point of growth allowed a reduction of roughly 4 per cent in poverty (measured as the number of people living on less than one dollar a day). In countries with high levels of economic inequality, the effect of a growing GDP on the level of poverty was practically zero. "The more unequal a society, the higher the growth rate required to reach any given poverty reduction scheme (Machinea and Kacef 2007, 6).

Third, profound poverty and high levels of inequality hollow out democratic institutions, undermining democracy. "Deep inequalities in life chances limit substantive freedoms, rendering hollow the idea of equality before the law" (UNDP 2005, 54). Inequality weakens important values that underlie a democracy, such as trust and social cohesion, limiting collective action and cooperation. This is true more for the poor than for the wealthy. Economic and social inequalities often reflect political inequalities and unequal access to state institutions. The state is then more easily captured by the elite, and loses state capacity. The higher the inequality, the more difficult it becomes to reform the economic structure that produces this inequality; the captured state then perpetuates this reality. Democracy lacks legitimacy in the eyes of its citizens, prompting the search for alternatives.

The degree of economic inequality (rather than the level of economic development) best explains democratic stability and instability. It is hard to build or sustain democratic institutions in a society divided sharply by income and wealth, especially one that gives the impression of doing little to redress the situation or, worse, of actively exacerbating it (Karl 1996, 78–9).

Analyzing countries from around the world, including those in Latin America, Sandbrook, Edelman, Heller, and Teichman (2007) suggested that in order for economic development and democracy to mutually benefit each other and the lives of citizens, the form of the state is critical. Strong democratic institutions within a state with high capacity can mediate conflicts over resources such as land, taxation, and labor regulation. The state ensures that social inequality is kept to a minimum and promotes economic distribution. Over time, this form of a state can reconcile capitalism and democracy to produce growth with equity.

INTERNATIONAL INFLUENCES ON DEMOCRACY

While the state, citizenry, and the economy are components of any democracy anywhere in the world, these are all domestic components. In the globalized world, it is important to analyze the impact of the international arena on democracy. There are many international influences on domestic democracy, and not all of them are quantifiable. For example, it is difficult to determine the impact that foreign aid, NGOs, migration, and the transmission of foreign ideas have on democracy. Common sense suggests that they operate like a soft power, influencing the debate within civil society. Without them, civil society might be different, possibly weaker. But this theory is difficult to prove.

Easier to demonstrate is the effect on democracy of neighboring countries. Neighboring countries can help democracy by acting against threats to it. International actors can thus offset the viability of coup d'états and electoral fraud by making the punishment for such offenses greater than the benefit of being in power. Neighboring countries can make symbolic statements in favor of democracy and apply economic sanctions against anti-democratic governments. For example, the General Assembly of the Organization of American States (OAS) approved the "Santiago Commitment to Democracy" in 1991, which committed Latin American nations to the defense and promotion of representative democracy and human rights in the region. In 1997, the OAS signed the Washington Protocol, which agreed that if a democratic government were overthrown by force then the OAS could suspend that member from the OAS. This was strengthened in 2001, when the OAS agreed that it would suspend non-democratic governments from the Free Trade Agreement of the Americas (FTAA). This was further reinforced by MERCOSUR, a regional trade agreement between Argentina,

Brazil, Paraguay, and Uruguay, which also has a democracy clause prohibiting non-democratic states from participating. More robustly, foreign states can engage in military actions to overthrow dictatorships. More subtly, international actors can foment antiauthoritarian, pro-democracy elements in society. The effect of a neighboring country's attitudes and support is so great that Hagopian and Mainwaring (2005) consider it the decisive difference in maintaining a democratic regime's durability. Foreign influence is mediated by factors such as a divided elite, geographical size and location, and the country's vulnerability to economic factors such as raw resources, energy, and debt repayments (Schmitter 2001, 48–9). There is a limit to the amount of intervention or support that a foreign nation can offer. While powerful countries or international organizations like the UN can insist on democracy, they are less capable of altering the depth of democracy, that is, the quality of the democratic procedures and institutions.

The impact of foreign powers on democracy has been overshadowed by the impact of globalization.[7] The meaning of globalization is under debate, as is the extent of its impact on individual nation-states. Broadly defined, globalization is the accelerating set of processes, including a greater number of peoples and spaces, leading to the interconnectivity and integration of the world. It can include labor, capital, products, technology, knowledge, information, belief systems, ideas, and values. It is the purposeful pursuit of objectives (economic, political, or social) to widen the activities of nations, institutions, and individuals across national boundaries (Kaplinksy 2005, 9). Economies are now integrated into the global economy through international financial institutions (IFIs) and trade agreements. These IFIs and trade agreements frequently shape political options by constraining and altering the political process, democratic institutions, and political participation. Globalization's clearest articulation is through international agreements that influence and shape trade, domestic regulation, and the organization of the state itself. These trade agreements include the General Agreement on Trade and Tariffs (GATT), which became the World Trade Organization (WTO) in 1995. It is a legal institution with an expanded mandate to regulate not only trade but also the service sector, intellectual property, and capital. The WTO constrains, limits, directs, and conditions decision-making in areas far removed from trade as it is traditionally understood, including areas such as health, the environment, and labor standards. Domestic policy must be changed to match the WTO's framework, or the offending country can be fined.

In theory, globalization as articulated through IFIs has meant a neoliberal structuring of economies to promote trade and improve efficiencies through the dominance of the market, with the hopeful result of improving a nation's GDP. However, IFIs helped to build an international trading regime that has "served the interests of the more advanced industrial countries—and particular interests within those countries—rather than those of the developing world" (Stiglitz 2003, 214). While Latin America's neoliberal nations outperformed non-trading nations, Asia's impressive economic growth without neoliberalism offers a potent alternative. It is now clear that globalizing the world's economy through neoliberalism has widened the gap between the rich and poor, both between and within countries by concentrating assets in the hands of fewer individuals and granting them disproportionate economic power (Cornia and Court 2001, 22). This economic influence has combined with existing authoritarian practices of clientelism and cronyism. In effect, authoritarian practices modernized themselves and are now well adapted to globalization (Teichman 2003, 45). So the globalization of the economy has exacerbated preexisting economic and social inequalities.

While global financial institutions have created markets on an international scale, the revolution in information technology has also created transnational networks of non-state actors. These international social movements and NGOs are connecting local issues and struggles to the global arena, including human rights, the environment, and maternal health. These organizations are able to mobilize resources internationally and to transfer expertise across borders in order to take advantage of political opportunities that will achieve change. These international social movements have the possibility of changing values and social norms, strengthening civil society, informing the citizens, and organizing mass protests such as those which took place in Seattle (1999), Quebec City (2001), and San José, Costa Rica (2007).

There is a lack of consensus about the effect of globalization on democracy. One perspective suggests that the state is transformed, but by necessity remains powerful in order to enact the international agreements, which is based on the assumption that the state was powerful in the first place. Ulrich Beck (Beck and Cronin 2006) suggests that globalization expands a nation's net power and embeds citizenship in a more cosmopolitan nation. Sassen (2006, chapter 4) is less sanguine. Her analysis suggests that globalization has a second, more subtle dynamic of micro-processes operating within national institutions to reorient themselves toward global agendas and systems. So globalization is reorganizing the state apparatus and, with that, the state's relationship with its citizens. With the insertion of a nation into the globalizing process, there has been a shift in power relations from the legislature to the executive. There is a rise in the number and power of executive agencies that specialize in regulatory oversight, with technical experts trained on multinational regulation of trade and finance. As a result, there is the loss of lawmaking capabilities and public oversight within the legislature. In such a way, globalization's institutions do not merely change domestic public policy on a wide range of issues but also become endogenous to the nation-state by reconfiguring the state apparatus. Teichman (2001) charted this phenomenon in three countries in Latin America.

An even more negative perspective suggests that the democratic state is getting weaker, with reduced state capacity. With international agreements acting as supraconstitutions, there is less ability for state institutions to form policies. The role of the citizen has shifted from political participant to consumer (McBride and Fossum 2004, 242, 256). The domestic elite realign themselves to meet the needs of the globalized system of capital accumulation, which rarely responds to the needs of the impoverished or appreciates the value of a deeper democracy (Robinson 2009). In the process, national sovereignty and self-determination are eroded. Multinational corporations have become less accountable to the nation-state, because it is now easier to shift production between states. International agencies such as INGOs and IFIs are non-accountable, although highly influential. With income and social inequality rising both within and between nations as a result of globalization, democracy has been hollowed out.[8] "In sum, the economic aspects of integration into the world economy are beginning to cause a decline in national democratic governance" (Li and Reuveny 2003, 53).

In recent years, the international debate has shifted from pro- versus anti-free trade to managing the best form of free trade so that everyone benefits. Even Jagdish Bhagwati, one of globalization's strongest proponents, calls for better management of the forces of globalization (2004, 35). Developing nations, in particular China, India, and Brazil, are insisting that the WTO be reformed to equalize the benefits from trading. The refusal by the developed nations, in particular the EU and the US, has blocked reforming measures, most recently at the Doha Round in July 2008. In this debate, the importance of the state has reemerged as a key operator. Domestic institutions and the domestic elite negotiate the extent to which the country is inserted into the globalized economy. Their ability to respond to the forces of globalization with appropriate public policies to protect democracy and offset the risk to citizens can profoundly affect the extent of the negative impact. Globalization, then, is neither a force to increase wealth through free trade, nor is it a force that weakens democracy. Rather, globalization is a neutral force capable of doing either. "Generally, countries with an effective institutional base appear to be better in a globalized world than countries where the rule of law is weak, corruption is rampant, property rights are unprotected, and civil society is not able to force accountability from the government" (Tulchin and Bland 2005, 221). In other words, those countries already enjoying a deep democracy stand to benefit from the advantages of globalization with minimum risk and cost. Those countries where the state and democracy are weak will likely experience substantial costs from globalization, with limited benefits.

CONCLUSION

Democracy is based on two contradictions. The first is based in assumptions about people. Democracy assumes that people are not to be trusted; thus, no single group or individual can gain power. Conversely, it assumes that people can create a society that benefits everyone, through creating values of trust, tolerance, and equality and then forging institutions to enact those values. Democracy does not promise or attempt to change human nature, to make us nicer or better people. Instead, it is a system that encourages and rewards good behavior (e.g., political participation, transparent actions) while either criminalizing bad behavior (e.g., corruption) or at least not rewarding certain actions, such as apathy.

Because a democracy rewards and punishes actions, it has moral content. That content is based on freeing humanity from oppression and domination, regardless of whether that domination is political, economic, or social. With freedom comes human agency, so people, both individually and as a group, can take charge of their own lives and live with mutuality, self-determination, and dignity. Thus, participation is central to democracy. A top-down democratic system with a weak civil society is almost not a democracy. Democracy's moral content must be clearly expressed and continuously rearticulated in appropriate language, or the ethical core of democracy becomes lost in the changing political and economic context, complex state structures, and new demands on citizenry and representatives.

There is a second contradiction built into democracy. Its ethical core is freedom, equality, and fairness. Yet the economic organization of democracies is capitalism. Capitalism creates inequality, which can easily subvert the values sustaining democracy and democratic institutions. Globalization has enhanced the ability of capitalism to increase inequality while decreasing the ability of the state to offset this negative impact.

Yet despite these unresolvable contradictions, democracy can flourish. It balances, organizes, and integrates politics with the economy and civil society. These three aspects of the polity, the economy, and society express themselves in the forms of laws, the structure of economic production, and social opportunities or constraints. Mitigating the importance of one aspect degrades the quality of the democratic system as a whole. Indeed, it is even difficult to fully examine one aspect without engaging with the other two.

To articulate and implement a democratic ethos with a structural balance of power, a democracy must have state capacity, excellent institutions with an embedded bureaucracy, a densely active civil society, and high levels of social and economic equality. Depending on its specific organization, a democracy which supplies those goods is called different things, including full democracy, social democracy, thick democracy, and deep democracy.

Alternatively, if there are high levels of socioeconomic inequality, then a group or individual, usually the elite, the military, or an alliance between the two, can capture the state. If the state is weak and lacks capacity, then it is not the dominant force in society. As a result, it cannot organize the polity with a high level of institutional sophistication or balance the polity with the economy and society. There is little dispersion of power through formal and informal institutions. As a result, the nation as a whole tends not to thrive. Positive social values, the state, democracy, and economic production are weakened. "Deep disparities based on wealth, region, gender and ethnicity are bad for [economic] growth, bad for democracy and bad for social cohesion" (UNDP 2005, 51).

NOTES

1 Freedom House is a non-partisan, not-for-profit organization that publishes global data about political and civil freedoms, freedom of the press, and democracy. The 1976 Freedom in the World survey only covered 29 of the 35 countries in the Americas. Freedom House provides a numerical score for each country's degree of political rights and civil liberties, from which it designates a country as free, partly free, or not free. Criticisms of its methodology will be dealt with in chapter 2.

2 Equality is also a contested term, which will be analyzed in greater detail later in this chapter.

3 In theory, social capital can be measured. However, it is difficult to do this in practice. Any statistics measuring social capital or the depth or density of civic engagement should be regarded with caution. Similarly, definitions of civil society range. I have chosen Larry Diamond's definition because it is most widely used in Latin American studies.

4 Political culture is a problematic concept because it implies that a nation has a homogenous set of values. Instead, national values are fractured by class, age, gender, education, ethnicity, rural/urban residence, and so on. Despite the difficulty in collecting sophisticated data, political culture can be a useful tool for understanding institutional performance, policy changes, and citizen commitment to democracy.

5 It is difficult to establish causal links between amorphous civil society relations and economic development. Increasingly, however, even conservative international financial institutions, such as the Inter-American Development Bank, are endorsing this view.

6 In this debate, the definitions of both democracy and capitalism frequently lack clarity, and care should be taken with terminology.

7 It is possible to consider globalization as an extension of American foreign policy, given the high level of American support for it, and the extent to which the US dominates international financial institutions. Indeed, while

he was Bill Clinton's undersecretary of state, Lawrence Summers linked American security to a globalist economic policy (Laxer 2004, x).

8 There are powerful arguments suggesting that inequality is lessening due to globalization; however this is a view espoused by the minority. For more on this debate, see Bhagwati (2004); Held and Kaya (2007); Weinstein (2005).

REFERENCES

Beck, Ulrich, and Ciaran Cronin. 2006. *Cosmopolitan Vision*. Cambridge: Polity Press.

Bhagwati, Jagdish. 2004. *In Defense of Globalization*. Oxford: Oxford University Press

Boron, Atilo. 1995. *State, Capitalism, and Democracy in Latin America*. Boulder: Lynne Rienner Press.

Chang, Ha-Joon. 2007. *Stranger Than Fiction? Understanding Institutional Changes and Economic Development*. Policy Brief No. 6. Helsinki: United Nations World Institute for Development Economics Research.

Cornia, Giovanni Andrea. 2004. "Inequality, Growth and Poverty: An Overview of Change over the Last Two Decades." *Inequality, Growth, and Poverty in an Era of Liberalization and Globalization*. Ed. Giovanni Andrea Cornia. Oxford: Oxford University Press. 3–25.

Cornia, Giovanni Andrea, and Julius Court. 2001. *Inequality, Growth and Poverty in the Era of Liberalization and Globalization*. Policy Brief No. 4. Helsinki: United Nations University and World Institute for Development Economics Research.

Dahl, Robert. 1971. *Polyarchy: Participation and Opposition*. New Haven: Yale University Press.

Diamond, Larry. 1999. *Developing Democracy: Toward Consolidation*. Baltimore: Johns Hopkins University Press.

——. 2008. *The Spirit of Democracy: The Struggle to Build Free Societies throughout the World*. New York: Henry Holt.

Eicher Theo S., Ceclia García-Peñalosa, and Utku Teksoz. 2006. "How Do some Institutions Lead Some Countries to Produce So Much More Output per Worker than Others?" *Institutions, Development and Economic Growth*. Ed. Theo S. Eicher and Celia García-Peñalosa. Cambridge, MA: MIT Press. 65–80.

Evans, Peter. 1995. *Embedded Autonomy*. Princeton: Princeton University Press.

Freedom House. June 10, 2010. www.freedomhouse.org.

Friedman, Milton. 1962. *Capitalism and Freedom*. Chicago: University of Chicago Press.

Garretón, Manuel Antonio, and Edward Newman. 2001. "Introduction."*Democracy in Latin America: (Re)Constructing Political Society*. Ed. Manuel Antonio Garretón and Eward Newman. New York: United Nations University Press. 3–15.

Gaviria Trujillo, Cesar. 2007. "Foreign Direct Investment and Income Inequality in Latin America." Paper presented at Social and Political Exclusion: The Challenge of Inequality in Latin America, London, England, November 5.

Hagopian, Frances, and Scott Mainwaring, eds. 2005. *The Third Wave of Democratization in Latin America: Advances and Setbacks*. Cambridge: Cambridge University Press.

Halperin, Morton H., Joseph T. Siegle, and Michael M. Weinstein. 2005. *The Democracy Advantage: How Democracies Promote Prosperity and Peace*. New York: Routledge.

Hayek, von Friedrich. 1944. *The Road to Serfdom*. London: Routledge.

Held, David, and Ayse Kaya. 2007. *Global Inequality: Patterns and Explanations*. Cambridge: Polity Press.

Inglehart, Ronald. 1999. "Trust, Well-Being and Democracy." *Trust and Democracy*. Ed. M.E. Warren. Cambridge: Cambridge University Press. 88–120.

International Monetary Fund. 2005. *World Economic Outlook*. New York: IMF.

Itzigsohn, José. 2006. "Neo-liberalism, Markets, and Informal Grassroots Economies." *Out of the Shadows: Political Action and the Informal Economy in Latin America*. Ed. Patricia Fernández-Kelly and Jon Shefner. University Park: Pennsylvania State University Press. 81–96.

Kaplinsky, Raphael. 2005. *Globalization, Poverty and Inequality: Between a Rock and a Hard Place*. Cambridge: Polity Press.

Karl, Terry. 1996. "How Much Inequality Can Democracy Stand? Or How Much Democracy Can Inequality Stand?" In National Endowment for Democracy and the Pacific Council on International Policy, *Constructing Democracy and Markets; East Asia and Latin America: Conference Report*. New York: International Forum for Democratic Studies and Pacific Council on International Policy. 75–83.

Laxer, Gordon. 2004. "Preface." *Governing Under Stress: Middle Powers and the Challenge of Globalization*. Ed. Stephen Clarkson and Marjorie Griffin Cohen. London: Zed Books.

Levine, Daniel H. 2008. "Evangelicals and Democracy: The Experience of Latin America in Context." *Evangelical Christianity and Democracy in Latin America*. Ed. Paul Freston. Oxford: Oxford University Press. 207–23.

Li, Quan, and Rafael Reuveny. 2003. "Economic Globalization and Democracy: An Empirical Analysis." *British Journal of Political Science* 33: 29–54.

Linz, Juan J., and Alfred Stepan. 1996. *Problems with Democratic Transition and Consolidation: Southern Europe, South America and Post-Communist Europe*. Baltimore: Johns Hopkins University Press.

——. 1978. "Crisis, Breakdown, and Reequilibration." *The Breakdown of Democratic Regimes*. Ed. Juan Linz and Alfred Stepan. Baltimore: Johns Hopkins University Press. 3–124.

Lowri, Theodore J. 2002. "Progress and Poverty Revisited: Toward Construction of a Statist Third Way." *Democratic Governance and Social Inequality*. Ed. Joseph S. Tulchin (with Amelia Brown). Boulder: Lynne Rienner Press. 41–74.

Machinea, José Luis, and Osvaldo L. Kacef. 2007. "Growth and Equity: In Search of the 'Empty Box.'" *Economic Growth with Equity: Challenges for Latin America*. Ed. Ricardo French-Davis and José Luis Machinea. London: Palgrave MacMillan. 1–23.

MacPherson, C.B. 1977. *The Life and Times of Liberal Democracy*. Oxford: Oxford University Press.

McBride, Stephen, and John Erik Fossum. 2004. "The Rule of Rules: International Agreements and the Semi-Periphery." *Governing under Stress: Middle Powers and the Challenge of Globalization*. Ed. Stephen Clarkson and Majorie Griffin Cohen. London: Zed Books. 239–59.

Miliband, Ralph. 1973. *The State in Capitalist Society: The Analysis of the Western System of Power*. London: Quartet Books.

North, Douglass C. 1990. *Institutions, Institutional Change and Economic Performance*. Cambridge: Cambridge University Press.

North, Douglass C., and Robert P. Thomas. 1973. *The Rise of the Western World: A New Economic History*. Cambridge: Cambridge University Press.

O'Donnell, Guillermo. 1999. "Horizontal Accountability in New Democracies." *The Self-Restraining State*. Ed. Andreas Schedler, Larry Diamond, and Marc Plattner. Boulder: Lynne Rienner Press. 29–51.

Offe, Claude. 1999. "How Do We Trust Our Fellow Citizens?" *Democracy and Trust*. Ed. Mark E. Warren. Cambridge: Cambridge University Press. 42–87.

Pearce, Jenny. 2004a. "Collective Action or Public Participation? Complementary and Contradictory Democratisation Strategies in Latin American." *Bulletin of Latin American Research* 23(4): 483–504.

———. 2004b. "Civil Society, the Market, and Democracy in Latin America." *Civil Society in Democratization*. Ed. Peter Burnell and Peter Calvert. London: Frank Cass Press. 90–116.

Peruzzotti, Enrique, and Catalina Smulovitz, eds. 2006. *Enforcing the Rule of Law: Social Accountability in the New Latin American Democracies*. Pittsburgh: University of Pittsburgh Press.

Przeworski, Adam, Michael E. Alvarez, José Antonio Cheibub, and Fernando Limongi. 2000. *Democracy and Development*. Cambridge: Cambridge University Press.

Putnam, Robert, Robert Leonardi, and Raffaella Y. Nanetti. 1994. *Making Democracy Work: Civic Traditions in Modern Italy*. Princeton: Princeton University Press.

Robinson, William I. 1996. *Promoting Polyarchy: Globalization, US Intervention and Hegemony*. Cambridge: Cambridge University Press.

———. 2009. *Latin America and Global Capitalism: A Critical Globalization Perspective*. Baltimore: Johns Hopkins University Press.

Rodrik, Dani, Arvind Subramanian, and Francesco Trebbi. 2002. *Institutions Rule: The Primacy of Institutions over Geography and Integration in Economic Development*. NBER Working Paper 9305. Cambridge, MA: National Bureau of Economic Research.

Sandbrook, Richard, Marc Edelman, Patrick Heller, and Judith Teichman. 2007. *Social Democracy in Global Periphery*. Cambridge, MA: Cambridge University Press.

Sassen, Saskia. 2006. *Territory, Authority, Rights: From Medieval to Global Assemblages*. Princeton: Princeton University Press.

Schedler, Andreas. 1998. "What is Democratic Consolidation?" *Journal of Democracy* 9(2): 91–107.

Schedler, Andreas, Larry Diamond, and Marc F. Platter. 1999. *The Self-Restraining State: Power and Accountability in New Democracies*. Boulder: Lynne Rienner Press.

Schmitter, Philippe C. 2001. "The Influence of the International Context upon the Choice of National Institutions and Policies in Neo-Democracies." *The International Dimension of Democratization: Europe and the Americas*. Ed. Laurence Whitehead. 2nd ed. Oxford: Oxford University Press. 26–54.

Schmitter, Philippe C. (with Claudius Wagemann, and Anastassia Obydenkova). 2005. "Democratization and State Capacity." Paper presented at the XV Congreso Internacional del CLAD sobre la Reforma del Estado y de la Administración Pública. Santiago, Chile, 18–21 October.

Schumpeter, Joseph A. 1942. *Capitalism, Socialism, and Democracy*. New York: Harper and Bros.

Sen, Amartya. 1992. *Inequality Re-examined*. Cambridge, MA: Harvard University Press.

———. 1999. "Democracy as a Universal Value." *Journal of Democracy* 10(3): 3–17.
Shapiro, David. 2003. *The State of Democratic Theory.* Princeton: Princeton University Press.
Skocpol, Theda. 1979. *States and Social Revolutions: A Comparative Analysis of France, Russia, and China.* Cambridge: Cambridge University Press.
Stalher-Sholk, Richard, Harry E. Vanden, and Glen David Kuecker. 2007. "Globalizing Resistance: The New Politics of Social Movements in Latin America." *Latin American Perspectives* 34(5): 5–16.
Stiglitz, Joseph E. 2003. *Globalization and Its Discontents.* New York and London: W.W. Norton Press.
Teichman, Judith A. 2001. *The Politics of Freeing Markets in Latin America: Chile, Argentina, and Mexico.* Chapel Hill, NC: University of North Carolina Press.
———. 2003. "Latin America: Inequality, Poverty and Questionable Democracies." *Civilizing Globalization: A Survival Guide.* Ed. Richard Sandbrook. Albany: State University of New York. 39–52.
Tilly, Charles. 2007. *Democracy.* Cambridge: Cambridge University Press.
Tulchin, Joseph S., and Gary Bland. 2005. "Inequalities and the Globalization Debate," *Getting Globalization Right: The Dilemmas of Inequality.* Ed. Joseph S. Tulchin and Gary Bland. Boulder: Lynne Rienner Press. 221–29.
United Nations Development Program. 2005. *Human Development Report.* New York: UNDP.
Weinstein, Michael M. 2005. *Globalization: What's New?* New York: Columbia University Press.
Whitehead, Laurence. "Bowling in the Bronx: The Uncivil Interstices Between Civil and Political Society." *Civil Society in Democratization.* Ed. Peter Burnell and Peter Calvert. London: Frank Cass. 22–42.

E-RESOURCES

International Centre for Human Rights and Democratic Development (www. ichrdd.ca). A Canadian parastatal organization devoted to the promotion of democracy and international human rights as defined by the United Nations.

National Democratic Institute for International Affairs (www.ndi.org). Funded by the US and foreign governments as well as NGOs such as the Bill and Melinda Gates Foundation, it promotes international human rights and democracy, especially elections, transparency, and civil society.

National Endowment for Democracy (www.ned.org). A US government website for information about democracy. The site is considered somewhat controversial because of a built-in bias in favor of governments supportive of the US.

International Foundation for Electoral Systems (www.ifes.org). An American NGO funded by US and foreign governments as well as international institutes like the United Nations, it helps foreign governments to create free, fair, clean, competitive elections, with a high level of citizen participation.

United Nations Research Institute for Social Development (www.unrisd.org). A list of academic works examining social issues such as healthcare and education.

TWO

Democracy in Latin America: A Political History

KATHERINE ISBESTER

In these quantitative scientific times, history is a hard sell. Yet, to understand Latin Americans' skepticism about their democracies and the continuity of non-democratic practices, history must be addressed. In his magisterial history of democracy (2009, 875), John Keane wrote, "Treat the remembrance of things past as vital to democracy's present and future ... 'history' should be posted on the mirrors and doorframes of all democrats, to serve as a daily reminder of the reasons why today and tomorrow depend on yesterday."

Since 1809, when Latin American nations started rebelling against Spanish colonialism and forging their own independent countries, the region has been wracked by civil wars, invasions, revolutions, dictatorships, and sham democracies.[1] Throughout its postcolonial history, there has been a persistent struggle to create a truly democratic state. "Latin America made consistent, repeated, and intensive efforts to implant electoral democracy over the course of the twentieth century.... Indeed, the struggle for democracy has been one of the defining features of the region's recent history" (Smith 2005, 19). Consequently, the recent transition to democracy in Latin America should more accurately be called the re-democratization of Latin America because many of these countries had previously celebrated transitions to democracy only to see those democratic gains erased. The autocracies of the 1930s gave way to electoral democracies throughout most of Latin America, and by 1959 only four Latin American nations were dictatorships. These electoral democracies were overthrown by the military in the 1950s, and by the 1960s were again replaced by electoral democracies or democratic-ish governments, making the majority of the nations of Latin America either electoral democracies or regimes with strong democratic credentials. However, the military reimposed its power throughout the 1960s and 1970s through increasingly brutal dictatorships. By the mid-1970s, only three Latin American countries were democratic, that is, having both civil liberties and political rights. Starting in 1978, the cycle reversed itself and electoral democracy again emerged. Today, almost every country in Latin America has constitutionalized its civil liberties and democratic procedures to some degree.

In order to understand these cycles of democracy it is useful to examine the Latin American state for its degree of autonomy from the elite, and the degree of state intervention in the economy, that is, state capacity. Many of Latin America's experiments with democracy were overshadowed by the state's inability to gain autonomy from the nation's elite. Without state capacity, economic development protected elite control over the economy and authoritarian practices continued within the state. This perpetuated socioeconomic inequality. With time, it also eroded democratic norms, institutions, and procedures. Despite Latin American democracies reaching a minimum democratic standard, they were never able to deepen or safeguard democracy and, instead, reverted to authoritarianism.

An autocracy or authoritarianism is a form of dictatorship. Like a democracy, it is a system that disperses power. Unlike a democracy, it disperses power through a small set of political actors and has little moral content. Power generally resides in the supreme leader. Civil society is either controlled or oppressed. While there is some limited mobilization of civilians and some political pluralism, what there is tends to be controlled.

ELITE CONTROL, CONSTITUTIONS, AND *CAUDILLOS*, 1820s-1930

After the wars of independence ended in the 1820s, new struggles arose between various regional and state leaders for control of the nascent state. The ex-colonies inherited a feudal organization of power with profound inequalities. It was unclear whether the best form of government was a monarchy, albeit a Latin American one, or a republic. Mexico initially decided in favor of a monarchy, shifted to a republic in 1823, and then reinstated the monarchy from 1864 to 1867. Brazil maintained its monarchy until 1889. The rest of Latin America compromised on political representation that was restricted to an elite 10 per cent of the populace (i.e., an oligarchy) but was legally inscribed in a constitution. A constitutional oligarchy, also known as a democratic oligarchy, is a form of autocracy in which the state exists to protect and advance one social group instead of another, both of which are generally elite. The oligarchic elite controlling the state could legally suspend civil liberties and political rights, confiscate private property, and establish authoritarian practices. Latin Americans decided that the solution to these political acts was to have better written constitutions. Between the 1820s, when Latin America obtained its independence, and the end of the nineteenth century, Latin America averaged six constitutions per country (Smith 2005, 22).

Although the state was weak, it created a powerful military for three reasons. First, Latin America had to defend itself. Europe and the United States were deciding whether to claim this newly independent territory for themselves and were weighing the costs and benefits. Latin America's ability to defend itself substantially raised the cost of foreign intervention. Second, without clear borders, the new nations quarrelled diplomatically and militarily with one another. Third, the military helped to centralize power and integrate the sparsely populated regions into a nation. The military became such a strong actor that its support became pivotal in transferring political power between parties. Latin America's new states, then, were simultaneously too weak to gain autonomy from the elite yet too strong militarily.

A form of intra-elite conflict was *caudillismo*, a non-democratic rule by strongmen, who generally arose via the military, possibly had humble beginnings, and usually ruled with the support of the rural aristocracy. *Caudillos* and their militias fought each other for control of the state. Typically, *caudillos* did not institutionalize their power, letting it reside wholly in themselves. Conversely, a folk *caudillo* could solidify his rule through representing the will of the people and opposing the elite. Rafael Carrera, president of Guatemala 1839–65, is an example of a folk *caudillo*. *Caudillismo* slowly waned throughout the nineteenth century as Latin America increased its export markets. International trade gave greater strength to the commercial urban elite, weakening the influence of the rural elite and, in the process, undermining a power base for *caudillismo*. However, *caudillos* persisted as regional leaders.

Both oligarchies and *caudillismo* thrived on informal relations of power, such as clientelism or bureaucratic patrimonialism. Clientelism is the unequal relationship between a powerful patron and a weaker client that is based on an exchange of goods and services. The patron offers security and resources in exchange for support and/or labor. The patron benefits far more from this system than the client does, and the patron may act violently to protect his network of clients. Clientelism can operate within a governing system, including a democratic one, by using political parties or the political machinery of government to distribute rewards through patron–client networks. Bureaucratic patrimonialism is similar to clientelism in that political authority is based on personal relationships and the distribution of public goods such that the property of the rulers and the state are indistinguishable. Clientelism and bureaucratic patrimonialism within a democracy disrupt the ability of political parties to run a meaningful campaign, of a government to respond to popular needs, or of civil society to participate in the formation of policies and values. These hierarchical and authoritarian practices, which run through relationships between citizens, are more likely found in a society with high rates of poverty, economic inequality, and lack of state welfare. These authoritarian practices create their own set of rules, which can be communicated and enforced outside the official channels. These rules are common knowledge despite being unspoken or illegal.[2] There is the expectation that everyone will behave in a certain manner and will be punished if they do not. Because of this disciplinarian element combined with the inequality between patron and client, these practices are authoritarian. Because these practices are rule-bound, communicated and enforced, they operate as institutions. Because they are illicit, or at least non-transparent, they are called informal institutions. These informal institutions still operate today. They are supplemented by other non-democratic practices that perpetuate injustice and undermine democracy, such as crony capitalism and corruption.

Postcolonial Latin America's integration into global trade modernized both the economies and attitudes to governance. Immigration, the construction of national infrastructure, and policies to reform inefficient modes of socioeconomic organization such as the *latifundia* began, although not in Central America and not without setbacks. To service the growing industrialization of Europe and the United States, Latin America exported raw resources (foodstuff, minerals, wool, and hemp) and imported finished products. Between 1825 and 1850, the value of exports leaving the port of Buenos Aires nearly tripled. The number of ships carrying goods from Chile to England increased by almost 300 per cent between 1820 and 1847 (Burns 1994, 101). The economic infrastructure was built to facilitate export-based trade, which was funded almost exclusively by European or American investments. There was little development of the internal economic infrastructure to move goods around the nation for domestic consumption, and little development of domestic manufacturing or of finished goods. An export-oriented economy generally meant that the state had more autonomy from its elite than an agricultural state (such as Central American nations) because exporting states could raise money from taxing exports rather than from tariffs or consumption, income, or land taxes. Nonetheless, the state still lacked capacity because of the collapsing of state and elite interests and the overlapping of actors from the political and economic sectors of society.[3]

This export-led economic organization was the ideology of a small government (also known as liberalism because power would then reside with individuals protected through civil liberties). Supporters of liberalism were predominantly exporters and organized themselves into liberal parties throughout Latin America. Landowners and the Church organized themselves into conservative parties. The divisions between the two groups should not be overemphasized. In fact, when liberal parties held power they did not engage in agrarian reform. When conservative parties were in power, they offered concessions to foreign companies and supported the modernization of the economy. Both liberals and conservatives participated in systematically oppressing the indigenous population so that there would be a ready supply of cheap labor. To promote stability and to attract foreign investment, both parties placed a premium on law and order that meant ruthlessly suppressing uprisings and political mobilizations. Neither party invested in the development of state institutions; public administration was of poor quality; and public financing was limited due to low tariff levels and minimal taxation.

The economic dependency on exports and the political restrictions on participating in the polity slowed the development of the middle and working classes in Latin America. The middle class was made up of a number of middle-class groups reflecting the constrained industrialization of the economy, that is, urban professionals, small entrepreneurs, artisans, and medium-sized farmers. The working class was limited by numerous small enterprises, a high number of immigrants who eschewed political involvement, and surplus labor, in addition to the capital intensive nature of Latin American industrialization. Nonetheless, by the 1870s, labor unions began to organize in the port cities and capitals. The middle class, the political parties, and the state shaped the labor movement, although the extent of the influence varied from country to country. It was the middle class who consistently pushed for democratization and, in conjunction with the working class, were able to deepen democracy (Rueschemeyer, Huber Stephens, and Stephens 1992, 181). As the nineteenth century closed, new political parties—driven by the middle class and extolling nationalism, industrialization, and modernization—gained power in Argentina, Brazil, Chile, and Uruguay. Although these parties challenged oligarchic rule, once in power, they proved to be remarkably conservative and did little to transform their societies. Always the exception to the rule, Costa Rica began electoral democracy in 1899. In Mexico, the *caudillo* leader Porfirio Díaz (1876–1911) used the military and constitutionalism to gain power and then stripped the state of what democratic procedures it had. His tenure as dictator sparked the Mexican Revolution (1910–20). Mexico's triumphant national party imposed single-party corporatist democracy on Mexico from 1929 to 2000.

In the nineteenth century, Britain was the dominant global power and the largest investor in Latin America, shaping it to suit British needs. The British navy defended British commercial production in Latin America, while the British government, highly experienced in the mechanics of running an empire, negotiated trade agreements and treaties beneficial to itself. The Latin American elite, having already embraced liberalism, discounted the value of any policies that might have mitigated the impact of Britain. This pattern of commercialism persisted with the rise of the United States as the dominant regional power. By the early twentieth century, the US supplanted Britain as Latin America's largest investor.

In addition to the techniques that the British employed to protect its business or strategic interests, various US governments invaded, militarily threatened, or overthrew Latin American governments, including those democratically elected. The United States further threatened to control the banks and custom houses of Latin American nations. This combination of military intervention with economic sanctions is called gunboat and dollar diplomacy. Starting in 1845, the United States militarily intervened 30 times in Latin America, excluding wars by proxy. This form of American foreign policy was most overt in Mexico and Central America where the United States claimed possession of the independent (previously Mexican) State of Texas in 1845 and then invaded Mexico in 1846. Until the Great Depression caused a reduction in American military funding, the US invaded Central American and Caribbean countries to support their dictatorships, sometimes invading the same country more than once. Post–World War II, the US continued its intervention in the name of anticommunism. Unfortunately, the legacy of gunboat and dollar diplomacy has left a bitter aftertaste in the mouths of many Latin Americans.

In the early decades of the twentieth century, the Latin American nation was notably modern, with an established banking and economic infrastructure and showing impressive economic growth. Political participation in the wealthier nations had stabilized around an export-oriented elite with a slowly widening franchise. However, the state was weak and captured by the elite, and lacked transparent and effective institutions. While civil society was elite-dominated, the masses were frequently excluded from deliberative decision-making, rising up in protests or supporting folk *caudillos*. This combined reality hampered the deepening of democracy with its inclusionary moral code, processes and norms, viable institutions, and dispersion of power. The ruling legacy of Latin America's constitutionalized elite of the late nineteenth and early twentieth century persists today—it continues its obsession with (but disregard for) the rule of law, its emphasis on constitutionalism, its profound inequalities, and its deeply embedded authoritarian practices.

In 1929, when the New York Stock Exchange collapsed and Europe and North America slid into the Great Depression, Latin America's economies also crashed. Exports to Europe declined by almost 50 per cent. Because global demand for Latin American goods contracted, there was a glut on the world market and prices fell, so the goods Latin America did sell internationally earned less. Furthermore, between 30 per cent and 40 per cent of Latin America's productive capital was controlled by foreigners who repatriated it. All of Latin America except Argentina suspended their debt payments, which made it difficult to obtain the foreign capital necessary to buy needed imports.

STATE-LED DEVELOPMENT, 1930–1982

The economic collapse brought to the fore the failures of Latin America's development. By the time Europe and North America were again importing goods to fight World War II, the constitutionalized oligarchies were erased. Instead, Latin America experimented with various forms of governance. Electoral democracies with developmentalist states emerged in Chile, Uruguay, and Colombia (1942), Guatemala and Peru (1945), Argentina, Brazil, and Venezuela (1946), and Ecuador (1948). Costa Rica reestablished its electoral democracy in 1948 after political strife in 1947. Dictatorships that modernized the economy emerged in the rest of Latin America. Some nations flipped between electoral democracies and dictatorships. These experiments with ballots versus bullets disguised the greater impact of state-led development.

It seemed obvious in the wake of the collapsing export market that Latin America should free itself from dependency on foreign markets and offset declining terms of trade by manufacturing its own goods for domestic consumption. In theory, through meeting local needs, Latin American nations could finance economic infrastructure appropriate to domestic development and create backward linkages into the economy to enhance diversification. Industrialization would also employ the cities' surplus labor, which was expanding rapidly due to urbanization. Trade would later expand to the regions that allowed comparative advantages to emerge, and, in the fullness of time, Latin America would once again trade globally as an equal of Europe and the United States. This economic strategy was called import-substitution industrialization (ISI), also known as inward-oriented growth.

Latin American states raised tariffs, favored multiple exchange rates, controlled imports, subsidized or gave tax credit to domestic manufacturing, and subsidized food and public transport to keep down labor costs. Agriculture was used as a mechanism to increase the supply of money because crops could be sold internationally and domestically. From the mid-1930s to the mid-1940s, the first businesses were typically basic food and clothing manufacturers in Chile, Argentina, Brazil, Uruguay, and Mexico. Colombia, Costa Rica, and Venezuela joined in the 1950s, and Peru by the 1960s. By the 1960s and 1970s, production had expanded to consumer durables, intermediate goods, and even capital goods.

Initially, ISI was successful. By the mid-1950s, Latin American economies were growing faster than those in Europe. Between 1950 and 1970, the region's GDP tripled and per capita income increased by two-thirds. Infant mortality fell and life expectancy increased. By the 1960s, Mexico supplied 95 per cent of its own domestic consumption, and Brazil supplied 98 per cent (Green 2003, 23). Dependency on Europe and the US declined. The working class grew in strength and political importance, rapidly unionizing and gaining a higher standard of living. To a degree, income was redistributed downwards through offering the benefits of the growing economy to the working class, although, it is important to note, not through structural changes to the distribution of income. An alliance between the middle and working classes helped to provide and improve state services and social welfare. A new industrial entrepreneur emerged, skilled not so much in laissez-faire economics but in extracting concessions from the state. The problem of the current account deficit was temporarily solved. Horizontal diversification of finished products improved. The state built physical infrastructure and institutions to assist production, and either created or invested in new industries. Over time, several nations developed powerful domestic industries that did compete globally. Brazil, for instance, produced a competitive shoe industry, set up its own aviation industry, developed bio-fuel technology well in advance of other nations, and worked with multinational corporations to produce cars for the regional consumer. Regional trade increased substantially and was mediated by new regional integration agencies such as the Central American Common Market (CACM) (1960), the Andean Pact (1969), and the Latin American Free Trade Area (1960).

However, industrialization was sporadic and confined to the larger countries of Argentina, Brazil, and Mexico. Backward linkages rarely happened, and problems of scale emerged, that is, a nation would have several very large and powerful firms and very small firms with little in between. This gave large firms disproportionate influence over the state. The expanded bureaucracy was inefficient, and the decision-making about who would get which subsidy or tax break and for how much deepened both corruption and bureaucratic patrimonialism. Goods were expensive or shoddily made due to the lack of competition, and markets were inevitably small with a limited number of consumers. The benefits of regional markets were eroded by a beggar-thy-neighbor competitiveness. Latin American nations still needed to import intermediate goods as well as capital and technology, creating supply bottlenecks, increasing their reliance on foreign currencies (i.e., debt), and incorporating technology that was inappropriate to Latin America's labor surplus. Ironically, using foreign currencies to modernize industrial production made the state more reliant on a reinvigorated agricultural sector despite the global decline in prices for its goods. Industrialization could not absorb the jobless. To offset the political instability arising from high unemployment, the state expanded beyond its needs, bloating bureaucracy. By the 1960s, the ISI model was stagnating.

ISI spurred a specific form of state. ISI was not laissez-faire free market enterprise but rather state-led development. Its purpose was not merely to increase the GDP but also to improve the lives of the working class. This was its democratic ethos, its moral code. As a developmentalist state, it engaged in approving and negotiating with different sectors of society, ordering and implementing from above an economic and social model for the good of all. The urban middle class and some blue-collar workers had access to relatively generous social provisions such as healthcare, education, and pensions. But the informal sector and rural workers did not. Social spending became tied to occupation, rather than being a universal social good (Haggard and Kaufman 2008, 112). Because the state expanded before an autonomous and influential working class did, the political and economic elite could use state institutions to "intervene in the development of civil society in order to prevent disruptive consequences of industrialization" (Rueschemeyer, Huber Stephens, and Stephens, 1992, 184). As a result, civil society was weak overall with political participation concentrated in the urban centres. In Brazil, where the state took the strongest role in absorbing both new groups and the labor movement, an autonomous civil society did not emerge until the 1970s. In Chile, Peru, Venezuela, and Bolivia, which all exported minerals rather than manufactured or agricultural goods, proceeds from export taxes gave the state some autonomy from the elite and the opportunity to promote a middle- and working-class alliance. Unsurprisingly, Chile and Venezuela were able to deepen democracy earlier than other nations, and Bolivia had a revolution. The Argentine state absorbed the labor movement and the middle class through political parties. In an entirely different manner, the Mexican state absorbed its labor movement and negotiated societal conflict between the classes with the result that an autonomous civil society did not emerge until the 1990s. With a prominent state apparatus, a weak civil society, and an economy dominated by large firms and landowners, political parties became a new source of power. In many Latin American nations, political parties were taken over by populists or new political parties were created around a populist leader.

Populism was a morally driven political movement with a heterogeneous social and economic base. Democratically elected populist leaders arose when changing economic structures split the traditional governing elite and produced new economic actors operating in new alliances, for example, unions and industrialists. Charismatic leadership and the cult of the individual were features necessary to override the conflicts inherent within these broad alliances. Populism performed some important positive functions such as extending the franchise to include all the electorate, mobilizing the working class, and decreasing economic and social inequality in society. The famous Latin American populist leaders Juan Perón of Argentina and Getulio Vargas of Brazil led multiclass urban-based alliances to power in the late 1930s and early 1940s.

Although populist leaders were democratically elected and the countries were at least superficially democratic, the populist state was authoritarian in character and practice. Populist leaders claimed to be one with the people and persuaded the people that they could be fully represented by the leader. Thus, intermediary political structures like opposition parties, autonomous branches of government, and the rule of law were deemed to inhibit the connection between the leader and his people, and were consequently bypassed. Other components of a democratic state like an autonomous civil society and a critical free press had the treasonous aura of the enemy and were either co-opted by the state, ignored, or oppressed. Unions and other civil society organizations that cooperated with populism exchanged their autonomy and legitimacy for participating in government. There was no loyal opposition critiquing government policy. Corruption became institutionalized and normalized within the state, erasing transparency and horizontal accountability. Populism did not eliminate authoritarian practices or inequalities; instead, it absorbed all conflict into a nationalist, corporatist, reformist movement-cum-government-cum-state. Thus populism reduced the deliberative mechanisms of democracy. As a result, conflict could not be resolved through compromise, accommodation, and deliberative negotiation, that is, democratic governance.

The call for a deeper democracy and a better standard of living for the dispossessed ignited revolutionary movements. From the 1950s and into the twenty-first century, guerrilla groups confronted dictatorships and minimum democracies. Occasionally, revolutionary groups won important concessions from the government, such as EZLN in Chiapas, Mexico, setting up autonomous local governments (1994). Occasionally the conflict between the revolutionary groups and the government brought civil war, which no side clearly won, as in El Salvador (1980–92). Rarely, revolutionary groups overthrew governments as they did in Nicaragua (1979). Mostly however, the low-intensity guerrilla campaigns and military response frightened citizens, drained resources, and served as a pretext for militarization.

Even in those countries without revolutionary movements, ISI's stagnating economies produced widespread street protests. The middle class, fearful of the chaos of the uprisings, broke its interclass alliance with the working class and lent its support to non-democratic options. The military was used to quell dissent, impose order, and return the nation to the military's definition of normal. Without any democratic check on the military, with a weak civil society, and with charismatic leaders losing their appeal, civilian governments were overthrown in Brazil (1964), Argentina (1966), Chile (1973), and Uruguay (1973).

The coups ushered in bureaucratic-authoritarian regimes (B-A regimes), which tortured, murdered, exiled, and terrorized in the name of order, normalcy, and economic development. Like all authoritarian governments, B-A regimes had limited pluralism so there was some competition within the elite to rule. However, mass participation, class interests, and civil society mobilization were oppressed. To this day, a fearfulness of mobilizing and confronting the powerful hinders the process of deepening democracy. B-A regimes were unique in the extent to which they embraced specialist and technocratic approaches without any ideological commitment or moral judging. This technocratic approach to governance has dominated Latin America until the rise of the Pink Tide (which began in 1999 and continues). Mexico's own version of this system was a slow and peaceful transition from its populist leader, Lázaro Cárdenas, to a B-A regime while maintaining its elite cohesion and societal order despite declining terms of trade and occasional powerful eruptions of mass unrest. Central America never escaped its dictatorships (with the exception of Costa Rica). Its agricultural elite merged with its exporters to support a coercive state. In Guatemala, the military split between the reformists and traditionalists with the reformists obtaining power and initiating a developmentalist state. With the support of the CIA, that effort was overthrown in 1954, sowing the seeds for the tragic civil war from which Guatemala is still recovering.

All the economies were vulnerable due to high debt and inflation, declining terms of trade for agricultural products, and limited manufactured exports. (Venezuela had its oil, which protected it from the failures of ISI, and Colombia hardly borrowed any funds.) Vulnerability was enhanced by global changes, predominantly the oil shocks of 1973–74 and 1978–79. The cost of producing manufactured goods rose but Latin American nations borrowed their way out with easy access to credit. Between 1975 and 1982, Latin America borrowed $60 billion (Green 2003, 28). The money was used to subsidize production and was sent back to the United States in the form of capital flight,[4] that is, it was spent by the military to buy American-made weapons and poured into large development projects of dubious value built by American contractors, such as hydroelectric dams. The revolving circuit of money from predominantly American sources to Latin America and back to the US has been dubbed the Dance of Millions.

The rise in global interest rates in 1981 changed all that. Latin American nations could no longer afford to borrow or make their debt payments.

By 1982, when Mexico defaulted on its interest payments, Latin American economies were in crisis. The debt crisis was so profound that it made the public accept radical economic reform. The global banking community was fearful that Latin America's imminent bankruptcy could destabilize the global financial market. Working with international financial institutions (IFIs) such as the International Monetary Fund and the World Bank, the United States and other governments restructured Latin American debt payments to make them affordable. In exchange, Latin American nations agreed to insert their economies into globalized forces of production. This reorganization was called monetarism, also known as neoliberalism, the Washington Consensus, or structural adjustment.

EXPORT-LED SMALL-STATE DEVELOPMENT, 1982–2008

In 1982–83, 17 nations of Latin America agreed to neoliberalize their economies; the remaining nations did so later. The goal was to increase the GDP through prioritizing exports and freeing the market (liberalization) to attract direct foreign investment and transnational corporations. But this could only be achieved once inflation was reduced through controlling the supply of money (monetarism). Monetarism included stabilization through cutting wages, increasing interest rates, and devaluing the currency. Market liberalization included privatizing state-owned companies; stripping state subsidies on food and transport; deregulating the trade, investment, and financial sectors; replacing tariff barriers with a sales tax; dismantling various forms of price controls; and weakening labor rights to "flexibilize" labor in order to keep wages low, unions inhibited, and employers' contributions to the minimum. Despite the rhetoric, the free market principle was not universally applied, and some policies allowed the emergence of monopolies or near monopolies and subsidized exports.

While the lion's share of the attention has been given to the economics of neoliberalism, it would be a mistake to think of neoliberalism as being merely an economic strategy.[5] It was also a reworking of the state and of the relationship between the state and the citizen. The state was to be reduced in an effort to diminish its politicized nature, and thereby avoid neoliberal politics from being subverted by rent-seeking elites or groups mobilizing to protect their interests. The state was not to be autonomous (as the ideology presented it) but rather apolitical and disengaged from democracy itself (Grindle 2001). Furthermore, it remained captured by technocratic elites.

Citizenship was reconfigured to be more atomized and individualistic, with a corresponding reduction of the role of the group and the community. Human agency became synonymous with market activity and consumer choice. Neoliberalism "celebrated the individual as the political subject of citizenship" (Yashar 2007, 70). This did not necessarily have to be detrimental to democracy as long as the individual was embedded in a powerful and autonomous civil society. However, weakened by authoritarianism and then by the economic crisis, civil society became little more than an arena for consumption, and citizenship became a form of consumerism. This depoliticized both citizenship and civil society, eroded the image of the active citizen engaged in moral action, and impeded the creation of horizontal bonds and social trust that Putnam and Tocqueville felt were critical to a democracy (O'Donnell 2004).

The reconfiguration of citizenship and the state was heavily negotiated, with different nations arriving at different compromises, depending on the balance of power between the supporters of neoliberalism and its opposition. The severity of the economic crisis, the strength of civil society organizations, and the power of political parties and key political actors affected the compromises reached. Generally, the more severe the crisis, the more latitude the state had to impose harsher adjustments. Similarly, a strong executive could frequently overcome resistance. So Chile under Augusto Pinochet, Argentina under Carlos Menem, Peru under Alberto Fujimori, and Mexico under Carlos Salinas experienced a harsher implementation of neoliberalism than Uruguay, Brazil, and Costa Rica,[6] which had more open and competitive political systems and more mobilized civil societies (Huber 2005, 94). Consequently, neoliberalism was not monolithic, all-powerful, or static. Instead, it was and remains continuously reworked in a fragmentary, heterodox, and indeterminate fashion.

The economic impact of neoliberalism on Latin America was profound. The 1980s were called the "Lost Decade." In 1982, Latin America's economy shrank for the first time since World War II. Imports were halved between 1981 and 1983, and exports exceeded imports until 1992. The accumulated trade surplus between 1982 and 1992 was $243 billion, which was slightly more than the total debt service payment of $219 billion. Nations attempted different policies. These included free trade deals (NAFTA), debt restructuring programs (Paris Club, Brady Plan), and new currencies (*cruzado* in Brazil, the *austral* in Argentina). They temporarily stabilized Latin American economies, which were no doubt helped by favorable global conditions. However, with rising global interest rates in 1988, any macroeconomic stability was lost and economies continued to contract (Green 2003, chapter 3).

Neoliberalism was also expressed through international free trade deals. These inserted the newly liberalized economies of Latin America into global trade regimes. The North America Free Trade Agreement (NAFTA) between Mexico, the United States, and Canada was signed in 1993 and came into effect in 1994. Like the World Trade Organization (WTO), NAFTA has been called a supraconstitution because of the profound impact it can have on the state, the economy, and the organization of power relations within a country (Clarkson 2004, 155; Wise 2009). The attempt to expand NAFTA to include all the countries in Latin America creating a Free Trade Area of the Americas (FTAA) has been unsuccessful due to the concerns raised in Latin America over the impact the agreement would have on patents and copyright, foreign investment, the codification of corporate rights over individual rights, and the reduced scope of the judicial system to resolve potential conflict over trade. The fear over US abuse of its economic might has been effectively used by reformist and populist governments as a spur to seek alternative means of stimulating the economy. Luiz Inácio Lula de Silva of Brazil successfully used the fear of FTAA as a way of attracting uncommitted voters to his presidential bid. The US also had its concerns of job losses, environmental standards, and human rights abuses, which have slowed the passing of free trade agreements with Latin American nations.

More politically feasible were bilateral free trade deals between individual nations. These smaller deals galvanized less public protest in the US and Canada. Smaller nations, unable to stand alone against American demands, folded more quickly at the bargaining stage. For example, when protests against the bilateral free trade deal threatened its passing in Nicaragua, US President George W. Bush wrote a letter to the president of Nicaragua strongly urging him to ensure that the bill be passed. It quickly was. The United States and individual countries have signed bilateral free trade deals with Chile (2004), Peru (2006–09), the Central American Free Trade Agreement plus the Dominican Republic (DR-CAFTA) (2005–07), and has negotiated one with Colombia (2008; which has the potential of passing through Congress in 2010).

With the failure of FTAA and the slow pace of bilateral trade deals, agreements with the EU and Asia expanded. This increased exports to Asia-Pacific, especially from the Southern Cone countries. However, imports into Latin America, predominantly intermediate and high technology goods, were greater than exports and created current account deficits.

The economic crisis continued to spur capital flight from the region. Between 1980 and 1990, Latin America became a net exporter of capital at an annual rate of 3.5 per cent of the region's GDP (Huber 2005, 79). But by 1991, capital inflows were greater than outflows. Capital returned to Latin America predominately in the form of speculative capital taking advantage of the deregulated financial markets. Financial liberalization reduced banking regulations, restrictions on foreign investments, bank-required lending reserves, and rules governing credit. A credit bubble emerged and then burst in Chile (1982), Mexico (1994), Argentina (1995), Brazil, Ecuador, Peru, Colombia (1998), and Argentina (1999). While financial markets were partially reregulated and stabilized currency and investors' risks, the volumes of capital did not return. Instead, capital flight from the region continued with weak financial markets becoming an ongoing concern. Between 1995 and 2005, the number of companies listed on Latin American stock markets shrank by 10 per cent. In comparison, the number listed on Asian stock markets during the same period expanded by 33 per cent.

The deregulation of the financial market had the unintended consequence of facilitating organized crime, in particular narco-trafficking. Colombia, Bolivia, and Peru are the world's suppliers of cocaine. In 2004, the potential value of the cocaine trade was estimated at $565 million (Goehsing 2008, 96). The Cali Cartel began buying banks in Colombia in the 1970s to launder its earnings. As it became easier through neoliberalism and NAFTA to own or create banks both nationally and internationally, cocaine smugglers began owning banks in the rest of Latin America, especially those with ties to American banks. This strategy was adopted by Mexican crime cartels in the 1990s. Furthermore, liberalized banking permitted the rapid financial transactions without state oversight that are essential to money laundering. By facilitating the laundering of money across national borders, by turning drug smugglers into bankers, narco-traffickers and crime lords became powerful and legitimate actors.

Nonetheless, neoliberalism had some successes within a narrow economic definition. The tight control of money eventually reduced inflation and kept it low and stable. This was not a minor success. Inflation punished the poor more than other classes because they had fewer convertible assets and even fewer savings in foreign currencies. Exports did increase; the total volume of Latin America's trade doubled in the 1990s. Labor was once again cheap in Latin America. Trade and labor liberalization allowed the ready exploitation of resources and the creation of export processing zones (also known as *maquiladoras* or simply *maquilas*). *Maquilas* were assembly plants mostly for sewing together garments or building parts for the auto industry. They were originally built along the US–Mexican border to take advantage of the proximity to the American market. Later, they were built in Central America to take advantage of both its relative proximity to the American market as well as wages that were cheaper than Mexico's. *Maquilas* benefited from NAFTA, which gave them access to the American market. However, *maquilas* have appalling working conditions and wages, making them politically controversial.

While some aspects of Latin America's political economy were thriving, as a whole Latin American economies stagnated until 2004. Latin America's average annual growth in real GDP per capita from 1990 to 2003 averaged 1.2 per cent, which is hardly impressive (UNDP 2004, 50). The percentage of the population living in poverty increased between 1980 and 2004 because of the rise in unemployment and underemployment in practically every country (Machinea and Kacef 2007, 2). Furthermore, neoliberalism hurt women more than men, "feminizing" poverty and inequality that hurt female-headed households more so than dual-headed households. With rising unemployment, employment-based social spending on healthcare and pensions declined. Social indices of health, mortality, and literacy worsened and have only recently seen an improvement. When the economies began to grow again, the growth was fueled by global demand, particularly China's increasing consumption of Latin America's raw resources, rather than its own organization of production.

The underperformance of the neoliberalized economies is partially due to low state capacity. The Latin American state, colonized by the elite and eroded by clientelism, has always been weaker than it should be. Neoliberalism's restructuring of the state further weakened it by removing its regulatory agencies and reducing the caliber of state institutions, which diminished its mandate to provide primary services and infrastructure. Through minimizing the state's ability to act with capacity, neoliberalism reduced the ability of the economy to function as it could or workers to be as productive as they could be. A weak state without quality institutions permitted authoritarian practices to operate unchecked. Clientelism, cronyism, and bureaucratic patrimonialism operated within the neoliberal state, not only reducing accountability and transparency but also raising the costs of doing business. With weak state institutions, tax evasion became rampant. A substantial informal market, enlarged by neoliberalism to be between 45 per cent and 50 per cent of the economy, was outside the area of regulation and taxation (Durán 2007, 6). Unable to tax the wealthy or those working in the informal market, the state was incapable of building quality institutions or funding public goods, which could safeguard the market and spur economic and social development. For example, state expenditure on the police was low. Unsurprisingly, crime in Latin America flourished. The Inter-American Development Bank estimated that per capita GDP in Latin America would be 25 per cent higher if its crime rates were to drop to world levels (Buckley 2005, 10). The most important role for the state was to guarantee the market through protecting property rights, enforcing contracts, and collecting data. But without investing in primary institutions, the state could not even do that.

A second reason for economic underperformance was the high level of economic inequality in Latin America. Economic inequality measures the gap between the amount of capital (assets and income) that the wealthiest part of the society has versus the poorest. This gap is expressed as the Gini coefficient, a number between zero and one, where zero is perfect equality and no one has more money than anyone else, and one where all the wealth resides in the hands of one person. A society that has a Gini coefficient greater than 0.4 or 0.5 is considered to have a wide disparity of wealth. Latin America's Gini coefficient is 0.57 and has been steadily rising since the 1980s.[7] In Latin America, the richest 10 per cent of individuals receive between 40 per cent and 47 per cent of the total incomes, while the poorest 20 per cent of individuals receive only 2 per cent to 4 per cent. These differences are greater than elsewhere in the world. For example, in the US, which has the highest divisions of wealth of all OECD nations, the richest 10 per cent receive 31 per cent of the total income (World Bank 2000, 7). A high Gini coefficient acts as a drag on the economy.

Neoliberal policies fostered economic inequality by squeezing the middle and working classes and reducing the state's ability to intervene. Workers' wages and opportunities were reduced. State institutions that assist equality of opportunity shrank, like laws equalizing access to credit and an embedded bureaucracy, among others. Costs rose through the privatization of public services like healthcare, pensions, and education. Income inequality grew between the highly educated worker and the low-skill laborer.[8] Banking liberalization led to increased wages for those working in the financial sector. Fiscal decentralization of the national government to regional and sub-regional governments heightened the internal wealth differences within a country, so that the poorer regions became poorer still. The reforms concentrated assets in fewer hands, delivering economic power to a small group of people who then created a political power base to perpetuate their advantages. In effect, wealth and power were transferred from the poorer people in society to the wealthier, and neoliberalism was one of the mechanisms that made this possible. Thus, poverty was structurally inherent within neoliberalism.

The failure of neoliberalism to bring its promised prosperity to Latin America caused considerable debate within IFIs, governments, and civil society. The debate reflected changing understandings of how poverty is integral to neoliberalism, and how the rising Gini coefficient acted as a drag on economic growth. Furthermore, civil society agitation for better welfare provisions led to a positive reevaluation of the role of the state in resolving social conflict and promoting social and economic development. In 1998, the World Bank endorsed cooperation between the state and market in order to increase economic productivity. State regulation and social protection, as well as quality institutions and policies enhancing competitiveness were once again promoted. There was an emphasis on increasing state capacity, the rule of law, and accountability. The World Bank called this approach "structuralism with a human face" or neostructuralism. However, it was rapidly named the post-Washington consensus or postneoliberalism. It neither fundamentally reformed neoliberalism's tight fiscal policy that restricted social spending nor altered the structural concentration of wealth in ever fewer hands. However, it did allow support for reform.

What exactly these new reforms entailed was unclear. There was much debate over the value of universal access to social welfare versus targeted relief from poverty with increased access to social services for the extreme poor. It was felt that poor nations could not realistically afford universalism. In comparison, targeting the extreme poor was supported financially by IFIs and morally by the domestic elite. In a divided continent, a consensus emerged for expanded and targeted social welfare.[9] As a result, between 1990 and 2000, social spending increased by 50 per cent. Unfortunately, programs lacked uniformity and coherence (Green 2003, 163; Molyneux 2008, 785, 794). Nonetheless, rates of extreme hunger and poverty decreased between 2004 and 2007 because of rising employment, smaller families, and increased social spending. Primary school education has expanded through Latin America, and indices on child and maternal mortality are dropping (ECLAC 2008b). In some countries, like Chile and Costa Rica, a universal social welfare floor is emerging.

The most popular, and most criticized, mechanism for addressing poverty has been conditional cash transfers (CCTs) in which money is given directly to the poor. In exchange, the poor have to send their children to school, have their children inoculated, or other similar actions. These CCT programs have been implemented in Brazil, Honduras, Colombia, Nicaragua, Mexico, and Chile. Other poverty reduction schemes, perhaps more traditional or smaller, have been strengthened and/or integrated as a way to provide better outcomes. CCTs give an almost immediate and measurable result, which is highly unusual for any public policy. They are relatively cheap to administer, enjoy multiclass support, and reduce the Gini coefficient. However, important criticisms of CCTs remain unanswered. It excludes some of the deserving poor who do not fulfill the criteria, such as the elderly and the childless. This divides communities rather than creating community solidarity. There is no public participation in setting the criteria or choosing the families; instead, they are imposed from above. There is the suggestion that CCTs shift a reformist government's emphasis from transforming structures that would benefit all the class to focusing solely on alleviating the status of the extreme poor (Teichman 2008).

Migration and remittances sent home by migrant workers have helped as well to offset poverty. Because remittances take the form of cash, consumer goods, and payment in kind, and can be sent via informal channels, they are difficult to measure. The global value of remittances from rich countries to poor ones is about $100 billion per annum. They are the second largest transfers of cash after direct foreign investment and they are substantially greater than what is received through development aid. Latin America and the Caribbean receive the largest amounts of global remittances (32 per cent) although they only have 9 per cent of the world's population. It is estimated that Mexico received $9 billion in remittances in 2001, and that same year, the highest level of remittances as a percentage of the GDP in Latin America went to Nicaragua, which received $600 million. That amount was 24 per cent of its GDP, equalled its development aid, and was greater than its total export earnings (Jennings and Clarke 2005). Remittances tend to be sent back to the lower or middle classes but not the extreme poor who lack the money to emigrate or the skills to thrive in a foreign nation. The migration of its workers and the remittances sent home have eased the pressure on governments to reform the state and society because the skilled, hard-working, and adventurous have found countries more welcoming to what they have to offer where they can obtain consumer goods, food, and even social assistance and healthcare.

After two and a half decades of export-led, small-state economies with unfettered markets in a variety of countries, it is possible to take a balanced view of neoliberalism's successes and deficits. Undoubtedly, its greatest success has been to restructure the state, the economy, and the polity without incurring revolution, civil war, or even prolonged mass uprisings. Instead, the dispossessed became migrant laborers and offset political instability through their sending home remittances. Another major success has been to create a strong structure for its own continuity. Neoliberalism will now be hard to fundamentally alter. It has been constitutionalized domestically and codified through international trade agreements. A political elite has renovated itself and now operates through the neoliberal state, and the traditional mechanisms once able to robustly forge reform have been weakened such as civil society, labor unions, and cohesive communities. Policy creation lies within closed networks of senior government officials, private sector executives, and IFIs.

Neoliberalism's other successes were mixed. While it was successful in implementing macroeconomic stability, debt in 2003 was double what it was at the start of the debt crisis in 1982, with service payments on the debt consuming one-third of the earnings from exports. This can hinder sustainable economic growth by placing inflationary pressures on currencies (Green 2003, 117). While neoliberalism has been successful in promoting exports, increasingly to Asia and other Latin American nations that lessens dependency on the US and diversifies trade, export-led growth has been based on low-skilled, low-paying jobs. While many of the state-owned industries were unproductive, privatizations of those industries, especially in the early days, have been dogged by corruption. This engendered distrust, which tarred the more transparent privatizations that followed. Privatization's successes in lowering prices and increasing profits have been overshadowed by layoffs, poor regulation, and the occasional bankruptcy. The liberalized economy that eventually did emerge has become dominated by large conglomerates, which sometimes have monopolies in essential services.

While the state has shed unnecessary jobs and agencies, the informal labor market has correspondingly expanded, increasing the number of people who are living more precariously without access to healthcare and pension plans and making the state poorer without their taxes. While tax reform simplified the system, tax revenue remained too low. While the marginal tax rate was slashed for individuals and corporations and the tax on trade was abolished, actual tax collection remained ineffectual. Furthermore, the new tax system transferred the burden of taxation from corporate and income to consumption, which is both regressive and non-redistributive. State regulation and state extraction of revenue remain difficult because of the personal ties between the business elite and the political leaders. The state is now so underfinanced that it cannot afford to run its existing governmental institutions or increase social spending. While private investment in infrastructure between 1990 and 2001 was $360 billion, more was needed to overcome decades of underinvestment (Reid 2007, 146). Basic public services like roads, utilities, transport, schools, and healthcare are crumbling or have become non-existent.

Although neoliberalism inserted Latin American economies into a globalizing world and codified new regulatory regimes to create markets appropriate to transnational capital, it facilitated organized crime and capital flight and produced speculative bubbles that destabilized the marketplace. While national differences between economic systems have been mitigated so that systems and institutions can be integrated transnationally for homogenous operations and regulations, elected governments are less able to alter neoliberal policies while democratic citizenship has weakened. Although free trade deals promised better economic growth than could be achieved under ISI, the benefits of protected access to the US market have evaporated with the emergence of China. China and the other three Asian Tigers (Hong Kong, Singapore, and South Korea) remain a tantalizing reminder of a route Latin America could have taken if it had not embraced neoliberalism. While there is general acceptance that the economies prior to neoliberalism were unsustainable, it is unclear that the restructured globalized economies are any better. Highly dependent on global consumption with weak financial markets, neoliberalism has created a continent vulnerable to international crises and to a boom–bust dynamic.

The weaknesses inherent with globalized economies became obvious in late 2008 when the subprime mortgage crisis in the US initiated a global financial meltdown that drew in nations as wide-ranging as Iceland, South

Korea, and Britain. The price of oil and other raw resources, which had been sufficiently high from 2003 to 2008 when there were fears of inflation in Latin America, plummeted and seriously restricted economic growth. Investors pulled their money from any country that even vaguely suggested a risk, such as those in Latin America. If OECD nations experienced a recession in 2009 and anticipated slow economic growth into 2010, it would have been almost impossible for developing economies to escape unscathed. By November 2008, Brazil's stock exchange, the largest in Latin America, had contracted 40 per cent, despite sound macroeconomic indicators and well-regulated banks. This was followed with the major currencies of Latin America sliding precipitously. In March 2009, the World Bank estimated that global trade would shrink for the first time since World War II, and "in 2009, the external sector will therefore no longer be a growth factor for the region" (ECLAC 2008a, 16). This is problematic because Latin American neoliberal economies are now led by exports.

DEMOCRATIZING LATIN AMERICA, 1977–

Simultaneous to the creation of the neoliberal state was the democratization of Latin America. They mutually reinforced each other with neoliberalism operating logically within a minimum democracy. In 1977, only Colombia, Venezuela, and Costa Rica had democratically elected governments. In 1978, after the withdrawal of its military, Ecuador wrote a democratic constitution and a year later held presidential elections. Also in 1978, the Peruvian military held elections for a legislative assembly and, in 1980, a democratically elected president entered office. Between 1981 and 1984, Honduras made a slow transition to democratic rule, as did Bolivia between 1978 and 1982. In 1983, Argentina elected a civilian assembly and president. In 1984, after a negotiated transition, Uruguay elected a president. Also in 1984, El Salvador, Guatemala, and Nicaragua held elections in the midst of civil wars, with Guatemala holding a second election for a civilian president a year later. In 1985, Brazil elected a civilian president. In 1989, Chile and Paraguay both elected civilian presidents. In 1990, a civilian government took over in Panama, and elections were held there in 1994. In 2000, Mexico elected its first president in 70 years who was not from the long-ruling Institutional Revolutionary Party (PRI). In 2001, Peru's backsliding into authoritarianism was halted and a civilian president was elected again.

There are competing attempts to explain why one nation democratized and another did not. One set of explanations is grounded in the transformative impact of capitalism. Industrialization in Europe produced a bourgeoisie (owners and managers of capital) who divided the elite, traditionally land-owning aristocrats, through commercializing agriculture. This in turn weakened the peasantry. In the process, the bourgeoisie weakened the alliance between the authoritarian state (generally the monarchy) and the feudal aristocrats. The balance of power inside the nation shifted to those who supported modernization, which included modernizing and rationalizing the system of governance, that is, elected assemblies, institutional capacity, and the rule of law. With time, this produced democracy (Moore 1966). In Latin America, however, ISI's industrialization strengthened the state alliance with the elite, co-opted the bourgeoisie, and absorbed working-class and peasantry discontent. Modernization theory suggests that when capitalism achieves a certain per capita income, the populace demands the political infrastructure and economic incentives to organize their own lives, meaning a change in the political economy to a capitalist democracy (Rostow 1971). However, there is little correlation between levels of development and the democratization of Latin America. Mainwaring and Pérez-Liñán (2003, 1033), in their comparative study of social and economic development and democratization, found little correlation: "In Latin America, the level of development is a weak predictor of regime type."

A second general approach is to examine warfare. Wars between states force governments to develop institutional capacity and dominate all groups within society, including the elite. Wars also force governments to seek the support of the masses in exchange for a broadening of the franchise. In addition, militarizing society standardizes language, education, healthcare, and values while eroding provincial networks, ethnic identities, and class cohesion. Latin America, due to Pax Britannica and Pax Americana, had relatively little interstate conflict. Therefore, a strong centralizing state developed late or intermittently and without bureaucratic rationality, organizational sophistication, national solidarity, or mass participation (Centeno 2002). Therborn (1977, 20) goes so far as writing, "The fragility of bourgeois democracy in Latin America may be partially attributed to the fact that it was never drawn into the mass slaughter of two world wars."

A third general approach is to look at the rise of civil society and its demands for a responsive state. B-A regimes failed economically and had to impose neoliberalism, which included the retreat of the state from a corporatist, developmentalist sanctioning of norms and activities between various sectors of society. Into the newly freed public spaces, civil society organizations emerged. Christian-based communities, soup kitchens, health clinics, and a variety of other social organizations protesting the dictatorship and the economic collapse supplemented existing civil society organizations. In other words, the economic crisis combined with an oppressive state in retreat created the conditions appropriate for the emergence of an autonomous civil society. The mobilization of civil society highlighted the authoritarian regime's lack of legitimacy and helped to create a broad multiclass alliance in favor of change. Civil society organizations did much to inculcate democratic norms, and their efforts forced the issue of democratization to be recognized. The mobilization of civil society forced military regimes to broaden their bases of support and start negotiating with the elite. In some cases, these negotiations involved labor and social movements.

These social movements operating in loose alliances never coalesced into a powerful enough political force to transform the status quo. The middle class was too small, the various soup kitchens and other civil society organizations were too disparate and underfinanced, and the labor movement too weakened by neoliberalism to force democratization. Indeed, neoliberalism's undermining of labor rights might have assisted the transition to democracy. "Flexibilizing" labor meant that the workers posed no redistributive threat to the status quo, making it easier for the elite to safeguard its economic interests in spite of democracy. So the rise of civil society did not lead to the transition to democracy, but rather shaped the extent of the implementation of democratic procedures.

A fourth common approach to understanding Latin America's democratization is how foreign governments' encouragement and assistance affected the transition to democracy. As the Cold War warmed up, American strategic concerns about communism in Latin America evaporated. Promoting democracy abroad became part of a comprehensive attempt to stabilize the international arena, and thereby safeguard the United States'—and that of other nations—domestic security. Collectively, international support for promoting democracy increased to $9 billion per annum, up from $2 billion a decade previously (Perlin and Wood 2007, 3). While the United States under the presidency of George W. Bush (2000–08) took a peculiar approach to this new foreign policy, both the US and Europe have broadly endorsed it (Youngs 2004, 28). "In several cases, US intervention helped to end dictatorships, and recent US policy has certainly promoted free and fair elections and respect for human rights [in Latin America]" (Peeler 2004, 71). However, the larger countries of the Southern Cone were not within the American geopolitical ambit and thus were minimally affected. Nonetheless, transitions to democracies seemed to have had cross-border influence (Hagopian and Mainwaring 2005).

While the rise of civil society and the impact of foreign nations may have assisted the democratization process, the strongest explanation for Latin America's transition to democracy is elite pacts. The Latin American elite pacts are considered to be, at their broadest, political parties and major political actors, the military, the unions, the Church, and the bourgeoisie. The classic definition of an elite pact is the explicit, but not always publicly explicated or justified, agreement among a select set of actors which seeks to define (or better, to redefine) rules governing the exercise of power on the basis of mutual guarantees for the 'vital interests' of those entering into it. (O'Donnell and Schmitter 1986, 36)

Political scientists refer to such negotiations as political pacts or elite pacts or elite settlements, with small variations of meaning between each term. Before and during the transition to democracy, there were negotiations between members of the elite who decided among themselves under what conditions the military would retreat and democracy be constructed. The specifics of each country meant that each agreement differed in its details. Nonetheless, certain truisms applied. In order for there to be a transition to democracy, the cost of paying imposed taxes and other fees set by a legislative assembly had to be cheaper than the cost of continued repression and civil strife. In addition, the level of uncertainty inherent within a democracy had to be less than the uncertainty generated by an authoritarian regime. In other words, an elite pact for democracy was a strategic choice rather than the embracing of a new ideology of politics.

The pacts were useful in reducing the level of political uncertainty and political competition, and thereby reducing the potential for political conflict. When socioeconomic or political conflict did arise, an elite pact allowed for the conflict to be more readily resolved. As a result, there was a remarkable level of peace and stability in the transition to democracy. This peace and stability allowed for economic growth, which then further legitimated the new democratic system. The elite pacts may have involved only some of the political actors in society, but they made political participation the norm, rather than apathy or acquiescence. In that way, elite pacts might act as models for the rest of society to emulate. The key importance of elite pacts in the transition to democracy in Latin America is difficult to overstate. "Stable democracies do not emerge simply by writing constitutions, holding elections, expanding human rights, accelerating economic growth, or exterminating leftish insurgencies. The vital step is the consensual unification of previously disunified elites" (Higley and Burton 1988, 28).

The three countries that were able to maintain their democracies post–World War II while the rest of the continent suffered under a wave of authoritarianism were products of previously negotiated elite pacts. Colombia negotiated one in 1957–58, Venezuela in 1958, and Costa Rica in 1948; although in the case of Costa Rica that pact was not formal. The peace and stability of these nations throughout the decades is a testimony to the power and advantages of elite pacts.

While elite pacts helped to bring about transitions to democracy, paradoxically they also weakened democracy. Elite pacts clearly subverted the ethos encouraged by a democratic state for meaningful engagement both individually and within a group with the goal of working toward a better end. Without clear statements of the values and ethics underpinning a democracy, the ultimate goal of a democracy remains unknown or is shrunk to the instrumental. For example, democracy is good because authoritarian governments mishandled the economy and people believe there is less chance of that with a democracy. Or, democracy is good because a democratic government will improve public services, reduce corruption, and involve the people in the decision-making process. Certainly, democracy is strengthened by these activities. Ultimately, however, democracy is more than a government service, a means to an end, or a mechanism for achieving something else. In Latin America, people understand democracy as an instrument to achieve a better quality of life economically (Camp 2001). Due to neoliberalism, economic growth in Latin America has not been as robust as expected nor has poverty been greatly diminished. This may well be one of the causes for the declining level of support for democracy in Latin America.

Civil society organizations were rarely included in the pacts. For example, the 1958 Punto Fijo pact democratized Venezuela but specified limits under which labor unions were able to organize, although a democracy permits civil society to make demands as it sees fit, not as an elite sees fit. A transition to democracy based on elite pacts does not need a robust civil society. Under an elite pact, civil society organizations become weakened, marginalized, fragmented, disillusioned, exhausted and ultimately depoliticized (Silva 2004). Yet the experience of participating in civil society changed the attitude of Latin Americans. To them, a democracy must include civil society participation with citizens actively involved in forging and implementing public policy. Top-down governing, regardless of whether the government is elected or not, is considered to be non-democratic. "The key variable mediating the relationship between government performance and citizen attachment to democracy is the nature and quality of political representation, and specifically the linkages between citizens, civil organizations, and political parties" (Hagopian 2005, 362).

Furthermore, the military across Latin America was able to negotiate amnesty for its crimes against humanity, papering over deep social trauma. Amnesty was granted in El Salvador in 1993, in Chile in 1978, and in Argentina in 1987. The issue has not been adequately dealt with in either Brazil or Guatemala. Democracy requires that all be equal before the law. The general amnesty given to the military meant that some were above the law and that the reconstituted democratic civil society could not demand justice for human rights abuses from its democratic state. The inability of civil society to be heard on this core issue produced a deep disappointment with the new democracy. This bred an indifference to the new system and to politics in general (Garretón and Newman 2001).

Equally problematic, elite pacts allowed authoritarian practices of clientelism and other non-democratic practices to be transmitted into the new democratic structures. Clientelism, crony capitalism, and bureaucratic patrimonialism operate with and through democracy's procedures, institutionalizing themselves and weakening democracy in the process. When a democracy has weak formal institutions, lacks accountability, or is insufficiently democratic, then informal institutions can structure the operating procedures of a democracy. The elite, such as the military, industrialists, bureaucrats, landed gentry, and politicians, uses democratic procedures in conjunction with informal institutions to perpetuate its own power bases. So political actors shift between formal and informal institutions depending on the context and assume that everyone else is as well (O'Donnell 2006, 286). For example, Brazil had several political pacts in its transition to democracy between 1974 and 1985. It included electoral laws that favored powerful regional elites that permitted the continuance of *caudillismo*, clientelism, and patronage (Hagopian 1992).

Unexpectedly, research suggests that informal institutions can improve democratic performance in weak democracies by resolving political deadlocks between the president and the legislature; using patron–client networks to distribute goods to the people, especially to those in rural areas; replacing government services such as policing; increasing cross-party power sharing; and supporting indigenous laws. Nonetheless, when informal institutions complement the state's institutions, demand for necessary reform is blunted. However, informal institutions can also compete with formal institutions where the rules of formal institutions violate those of informal institutions. If this becomes too blatant, the competition can reform democracy (Helmke and Levitsky 2006). Thus, the institutionalized relationships between citizens, formal and informal, legal and illegal, shape democracy and in turn influence the civil society power relationships.

While elite pacts may have dominated the region's transition to democracy, there were nonetheless two exceptions. Neither Argentina nor Ecuador had external support from the United States and neither had an elite pact. Ecuador's odd democracy emerged as the military voluntarily stepped back from power, allowing for the rise of *caudillo* leaders who were unsupported by political parties and who built a power base through patronage and populism. At a superficial level, the elite competed for power through democratic mechanisms, although once in power, had enormous difficulty governing. In comparison, Argentina's military junta fell from power over the 1982 invasion of the British-owned Falkland Islands. The military junta invaded to distract the populace from the economic crisis and to distract its own elites from their internal conflict over the transition to democracy. After the failure of the invasion, the governing military was so weak that it withdrew from power without negotiating a formal pact. The multiparty democracy that emerged (and is still being created) was more by trial and error than an elite pact (Peeler 2004, 67–72).

As the new democracies in Latin America dealt with economic crises, it was unclear that the pacts would hold, that the military would stay in their barracks, and that democracy would become the only way to govern a country. Peru suffered a temporary reversal of democracy in 1992–2001. Venezuela had two attempted coups, one by Hugo Chávez in 1992 and one against Chávez in 2002. Paraguay had two attempted coups in 1996 and 2000, and a political assassination of the vice president in 1999. Guatemala's president attempted to dissolve democracy by overthrowing himself in 1993, called in Spanish an *auto-golpe*. Between 1997 and 2006, Bolivia had four governments, demonstrating how weak its democratic political system was. Argentina went through five governments in two weeks in 2001 as it struggled with its economic crisis. Ecuador's populace drove four presidents from power between 1997 and 2006. The possibility of electoral irregularities in Mexico's 2006 presidential election roiled Mexican politics and undermined the legitimacy of the new government. In the summer of 2009, the Honduran president was deposed and the usurping president refused to reinstate him despite considerable international pressure. The issue was not resolved until a new election was called and a candidate acceptable to both the people and the elite was elected. So it was fair to wonder whether Latin America's new democracies would last or whether the transition to democracy would be "consolidated."

According to Peeler (2004, 93), once a democratized regime has had at least two changes of power from the ruling party to an opposition party without the threat of military intervention, foreign meddling, or generalized non-cooperation from the elite, it can be said that the democracy has been consolidated. On the basis of that definition, there is nothing to suggest that a consolidated democracy is a permanent state of affairs and that threats to democracy can never arise—only that threats and attempts to overthrow democracy are less likely to occur. A more challenging definition of a consolidated democracy is that it is able to defend itself against threats, while deterring regime breakdown, erosion of democratic principles and procedures, and ideally working toward an improved democracy. In effect, democracy then becomes "the only game in town" (Linz and Stepan 1996, 15.) The range of definitions suggests that there is a lack of consensus about the criteria necessary to determine when a democratizing country becomes democratic, that is, when the transition is complete. One frustrated theorist called the concept of the consolidation of democracy "a garbage-can concept, a catch-all concept, lacking a core meaning" (Schedler 1998, 105).

The issue of whether or not a democracy has been consolidated is less important than an analysis of what kind of democracy has been consolidated. The hope that accompanied the transition of democracy in Latin America was that elections would allow opposition parties and individuals to rise to positions of power which would make the government more responsive to the voters' demands, more transparent, and more efficient. Civil liberties would be constitutionalized, democratic procedures would be normalized, and a deeper democracy would organically emerge. Instead, most Latin American nations have consolidated around a democracy that allows for intra-elite competition to control a governing system with weak formal institutions, weak civil society participation, and strong informal institutions. In order to maintain this weaker democracy, political rights, the rule of law, and democratic procedures are not fully enacted.

Smith (2005, 280–81) shows declining civil liberties as democracies consolidated in Latin America. In comparing minimal (hardly any), partial (more of them), and extensive civil liberties in Latin American countries from 1972 to 2000, he noted a marked shift from minimal civil liberties under authoritarian governments to extensive civil liberties as nations democratized. However, as the newly formed democracies consolidated, their extensive civil liberties contracted until the amount of civil liberties that most citizens in Latin America had was merely partial. This falls short of the extensive civil liberties that citizens in deep democracies enjoy.

Suppressing civil liberties can be entirely legal, obscuring the reality of oppression. The rules under which parties run for power can be biased against smaller, more radical parties, which then cannot compete. This concentrates electoral competition between fewer people and fewer parties, which are almost always those of the elite. Political actors and the business elite generally come from the same economic class and might be so extremely close that collusion, cronyism, and corruption are normal practices. Protests organized by social movements to change the system might be hampered by excessive red tape and prohibitive regulations. It is not illegal to agitate for change; it is just very, very difficult. This stifles civil society from organizing on its own behalf.

While there are opposition newspapers and occasionally critical press, investigative journalists have lost their jobs, experienced threats or had their families threatened, or have been assassinated. More subtly, television, radio, and print media are frequently controlled by big political parties. Through abusing regulations, licensing, and advertising, governments can obtain positive coverage and discourage critical press. Government officials have pressured newspaper editors and journalists, denied journalists critical of the government access to officials or information, or simply bought positive coverage from journalists. Freedom House has charted the increased restrictions on the freedom of press as democracies in Latin America became consolidated. In 1986, in the midst of the transition to democracy, six nations in Latin America had full press freedom: Venezuela, Colombia, Ecuador, Peru, Costa Rica, and Honduras. The press in the three countries of Central America in the midst of a civil war, El Salvador, Nicaragua, and Guatemala, was not free. And the rest of Latin America had a press that was partly free. By 1989, as democratic reforms became normalized, only Paraguay and Central America (excepting Costa Rica) did not have a free press, Mexico and Bolivia had a partly free press, and the rest of Latin America (ten countries), was experiencing full freedom of the press. But by 2004, fifteen years after democracy, only Costa Rica, Chile, and Uruguay continued to enjoy full freedom of the press. Venezuela's press alone was deemed not free, and the press in the remaining 14 countries of Latin America was partly free. This partial oppression of free speech allowed leaders to present to the world and to themselves a society that permitted dissent, built on a political system that incorporated freedom of speech and freedom of the press. However, any system that allows systemic—if limited—suppression of speech acts as a disincentive for genuine, uncontrolled, and profound free speech. When that happens, the abuse of free speech "remains largely invisible to the general public, while casting a long, insidious shadow on free expression" (ADC 2008, 1). Without genuine free speech or the ability to easily organize civil society, the failure of individual political actors, democratic procedures, and state institutions cannot be adequately criticized.

Because civil liberties and democratic procedures mutually affect each other, a decline in one generally erodes the other. Without the rule of law, citizens cannot obtain a fair hearing or appeal a ruling. The court system will not necessarily support the investigation of those accused of corruption or, when presented with the evidence, find the accused guilty. Instead, bringing charges against a government figure is redefined as disrespecting the government, and this carries stiff penalties.[10] Judges' appointments might be political patronage from which judges enrich themselves through corruption. In these cases, justice becomes accessible through the pocketbook.

The lack of some fundamental civil liberties and democratic procedures has created controversy about calling these nations democratic. By not making the definition of democracy more rigorous, organizations such as Freedom House, which is extensively quoted in this book, have been criticized as legitimating these new forms of constitutionalized elite rule.[11] This phenomenon of new democracies that are constrained at their most basic definitions has given rise to new names for them, names in which "liberal democracy" is no longer used. One example is "hybrid democracy," meaning that it has elements of both authoritarianism and a democracy. A democracy that permits the populace to vote but restricts other democratic functions is called an "electoral democracy" or a "minimum democracy." Fareed Zakaria, in a widely quoted article in *Foreign Affairs*, called these newly consolidated regimes "illiberal democracies," meaning that they have free and fair elections and mass participation but lack the civil liberties that only the rule of law can protect. Zakaria noted that a minimum democracy with its mass participation and adult suffrage but without civil liberties does not seem to lead to limits on governmental authority and thus the protection of the citizen from domination (Zakaria 1997, 28). If Zakaria is correct, then 75 per cent of the democracies in Latin America have consolidated as illiberal or minimum or electoral democracies. Only Chile, Argentina, Uruguay, Brazil, and Costa Rica can be said to be genuine democracies with both civil liberties and political rights (Wiarda and Kline 2007, 85). According to Zakaria, that number is unlikely to change.

THE RISE OF THE PINK TIDE, 1999–

Despite the impact of migration, remittances, and CCTs, there remains a strong demand for deeper reforms to Latin America's political economy. A number of international institutions support the call for reforms—from the World Bank to the Economic Commission on Latin America and the Caribbean (ECLAC), to the regional bank and Inter-American Development Bank (IADB). ECLAC and IADB have attempted to weave together many of the understandings and criticisms of neoliberalism into an alternative coherent intellectual framework called neostructuralism. It calls for greater public participation in decision-making, including integrating excluded groups, expanding human rights to include economic and cultural rights, and reactivating the economy through reducing socioeconomic inequalities. In general, neostructuralism suggests that a deeper democracy leading to greater dignity, more options and a better standard of living for all can be achieved through institutional reform, an interventionist state with capacity, and improved democratic governance (ECLAC 2001).

The international and domestic consensus for reforming neoliberalism has ushered in left-leaning reformist governments across Latin America: Hugo Chávez in Venezuela (1999–2012); Luiz Inácio Lula da Silva in Brazil (2002–11); Alejandro Toledo in Peru (2001–06); Néstor and Cristina Kirchner in Argentina (2003–11); Tabaré Vázquez in Uruguay (2005–10); Evo Morales in Bolivia (2006–10); Daniel Ortega in Nicaragua (2006–); Rafael Correa in Ecuador (2007–10); Fernando Lugo in Paraguay (2008–2013); and Mauricio

Funes in El Salvador (2009–). Some also include the election of Michelle Bachelet (2006–10) of Chile's Socialist Party in this group. This electoral success of leftish governments has been dubbed "the Pink Tide."

The success of the Pink Tide governments in Latin America highlights a conundrum for politics in the region: neoliberal democratization raised the expectations of the populace but did not create the mechanisms to fulfill those expectations. The weak state lacks autonomy from the elite class but the elite no longer control the vote. Voters are now using their most powerful tool—their sheer numbers—and electing into power those who promise to make the system work for them. The agendas of Pink Tide governments intend to improve social justice. Yet most Pink Tide countries have compromised with the neoliberal structuring of their political economy and the insertion of their nations into globalization. This approach has been called pragmatic economics, pragmatic socialism, or even modernization. In making these compromises, these countries generally accept as their starting point export-based, privatized, and deregulated economies with flexibilized low-wage, low-skill labor and tight fiscal spending, dominated by capital-intensive TNCs and domestic conglomerates. But these Latin American nations, with the support of the IFIs, American government and INGOs, are nonetheless engaged in the slow and frequently frustrating struggle to achieve state capacity and deeper democratization.

There are two ways this compromise with neoliberalism can be interpreted. The first perspective understands the resolution of the paradox of consolidated democracies as having only contingent support. According to this viewpoint, the democratic system is responding to the challenges it has encountered. These reforms may be piecemeal, fragile, and idiosyncratic but they enjoy a domestic and international consensus that democracy has to be deepened, the state has to be strengthened, and inequalities have to be overcome. Such a consensus is rare. Politicians, political parties, and social movements must seize the opportunity to change as much as possible both peacefully and democratically before the consensus dissipates. According to this perspective, the democratic system is working as it should. Those critical of it are idealistic (from either the right or the left of the political spectrum) or unappreciative of the complexity of power relations. The validity of this perspective will be seen after the world pulls through this most recent global recession. If Latin American nations are able to protect their social services during reduced economic downturns while continuing to strengthen state institutions and good governance, then these likely will become standard operating practices, normalized, even "common sense." Once the global economy reactivates and GDPs improve, then it is entirely possible that reforms can be deepened and extended. In this case, the democratized neoliberal political economics of Latin America might well experience growth with equity.

The second perspective is more jaundiced. It sees Latin America's reforms as necessary but insufficient, with the divisions within Latin America's societies continuing. It suggests that these efforts were not to reform neoliberalism but rather to safeguard it from the frustrated citizens of Latin American democracies who tie their votes to concrete measures that can improve their lives (Leiva 2008). So building state capacity and improving social justice is tactical, a strategy to absorb discontent about neoliberalism (Prevost 2005, 386). Some reforms might well have lasting impact, such as strengthened legislatures. But other reforms can only accomplish so much. Participatory democracy cannot by definition operate within larger political units such as regional governments and is highly dependent on the caliber of local political actors. Some reforms look better on paper than how they play out in reality. For example, decentralization has in some cases replicated clientelism and corruption, or strengthened local *caudillos*. With preferential free trade deals, NAFTA, DR-CAFTA, and the WTO locking in neoliberalism, the room for deep reform to the organization of the economy is limited. Even the governments of Venezuela and Bolivia, the reddest of the Pink Tide governments, accept the reality that their nations are inextricably bound by the global marketplace and, as a result, there is only so much that even a radical reworking can accomplish. Economic growth in Venezuela is increasingly dependent on its oil, making the country vulnerable to changes in the global price of oil, which is affected by international events far from Venezuela. In 2009, Venezuela's exports dropped by 24 per cent due to the global recession (ECLAC 2009). In January 2010, Chávez's Venezuela had to devalue its currency, which inevitably will reshape the domestic economy. Venezuela's dependency on the global marketplace diminishes its sovereignty and increases its vulnerability to the forces of globalization. Similarly, in 2006, Bolivia's Morales announced with great fanfare that he was "nationalizing" oil and natural gas contracts, which were predominantly held by foreigners. In fact, he did not. Recognizing that Bolivia did not have the technology or skills to efficiently extract its natural resources, he renegotiated the contracts with terms more favorable to the Bolivian people. Morales and Chávez need the world economy more than it needs them.

The limits of reform in all the Pink Tide countries are most obvious in the debate over the distribution of gains from economic growth. The consensus to overcome inequality has never confronted the reality of the elite's refusal to reduce its share of the wealth. The battle to increase redistributive taxes has failed in the larger countries of Latin America and in many of the smaller ones as well. "The beneficiaries of neoliberal reforms, the large

economic conglomerates and the top five to ten per cent of income earn-
ers, oppose increases in their tax contributions commensurate with their
relative ability to pay, and they have the resources to make their opposition
effective" (Huber 2005, 104).

As these governments embark on a range of political economic reforms,
it is difficult to draw conclusions about how the reforms affect democracy.
Analysis is hampered by the range of diverse approaches that emerge as
each government attempts to find a path for sustainable development specific to its own nation, culture, and history. The most well known analysis
for understanding Pink Tide governments came from Mexican intellectual
Jorge Castañeda (2006), who separated them into "good left" and "bad left"
governments.[12] Good left governments were those which abided with the
fundamental tenets of democratic neoliberalism while addressing social
injustice. According to Castañeda, bad left governments were those which
approached social equity through rejecting the gains of neoliberal democracy and promoting populism. This included rejecting the rule of law and
other democratic norms, fiscal responsibility, and monetary stability.

This analysis, however, overly simplifies the complexities of these reformist governments, which rarely are either black or white. It also ignores the
reality of doing politics: the gap between politicians' speeches and the policies that are implemented, the variety of reasons why candidates get elected,
and the influence of institutions and individuals on shaping policies. For
example, according to Panizza (2009, 169), there has been little change since
1996 in the percentage of the population that defines itself as "left," assuming
that there is one accepted definition of what that is. Reformist governments
are being elected by citizens who are not necessarily left-of-centre but rather
who are disenchanted with the functioning of government. This can be seen
with the broad alliances with which Lula governs Brazil, Lugo governs
Paraguay, and Bachelet governed Chile.

Despite differences between countries, Pink Tide governments do share
common traits. First, they have injected back into the polity an ethos,
a moral goal of social justice. With an emphasis on moral content, the
technocratic approach to governance that has dominated Latin America
since B-A regimes were in power has been sidelined. Secondly, they try
to mitigate the effects of neoliberalism by acknowledging that the market
cannot solve all problems. This opens the door for a stronger state. Thirdly,
Pink Tide governments are attempting to enhance regionalism through
increased trade and diplomacy. In theory, these three endeavors have a
mutually reinforcing impact so that social justice policies will increase
incentives to act in the marketplace and decrease the Gini coefficient.
The resulting increased economic productivity will be assisted by better
regional trade opportunities that are created through regional diplomacy.

Combined, these actions will diminish the influence of globalization and strengthen the state. A stronger state will then be better able to overcome the problems inherent within neoliberalism, such as inequality (Lievesley and Ludlam 2009; Spronk 2008). Regardless of how successful the Pink Tide governments are, they have already shifted the political and ideological center, changing the agenda and priorities of whichever government succeeds them.

Ultimately, the term "the Pink Tide" is not a useful analytical tool as it encompasses too wide a range of governments and policies. It includes those actively overturning neoliberalism (Chávez and Morales), those reforming neoliberalism while abiding by its fundamental tenets (Lula), those attempting a confusing mixture of both (the Kirchners and Correa), those having the rhetoric but lacking the ability to accomplish much (Toledo), and those using anti-neoliberal rhetoric to consolidate power through non-democratic mechanisms (Ortega). A better way of understanding reform in Latin America is to look at its impact on social relations and economic growth and governance, which is done in the conclusion of this book.

CONCLUSION

There are no guarantees in politics. Just because Latin America is a form of a democracy now does not mean that this will be a permanent state of affairs. As Latin America's 200 years of sovereignty demonstrates, democracy is under considerable flux. Nonetheless, a pattern emerges. Elite rule that is constitutionalized into minimum democracies operating through weak states has been the dominant form of democratic rule since the Spanish were pushed out. Embedded in this organization of governance has been non-democratic practices ranging from exclusion, economic exploitation, and inequality to informal institutions of clientelism, bureaucratic patrimonialism, and crony capitalism. A partial exception was during ISI with its middle-working-class alliance, social justice ethos, and interventionist state. Even then, however, the necessary components for a deeper democracy were not there: an autonomous and powerful civil society, a state autonomous from its elite with capacity to intervene or to resist any group, and socioeconomic equality. As a result, the state never redistributed resources or eliminated its authoritarian practices. Ultimately, the failure to establish a deep democracy under ISI erased democracy itself.

Latin America most recently democratized through elite pacts that had little to no moral content. By focusing on its procedural component, the Latin American state has produced a minimum, electoral, or illiberal democracy. These democracies have free, fair, contested, and regular elections, but do not acknowledge the structural exclusion of many people socially, politically, and economically. The rule of law is not always respected and freedom of speech can be curtailed. This reality has meant that the benefits of the reorganization of the economy and the transition to democracy might well be lost on broad swathes of the populace. Democratization may not have improved lives in a real and meaningful way. This is the ugly truth that underlies the statistics about Latin America's support for democracy. In 2007, less than 50 per cent of the population of Latin America agreed that democracy is preferable to any other kind of government. With the exception of only five countries,[13] support for democracy as the best form of government declined from 1996, although it did rise from a historic low in 2001. As well, since 1996, nine countries showed an increase in their support of the idea that under certain circumstances an authoritarian government would be preferable to a democratic one. While democracy was still the preferred system of government for almost half the population, support for authoritarian regimes averaged 19 per cent of the population. And this was after four years of steady economic growth and low inflation. These statistics are hardly a ringing endorsement of democratization (Latinobarómetro 2007; Camp 2001).

Simultaneous to democratization was the imposition of monetarism or structural adjustment to facilitate the insertion of Latin American economies into globalization. This produced a neoliberal state. The neoliberal state was weak and had even less autonomy from the elite and less capacity to intervene than it had previously. This cotransition had a high degree of continuity with the previous authoritarian regimes through technocratic governance and exclusion of the marginalized. As Friedman (2002, 13) and Hagopian (2004, 86) noted, the spread of democracy in Latin America accompanied a declining ability of the state to address the inherent weakness of its political economy and the social problems that resulted. Whitehead (2006, 24), noting that democratization in Latin America was accompanied by a shift away from policies of social justice and redistribution, wrote that "social justice has been conspicuous by its absence." Instead, the state has lowered expectations about what a democracy can achieve. The neoliberal democratic state has not redistributed income or even reactivated sustainable economic growth, but instead has tight fiscal discipline and widening inequality. Democracy in many countries of Latin America has come to mean "an absence of overt coercion, not an opportunity to shape the public destiny" (Friedman 2002, 17). The inequality of wealth and power that this process engenders seriously undermines the basic functioning of democracy. The extension of social welfare to the poorest does not alter this sad state of affairs. "The promise of democracy is an empty one in the absence of the ability of the state to extract adequate resources to offset the risks of the market" (Haggard and Kaufman 2008, 367). If democratic politics assumes that citizens organize, cooperate, and compete with each other through appropriate institutions in order to govern themselves, then the new democracies of Latin America have been depoliticized and de-democratized. This is the paradox of Latin America's strengthening political economy, yet the citizenry's modest endorsement of it.

With the rise of the Pink Tide governments, that paradox has been acknowledged and to a degree addressed. With an explicit agenda of social justice, democracy now has a moral content of creating a better life for its most destitute. The role of the state as a means to redress the failures of neoliberalism has been acknowledged. What remains unclear is how best to achieve those social justice goals. Despite being elected on a reform mandate, Pink Tide and other reformist governments have difficulties altering neoliberal democratic states or even improving the performance of state institutions. Strengthening state institutions, extending social welfare, and transferring money directly to the poor is the dominant response. However, these measures make little structural change to the fundamental organization of Latin America's political economy. More radical, if not necessarily more democratic, reforms are being carried out in Venezuela and Bolivia. The future of Latin America's democracies depends on the depth and scope of its reforms.

NOTES

1 For the purposes of this book, Latin American countries include the Spanish-speaking nations south of the United States but excluding Spanish-speaking islands in the Caribbean. These number 18 in total.

2 The classic—if overly simplistic—example is not stopping at a red light in a tough neighborhood at night.

3 Dependency theory considers an export economy to be a form of dependent development, that is, there might be some industrialization and agricultural production but it is for the benefit of the developed nations at the expense of the developing ones. Dependency theory is the dominant theoretical framework used to explain Latin America's continued status as a third world. The Argentine economist Raúl Prebisch suggested in the 1940s that Latin America suffered from declining terms of trade due to surplus labor depressing wages while importing increasingly expensive manufactured goods from developed nations. As a result, Latin American economies were and would remain structurally impoverished. This theory, called structuralism, evolved into dependency theory when economists and sociologists in the 1960s included social relations of power both inter- and intra-nations. Ultimately, it depoliticized and disempowered citizens in Latin America from reforming what they could and promoted a sense of victimhood. Dependency theory has fallen from favor without being adequately replaced by a better theory.

4 Capital flight between 1976 and 1982 has been estimated at $25 billion from Mexico, $22 billion from Argentina, $21 billion from Venezuela, and $6 billion from Brazil (Huber 2005, 97).

5 Many fine thinkers, predominantly economists, define neoliberalism through the narrow prism of economic policy. Political scientists generally define neoliberalism more broadly as a relation of power residing in the state.

6 Costa Rica, once again, breaks the generalized rule because it was also granted more generosity by IFIs in an effort to protect its political stability during the crisis with Nicaragua.

7 Both Brazil and Panama have recently been able to make a modest reduction in their disparity of wealth.

8 According to the Human Development Report (2005, 124), a college education in Latin America now generates a higher economic return than it does in the US.

9 Social welfare means healthcare and pensions. In some nations it includes housing credits. It does not include unemployment insurance or education. However, social spending is broader and includes education, potable water, and other infrastructure improvements, as well as programs like school lunches.

10 Peter Smith (2005, 269) gives an excellent example of how freedom of speech is curtailed in Guatemala with the assistance of the judicial system, the president of Guatemala, and legislative committees.

11 I use Freedom House as a source because it reviews the political organization of power for every country in Latin America for every year. As well, it is easily accessible through the Internet and is widely quoted by other sources, both of which assist students with their research. However, its data base remains flawed due to its narrow definition of democracy.

12 See also Arditi (2008); Burdick, Oxhorn, and Roberts (2009).

13 Costa Rica, Bolivia, Venezuela, Ecuador, and Nicaragua are the five exceptions. Likely they are more supportive of democracy because Bolivia, Ecuador, Nicaragua, and Venezuela have targeted the poor in the operating of their governments and Costa Ricans fought a referendum over the legalization of CAFTA.

REFERENCES

Arditi, Benjamin. 2008. "Arguments about the Left Turns in Latin America: A Post-Liberal Politics?" *Latin American Research Review* 43(3): 59–81.

Asociación por los Derechos Civiles (ADC) and Open Society Justice Initiative. 2008. *The Price of Silence: The Growing Threat of Soft Censorship in Latin America*. Open Society Institute.

Buckley, Richard. 2005. *Winds of Change in Latin America: Populism versus US Imperialism*. UGI Briefing 136. Cheltenham, UK: Understanding Global Issues.

Burdick, John, Philip Oxhorn, and Kenneth Roberts, eds. 2009. *Beyond Neoliberalism in Latin America? Societies and Politics at the Crossroads*. New York: Palgrave MacMillan.

Burns, E. Bradford. 1994. *Latin America: A Concise Interpretative History*. New Jersey: Prentice Hall.

Castañeda, Jorge. 2006. "Latin America's New Left." *Foreign Affairs* 85(3): 28–43.

Camp, Roderic Ai, ed. 2001. *Citizen Views of Democracy in Latin America*. Pittsburgh: University of Pittsburgh Press.

Centeno, Miguel Angel. 2002. *Blood and Debt: War and the Nation-State in Latin America*. University Park: Pennsylvania State University Press.

Clarkson, Stephen. 2004. "Global Governance and the Semi-Peripheral State: The WTO and NAFTA as Canada's External Constitution." *Governing under Stress: Middle Powers and the Challenge of Globalization*. Ed. Marjorie Griffin Cohen and Stephen Clarkson. London: Zed Books. 153–74.

Durán Martínez, Angélica. 2007. *Organized Crime, the State and Democracy: The Cases of Central America and the Caribbean*. Conference Report. Madrid: Fundación para las Relaciones Internationales y el Diálogo Exterior, and New York: United Nations Department of Political Affairs.

ECLAC. 2001. *Equity, Development and Citizenship*. Washington, DC: ECLAC.

——. 2008a. *Latin America and the Caribbean in the World Economy: 2008 Trends*. Washington, DC: ECLAC.

——. 2008b. *Millennium Development Goals: Progress towards the Right to Health in Latin America and the Caribbean*. Washington, DC: ECLAC.

——. 2009. *International Trade in Latin America and the Caribbean 2009: Crisis and Recovery*. Washington, DC: ECLAC

Friedman, Steven. 2002. "Democracy, Inequality and the Reconstruction of Politics." *Democratic Governance and Social Inequality*. Ed. Joseph S. Tulchin with Amelia Brown. Boulder: Lynne Rienner Press. 13–39.

Garretón, Manuel Antonio, and Edward Newman. 2001. "Introduction." *Democracy in Latin America: (Re)Constructing Political Society*. Ed. Manuel Antonio Garretón and Edward Newman. New York: United Nations University Press. 3–15.

Green, Duncan. 2003. *Silent Revolution: The Rise and Crisis of Market Economies in Latin America*. New York: Monthly Review and LAB.

Grindle, Merilee. 2001. "In Quest of the Political: The Political Economy of Development Policymaking." *Frontiers of Development Economics: The Future in Perspective*. Ed. G.M. Meier and Joseph Stiglitz. New York: World Bank and Oxford University. 345–80.

Goehsing, Julia. 2008. "Beyond the North-South Divide: A Multi-Pronged Approach to Transnational Criminal Networks in Latin America and the Caribbean." *State of Corruption, State of Chaos: The Terror of Political Malfeasance*. Ed. Michaelene Cox. Lanham: Lexington Books. 93–126.

Haggard, Stephen, and Robert R. Kaufman. 2008. *Development, Democracy and Welfare States: Latin America, East Asia and Eastern Europe*. Princeton: Princeton University Press.

Hagopian, Frances. 1992. "The Compromised Consolidation: The Political Class in the Brazilian Transition." *Issues in Democratic Consolidation: The New South American Democracies in Comparative Perspective*. Ed. Scott Mainwaring et al. Notre Dame: University of Notre Dame Press. 243–93.

——. 2004. "Authoritarian Legacies and Market Reforms in Latin America." *Authoritarian Legacies and Democracy in Latin America and Southern Europe*. Ed. Katherine Hite and Paola Cesarini. Notre Dame: University of Notre Dame Press. 85–158.

——. 2005. "Government and Performance, Political Representation, and Public Perceptions of Contemporary Democracies in Latin America." *The Third Wave of Democratization in Latin America: Advances and Setbacks*. Ed. Frances Hagopian and Scott Mainwaring. Cambridge: Cambridge University Press. 319–62.

Hagopian, Frances, and Scott Mainwaring, eds. 2005. *The Third Wave of Democratization in Latin America: Advances and Setbacks*. Cambridge: Cambridge University Press.

Helmke, Gretchen, and Steven Levitsky. 2006. "Introduction." *Informal Institutions and Democracy: Lessons from Latin America*. Ed. Gretchen Helmke and Stephen Levitsky. Baltimore: Johns Hopkins University Press. 1–30.

Higley, John, and Michael G. Burton. 1988. "Democratic Transition and Democratic Breakdowns: The Elite Variable." Texas Papers in Latin America No. 88-03. Austin: University of Texas.

Huber, Evelyn. 2005. "Globalization and Social Policy Developments in Latin America." *Globalization and the Future of the Welfare State*. Ed. Miguel Glatzer and Dietrich Rueschemeyer. Pittsburgh: University of Pittsburgh Press. 75–105.

Human Development Report. 2005. Human Development Report. 2005. New York: UNDP.

Keane, John. 2009. *The Life and Death of Democracy*. London: Simon and Schuster.

Jennings, Allan, and Matthew Clarke. 2005. "The Development Impact of Remittances to Nicaragua." *Development in Practice* 15(5): 685–91.

Latinobarómetro. 2007. Opinion Pública Latinoamerica. June 10, 2010. www. latinobarometro.org.

Leiva, Fernando Ignacio. 2008. *Latin American Neostructuralism: The Contradictions of Post-Neoliberal Development*. Minneapolis: University of Minnesota Press.

Lievesley, Geraldine, and Steve Ludlam. 2009. *Reclaiming Latin America: Experiments in Radical Democracy*. London: Zed Books.

Linz, Juan J., and Alfred Stepan. 1996. *Problems with Democratic Transition and Consolidation: Southern Europe, South America and Post-Communist Europe*. Baltimore: Johns Hopkins University Press.

Machinea, José Luis, and Osvaldo L. Kacef. 2007. "Growth and Equity: In Search of the 'Empty Box.'" *Economic Growth with Equity: Challenges for Latin America*. Ed. Ricardo French-Davis and José Luis Machinea. London: Palgrave MacMillan. 1–23.

Mainwaring, Scott, and Aníbal Pérez-Liñán. 2003. "Level of Development and Democracy: Latin American Exceptionalism, 1945–1996." *Comparative Political Studies* 35(9): 1031–67.

Molyneux, Maxine. 2008. "The 'Neoliberal Turn' and the New Social Policy in Latin America: How Neoliberal, How New?" *Development and Change* 39(5): 775–97.

Moore, Barrington Jr. 1966. *Social Origins of Dictatorship and Democracy: Lord and Peasant in the Making of the Modern World*. Boston: Beacon Press.

O'Donnell, Guillermo. 2004. "Human Development, Human Agency, and Democracy." *The Quality of Democracy: Theory and Applications*. Ed. Guillermo O'Donnell, Jorge Vargas Cullel, and Osvaldo M. Iazzetta. Notre Dame: University of Notre Dame Press. 9–92.

——. 2006. "On Informal Institutions Once Again." *Informal Institutions and Democracy: Lessons from Latin America*. Ed. Gretchen Helmke and Stephen Levitsky. Baltimore: Johns Hopkins University Press. 285–89.

O'Donnell, Guillermo, and Philippe Schmitter. 1986. *Tentative Conclusions about Uncertain Democracies*. Baltimore: Johns Hopkins University Press.

Panizza, Francisco. 2009. *Contemporary Latin America: Development and Democracy beyond the Washington Consensus*. London: Zed Books.

Peeler, John. 2004. *Building Democracy in Latin America*. 2nd ed. Boulder: Lynne Rienner Press.

Perlin, George, and Bernard Wood. 2007. "Co-Chairs' Report on 'A Dialogue on Canada's Approach to Democratic Development.'" Ottawa: Canadian International Development Agency.

Prevost, Gary. 2005. "Contesting Free Trade: The Development of the Anti-FTAA Movement in the Streets and in the Corridor of State Power." *Journal of Developing Societies* 21: 369–87.

Reid, Michael. 2007. *Forgotten Continent: The Battle for Latin America's Soul*. New Haven: Yale University Press.

Rostow, Walt. 1971. *The Stages of Economic Growth: A Non-Communist Manifesto*. 2nd ed. Cambridge: Cambridge University Press.

Rueschemeyer, Dietrich, Evelyne Huber Stephens, and John D. Stephens. 1992. *Capitalist Development and Democracy*. Cambridge: Polity Press.

Schedler, Andreas. 1998. "What is Democratic Consolidation?" *Journal of Democracy* 9(2): 91–107.

Silva, Eduardo. 2004. "Authoritarianism. Democracy and Development" *Latin America Transformed: Globalization and Modernity*. Ed. Robert N. Gwynne and Cristóbal Kay. 2nd ed. London: Edward Arnold. 141–56.

Smith, Peter. 2005. *Democracy in Latin America: Political Change in Comparative Perspective*. Oxford and New York: Oxford University Press.

Spronk, Susan. 2008. "Pink Tide? Neoliberalism and its Alternatives in Latin America." *Canadian Journal of Latin American and Caribbean Studies* 33(65): 173–86.

Teichman, Judith. 2008. "Redistributive Conflict and Social Policy in Latin America." *World Development* 36(3): 446–60.

Therborn, Goran. 1977. "The Role of Capital and the Rise of Democracy." *New Left Review* (103): 3–41.

United Nations Development Program. 2004. *Democracy in Latin America: Towards a Citizens' Democracy*. New York: UNDP.

Wiarda, Howard A., and Harvey F. Kline. 2006. "The Struggle for Democracy in Latin America." *Latin America: Politics and Development*. Ed. Howard Wiarda and Harvey F. Kline. 6th ed. Boulder: Westview Press. 81–93.

Whitehead, Laurence. 2006. *Latin America: A New Interpretation*. New York: Palgrave MacMillan.

World Bank. 2000. *Poverty in the Age of Globalization*. New York: World Bank.

Wise, Carol. 2009. "North America Free Trade Agreement." *New Political Economy* 14(1): 138–48.

Yashar, Deborah J. 2007. "Citizenship Regimes, the State and Ethnic Cleavages." *Citizenship in Latin America*. Ed. Joseph S. Tulchin and Meg Rutherburg. Boulder: Lynne Rienner Press. 59–74.

Youngs, Richard. 2004. *International Democracy and the West: The Role of Governments, Civil Society, and Multinational Businesses*. Oxford: Oxford University Press.

Zakaria, Fareed. 1997. "The Rise of Illiberal Democracy." *Foreign Affairs* 76(6): 22–43.

E-RESOURCES

BBC country profiles (http://news.bbc.co.uk/1/hi/world/americas; choose a country). These offer a timeline of each nation's history.

Centro de Investigación y Adriestramiento Político Adminstrativo (CIAPA) (www.ciapa.org). A think tank to promote research in the social sciences and contribute to the formation of public policy to solve problems in Latin America, particularly Central America.

CIA The World Factbook (www.cia.gov/library/publications/the-world-factbook/). A wealth of facts from geography to the level of electrification.

Economic Commission on Latin America and the Caribbean (www.eclac.org). A left-leaning think tank devoted to Latin America's development.

Foreign Policy in Focus (www.fpif.org). An American think tank devoted to diplomatic solutions to US issues in foreign policy.

Fundar Centre for Analysis and Research (www.fundar.org.mx). A Mexican think tank with wide-ranging research on politics of Latin America.

H-LatAm (www.h-net.org/~latam). Scholarly netgroup to discuss Latin American history.

Inter-American Development Bank (www.iadb.org). The largest development bank in Latin America. It publishes economic and other data.

Inter-American Dialogue (www.thedialogue.org). An American political website broadly funded from progressive organizations and countries.

Latin American Media and Marketing (www.zonalatina.com). A gateway for international and domestic newspaper articles, radio reports, magazine articles, and TV shows about Latin America in English. It also has information about music movies and the Internet.

Latin American Network Information Center (www.lanic.utexas.edu). A gateway to more websites and e-resources about Latin America.

Organization of American States (www.oas.org). A political organization of Latin America that publishes regional agreements.

Pan-American Health Organization (www.paho.org). A website that offers surprisingly wide-ranging data on Latin America.

Washington Office on Latin America (www.wola.org). A program to promote human rights, democracy, and social justice.

Upside Down World (http://upsidedownworld.org). An alternative media site dedicated to activism in politics in Latin America. It features current events based on investigative reporting.

THREE

Issues and Institutions in Latin American Governance

KATHERINE ISBESTER

Democracy is a structure for organizing power through institutions, which reside in both the state and civil society. Institutions are formal and informal, legal and illegal, explicit and invisible, and political, social, and economic. However, they all help structure opportunities and incentives or, conversely, constraints and punishments. Latin America's institutions are famously weak and can be complex and difficult to grasp. Two examples of this are Brazil's complicated constitution and Bolivia's form of presidentialism, both which require substantial investments of time to understand. To understand Latin America's democracies, these institutions and structures of power must be analyzed, because they describe the broader political dynamic of the state, its relationship with its citizens, and the effect both have on democracy and development.

STATE INSTITUTIONS IN LATIN AMERICAN DEMOCRACIES

Political institutions are organized so that political actors can make legislation and civil society can participate in the democratic process. Political institutions are also known as the organization of power, or power relations. Poorly structured political institutions make reform more difficult, heighten the chance of political instability, and delegitimize democracy. A great deal of scholarly attention has been focused on Latin America's political institutions because they are regarded as a major cause of Latin America's underperforming democracies. The organization of power in Latin America is constantly changing as political systems are reformed, generally for the better. Legislatures are gaining power, supreme courts are gaining autonomy, and executives are having their power curtailed. In Chile, Costa Rica, and Uruguay, the rule of law prevails. Military amnesty is being rolled back in many countries. As a result, there is cause for cautious optimism about the potential for democratic governance to improve.

CONSTITUTIONS

In a quality democracy, a social contract of consent underlies the relationship between the governed and the governing. This consent is expressed through laws and/or is outlined through a constitution. Constitutions establish procedures, create democratic institutions, and also constrain the power of those institutions. They also establish the rights of citizens, judicial functions to interpret the constitution, mechanisms for enforcing judicial rulings, and procedures for amending or repealing rules. A constitution establishes political, social, and legal norms, which then become inviolate. In its essence, a constitution organizes power relations within a society and creates mechanisms to allow for the reform of those relations. The struggle over a constitution is a social, political, and economic struggle for control over the organization of power.

Latin America never developed the concept of a social contract between the rulers and the ruled. Instead, constitutions are a comprehensive framework detailing the perfect society. There is no case law (i.e., common law) which interprets the constitution to make it appropriate for unforeseen demands, but rather strict deductions from constitutional principles or truths. This is called code law. This results in a formal, even rigid, adherence to law on paper, but in practice a well-accepted disregard for it. Judges and lawyers are bureaucrats rather than interpreters of law, and are not as respected or trusted as they are under other democratic regimes.

While Latin American constitutions establish the separation of powers into three branches of government (sometimes four),[1] these branches are rarely equal and autonomous. The judiciary and legislature generally are granted less power than the executive. Emergency powers—which the executive can invoke—allow for the suspension of civil liberties and democratic procedures and the ability for the president to rule by decree. However, emergency powers must be approved by the legislature and are for a limited time period (although this can be extended). Typically, the courts do not have the right to judicial review, the process by which the courts rule on whether or not legislation or its implementation is constitutionally legal. In Latin America, there is less recognition of individual rights, but more recognition of a group's rights (amparo), for example, children's, women's, and workers' rights. They have specific rights because they clearly belong to groups who need special protection. Civil society organizations and social movements have worked hard to ensure that their groups became recognized and protected by the new constitutions. Constitutions vary from country to country and can be contradictory within a nation.

RULE OF LAW

Constitutions prescribe the balance of powers. Laws stem from constitutionally prescribed rights and institutions. The rule of law is defined as enforcing laws so that they are the same for every member of society, regardless of race, religion, class, sex, age, or ethnicity. This is critical in a democracy, because it creates predictability in the economy by protecting property rights and contracts, which then encourages economic development. Furthermore, the rule of law encourages respect for judicial institutions and practices, which supports the acceptance of democratic norms.

As poorer Latinos have discovered, the existence of laws does not mean that there are resources to access them and turn them into reality. The rule of law is often poorly respected in Latin America. The judicial system is inefficient and corrupt. The judges and their staff are undertrained and underpaid. Low wages have induced corruption, yet the state is too poor to increase wages. In Colombia, Central America (except Costa Rica), and Mexico, the drug trade, with its violence and wealth, strongly affects the rule of law. People, especially those in rural areas, have varying levels of access to the courts, sentencing is unpredictable, and time lags are too long. The judiciary lacks autonomy from executive interference and manipulation. Between 1980 and 1994, over a billion dollars were spent on judicial reform in Latin America and "the results have been singularly disappointing" (Sieder 2004, 138). Nonetheless, several Latin American nations have managed to impose the rule of law. Their judiciaries are better trained, funded, and respected than those found in the rest of the region.

PRESIDENTIALISM

The political organization of power is presidentialism, which means that the people elect the president separately from the legislature. Power is concentrated in the executive rather than dispersed through the branches of government, or residing predominantly in the legislature. The president is the commander in chief of the armed forces, leader of a political party, and head of the state. She or he is seen as a strong, unifying force for a competitive elite and a fractious society. The compromises, accommodations, and negotiations necessary to create policies in a parliamentary system could well be seen as weaknesses for a Latin American president. This seriously hampers deliberative democracy, especially given the strength of the executive.

Presidentialism in Latin America also includes *personalismo*, which emphasizes the person as president, rather than the office itself. *Personalismo* is probably best understood as charisma. The meshing of so many roles and functions in one person imbues the presidency with a mysticism and a legitimacy beyond the needs of democratic governance. These variables, combined with Latin America's authoritarian past, turn the president into the modern equivalent of a *patrón* or *caudillo*.

The president's extensive powers to act include the ability to appoint ministers who may not be from the ruling party or who reflect the balance of political parties in the legislature. Most draft legislation and the budget both come from the president. She or he can interfere with supreme court rulings, convene extraordinary sessions of the legislature (for which the president sets the agenda), and suspend the constitution. She or he can also veto laws passed by the legislature. The president can even prioritize or delay bills, or issue laws that the legislature can only pass or reject within a certain time period. These actions shape the policy agenda. By means of extensive appointing, the president can reshape the entire bureaucracy. He or she can also affect the party nominations of local, city, and regional leaders. The president can insist that a policy rejected by the legislature be made law, through ruling by decree. Argentine President Carlos Menem (1989–94) passed more than 300 laws by presidential decree, abusing his power so much that the legislature amended the constitution to limit the use of presidential decrees in 1994. Brazilian President Fernando Cardoso (1995–2003) averaged 36 presidential decrees a month. However, it must also be noted that not every president uses the available powers. For example, in Chile, General Augusto Pinochet (1974–90) created a powerful executive, but the elected presidents who followed him have not used all the powers formally available to them.

Presidents can be elected by a plurality of votes, meaning the person who has the most wins, even if the total number of votes for the individual amounts to less than 50 per cent of the vote. If three or more people ran for office, then it can mean that the president elected might have only one-third of the vote. In some nations such as Costa Rica, Argentina, and Nicaragua, if the leading candidate has reached a certain minimum per cent (between 35 per cent and 45 per cent), and/or if the gap between the candidates is large enough, then the candidate has won the presidency. Nonetheless, with three or more candidates for president, a plurality hardly amounts to a popular mandate. Generally, there is a second vote (a majority runoff), between the two leading candidates to coalesce power around just one individual. (The exception to this rule is found in Bolivia, which allows the congress to choose the president from the top three candidates, if no one has a clear majority.) Runoffs ensure that radicals are limited in their ability to gain power, and that if reformers wish to gain power, they must seek the middle ground.

Presidents have a limited term in office, typically only one, although it is being changed to two in some countries. Because the office wields disproportionate power and the president obtains financial gains from it, the elite could be destabilized if one person held power for too long. A rotating presidency allows the elite to share power among themselves. However, a single term in office also means that the people have no ability to vote someone out of office, since he or she is leaving regardless. Without accountability, there is little incentive for the president to be an effective leader.

Presidentialism does have some advantages. First, it stabilizes the running of the government. The president cannot fall from power as the result of a vote of non-confidence in the legislature. If he resigns, the vice president automatically assumes power. In the event of a crisis, there is a high level of predictability about who will do the decision-making. Furthermore, because the president is directly elected, usually with a runoff, a minimum per cent of the populace had to vote for him. Consequently, the president has substantial legitimacy. Should the president want to reform the system or engage in new economic development programs, his or her extensive powers allow for minimal delay and maximum stability. For example, when Carlos Memen of Argentina, Alberto Fuijimori of Peru, and Victor Paz Estenssoro of Bolivia enacted sweeping economic reforms, they were able to do so using presidential powers, despite public protests and with limited legislative support.

The disadvantages of presidentialism are more numerous. The same stability that can be an advantage can also be a disadvantage, in the event that the president or vice president cannot handle a crisis, or is dogmatically pursuing a policy destructive to the economy, the nation, or the party. As a result, Linz (1994) argues that the presidential system is overly rigid. He also criticizes the impact of a winner-take-all system. Democratic politics, which have often been characterized as the art of compromise, are undermined by organizing power around one office. Presidentialism ensures that there is little need to compromise with legislators or respond to criticism of a public policy. This then becomes the political norm, reducing the ability of other political actors to broker deals, create alliances, or engage with dissenting voices. Presidentialism also perpetuates patron–client relations in which the president is the biggest boss. The president can use patronage to buy off or co-opt dissenting voices, rather than having to engage with reform. Presidentialism is also idiosyncratic. The policies embraced by the president can be completely unpredictable, even the exact opposite of his campaign platforms.

Finally, the concentration of both formal and informal power in the executive means that there can be confusion about which body governs the country—the president, or the legislature. If the president is elected from one party and the legislature is dominated by another, it can be unclear which office has the greater authority to create policy in the name of the people. This lack of clarity about the separation of powers can lead to gridlock between the executive and the legislature, with little being accomplished as a result. If the president does not have a majority in the legislature, or at least a sizable following within it, then the likelihood of conflict between the branches of government, along with governmental breakdown, increases. Presidents with a minority in the legislature must seek coalitions and negotiate alliances. Yet there is little incentive for the president to do so, and few political structures that allow it.

The chance of political gridlock increases if the legislature is chosen by proportional representation (PR), that is, the party receives seats on the basis of its share of the popular vote. Latin American and many European nations choose their representatives through PR. This system works best when there is an ethnically homogenous population with high degrees of social and economic equality. Under these circumstances, PR usually produces a median representative who reflects the median voter. But in the context of ethnic divisions and socioeconomic inequality, PR facilitates the existence of multiple smaller parties which reflect the microcosms of the polity. Once these parties gain seats through PR, there is rarely a legislative majority of one party. As a result, shifting alliances of parties decide policy in an unpredictable fashion. The chance of political gridlock is further increased if there are midterm elections for representatives and a bicameral system. If there is political gridlock, without the ability to remove the president with a vote of non-confidence, political actors seek other means, generally non-democratic, to resolve the conflict. This destabilizes the government and democracy itself (Cheibub 2002).

The effect of an overly powerful executive on the entire functioning of the political system makes it the dominant characteristic of the democracies of Latin America. O'Donnell (1994) coined a term to refer to this phenomenon: "delegative democracy." He defined it as having a powerful president who governed as he or she saw fit and to the extent that the power relations permitted for the duration of the term in office. Being elected president meant that he or she had the authorization to chart a course without any expectation of enacting campaign promises, following party platforms, using democratic institutions, or respecting the separation of powers and the checks and balances in democratic governance. In a delegative democracy, the president is above politics and its political negotiations and compromises. The president is more of a term-defined autocrat than a "first among equals" elected to carry out policies.

There have been attempts to reform the concentration of power in the presidential office, so that power is shared equally between the branches of government and civil liberties are strengthened. Not all these reforms have been successful. However, Chile, Costa Rica, Colombia, and Venezuela all have a different tradition of strong and independent legislatures, with correspondingly weaker presidents. Brazil, Bolivia, Mexico, and Uruguay have recently joined that group, with their legislatures defying executive orders and empowering themselves.

Furthermore, the social norms that supported an all-powerful executive are being eroded. For example, while the president may distribute favors to cement his hold on power, it has also been typical for him to enrich himself while in office. Now, Latin American presidents are finding themselves being accused of corruption because the behaviors expected from leaders are changing. Costa Rica and Chile, both with reputations of minimal corruption, are charging some of their ex-presidents with fraud, bribery, and kickbacks. Ex-presidents of Guatemala, Nicaragua, Brazil, Panama, Argentina, Paraguay, and Peru have been charged or found guilty of corruption (and as a result, many ex-presidents have retired to neighboring countries, thereby avoiding court trials and sentencing).

LEGISLATURES

Electing the legislature can be complicated by choosing some seats on the basis of plurality and others by PR. The electoral system can also be open ballot or open list (where you know both the person and the party for which you are voting) or closed ballot or closed list (you only know the party). Open lists can break the power of the elite to choose who runs and thereby allow greater participation in the party. Closed lists act as an incentive for clientelism and as a disincentive for the elected representative to respond to constituents. Closed lists also exacerbate elite control over the political process. Argentina, most countries in Central America, and Peru still use closed lists.

In Latin America, legislatures are usually malapportioned—that is, there is a wide discrepancy between the number of seats in an electoral district and its share of the population. Simply put, some people's votes count more than others. Malapportionment undermines democracy. Argentina, Bolivia, Brazil, Chile, Colombia, and Ecuador, countries which include two-thirds of the population of Latin America have extremely high levels of malapportionment, while Costa Rica has the lowest. It is difficult to understand malapportionment, yet it has a substantial impact on the distribution of seats in the legislature. Malapportioned legislatures tend to overrepresent rural areas, which tend to be more conservative. The president is elected by the entire nation on the basis of one person/one vote, rather than through a constituency. Because Latin America's population is predominantly urban, the president's platform has to appeal to the urban voter, and differs from a party reflecting rural interests. Yet a malapportioned legislature will increase the likelihood that a rural-based party will be strongly represented. This increases the chance of the president having to serve without a majority in the legislature. As a result, the president has to build coalitions with rural groups using pork-barrel politics to get legislation passed. These "fiscal favors" maintain clientelism, regional elite, and authoritarian enclaves in rural areas (Synder and Samuels 2006).

While Latin America was under authoritarian governments, legislatures met but were limited in their ability to accomplish anything. The legislature acted more as an assistant to the president than as a separate, equal, lawmaking body. This assistance ranged from giving advice, representing different national perspectives when debating legislation, and occasionally providing slight reforms for the president's policies. Even with the transition to democracy, legislatures have remained undervalued. Most legislatures in Latin America today are bicameral, with the exception of those in Central America and Venezuela, which are unicameral. Elected representatives have few research staff, and the committee system does not function adequately. Sessions tend to be noisy, acrimonious, and short. Reelection is rarer there than it is in the US, making it difficult for representatives to develop expertise, focus on long-term policy development, or build alliances and their own base of support, which would grant them some autonomy from party leaders and the executive. In Mexico and Costa Rica, representatives cannot run for their seat in consecutive elections, making it harder still to be competent representatives. In both of these cases, representatives use their term in power to seek better positions outside electoral politics. In the case of Mexico, this is generally a presidential appointment. The most common function of Latin American legislatures is to block or reform presidential initiatives. In both situations, the legislature can be bought off through patronage and pork barrelling, be overpowered by a presidential veto, or more rarely, it can form an alliance with the president to achieve other political goals.

POLITICAL PARTIES

Because individual representatives lack accountability, this makes it difficult for the electorate to judge the quality of political parties. Even so, parties perform a number of important functions. Primarily, they link the electorate to the legislature through structured mechanisms for participation, debate, and competition for office. Political parties analyze and distribute information, criticisms, and alternate approaches about issues and legislation. They are mediating structures that articulate civil society's demands. A political party can reduce the "noise" of politics, making it easier for the public to choose between candidates and ideologies. Political parties raise money for the party and for the representatives, choose candidates for office, and mobilize participation. Debates between political parties expose the strengths and weaknesses of specific pieces of legislation, and general approaches to governing. Disciplined political parties are able to ensure that their representatives vote coherently and consistently, and thus do not contradict each other.

This contributes to the effectiveness of the legislature and enormously assists coalition-building, which also helps the legislature to be effective. Institutionalized political parties have stability in membership, internal structures, and political ideology. They abide by the rules of democracy and inter-party competition. They have an established presence in a region or area, and have established relationships with civil society organizations, such as union groups or business groups. All these functions serve to institutionalize political parties in that they ground the mechanics of politics in society and in other democratic institutions such as the legal system and civil society organizations (Mainwaring and Scully 1995). Steven Levitsky (2003) gave an example of the positive role that a disciplined political party can have in his analysis of the relative calm during the Argentine economic crisis of 1998. He suggested that the Peronist Party, with its deep ties to unions and the working class, was able to diffuse anti-democratic threats, and to ease social chaos to some extent. Nonetheless, throughout Latin America, political parties reflect socioeconomic development, so that poorer people are represented by less institutionalized political parties (Luna and Zechmeister 2005, 389). Without the money to communicate effectively in the political arena, parties representing the poor have a harder time attracting votes.

With neoliberal economic reforms restructuring South American states in recent years, the political parties that had been successful in the past have gone into decline. These include political parties supported by the labor movement and the Catholic Church. Instead, parties that epitomize consumerism and individualism have gained strength. The newer political parties tend not to have collective affiliation or grassroots support. Instead, they foment support through mass media, negative campaigning, and image control. Mass media, neoliberalism, and a global consumer culture have eroded group-based or ideologically-based patterns of political representation, and replaced them with individualized or tailored preferences.

This trend weakens civil society by replacing group-based participation with professional teams using TV advertising and mass mailings. Linkages between citizens and political parties weaken and might last only until the next election, when they might be reassessed (Roberts 2002). This makes it easier for the electorate to shift loyalties when a better-packaged candidate appears. The lack of long-term loyalty and a tendency to flip between political parties from one election to the next is called electoral volatility. This dynamic, enhanced by a PR electoral system, leads to a proliferation of smaller parties which rise and fall with each election. Small, endlessly new parties are problematic for democracy, because they are weakly institutionalized. Because political parties help to structure the political process, weakly institutionalized political parties mean that the political process is also less institutionalized, and hence more unpredictable. Legislative politics are thereby weakened, permitting the elite and the technocrats to have disproportionate influence. This enhances presidentialism with all its accompanying problems. In the process, voters become more vulnerable to charismatic leaders, which is bad for democracy and citizens in the long run. Latin America has substantially higher levels of volatility than Western European nations, some of which also have PR and a presidential system but have better institutionalized political parties.

BUREAUCRACIES

Political parties, the legislature, the executive, and the judiciary must all use the state's institutions to operate. Before Latin America's democratization, state institutions functioned poorly. The state was bloated, bureaucracy was inefficient, and the chain of command was unclear. Worker morale was low. Civil servants generally obtained their jobs through patronage and sometimes held second "real" jobs as well. Despite recognizing this problem and attempting to reform it, democratization has had limited impact on the caliber of state institutions. In order to obtain a necessary permit or license, citizens must bribe officials. It has been estimated that the average Mexican household spends 14 per cent of its income on bribes for state officials in order to obtain necessities such as a telephone connection or a driver's license. Colombia loses 1 per cent of its GDP per annum to corruption, and each Brazilian pays $6,000 per annum to corrupt officials. Corruption not only raises the cost of living, it also reduces foreign investment and the efficacy of development projects (Franko 2002, 155–56). Transparency International, which publishes a list of countries in the order of their level of corruption, found that Chile was the least corrupt Latin American nation. Nonetheless, at number 22 on the list, it was ranked behind the Scandinavian countries, Canada (9), the UK (12), and the US

(20). The next Latin American country was Uruguay (25) followed by Costa Rica (46). Brazil and Mexico, the two largest economies in Latin America, tied at 72. Most Latin American nations were on the bottom half of the list (Transparency International 2007).

Formal and informal networks between the state and the business class are characterized by clientelism, nepotism, and bureaucratic patrimonialism. With few exceptions (those being Chile and Costa Rica), Latin America does not have modern professional bureaucracies where hiring and promoting are based on merit, and incomes adequately compensate for the work involved. Even fewer are states where the bureaucracy has embedded autonomy, because the connections between the state, social, and business sectors are poorly institutionalized, especially among the poorer economic producers, such as small businesses and rural workers. Instead, linkages are based on personal access and are hidden from public scrutiny. Bureaucratic actors try to protect their projects from other state institutions, leading to intra-institutional secrecy and competition. Macroeconomic policies and social reform policies are controlled by a closed network of senior-level government officials, businessmen and women who are supported by international financial institutions. The tight control over policy-making has augmented their political power, which has given them access to economic assets. Equally, neoliberalism has concentrated wealth in fewer hands, creating a greater economic power, which gave these businesspeople access to political power. The personal ties between state actors and the business elite can lead to policy isolation, skewed influence over policy by the wealthy, and corruption (Teichman 2001). The low caliber of state institutions has left the state weak, lacking capacity to devise and implement policies, attract skilled workers, or overcome the vested interests of the elite. The low level of respect for bureaucracy has assisted neoliberalism in shrinking the powers of the state. Spending on the Latin American state as a percentage of its GDP is now half of that of most countries in the developed world (Franko 1999, 162).

Spearheaded by the OAS, there have been concerted attempts to improve bureaucracies by rewarding good performance, removing political control over appointments, and imposing new ethics codes for civil servants. Other reforms include attempts to reduce corruption, increase transparency, and improve efficiency. These reforms have faced significant resistance from the political elite because they reduce their clientelistic practices, and from public sector unions fearful of job losses. However, a weak state with limited extractive ability does not have the resources to fundamentally alter the reality of its bureaucracy. Those nations with stronger states, Chile, Costa Rica, and Uruguay, also perform the best on Transparency International's list, and have professional embedded bureaucracies.

DECENTRALIZATION

Attempts to reform state institutions to improve state capacity have been complicated by decentralization. Decentralization is the shifting of responsibilities and functions from the national level to sub-national levels of government, which can be both local and regional. Decentralization of the state was one of the reforms that neoliberalism has strongly endorsed. Political decentralization was more likely in nations with a geographically large land mass, federal structures, and ethnic diversity. The movement to decentralize power fundamentally changed the organization of power in Latin America in the 1980s and 1990s. Sometimes governments at the local or regional levels were completely new and had to be formed before holding their first elections. Sometimes the role of individual political actors at sub-national tiers, such as mayors, grew in financial strength and scope of responsibility. Decentralization was constitutionalized in Brazil in 1986, in Mexico in 1983 and 1999, in Guatemala in 1985, and in Venezuela in 1989. Argentina and Brazil are the most decentralized nations in Latin America (Montero and Samuels 2004, 21).

It was hoped that devolving power to the local level would increase community control and participation. It was thought it would be easier for citizens to monitor and influence programs. Governing structures would operate with increased transparency, accountability, and responsiveness. By increasing the participation of citizens and improving governance, social capital should develop, creating new norms of trust, mutuality, and tolerance. So decentralization was regarded as a mechanism which protected the people from authoritarian practices and governments. Decentralization would connect the citizen to the state, encourage new forms of participation, and produce appropriate—even innovative—solutions to local issues (Rondinelli and Shabbir 1983).

There are some examples of successful innovation and new forms of participation at the local level. In Guatemala, the indigenous people broke through centuries of oppression to participate in formal politics at the local level, running for office and winning mayoralties. Elements of participatory democracy have been integrated (with varying degrees of success) into the budgeting process, giving citizens and organized civil society opportunities to express and enforce their priorities at the local level. For example, Porto Alegre in Brazil has successfully practiced participatory democracy in its budget planning. Political decentralization has also empowered left-wing politicians to seek office at the local level, where they use mayoralties to criticize the national government's neoliberal policies and insist on increases in social spending. This has resulted in an "apparent schizophrenia. Right-of-centre pro-business regimes are voted in at the national level, while socially oriented administrations are elected at the municipal one" (quoted in Green 2003, 190). Some municipalities are beginning to use their new power and resources to create appropriate poverty alleviation programs and other kinds of social development.[2]

Nevertheless, political decentralization has its drawbacks. The benefits of political decentralization may not occur if there are no effective channels for citizen participation and representation at the local level. For example, in Oaxaca, Mexico, indigenous laws have been integrated into the electoral process, which has resulted in indigenous women being banned from running for office. Also, by devolving political power, there is less demand for political inclusiveness at the national level, thus protecting the national political elite. In Bolivia, decentralization was encouraged because the party elites had declining electoral support at the national level. Political and fiscal power was devolved to the sub-national level as a result, because the party was still powerful there (O'Neill 2004).

The central government is not the only political body that might benefit from decentralizing. Devolution may not boost democracy as much as it boosts the influence of regional *caudillos*, as has happened in Brazil, Argentina, and Mexico. Newly devolved regional and local governments in both Argentina (1998–2002) and Brazil (1998–99) used their budgets to establish their own networks of patronage and clientelism, which the central government was unable to stop. Without an active civil society demanding cost-efficient decentralization, there were few checks on spending. In Colombia, decentralization normalized and legitimized the control of drug cartels.

Decentralization is persuasive financially. Central governments, captured by political and economic elites, are inefficient. With fiscal decentralization, central governments lose control over a part of the budget. Political decentralization combined with fiscal decentralization offers more local control over devolved public services and activities, with the hope that policies will be better and more efficiently delivered. However, central governments can take the opportunity to devolve responsibility for supplying crucial services such as healthcare, policing, and education, without necessarily transferring enough money to the regional level to fund them. Or the conditions that the central government places on the spending can determine how the money must be used, and thereby shape the agenda at the local level. However, this problem can be resolved if the sub-national levels can generate their own revenue. Even so, while in theory the local level will have more financial oversight, there is no guarantee that regional or local governments will be any less profligate than national governments.

Fiscal decentralization can result in the loss of economies of scale when the national government withdraws from supplying services, so money may not be saved. Likely, regions differ on the quality of services, standards of care, and mode of delivery. The local level may not have the administrative power to set goals and implement policy. Even if they do, some regional governments may lack the capacity, knowledge, and experienced workers capable of supplying services requiring specialized skills. Without national standards or a national government integrating and coordinating services to ensure coherence, regional differences between rich and poor areas can be exacerbated. Richer areas, which might well receive more transfer funding, have proved better at supplying programs and care which help to overcome poverty and underdevelopment. Poorer areas have often become poorer. So decentralization can produce new forms of inequalities. Only Venezuela has asymmetrical decentralization, where the regions decide if they can offer high quality care or not, and the regions can return responsibility to the national government for any services they feel they cannot supply. Regional disparity highlights the weakness of the idea of decentralization, which requires, paradoxically, a strong central government to set standards and enforce them, to integrate bureaucracies so that there are economies of scale, and to adequately distribute income so that all people benefit.

It is difficult to measure the success of decentralization. Decentralization aspires to varying goals (enhanced democracy, better efficiency, alternative programs) and often has contradictory results. Local government might be less efficient in delivering a service but simultaneously does foster civil society participation. For example, Mexico decentralized political and fiscal power to the local and regional level, which assisted with the transition to democracy at the national level. However, these decentralized govern-ments are now being accused of authoritarian practices, corruption, and economic inefficiency (Mizrahi 2004). Thus, it is difficult to judge the suc-cess of Mexico's decentralization.

Where decentralization has been successful, it has promoted changes for the better. Civil society is more vibrant, participation is increased, and political structures are more horizontal. Electoral competition is more intense, opposition parties and new political actors are gaining power, and progressive change is happening, sometimes using innovative strategies. While the issues over which local people are struggling may seem trivial, the process does strengthen democratic norms and procedures, albeit at a modest pace. Where decentralization has not been successful, due to endemic poverty, powerful regional *caudillos*, and poorly structured insti-tutions, then the process has acted as a force to de-democratize political structures. Thus, depending on the circumstances, decentralization can seriously undermine democracy rather than enhance it. Within any nation, decentralization can have both effects.

THE MILITARY

Despite its history of supporting authoritarian governments and the elite, committing human rights abuses, and mismanaging the economy, the military remains one of the most respected state institutions in Latin America (Latinobarómetro 2007).[3] As Latin America democratized, the military voluntarily retreated to the barracks, handing over the power and authority to run the country to civilians. In some countries, the military even permitted the public to participate in discussions about constitutional reform (Brazil), the state to professionalize it (Nicaragua), neoliberalism to cut its funding (practically every country in Latin America), and the judiciary to try its generals for human rights abuses (Argentina, Uruguay, Bolivia, and Chile). The military has acquiesced to civilian control; but that does not necessarily mean that it has submitted to democratic control.

In order to establish control over the military, a democracy must employ two essential functions. First, military control must be institutionalized into democratic governance so that the military is accountable to elected representatives and is submissive to democratic principles, procedures, and institutions. Logically, then, the military cannot have political autonomy[4] or political influence, nor can it be a political actor in any sense of the word. The military also cannot be the guardians of the state, nor can it be above the law. Yet the military in Latin America continues to protect *la patria*, the fatherland, safeguarding it from dishonor, underdevelopment, and subversion, rather than investing that function in the legislature. Furthermore, the military is still above the law. The elite pact, which produced the transition to democracy, protected the military for a long time. The militaries and civilian governments negotiated over the status of amnesty for human rights abuses, with the military ultimately gaining substantial concessions from the government (Hunter 1998). More critically, the voluntary return to the barracks meant that the military felt it had been successful in its taking of power. Democratization did not change the military's fundamental belief that it had been right to intervene to safeguard *la patria*. Rather, the retreat to the barracks realigned the balance of power within the military. As the democracies consolidated, amnesty began to deteriorate to a degree. While some members of the military in certain countries have been found guilty of human rights abuses, the vast majority continue to enjoy effective amnesty.

Second, for democratic control of the military, elected representatives must identify threats to the regime and formulate defense policies, allocate the budget and resources, assign missions, and exert oversight of the management of the armed forces. With the pacted transition to democracy, the military retained some policy-making roles: helping to create or approve public policy; defining and watching for subversion through intelligence-gathering; and controlling the fight against crime, including drug trafficking (Colombia, Peru, Bolivia, Mexico, and Guatemala). The military tend to exert undue influence on the police (Diamint 2007, 162). The military may also put restrictions on the ideology of the political candidate running for office, constraints on democratic authority, or limitations on democratic procedures. Fear of a coup d'état could affect democratically elected leaders' decisions, producing policies that are amenable to the military. "The establishment of democratic control [of the military] remains elusive" (Díez 2008, 117).

In several countries, the military has made it clear that it voluntarily left power but can return should it feel so inclined (Brazil, Chile, Colombia, Argentina, Uruguay, Honduras, Nicaragua, Paraguay, and Peru). If it does return, then this action could be legal because the military has maintained the constitutional authority to protect *la patria*, in contradiction to its submission to civilian control. Loveman (1994) called this form of democracy a "protected democracy" because the military has the authority to protect the state rather than its elected representatives. This constitutional ambiguity over the role of the military in a democracy provides a legal cover for a coup d'état. The military also has the legal right to intervene during an emergency or time of crisis, when normal civil liberties are suspended. In Venezuela, the 1999 constitution increased the legal power of the military and its autonomy from legislative oversight.

To protect itself from government cutbacks, the military in many countries has taken over the operation of certain businesses, using its networks within the government and the business elite (Brazil, Guatemala, Ecuador, Colombia, and Paraguay). This highly organized but private source of income grants the military some autonomy from the state; the military is able to marshal resources to defend itself against political control, persuade citizens of its value, and influence the political economy. With its own private source of income, in most countries the military has become the single most organized and coherent sector of the elite. As it has with the rest of the elite, the running of businesses offers the military opportunities for corruption, including organized crime and drug trafficking (Guatemala, Colombia, and Paraguay). The depth of the involvement of the military in the political economy led one academic to call it an "expansive entrenchment" of the military in society (Agüero 1992, 155).

In all of Latin America, only Costa Rica, Mexico, and Panama have complete civil control over their militaries.[5] The rest of Latin America has a military involved in politics and the economy to the point that it is unhealthy to a democracy, although the military's involvement is hard to see. Under such circumstances, it is difficult to accept that the military has retreated to the barracks, as is claimed. Rather, the military has diminished some of its political involvement, changed the nature of its involvement in some ways, and made the lack of its overt involvement conditional on how well democracy is functioning. Nonetheless, so long as the elite remains united, and democracy has substantial mass support, the military will likely abstain from coup d'états and forming governments.

As this section on state institutions shows, the Latin American state still lacks the capacity to act autonomously from its elite in order to act in the name of all its citizens, and to shed its authoritarian, non-democratic practices. State institutions still lack professionalism, and some reject the ethos underlying democracy. However, the weakness inherent in state institutions is well recognized, and many state institutions are being critically examined and reformed, leaving room for optimism.

SOCIETAL INSTITUTIONS IN LATIN AMERICAN DEMOCRACIES

Many of the social institutions that helped with Latin America's transition to democracy, such as labor unions and the Catholic Church, were, paradoxically, weakened in the process. Democracy changed the political landscape, encouraging different forms of organization through different institutions.

CHURCHES

During the time of authoritarianism, many Roman Catholic churches in Latin America protected dissidents, organized protests, and helped offset the worst effects of economic dislocation through food banks and soup kitchens. As the labor movement weakened and universities were closed, the Catholic Church became a louder voice for the oppressed, if only because of lack of competition. The Church's activities grew from Christian-Based Communities (CEBs) and were supported by a theological movement called liberation theology, which strongly endorsed human rights, democracy, and freedom. CEBs numbered between 150,000 and 200,000 in the 1980s. These communities combined theology with their ability to mobilize participants in order to undermine the legitimacy of the ruling elite. CEBs also assisted in the transition to democracy by creating spaces for people to engage in critical enquiry, by training leaders and citizens, by mobilizing political participation, by normalizing responsibility for vulnerable sectors of society, and by permitting their contacts and networks to be used to exchange ideas and information. These skills are essential to a democracy. The CEBs also served as a political base for Christian democratic parties. During the pacted transition to democracy, the Catholic Church was frequently a political player. It managed to secure constitutional protection for itself in Costa Rica, Argentina, and Bolivia.

Christian democratic parties were elected in Chile, Costa Rica, El Salvador, Guatemala, Mexico, Venezuela, and Ecuador. The leaders of these political parties were prominent in resisting authoritarian governments. Although autonomous from the Catholic Church, Christian democratic parties were supported institutionally by the Church through the development of a unique perspective, support from students, and access to religious communities. While in power, however, Christian democrats were faced with the perennial problem of those in positions of power: the conflict between ideals and the reality of politics. As the Christian democrats compromised their ideals or cooperated with the elite, their value as an alternative to the status quo evaporated. In the end, Christian democratic parties were on both the right and the left of the political spectrum, and are now substantially weaker than they were in the 1980s and 1990s. Only Costa Rica's Christian Democratic Party has been able to hang onto power, although it must be noted that its attachment to the Catholic Church is nominal.

With the transition to and consolidation of democracy, the impetus for the Church's political involvement declined. In many countries, the Catholic Church returned to religious activities and other forms of devotion, and turned away from overt politicking. Unsupported by the hierarchy of the Catholic Church, CEBs slowly dissolved. There is also the suggestion that the CEBs were not necessarily in favor of individual civil liberties due to the corporatist tradition of Catholicism and Latin American society (Smith 1994, 127). The legacy of the Church's political activities is smaller than predicted. In Central America, one of the areas where the progressive Catholic Church had been most active, there has been a contraction in the number of CEBs and a reduction in their political militancy. Priests and laity in parishes known to be progressive now support protest less than those who were areligious (Stein 2000).

Civil liberties produced new forms of social identity, new mechanisms for expressing dissent, and new kinds of religious affiliation. Churches, chapels, street preachers, charismatic movements, religious radio stations, and TV programs have multiplied. While religiosity is on the rise, the Catholic Church is losing parishioners to the fast-growing evangelical churches. Protestantism has grown from 15 million adherents in the late 1960s to 50 million by 2008. It is particularly powerful in Brazil, Chile, and Guatemala. It has grown as a result of dissatisfaction with Catholicism, but also because it offers refuge from social upheaval and violence. Protestantism is any Christian church that is not Roman Catholic, and thus spans the political and theological spectrum. However, there are common traits. Protestantism preaches individual redemption, with an emphasis on the need to change one's life, an approach more in step with neoliberalism than corporatist Catholicism. Protestantism has the reputation of being less tolerant than the Catholic Church of sins such as womanizing and drinking; of having poorer, darker-skinned, less-educated congregations; of being a group to belong to if you want to get ahead in society; and of being resolutely apolitical. Nonetheless, there are Protestant political parties and elected representatives. Guatemala has had two Protestant presidents, and Brazil elected 60 Protestant representatives in 2002. However, the political impact of Protestantism is muted. Voter support is low. The Protestant movement is fragmented and lacks theological unity. "It is unlikely that any of the existing Protestant Latin American parties will evolve into cohesive and competitive political actors" (Freston 2008, 27). Like the CEBs, the Protestant churches open spaces for critical enquiry, to train community leaders, and to foster respect for the rule of law, freedom of speech, and freedom of religion. If only because of their growing communities, Protestant votes will be increasingly courted. Although the Catholic Church is still the most powerful church in Latin America, the rising force of the evangelical churches weakens its traditional centrality in the religious, social, and political life of Latin America.

SOCIAL MOVEMENTS, NGOs, AND INGOs

Social movements were also instrumental in the transition to democracy in Latin America by organizing civil society and demonstrating against the state. Under populist and B-A regimes, Latin American states either co-opted civil society through managing unions or other civil society organizations, or else oppressed them. Consequently, legal citizen activity was fragmented, partial, and conditional on state approval. With economic crises and human rights abuses, social movements arose to demand democracy. Their persistence eroded the legitimacy of the dictatorship while simultaneously eroding the fear of citizens to protest. For example, in Argentina the mothers of those who were "disappeared" by the government marched around a central plaza every Thursday, sometimes carrying pictures of their children. While the women were threatened with torture or even assassination, the government was ultimately weaker than they were. However, not all social movements had the protection that symbolism offered those mothers, and many suffered accordingly. Yet despite exile, torture, threats, and murder, social movements were sufficiently powerful enough to become part of the process of forcing the military to negotiate pacts. With democratization, representation replaced the overwhelming need for social movements. The vast majority of social movements demobilized.[6] However, the vital political skills learned from participating in the social movement were retained by those who took part, and can be called upon in another civil setting. Thus, the social capital of those movements has not necessarily been lost.

In most countries in Latin America, social movements lack the political influence they once had. It is difficult to quantify the number of social movements and their precise impact. Social movements, inherently fluid, local, and dealing with immediate issues, dissolve and reconstitute regularly. Increasingly however, social movements in Latin America are networked into associations that link communities, movements, churches, activists, and the occasional political party. They have international connections and support. These networks share common values and a common discourse, rapidly spread ideas and concerns internationally, and can cooperate to achieve a short-term or immediate goal. Bringing national and international attention to a specific issue can force any state to act, even the weak states of Latin America. For example, international advocacy networks assisted survivors of human rights abuses and their families to obtain national recognition of the military's actions. The Inter-American Commission on Human Rights provided legal support and political support, and the Inter-American Court for Human Rights ruled against amnesties and pardons in Argentina, Chile, and Uruguay, and adjudicated on Honduras and Guatemala. This integration of the local, national, and international was instrumental in dissolving military amnesty and enhancing democratic norms.

The constituents of NGOs became those who are left out of formal institutions due to the retreat of the state, weak governance, economic crises, and neoliberal policies. The poor not only lack secure, well-paying jobs and formal education but also social and political connections and influence. As a result, they find it difficult to organize or access democratic procedures. In effect, political rights and freedoms belong predominantly to the middle and upper classes. NGOs help to mobilize poorer citizens to demand goods and services from the government, and to develop community networks and cohesion.

Furthermore, NGOs and INGOs have replaced some of the state's activities by running a host of programs including schools, health clinics, retraining centers, businesses, and banks offering credit to the poor. Sometimes the skills and understanding that NGOs bring are superior to what is available through the state. NGOs tend to espouse greater gender sensitivity and environmental consciousness, passing on these concepts to the communities they serve. Yet however necessary their contributions are, NGOs and INGOs replacing state services can only produce a patchwork of approaches and results. Meanwhile, the state has been able to offload some of its responsibility to supply basic services, because the private sector (for the rich) or civil society organizations (for the poor) supplies them.

Due to their connections with local people working at ground level, NGOs are best at giving the state feedback about how its programs are working: they can analyze the weak points of a system, showing how individuals or groups are hampering or assisting development, and how programs could be improved. For example, in Mexico, an OECD nation, maternal mortality remains high, at 83 deaths per 100,000 live births in 2000. Improving maternal health indicators and ensuring universal access to reproductive health services was a UN Millennium Development Goal that Mexico endorsed. By acting between formal healthcare institutions and the women who are outside the system, and by using the political influence of larger INGOs, maternal health NGOs are able to act as advocates for better maternal healthcare provision (Mills 2006).

There is, nonetheless, a failure of logic in having networks and alliances represent and agitate on behalf of the population. If people join NGOs because the weak state and minimum democracy have excluded them, then advocacy has limited impact. The state lacks the capacity to address the issues being raised, and there are few mechanisms to ensure that the state will change its policies. In some countries, this paradox is resolved by connecting social movements to political parties, such as ethnic-based mass mobilizations cum political parties.

ETHNICITY

A new political movement arose from civil society in the 1970s and 1980s, gained power in the 1990s, and is becoming the dominant political movement of the twenty-first century. The emergence of ethnicity as a key political factor in Latin America is sufficiently complex that academics are scrambling to explain it. It is a measure of how little is known about the indigenous peoples, and the difficulty in deciding what constitutes "indigenous," that explains why numbers are unclear. There are 35 to 40 million indigenous people living in Latin America, forming 600 to 700 ethnic groups or tribal affiliations, and speaking even more languages. They are disproportionally the continent's poorest people. Racist ideology and exploitative economic structures in the nineteenth and twentieth centuries ensured that the indigenous peoples of Latin America were politically excluded, socially discriminated against, and economically impoverished even while nations struggled to democratize. The exceptions to this rule were those peoples living in remote areas where the nation-state could not penetrate, such as the Amazon Basin, or those living in areas of little interest to the nation-state, such as the highlands of Peru, Guatemala, and Bolivia. Thanks to technology, by the late twentieth century even these areas were colonized. Furthermore, in Colombia, Brazil, Venezuela, and Chile, some indigenous people live close to areas or border regions where drug traffickers operate. This attracts military incursions into their territories and prompts the state to redefine the indigenous as a national security threat (Langer and Muñoz 2003).

The indigenous peoples of Latin America have fought back in a variety of ways, using both domestic and international mechanisms. Domestically, they are increasingly demanding inclusion in the polity, and requiring state and social recognition of the uniqueness and validity of their demands. These demands focus mostly on cultural rights, but also focus on the control of natural resources found on traditional lands. Generally, the Latin American state has permitted indigenous populations control over their own affairs so long as they do not violate national laws, although national laws take precedence in the event of a conflict. Thus, there are criminal proceedings in customary (also known as traditional) laws. Utilizing customary law and strengthening cultural identity and rights helps indigenous peoples to protect their right to make other demands on the state, such as gaining control over natural resources or administrative autonomy (Warren and Jackson 2002, 19). Using elements of globalization such as cheap airfare and the Internet, the indigenous connect with regional groups in order to act in ways that are supportive of each other. Other strategies include forging their own NGOs and linking with INGOs to replace state services, petitioning the state, and evoking liberal international legal norms to pursue land claims or codified rights (Brysk 2000). The range and complexity of these strategies dispel the myth that the indigenous peoples of Latin America are, in some way, "backward."

Even recently, left-leaning parties and revolutionary groups marginalized indigenous concerns and cultural identities. The legacy is an antipathy among the indigenous toward these political leanings. Instead, indigenous movements are embracing the opportunities offered by democratization, and using their numerical clout to assist the rise of political parties, platforms, and leaders who are either supportive of indigenous rights or indigenous people themselves. For example, Rafael Correa, a political outsider supportive of indigenous rights, won the 2006 presidential election in Ecuador predominantly because of the indigenous vote. Yashar (1998) further suggests neoliberalism ruptured ties of clientelism between the state and the indigenous and in doing so, increased the precariousness of their existence. With neoliberalism's smaller state, its inability to adequately respond to ethnic demands has strengthened ethno-nationalism. Neoliberalism also reduced the formal working class, sending ex-union workers with excellent organizational skills back to the community. Finally, the neoliberal state with its party fragmentation, minimum democracy, and weak rule of law reduced the reasons to work within the political system. So neoliberalism deepened the logic of the indigenous mobilizing on behalf of their own interests. To summarize, globalization, democratization, and economic dislocation assisted the rise of ethnic political parties cum social movements. Examples are the Pachakutik Party (MUPP-NP) of Ecuador, and the Movement Toward Socialism (MAS) of Bolivia. Both have been successful in propelling their candidates to the presidency, although MUPP-NP has been less successful in maintaining it. Both rhetorically endorse an inclusive political ideology of shared national interests. Nonetheless, the interplay between democratic structures, ethnic-based political parties and their indigenous constituency is complex, the meaning of which can sometimes be lost on outsiders. This enhances an exclusionary dynamic between ethnic-based politics and the broader polity (Rice forthcoming).

To make the dynamic more unpredictable, ethnic-based political parties require at least partial accommodation within Westernized society, while cultural identity must constantly be reforged, as the definition of "ethnic" is constantly changing. Furthermore, linguistic and cultural differences keep the indigenous from easily creating alliances with each other, even within the same nation. The diversity of ethnic groups means that they often have quite different economic needs, and compete with each other. The debate over what entails a cultural identity, how to organize in a way appropriate to that identity, and what limits the state raises questions about citizenship, and the relationship between citizens and the state. Ironically, this debate, originating within the indigenous and intellectual community, has spurred the *ladino* community to ask the same questions, and galvanized the emergence of a *ladino* ethnicity movement (*ladinidad*).

CONCLUSION

In many countries of Latin America, a deep democracy has not been achieved because the institutions necessary to extend the deliberative processes are weak. While no democracy in the world functions perfectly, in Latin America, the combined weaknesses of many state and civil society institutions cripple deliberative democracy. Limited rule of law, code-law constitutions, fragmented political parties, malapportioned legislatures, presidentialism, and weak bureaucracies have undermined democratic institutions, procedures, and norms. Vertical accountability may function, in as much as there are elections, but horizontal accountability has been nominal, and with the censoring of free press, social accountability has been weakened. Apolitical churches, smaller labor unions, and a splintered civil society still skittish from years of authoritarianism and preoccupied with replacing state services mean that civil society lacks robustness and dense organization. Without these institutions functioning as they should, corruption, clientelism, cronyism, and bureaucratic patrimonialism continue to thrive. These powerful, informal institutions have been able to adapt to and integrate themselves into newly democratized political structures and globalized economic restructuring through transfer payments, state support for NGOs, and the distribution of state goods and services. This combination of weak formal and powerful informal institutions has allowed the elite to unduly influence or even control the state, ensuring their position of dominance. In the process, democratic institutions and procedures have been hollowed out, producing electoral or minimum democracies throughout the region. The state in Latin America lacks the capacity to act autonomously, overcome social and economic inequalities, and deny non-democratic practices. Weak states with minimum democracies are vulnerable to the negative impact of globalization, which heightens anti-democratic and non-egalitarian practices.

Despite this gloomy picture, there is much to be optimistic about in Latin America's continuing construction of democracy. The Pink Tide governments are strengthening the state and improving governance. The state is addressing the inequality of wealth distribution through extending state services. Many countries are slowly reforming their organization of power. Core problems with the organization of the state are being addressed. These problems include corruption, bureaucratic incompetence, lack of an autonomous judiciary, inadequate rule of law, inappropriate use of presidential powers, legislative competition between the governing bodies, an imbalance of power between the branches of government, and weak revenue collection. In addition, new political actors arising from new civil society organizations, ethnic bases, and decentralized policies are creating new policies and opportunities for change, strengthening civil society in the process. Traditionally oppressed groups are expressing themselves through the vote, powerful NGOs, or political parties. The quality and quantity of these reforms suggest a vibrancy and responsiveness within Latin American democracies, a resilience to forge a better—more democratic—organization of power.

NOTES

1 The occasional fourth branch of government is the electoral tribunals. These are autonomous bodies with their own budgets which answer only to themselves. They oversee elections to ensure electoral fairness and transparency. They have generally been a force to preserve free and fair elections, and as such are important mechanisms for safeguarding democracy.

2 It is also possible that the historical practice of Latin Americans making political demands by demonstrating on a massive scale, sometimes repetitively, works better with decentralized power. These demonstrations can

actually paralyze a city, politicize more people easily, and influence government actors more readily. However, there is little comparative data on these.
3 That respect seems to be diminishing in relation to other state institutions, which is a testimony to the increasing strength of the Latin American state. See Latinobarómetro (2009).
4 Some institutional autonomy is necessary for the professionalization of the military, but it must be clearly bounded.
5 Given the ambiguity of constitutions and the nature of negotiation between the military and democratic governments, it is difficult to state emphatically which countries have decisive control over their militaries and which do not. Costa Rica may not have a military, but it does have a Home Guard with clearly defined functions.
6 The mothers who marched in Argentina are one of the exceptions. They have branched into other areas of human rights, pushing the government to investigate the disappearances.

REFERENCES

Agüero, Filipe. 1992. "The Military and the Limits to Democratization in South America." *Issues in Democratic Consolidation.* Ed. Scott Mainwaring, Guillermo O'Donnell, and Samuel Valenzuela. Notre Dame: Notre Dame University Press. 153–98.
Brysk, Alison. 2000. *From Tribal Village to Global Village: Indian Rights and International Relations in Latin America.* Stanford: Stanford University Press.
Cheibub, José Antonio. 2002. "Minority Governments, Deadlock Situations, and the Survival of Presidential Democracies." *Comparative Political Studies* 35(3): 284–312.
Diamint, Rut. 2007. "Military, Police, Politics and Society: Does Latin America Have a Democratic Model?" *The Construction of Democracy: Lessons from Practice and Research.* Ed. Jorge I. Domínguez and Anthony Jones. Baltimore: Johns Hopkins University Press. 148–76.
Díez, Jordi. 2008. "Legislative Oversight of the Armed Forces in Mexico." *Mexican Studies* 24(1): 113–45.
Franko, Patrice. 1999. *The Puzzle of Latin American Economic Development.* Oxford: Oxford University Press.
Freston, Paul. 2008. "The Many Faces of Evangelical Politics in Latin America." *Evangelical Christianity and Democracy in Latin America.* Ed. Paul Freston. Oxford: Oxford University Press. 3–36.
Green, Duncan. 2003. *Silent Revolution: The Rise and Crisis of Market Economies in Latin America.* New York: Monthly Review and LAB.
Hunter, Wendy. 1998. "Negotiating Civil–Military Relations in Post-Authoritarian Argentina and Chile." *International Studies Quarterly* (42): 295–318.
Langer, Erick D., and Elena Muñoz. 2003. *Contemporary Indigenous Movements in Latin America.* Wilmington, DE: Scholarly Resources.
Latinobarómetro. June 10, 2010. www.latinobarometro.org.
Levitsky, Steven. 2003. *Transforming Labour-Based Parties in Latin America: Argentine Peronism in Comparative Perspective.* Cambridge: Cambridge University Press.

Linz, Juan J. 1994. "Presidential or Parliamentary Democracy. Does it Make a Difference?" *The Failure of Presidential Democracy*. Ed. Juan Linz and Arturo Valenzuela. Baltimore: Johns Hopkins University Press. 3–87.

Loveman, Brian. 1994. "'Protected Democracies' and Military Guardianship: Political Transitions in Latin America 1978–1993." *Journal of Interamerican Studies and World Affairs* 36(2): 105–89.

Luna, Juan P., and Elizabeth J. Zechmeister. 2005. "Political Representation in Latin America: A Study of Elite-Mass Congruence and Nine Countries." *Comparative Political Studies* 38(4): 388–416.

Mainwaring, Scott, and Timothy Scully. 1995. "Introduction: Party Systems in Latin America." *Building Democratic Institutions: Party Systems in Latin America*. Ed. Scott Mainwaring and Timothy Scully. Stanford: Stanford University Press. 1–34.

Mills, Lisa. 2006. "Maternal Health Policy and the Politics of Scale in Mexico." *Social Politics International Studies in Gender State and Society* (3): 487–521.

Mizrahi, Yemile. 2004. "Twenty Years of Decentralization in Mexico: A Top-Down Process." *Decentralization, Democratic Governance and Civil Society in Comparative Perspective*. Ed. Philip Oxhorn, Joseph Tulchin, and Andrew D. Selee. Baltimore: Johns Hopkins University Press. 33–58.

Montero, Alfred P., and David J. Samuels. 2004. "The Political Determinants of Decentralization in Latin America." *Decentralization and Democracy in Latin America*. Ed. Alfred P. Montero and David J. Samuels. Notre Dame: University of Notre Dame Press. 3–32.

O'Donnell, Guillermo. 1994. "Delegative Democracy." *Journal of Democracy* 5(1): 54–69.

O'Neill, Kathleen M. 2004. "Decentralization in Bolivia: Electoral Incentives Outcomes." *Decentralization and Democracy in Latin America*. Ed. Alfred P. Montero and David Samuels. Notre Dame: University of Notre Dame Press. 35–66.

Rice, Roberta. Forthcoming. *The New Politics of Protest: Indigenous and Popular Mobilization in Latin America's Neoliberal Era*. Tucson: University of Arizona Press.

Roberts, Kenneth. 2002. "Party Society Linkages and Democratic Representation in Latin America." *Canadian Journal of Latin American and Caribbean Studies* 27(53): 9–34.

Rondinelle, Dennis A., and Cheema G. Chabbir. 1983. *Decentralization and Development Policy Implementation in Developing Countries*. London: Sage.

Seider, Rachel. 2004. "Renegotiating 'Law and Order': Judicial Reform and Citizen Responses in Post-War Guatemala." *Democratization and the Judiciary: The Accountability Function of Courts in New Democracies*. Ed. Siri Gloppen, Roberto Gargarella, and Elin Skaar. London: Frank Cass Press. 137–60.

Smith, Christian. 1994. "The Spirit and Democracy: Base Communities, Protestantism, and Democratization in Latin America." *Sociology of Religion* 55(2): 119–43.

Stein, Andrew. 2000. "Religion, Political Preferences, and Protest Action in Central America: Nicaragua, El Salvador and Guatemala." *The Church at the Grassroots in Latin America: Perspectives on Thirty Years of Activism*. Ed. J. Burdick and W.E. Hewitt. Westport: Praeger Press. 3–30.

Synder, Richard, and Samuels David. 2006. "Devaluing the Vote in Latin America." *Electoral Systems and Democracy*. Ed. Larry Diamond and Marc F. Plattner. Baltimore: Johns Hopkins University Press. 168–81.

Teichman, Judith A. 2003. "Latin America: Inequality, Poverty, and Questionable Democracies." *Civilizing Globalization: A Survival Guide*. Ed. Richard Sandbrook. Albany: State University of New York Press. 39–52.

Transparency International. June 10, 2010. www.transparency.org.

Warren, Kay B., and Jean E. Jackson. 2002. "Studying Indigenous Activism in Latin America." *Indigenous Movements, Self-Representation and the State in Latin America*. Ed. K.B. Warren and J.E. Jackson. Austin, TX: University of Texas Press. 1–46.

Yashar, Deborah J. 2008. "Contesting Citizenship: Indigenous Movements and Democracy in Latin America." *Comparative Politics* 31(1): 23–42.

FOUR

Mexico:
From Perfect Dictatorship
to Imperfect Democracy

JUDITH TEICHMAN

Claudia Cortes, a single mother of two young boys, died at the age of 26 in a hail of gunfire in her hometown of Apatzingan, Michoacán, in southern Mexico. Claudia was poor. Only a cross marks her pauper's grave in the poorest section of the town's municipal cemetery. The daughter of a plumber, she struggled to support herself and her boys by selling used clothing, but saw her economic prospects improve once she was recruited by drug traffickers to work at one of their "safe houses." It was Claudia's "choice" to work there that cost her her life. When the army moved in, the occupants of the safe house opened fire. Three police officers were seriously wounded, and four alleged drug traffickers, including Claudia, were killed (Tobar and Sánchez 2007). Claudia's short life highlights the clash between the government and the drug traffickers, inequality, and the failure of democratic development.

Poverty, inequality, and violence are widespread in Mexico, and they are intertwined because the poor become easy targets for recruitment into criminal activities.[1] Many Mexicans from all walks of life participated in the struggle for electoral democracy, achieved in the year 2000 with the election of Vicente Fox as president. But a basic prerequisite for democracy is a state capable of controlling its national territory and providing some physical security for its citizens. Since 2000, the ability of the Mexican state to carry out these functions has diminished. Hence, although the country now has generally clean elections and an activist congress, its democratic deficits are substantial and growing. Furthermore, its 2006 presidential election was so closely contested that the country's avoidance of the region's electoral Pink Tide by no means signified an absence of social justice concerns among a substantial proportion of the electorate. As we shall see, the failure to effectively address these concerns has important implications for democracy.

Mexico's current predicament, as a weakening state facing increasingly serious threats to the quality of its democracy, has been shaped by the country's authoritarian legacies. Indeed, Mexico's current situation is very far from the optimistic predictions many observers made 40 years ago. While other countries faced political instability and, later, brutal military dictatorships, Mexico experienced 70 years of political stability under a benign form of authoritarianism, so effective in its ability to contain discontent it has been described as a "perfect dictatorship."[2]

Furthermore, while serious economic problems plagued other Latin American countries, the "Mexican miracle" witnessed steady GNP growth, averaging 6 per cent per year until 1970. The Mexican state appeared to be a relatively strong one by Latin American standards. It played an important role in the economy, and was often able to contain pressures from social forces. By the late 1960s, however, the country's political arrangements were showing signs of strain, and the country embarked upon a long period of political transition. Poverty and inequality, already rampant, worsened because of the economic crisis of the early 1980s and the financial collapse of 1995. Meanwhile, the unraveling of old authoritarian political arrangements accelerated through the 1980s. In the year 2000, Mexico finally made the transition to electoral democracy.

The features of the country's authoritarian, one-party rule shaped both the transition and current problems. These authoritarian features stemmed from an underlying historical context: social heterogeneity, involving stark racial and cultural (such as indigenous versus European) divisions, reinforced by important class and regional inequalities. Mexico's long period of authoritarian rule had managed these divisions, but had not resolved them. Faced with strong social forces and ongoing political unrest, the main concern of the state became the achievement of political stability. This objective would drive the country's institutional evolution well into the twentieth century and would shape the evolution of both formal and informal arrangements of political control.

POPULAR RESISTANCE TO POLITICAL AND SOCIAL EXCLUSION

The sharp inequalities that characterize Mexico today have long historical roots and are closely linked to the process of conquest and exploitation of the indigenous population by the Spanish invaders. The seat of the Aztec empire was located where Mexico City stands and the Mayan civilization extended into much of southern Mexico. While the indigenous population declined sharply with the conquest, it recovered thereafter. In 1810, a decade before independence, more than 60 per cent of the population of what is present-day Mexico was indigenous. Because Mexican policy was one of assimilation, the indigenous population declined in the following years and by the mid-twentieth century had dropped to somewhere between 28 per cent and 37 per cent of the population (Lambert 1967, 42). With a high level of miscegenation, mestizos (the descendents of European and indigenous peoples) came to constitute the majority of the population, probably 60 per cent in total. The white population was small in comparison. While the country's poorest citizens were indigenous peoples living in rural areas, particularly in south central Mexico, the white population generally occupied the highest levels of economic and political power and resided in the urban centers. Mestizos occupied an intermediate level in the social, economic, and political hierarchy, although many were poor urban and rural dwellers.

As in Central America and the Andean region, colonization involved large land grants to Spanish conquerors and the subjugation of Indian labor on large landholdings. Independence from Spain did not alter this unequal and racialized order, which persisted in the midst of the political anarchy that was the norm for much of the nineteenth century. Between 1821 and 1860, Mexico had 50 separate governments, each, on average, lasting less than one year. Many nineteenth-century political struggles had marked class and racial elements. In central Mexico (the region with the highest population density), the juxtaposition of large landed estates (haciendas) owned by American-born Spaniards (*criollos*), Indian communal villages (*ejidos*), and mestizo settlements gave rise to conflicts between mestizo and Indian villages, and between villages (Indian and mestizo) and big landowners. In addition, by 1857 an ongoing intra-elite conflict between liberals and conservatives had produced a three-year civil war. Meanwhile, Indian rebellions raged as commercial agriculture impinged on communal village property. Regional *caudillo* strong men (usually mestizos), whose power was based on the personal loyalty of poor Indian followers, often took advantage of the chaotic situation to build local armies and regional bases of power.

Centralized control of the national territory was finally achieved with the rise to power of the authoritarian dictator, Porfirio Díaz (1876–1911). While political repression was one of the Porfiriato regime's main mechanisms of gaining control of rebellious social groups, Díaz also selectively dispensed material rewards to buy the support of elite power contenders and new middle sector groups—a tactic that would become an integral feature of politics in the decades which followed and into the twentieth century. Indian lands were confiscated and those lands were used to buy off regional military *caudillo* leaders. Díaz handpicked governors, also allocating them large tracts of land to ensure their political support, and he expanded the government bureaucracy, providing many jobs for the emerging middle class.

The philosophical context of the Porfiriato modernization strategy was an important component of its highly exclusionary and unequal consequences. Positivism, a philosophy emphasizing the use of science to attain knowledge and material progress, believed that the key to development lay in the application of Western science and in the economic leadership of a modern business class of bankers and industrialists. Díaz's close advisors, a group of technocrats known as the *científicos*, believed in an extreme form of the philosophy that held Indians and mestizos in contempt, and believed that the country's leadership must be in the hands of the *criollo* oligarchy.

In an effort to stimulate domestic industrialization, Díaz created a close business–state relationship, and a concentration of economic power that would shape the future in powerful ways. New, foreign-financed railway links to the United States stimulated the growth of industry, giving northern Mexico, particularly the city of Monterrey, the edge in industrialization. Many of the firms established between 1890 and 1910 became the backbone of the industrialization process that would occur from 1940 (Haber 1989, 3). Supported by government-granted monopoly concessions, the manufacturing sector quickly developed into a relatively small number of vertically integrated firms, many owned by Díaz cronies. While in some respects the Porfiriato was positive—the volume of trade expanded rapidly, the public treasury went into surplus, and the country had acquired a solid international credit rating—the social consequences were devastating.

To promote foreign investment in infrastructure, the government granted generous land concessions to railway and survey companies. In the process, Indians were divested of their lands. By 1910, 96 per cent of the agricultural population was landless, the real wage of the rural laborer was one quarter of what it had been in 1800, and urban wages had dropped (Tannenbaum 1968, 140). Agriculture production for domestic consumption was insufficient, and famine stalked both dispossessed peasants and the working class. Life expectancy and infant mortality rates, already very low to begin with, deteriorated in the last decades of the Porfiriato. Brutal repression met both worker resistance and peasant unrest.

Meanwhile, the middle class chafed under the absence of political rights. Schoolteachers, shopkeepers, small- and medium-sized farm owners (rancheros), and even some wealthy landowners joined workers and peasants in support of the Revolution of 1910–17. Mexico once again descended into anarchy. In the course of the revolutionary upheaval, those revolutionary leaders drawn from the lower classes (Emiliano Zapata and Pancho Villa) were defeated, and middle-class individuals took over the leadership in the post-revolutionary period. The Porfiriato financial/industrial class survived and was able to establish an alliance with the new revolutionary leaders, since elite collaboration was needed for the reconstitution of the banking system. A new commercial, agrarian bourgeoisie soon emerged from among the middle-class revolutionary leadership. As we shall see, neither the old nor the new propertied interests were very interested in the redistributive aspirations of the working and peasant classes.

However, given the important role of workers and peasants in the revolution, the revolutionary leaders could not afford to completely ignore the demands of the poor. Worker militancy, including involvement in military action, had been important during the revolution and continued unabated in its aftermath. Indian peasants and mestizo farmers had fought under the leadership of Zapata and Villa. As a result, the new constitution contained a variety of liberal concepts (federalism, the separation of powers, and a bill of rights) and it recognized the social rights important to workers and peasants. It provided for land redistribution (Article 27) and guaranteed extensive labor rights, such as the eight-hour day and the minimum wage (Article 123). Meeting these goals would be a persistent and recurrent promise of every post-revolutionary administration until the 1980s.

As the post-revolutionary state continued to wrestle with repeated uprisings, political leaders drew heavily on past practices. The end to the ongoing upheavals appeared to be in sight when President Plutarco Elías Calles created a new political party, the National Revolutionary Party, in 1929. The new party incorporated state political machines and used patronage to keep violent conflict in check. Those who cooperated with Calles and his party were rewarded not only with personal wealth but also with state funding for irrigation works, roads, schools, and agricultural credit for their region.

Through the 1920s, the post-revolutionary leadership acquired increasing wealth, many becoming big landowners engaged in commercial export agriculture, especially in northern Mexico.[3] They used the state to shield their lands against redistribution and to provide their agricultural businesses with irrigation and generous credit facilities. Then the Great Depression, which saw unemployment rates soar and salaries drop, triggered a rise in political mobilization. As social unrest mounted, a younger generation of revolutionaries gained ground within the ruling party. By 1934 social reform, including agrarian reform, was firmly on the agenda. At the same time, foreign control of mining and petroleum stoked nationalist fervor against a post-revolutionary leadership that had failed to take measures to reduce the foreign control of key economic sectors.

STRONG POPULAR FORCES, RIGHT-WING REACTION, AND THE CONTAINMENT OF POLITICAL PRESSURES IN AUTHORITARIAN MEXICO

The demands of workers and peasants would soon push the state toward more radically redistributive measures. Popular pressures also laid the groundwork for a new set of non-legal institutional arrangements that would ultimately incorporate and contain the country's powerful social forces. These new arrangements, combined with the constitutional powers of the presidency, ultimately produced one of the most powerful presidencies in Latin America. Presidentialism would go on to become one of the outstanding features of Mexican authoritarianism. The 1917 constitution gives considerable formal power to the president: the power to initiate legislation, to veto legislation, exclusive powers over expenditures, and extraordinary decree powers in the case of an emergency. But this formal power had proved incapable of keeping presidential contenders and congress in check.

The first important step toward Mexico's long period of political stability occurred when President Lázaro Cárdenas (1934–40) strengthened the office of the presidency by subordinating the party to it. Once the president gained control of the party, the Mexican presidency acquired a variety of powers which were not bestowed constitutionally, through the ability to control the naming of all party candidates. In this way, national legislators and gubernatorial candidates became tied to the president not only for their initial entry into politics but also for continued career advancement after their term in office ended, in the party, in the state bureaucracy, or in a different electoral office. Presidential power stemming from control over political career advancement was reinforced by the prohibition on candidate reelection, instituted in 1940. From this point on, the exchange of loyalty for career advancement and the opportunity for personal enrichment was an arrangement that ensured loyalty and political control from the top to the bottom of the political system.

During the Cárdenas years, worker mobilization was intense in the foreign-controlled enclaves of mining, petroleum, and railways, inflamed by the better wages and working conditions afforded foreign workers. That mounting pressure was instrumental in the nationalization of the foreign-controlled railways and petroleum industry.[4] Also because of pressure from workers, Cárdenas turned the operation of the country's railways over to the railway union and, when the petroleum industry was nationalized, he gave workers four of nine positions on the board of directors of the state petroleum company. This arrangement gave the labor unions access to sources of wealth from higher-paying jobs and government contracts. Throughout the Cárdenas years, workers saw improvements in wages and benefits, while peasants made their greatest gains in land reform. Between 1935 and 1940, the government distributed 44 million acres of land, more than two times the amount distributed by all of the previous governments combined (Parkes 1960, 343). Most of this went into communal holdings or *ejidos*, making poor Indians co-owners of new, large farms. The government also invested in roads, irrigation systems, schools, and medical services, along with increasing credit to *ejidal* agriculture. Cárdenas's government spent more on social welfare than any government that came before it (Wilkie 1967, 158).

The incorporation of the various representative organizations into the party apparatus was another key ingredient in the political stability of later years. Cárdenas oversaw the establishment of the Confederation of Mexican Workers (CTM) to represent workers, the National Confederation of Peasants (CNC) to represent peasants, and the popular sector, known as the National Confederation of Popular Organizations (CNOP), representing a number of important middle-class interests and the urban poor. Incorporated into a reorganized political party, these sectoral organizations replaced regional ones.[5] With the Cárdenas redistributive reforms, the nationalist takeover of foreign companies, and the introduction of popular representation within the party, it became the party of the Mexican Revolution in the eyes of most Mexicans.

However, Cardenas's policies had profoundly alienated the increasingly powerful private sector based in the northern city of Monterrey. Business reaction pushed the political leadership to the right, put an end to redistributive measures, and ushered in a set of political arrangements that would increase inequality and fail to reduce widespread poverty in the years to come. As the economy turned sour, private sector opposition mounted. While the country's debt rose, oil prices declined and inflation increased. Business became particularly alarmed by the mobilization of the popular classes, by labor strikes, and by the incessant pressure for wage hikes. Business sent capital out of the country, a tactic it used repeatedly in the future to discipline the state. The Monterrey business group supported its own candidate for the presidency, prompting Cárdenas to throw his support behind the conciliation candidate, Manuel Ávila Camacho, who became Mexico's next president. In the years to come, the political right reasserted itself and worker and peasant power diminished.

From 1940, the Mexican leadership developed a highly effective system of containing strong social forces. Integral to that system was both corporatism (incorporation of popular organizations into the party) and clientelism (the exchange of material rewards in exchange for political support). With presidential control of the party apparatus (now appropriately renamed the Institutional Revolutionary Party, PRI), and with peasant and worker organizational incorporation into the party, presidents could now replace recalcitrant worker and peasant leaders with quiescent ones. The 1931 labor code, requiring labor and peasant organizations to obtain legal recognition from the state, further strengthened state control.

The exchange of material rewards for political support was integral to the system of political containment, and it became the basis for widespread corruption within the political system. In exchange for opportunities for personal enrichment, labor and peasant leaders quelled dissent and ensured that their rank and file voted for the PRI at election time. This exchange was particularly important to control the country's most powerful trade unions in sectors like mining and petroleum, where collective agreements provided labor leaders with the ability to dispense housing, loans, and scholarships to loyal supporters. Demands for social benefits were channeled through the PRI-affiliated labor organizations, with the most generous benefits going to the most powerful trade unions—public sector employers and workers in the big, government-owned public enterprises. The government bureaucracy, which expanded rapidly throughout this period, became a major avenue of upward social mobility for the increasingly educated mestizos. As each new president came to power every six years, the bureaucracy was almost completely replaced, giving the new leadership the opportunity to reward supporters and spread around state appointments among the middle class.

When, at times, these more benign forms of political containment proved ineffective, the state did not hesitate to violently remove uncooperative labor leaders and impose cooperative ones nor did it hesitate to violently repress strike or protest activity. However, until at least the mid-1960s, there were reasons for most people to support the PRI. The party continued to thrive on its legacy as the party of the Mexican Revolution. Land redistribution, although slowed, was continuing. Most people had hope of a better future, as long as the economy continued to grow as it had. Industrialization was supported by a successful agricultural commercial export sector, which, until the late 1960s, had also made the country self-sufficient in agricultural produce. Elections played an important role in affording legitimacy and stability to the regime.

However, the authoritarian containment of popular demands, combined with privileged access to the highest reaches of political power on the part of propertied interests meant that redistributive measures were stunted and benefits heavily skewed in the direction of the wealthy and powerful.[6] Close personal ties bound Mexican presidents before 1960 to the big farmers of the north. Later, both personal relationships and official representation on various government bodies such as on the boards of the Bank of Mexico and National Financiera (NAFINSA), the state development bank, gave big financial/industrial interests direct access to power. Over time, ownership in the Mexican economy became increasingly concentrated in the hands of a few financial/industrial conglomerates (or groups), each comprised of a major bank, industrial enterprises, and holding companies; the conglomerates came to dominate the economy. The Monterrey business sector was particularly powerful. By the mid-1960s, 37 businessmen controlling some 70 economic groups formed the Mexican Council of Businessmen (CMHN). The powerful business groups owned by these men also dominated most other entrepreneurial organizations.

Investment in agriculture had largely benefited the big northern agriculturalists, while poor Indian and mestizo peasant producers in south and central Mexico, dependent upon rain-fed lands, received a declining share of credit and none of the technological support (Hewitt de Alcántara 1976, 63, 66). In the face of declining government support, small and *ejidal* farmers went heavily into debt trying to maintain their farms, and eventually they went bankrupt. *Ejiditarios* were forced to rent their land and as a result, both *ejiditarios* and small landowners left farming. Land ownership became, once again, highly concentrated. Meanwhile, the big, highly mechanized farms had less and less need for paid labor, so peasants migrated to towns and cities. However, the capital-intensive (non labor-absorbing) nature of industry, a feature encouraged by a variety of public policy measures,[7] meant that industry in urban areas did not provide expanded employment opportunities, and hence the urban informal sector, which disguised unemployment, increased.

The result was that social inequality rose between 1940 and the late 1960s (de Navarrete 1967, 146). Inequality between regions increased, with greater prosperity and less poverty in the northern and central regions where industrialization occurred, while the southern rural areas, with the largest concentration of indigenous population engaged in traditional agriculture, fared the worst. Here, extreme poverty prevailed. The increase in income inequality was particularly notable in agriculture.

By the mid-1960s, the economy began to stagnate and, by the late 1960s, it was in crisis. As agricultural production (neglected by the government after 1960) slowed, the balance of deficit payments shot up. Unemployment and underemployment, a consequence of the expulsion of labor from agriculture and the failure of industry to provide jobs, stood between 50 per cent and 60 per cent for the economically active part of the population (Tello 1979, 76). Labor unrest was on the rise and guerrilla activity emerged in rural areas. Political unrest climaxed in 1968 with the massacre of an estimated 200 striking students by government troops at Tlatelolco. The legitimacy of its rule sorely damaged, the PRI scrambled to recoup both its image and its political support. In doing so, it would begin to open the electoral system to increased competition.

THE POLITICAL TRANSITION BEGINS

The most significant feature of Mexico's political transition was the focus on electoral reform. This focus stemmed, in part, from the fact that the PRI wished to bolster its legitimacy and maintain control through cultivating an image of political openness. It was also a consequence of the understandable focus on the part of the opposition on ending the single-party rule that had been so entrenched for so long. In the face of rising political opposition, President Luís Echeverría (1976–82) passed new legislation making it easier for small parties to gain seats in the chamber of deputies, and relaxed censorship. Unlike future administrations, he also took assertive measures to deal with pressing social justice issues, moving the regime concertedly to the political left. His government increased social spending, especially in health, education, and housing, and expanded the social security system to provide health services to nearly 2 million small farmers (Frenk, González-Block, and Lozano 2000, 359). Echeverría also put more resources into small and *ejidal* agriculture by expanding credit. Faced with a situation in which peasants were increasingly invading and taking over land, the administration redistributed land to *ejiditarios* in the states of Sonora, Durango, and Sinaloa. Unfortunately, Echeverría's strategy ran headlong into an unfavorable international climate, involving a drop in demand for Mexican exports from the US market and the 1973 oil crisis. This latter event increased the country's already pressing need for foreign exchange. Faced with stiff private sector opposition to increased taxes, the government resorted to foreign borrowing to fund its ambitious programs.

As with the redistributive policies of the Cárdenas years, business was extremely unhappy with the direction of government policies. It did not like the dramatic upsurge in state spending, price controls, wage increases, and attempts by the administration to control direct foreign investment. Land redistribution, however, triggered the most hostile reaction. By now, the big conglomerates controlled a new peak organization known as the Coordinating Business Council (CGE), which brought together all of the country's business representative organizations. This organization supported the country's big commercial farmers in opposition to the government land redistribution measures. The extent of business alienation was reflected by the fact that, by 1976, capital flight had assumed disastrous proportions. Fearful of the rising political unrest, the administration resorted to supporting corrupt union leadership once again to contain labor unrest.

The development of vast petroleum reserves (discovered in the southern states of Chiapas and Tabasco in 1972) seemed to provide an opportunity for Echeverría's successor, President José López Portillo (1976–82), to kick-start the economy and restore the government's economic leadership role. By the mid-1970s, as petroleum prices increased on the international market, the administration promoted the exportation of crude petroleum, and by the late 1970s, petroleum accounted for 75 per cent of total exports. The new president also needed to shore up the legitimacy of PRI rule and to do this he turned to the electoral system. Electoral reform in 1977 eased party registration requirements, and gave legal status to several long-standing left-wing parties. The new law also awarded parties government subsidies and guaranteed at least one quarter of the chamber of deputies seats for opposition parties. This reform was effective in revitalizing opposition party activity, and, for a time, the new petroleum export strategy seemed to have put the country back on the track of economic growth.

The bonanza of foreign exchange earnings provided by the petroleum export strategy did not last, however. Indeed, far from bolstering PRI rule, the petroleum export strategy would be an important factor in its ultimate demise. Petroleum-led economic growth was not a good job producer and it stimulated inflation, eroding the purchasing power of the population. But worst of all, it stimulated a binge of foreign borrowing that pushed the country's external debt up to unsustainable levels. Mexico's petroleum wealth made it a magnet for international lenders, who saw the country as an excellent investment opportunity. Meanwhile, political leaders, convinced that the petroleum bonanza would continue indefinitely, used foreign loans to develop petroleum exports and lubricate its extensive patronage apparatus. By 1981, Mexico's foreign debt stood at $84 billion, second only to Brazil's.

Petroleum prices declined in 1981. Business confidence plummeted, and capital flight accelerated through late 1981 and 1982. In an unsuccessful bid to stem capital flight, the president announced the nationalization of the banks on September 1, 1982—a move that solidified private sector opposition to the regime. Mexico declared that it was unable to make payments on its foreign debt, and the country fell into its worst economic crisis since the Great Depression. The economic crisis would trigger the next stage in the unraveling of much of the country's authoritarian structure. It would also set the stage for a substantial weakening of the state, once electoral democracy was achieved in 2000.

THE UNRAVELING OF TRADITIONAL AUTHORITARIANISM, 1982–1999

The impact of the debt crisis in the early 1980s and the structural adjustment policies that followed had devastating social consequences. These consequences not only triggered the unraveling of the traditional corporatist clientelist mechanisms of political control but also propelled reforms enhancing the opportunities of opposition forces, opening the way to electoral democracy. The 1995 financial crisis hammered the final nail in the coffin of PRI rule, as political unrest mounted and support for the PRI plummeted. While new civil society actors were beginning to emerge by the mid-1980s, the country's already dominant conglomerates became more powerful than ever. Although the way was now open for democratic reform, the legacies of Mexico's authoritarian past and its exclusionary development model would prove enormously resilient.

The 1982 economic crisis, followed by another economic downturn in 1985–86, coincided with the rise to policy predominance of a group of young technocrats without party experience. With graduate degrees (mostly in economics) from US universities, they pushed through a trade liberalization program under President Miguel de la Madrid Hurtado (1983–89). By 1989, with one of their own in the president's office (Carlos Salinas de Gortari, 1989–95), privatization of the country's mammoth public enterprise sector went forward rapidly. Both governments made drastic reductions in state expenditures. The biggest beneficiaries of the new economic thrust were the country's big conglomerates—executives of these economic groups became close allies of the technocrats. The losers were organized labor, along with the urban and rural poor. President Carlos Salinas locked in his pro-market reforms by negotiating the North American Free Trade Agreement (NAFTA), an agreement signed in 1993 with the United States and Canada. This agreement opened Mexico up to increased trade and investment from the United States and Canada.

Both President de la Madrid and President Salinas faced the challenge of winning back an intensely hostile private sector, angered at the bank nationalization. Now, the state was permeated by private sector interests like never before, as it sought to win business favors by offering favorable treatment. De la Madrid's export promotion program granted the big conglomerates preferential treatment in the allocation of credit and tax relief. Under President Salinas, privatization involved inside deals that privileged entrepreneurs close to the president. When faced with the 1995 financial collapse, the government of President Ernesto Zedillo (1995–2000) bailed out the big conglomerates with close ties to the PRI leadership (López Obrador 1999, 60). A number of conglomerate executives became presidential advisors and their representative organization, the Mexican Council of Businessmen (CMHN), maintained direct and immediate access to the president and cabinet ministers.

With economic power and political influence in the hands of a few conglomerates, and a high level of inequality, a particularly high concentration of income in the top 10 per cent of the population was not surprising (Dussell Peters 2000, 152). Poverty remained widespread, particularly in rural areas. Regional inequality also worsened (Díaz-Cayeros 2004, 201). The highest levels of poverty were in the rural areas of the southern states of Chiapas, Guerrero, and Oaxaca, while trade and investment liberalization and the signing of NAFTA benefited northern Mexico. Social spending, already very low by international standards at 6.1 per cent of GDP in 1990, contracted sharply following the 1995 financial crisis (Corbacho and Schwartz 2002, 18). Those who lost formal sector jobs also lost their social security protection and joined the ranks of the swelling informal sector. The removal of subsidies on basics such as corn and tortillas, following the 1995 financial crisis, also caused hardship in urban areas. Generous wage and benefit settlements for public sector workers became a thing of the past.

The collaboration of official labor leaders in agreements that failed to increase wages, reduced benefits, and sanctioned large-scale layoffs caused workers to stop supporting official labor unions. Agricultural policies also resulted in small and *ejidal* farmers, by far the most neglected social sector, concluding that the state had abandoned them. The government removed guaranteed prices from all products except corn and beans, and abolished import licenses for all agricultural products except corn, beans, wheat, and powdered milk. The decline in state subsidies, credit, and support institutions hit the *ejidos* particularly hard under President Salinas, leaving many indigenous communities worse off than before (Lustig 1998, 206, 209). Peasants repudiated local CNC leaders or left the organization with their followers, sometimes establishing new organizations. Indeed, the termination of commercial networks and technical assistance provided by the state coffee institution, INMECAFE, were important factors in triggering the 1994 Zapatista insurrection in the state of Chiapas (Harvey 1998, 177–83). The most instrumental act which eroded the support of peasants for the PRI, however, may have been the constitutional reform that ended the *ejido* by making it possible for *ejiditarios* to obtain personal title to land with the legal right to buy, sell, or rent it. With this reform, the state lost its status as the supporter of the long-standing peasant aspiration for land distribution to *ejido* communities.

An important initial feature of the Mexican political transition was a rise in civil society activism. As the old official popular organizations declined, new social movements emerged, initially in response to the debt crisis. They gathered momentum, especially after the government's failure to respond adequately to the 1985 earthquake. Many of the civil society organizations were concerned primarily with democratization. But with repeated economic crises, more and more of them united in a call for more democracy, with an increasingly sharp critique of neoliberalism. Rejecting clientelism and subordination to the state, the new social movements focused their attention on elections, often acting in concert with political parties.

From the early 1980s, elections were the barometer of increasing popular alienation from the PRI. In 1982, nine registered parties participated in the national election, and the PRI candidate that year, Miguel de la Madrid, received the lowest proportion of the vote hitherto received by a PRI presidential candidate—71 per cent. In this election, the right-wing opposition party, the PAN (Popular Action), was the PRI's major challenger. With the government's abandonment of electoral fraud in the 1983 local elections, the PAN won 17 municipal victories in 5 states, including 2 state capitals. Hence, early democratization efforts were focused on the state and local level elections (Rodríguez and Ward 1995). The PAN drew its support from the Mexican middle class, especially in northern Mexico. The economic difficulties of 1972 and of 1982, overwhelming evidence of electoral fraud in 1988, and the peso crisis in 1994–95 were all factors driving middle-class support for the PAN (Gilbert 2007). Small and medium business people in northern Mexico, angered at the privileges granted to big business, were especially active in the PAN.

A return to the use of electoral fraud in 1985, renewed economic difficulties, and mismanagement of the aftermath of the earthquake all combined to prompt public clamor for clean elections that the government could not ignore. A new electoral reform law in 1986 expanded the opportunities for the opposition by enlarging the chamber of deputies from 400 to 500 seats, and doubled the number of congressional seats filled by proportional representation to 200.[8] Opposition was also gathering momentum within the PRI, over both the government's neoliberal economic program and the authoritarian method of presidential candidate selection. In the summer of 1986, the Movement for Democratic Renewal, led by former PRI activists, emerged. Expelled from the PRI in 1987, this group joined with a number of civil society organizations to form the left-leaning National Democratic Front (FDN). With Cuauhtémoc Cárdenas, former governor of Michoacán and son of the country's most popular president, Lázaro Cárdenas, as its candidate, the FDN challenged the PRI in the 1988 presidential election.

The July 1988 federal election was a turning point in the process of democratization. While Carlos Salinas was declared the winner, the belief was widespread that he had gained victory because of electoral fraud and that the real winner had been Cárdenas and the FDN. Although the strong public showing for the anti-neoliberal FDN would soon wane, sympathies for the political left would later reemerge. The incoming PRI government was now compelled to take measures to diffuse political tensions. President Salinas, therefore, began to concede electoral victories to the opposition at the state level. In 1990, a new electoral law established the Federal Electoral Institute (IFE) to supervize elections and investigate complaints of irregularities. In 1994, citizen representatives were placed on the IFE board and international electoral observers were permitted, thereby making it more difficult for the PRI to impose its will.

The PRI was briefly able to recoup its electoral support, first with a solid showing in the 1991 midterm elections and, later, with the 1994 presidential election, which brought the PRI presidential candidate Ernesto Zedillo to power. However, the PRI was weakened by a series of events in 1994 and 1995. First, two political assassinations in late 1994 (one of whom was the PRI presidential candidate whom Zedillo replaced) reflected a deep fissure within the leadership. The inability of the regime to resolve the 1994 Chiapas insurrection added to the public perception of regime weakness. In 1996, a congressional commission and the Zapatistas signed an agreement that would have, among other things, given indigenous people control over their land and natural resources and guaranteed the use of indigenous practices in the administration of justice. President Zedillo, however, rejected the agreement on the grounds that it would give indigenous people special privileges that would violate national sovereignty. Post-electoral transition regimes would continue to struggle with this issue. The 1994–95 financial crisis, however, had the most devastating consequences. It caused a rapid rise in poverty levels, resulting in the political alienation of a wide swath of PRI voters (ECLAC 2007, 300).

As opposition criticism mounted, the Zedillo administration took a variety of conciliatory measures to move the system toward electoral democracy. Most of these measures contributed in important ways to the weakening of presidential power. In 1995, President Zedillo strengthened the federal judiciary by giving it the power to veto legislation through judicial review. In addition, his 1996 electoral reform eliminated government control of elections, including the counting of ballots, and stipulated that no party could exercise an absolute majority in the chamber without an absolute majority in votes. This electoral reform contributed to the PRI's loss of the legislature in the 1997 congressional elections. With that turn of events, an activist congress came to block many of the president's initiatives, including his budget, and forced the government to back down on its plans to privatize energy. In that same year, the PRI lost control of the mayoralty of Mexico City to a candidate of the political left, Andrés Manuel López Obrador. Meanwhile, discontent within the PRI prompted by its electoral losses generated the desire to strengthen the party by making it more democratic. In 1999, the PRI carried out primaries for its presidential candidate for the 2000 presidential election. The Zedillo administration also ceased using the strong-arm tactics of the previous administration toward labor and opened up the policy process to some of the more powerful civil society organizations, such as environmental groups (Díez 2006).

THE MEXICAN STATE AND DEMOCRACY IN THE TWENTY-FIRST CENTURY

Mexico has avoided the regional Pink Tide—but only barely. In an election widely recognized as free and fair in 2000, the PRI presidential candidate was defeated and power was transferred peacefully to an electoral alliance headed by Vicente Fox. However, many voters in this election practiced "strategic voting," in which voters who otherwise identify with the left voted for Fox, not because they necessarily adhered to his policy positions, but because they believed that voting for Fox was the most effective way to remove the PRI from power. Political party competition was much fiercer in the 2006 national election. In fact, the PAN presidential candidate, Felipe Calderón, defeated the left coalition candidate, former mayor of Mexico City López Obrador, by such a narrow margin that his victory was heavily contested by the opposition left Party of the Democratic Revolution (PRD). Calderón called for further market liberalization, privatization, and a campaign against the drug trade, while the left PRD took a strong anti-neoliberal stance.

The progress toward democracy in the formal institutional sense described above (clean elections, electoral success of opposition parties at national, state, and local levels) is important. However, this progress must be weighed against the failure of elected regimes to mitigate authoritarian legacies (both political and social), and their inability to stem the erosion of state power arising from political insurgency in the south and widespread drug trade-related corruption and violence. On balance, both state power and democratic quality have been declining in Mexico since 2000. This has occurred *despite* the fact that Mexico's last two presidents have taken measures to confront the southern insurgency, the drug trade, and a variety of institutional democratic deficits.

Fox, for example, enacted a new transparency law. President Calderón passed an electoral reform aimed at making electoral competition fairer by restricting the length of presidential campaigns and enabling the IFE to regulate primaries and other major electoral events. Of greatest significance is Calderón's April 2008 judicial reform that ended the practice of judges deciding guilt or innocence behind closed doors based upon written evidence. Now prosecutors and defense lawyers are required to argue their cases in open court. Observers hope that this reform will do much to strengthen the rule of law in a country where laws have often been applied discretionally. However, as explained further below, the corrupting impact of the drug trade is likely to override the positive impact that this reform might have.

As noted in chapter 1, both poverty and inequality[9] contribute to increased criminal activity (in this case, related to the drug trade) and civil strife. Neither of the governments elected since 2000 have had much success in tackling poverty and inequality. This policy failure may also contribute to the erosion of the legitimacy of the country's democratic institutions since a significant portion of Mexicans define democracy in terms of real policy outcomes that improve people's daily lives (Klesner 2001). Furthermore, without much success in reducing poverty and inequality, it is difficult to root out clientelism—an authoritarian legacy that threatens democracy through its potential for the political manipulation of the vulnerable. In Mexico, clientelism persists, especially between the poor and politicians (Tejera Gaona 2003).

The predisposition of the center-right Fox government to rely largely on the market meant that the state did not take a forceful role in poverty and inequality reduction. This government, like the PRI governments before it, was very much a government of big business. But now, the private sector received direct representation within the state through a variety of high-level governmental appointments. This greater penetration of the state by big business signified a state increasingly less able to distance itself from powerful vested interests. Fox himself was a former Coca-Cola executive, and members of the private sector, including executives of the country's most powerful conglomerates, received an unprecedented number of cabinet appointments (nine) during his time in office. Fox also failed to increase taxation on corporations. Instead, he pursued a regressive tax reform proposal (blocked by congress) which called for an increase in the value-added tax on all items, including food and medicine, a measure that would have worsened the situation of the poor. His poverty program, Oportunidades, was a continuation and expansion of the targeted conditional cash transfer program (Progresa) introduced by his PRI predecessor. While the program no doubt improves the lives of the extremely poor, critics have pointed to its neglect of the moderately poor and its disregard of the importance of employment-generating measures. On the other hand, President Calderón, with a greater predisposition to negotiate with congress, was more successful at getting through his tax reform, which, among other things, imposes a minimum income tax rate on companies of 16.5 per cent, rising to 17.5 per cent after three years (Economist 2007). However, this measure reflects the greater strength of congress more than independent initiative on the part of the executive to make its private sector allies pay up. Given the looming public deficit (always a private sector concern) Calderón was compelled to secure some sort of tax reform and the demonstrated intransigence of congress on the tax issue meant that, if there was to be a reform, it would have to involve an increase in corporate taxes. Moreover, even after this reform, the country's tax intake remains very low by international standards and there is considerable skepticism about whether the government will actually collect this recently legislated increase (Latin Business Chronicle 2007). Finally, the new funds generated by the reform are slated for infrastructure development, with the objective of encouraging private investment—a market-reliant strategy unlikely to have an appreciable impact on poverty and inequality.

The failure of governments to address severe poverty and the political exclusion of southern Mexico are important ingredients in the rural indigenous insurgency. Although the Zapatistas are the most well-known guerrilla organization operating in southern Mexico, by 1999 at least 14 rebel groups had been identified in the region, a compelling indication of the failure of national integration. Mexico's southern states remain highly militarized. On three occasions in 2007, the Popular Revolutionary Army (EPR), a Marxist guerrilla group many believed was in decline, resurfaced to bomb gas pipelines, shutting down hundreds of factories in 10 states (Tobar 2007). Following President Zedillo's rejection of the agreement negotiated with the Zapatistas, another proposal was drawn up under President Fox, which became law in 2001. This law fell far short of meeting indigenous aspirations, however. It allowed local indigenous communities relatively little autonomy, and failed to give them control over natural resources. The likelihood of a PAN government achieving an agreement is remote, since the most vociferous opposition to the originally negotiated agreement came from the private sector and from the PAN itself (Hérnandez Navarro and Carlsen 2004, 453). But it would likely be difficult for the Zapatistas to make an agreement with any Mexican government. Conflicts between indigenous practices and Mexican law are not uncommon. One of the key challenges is to harmonize local indigenous regimes of justice ("usages and customs") with liberal democratic practices, since the former does not follow democratic norms such as the secret ballot, universal suffrage, and political party affiliation.

The improvement of democratic quality will require not only the continued strengthening of civil society but also a greater openness to civil society participation. Also, strengthening of the state requires closer links with civil society and greater distancing from powerful vested interests because such a development would do much to bolster democratic legitimacy. However, governments with strong beliefs in the efficacy of the marketplace such as those of Vicente Fox and Felipe Calderón, are reluctant to open up to civil society participation, particularly when much of Mexican civil society remains highly critical of the market model. True, the Fox administration rose to power on a crest of widespread civil society support, and even appointed some key former civil society leaders to important positions within the new administration. Indeed, the Fox transition team involved thousands of civil society organizations in a broad, consultative process on public policy issues ranging from the economy, to social policy, to culture. However, the Fox administration quickly lost its enthusiasm for citizen involvement in policy. President Fox reduced the role of environmental groups and excluded civil society consultation on one of his key social programs, Oportunidades (Teichman 2009). Like other Latin American cases, the arrival of electoral democracy has resulted in the weakening of many civil society organizations, particularly those that participated in the electoral struggles. Once electoral democracy was achieved, many civil society leaders abandoned their organizations and took up positions in the parties or in government. For example, El Barzón, a debtors' relief movement, was galvanized by the financial collapse of 1995 and became a nationwide movement, but it dissolved into factionalism and its leaders left to join political parties (Olvera 2004, 425).

Adherence to the neoliberal economic model, which requires a flexible labor regime provides considerable incentive for the government to maintain some form of political control over labor to discourage truly independent trade unionism. Carlos Abascal, labor minister (2000–05) and former head of one of the country's business organizations, COPARMEX (Business Confederation of the Mexican Republic), was a strong supporter of labor flexibilization.[10] On the one hand, trade union autonomy from the state had been increasing since the late 1980s, placing labor in a better position to criticize government policy. When Fox came to power, he invited the new umbrella labor organization, the National Union of Workers (UNT) to talks on reforming the country's labor code. The UNT unites unions wanting an alternative to the traditional, official trade union organization. However, the UNT's proposals to dismantle the old (1931) labor legislation requiring that unions obtain legal recognition from the state and that union membership be a condition of employment were rejected by the government. Indeed, most of the restrictions on the trade unions imposed by the labor code remain intact: only officially recognized unions have the right to strike, and strikes must be approved by the government. The Fox/Abascal proposal for labor reform increased the requirements for holding a legal strike, called for a variety of measures discouraging to the establishment of new independent unions, and only partially addressed the serious discriminatory offenses against women workers (Human Rights Watch 2005). These developments echo the labor control mechanisms of the authoritarian PRI era.

Of all of the factors identified in this section, the most important contributor to both a weakened state and low-quality democracy is the enormous expansion of the drug trade. Although Mexico has been involved in the drug trade for some time, Mexican drug cartels have become more powerful since the demise of the Colombian Cali and Medellín cartels in the 1990s. There are currently seven cartels operating in Mexico, and their influence extends into most states of the republic (Cook 2007, 5). This expansion in activity has resulted in extensive human rights abuses perpetrated by various agencies of the state, as the Mexican government has carried out ongoing campaigns against drug traffickers. Unlawful killings by security forces, arbitrary arrests, the use of torture by police, and corruption and arbitrariness in legal/judicial proceedings are among the long list of transgressions that have been identified by the US Department of State's Bureau of Democracy, Human Rights and Labor (2007). Meanwhile, the drug cartels themselves carry out extensive violence, virtually taking control of entire towns, which are then left without formal law enforcement.

There is no question that the crackdown on the Colombian drug cartels was instrumental in shifting the locus of the drug trade from that country to Mexico, already favored for its proximity to the North American market. However, Mexico's political conditions have also been highly conducive to the expansion of the trade. In particular, high levels of political corruption (a legacy of the country's authoritarian mechanisms of political control) which existed long before the entrance of drug traffickers made police and government officials open to the corrupting tactics of these groups bent on pursing their illegal activities. In addition, a number of experts have pointed to NAFTA as an important factor fostering the growth of the drug trade. Many legitimate Mexican farmers forced out of business as a consequence of the inflow of North American agricultural products have apparently turned to drug cultivation. In addition, NAFTA has made smuggling drugs into the US easier (Miller 2008).

The most important factor in the rising drug trade-related violence is, paradoxically, the very efforts of recent governments to curb it. Drug production and trafficking has a long history in Mexico, going back to the 1930s. Long before the crackdown in Colombia, corruption already permeated the state apparatus, right down to the federal police who were supposed to be fighting the drug cartels. It is only since the achievement of electoral democracy, however, that the trade has engendered such high levels of violence. Indeed, as long as the PRI was in power the most reprehensible consequences of the drug trade were contained because high-level control of the drug trade was part of the panoply of hierarchical control mechanisms.

Power concentrated in the hands of the president made government protection of the trade possible, in exchange for a piece of the action. Hence, the biggest drug traffickers invariably had close ties to high-ranking PRI politicians who, if they were not directly involved in the drug trade, operated to protect it and benefited financially from it. Unfortunately, the advent of electoral democracy, has, in a number of respects, made the situation worse. For one thing, it has unraveled the past centralized control that kept drug violence in check. And, as President Fox and President Calderón have sought to reduce drug trafficking and its attendant corruption by increasing the numbers of soldiers and police involved in the anti-drug trade activities, violence and corruption have increased. Because profits are so high (due to the illegal nature of the drugs), drug cartels can afford to respond to government-sponsored police and military action against their operations with ever-increasing levels of violence (private armies) and bigger payments to police and government officials. Battles in northern Mexico between drug traffickers and police are becoming the norm. Journalists who write about the drug trade are now at serious risk. According to the Inter-American Commission on Human Rights (2007, 16–17), in 2006 Mexico outranked Colombia in the number of assassinated journalists. In addition to the execution of police and state prosecutors, judges are now targets (Schwartz 2008).

Increased zeal in pursing drug traffickers has resulted in human rights violations of innocent citizens, while Mexico's poverty and lack of economic opportunity mean the cartels will readily find people to join their ranks. Police officers receiving low pay are particularly vulnerable when given the choice between accepting a bribe and providing protection to drug traffickers versus rejecting the bribe and endangering not only their lives but those of their families. Law enforcement, problematic at the state and municipal levels at the time of political transition, has become even more so. In short, reforms to the country's legal system will accomplish little if corrupt officials and police ignore the rule of law.

CONCLUSION

From its earliest history, Mexico faced daunting challenges in attempting to achieve national integration. The republic was born with high levels of both regional and socioeconomic inequality, reinforced by racial divisions between indigenous, mestizos, and the descendants of the *criollo* elite. Mexico's post-revolutionary leadership eventually solved the severe challenges to political stability by constructing a highly effective form of authoritarianism that depended upon clientelistic and corporatist forms of political incorporation. These forms of political containment played an important role in providing nearly 70 years of political stability, but they also contributed to high levels of inequality and widespread poverty.

The importance of elections as a form of legitimization created opportunities for opposition parties, once the efficacy of authoritarian mechanisms of political containment began to wear thin. The Mexican transition process was a protracted one, occurring over more than 30 years and propelled forward by repeated economic crises. Unlike other Latin American cases, it was constrained not by an elite pact, but by the enormously resilient mechanisms of the "perfect dictatorship" that had kept the popular sector and prospective counter-elites politically quiescent. By the turn of the century, electoral democracy had been achieved.

As with other countries in the region, however, difficult challenges to democratic quality remain. In addition, the Mexican state has weakened in the face of rural insurgency and drug cartels, unable to provide basic physical security for its citizens in many parts of the country. The advent of electoral democracy combined with an activist congress is one of the few bright spots in the Mexican political scenario. The legislature remains an important bastion of pressure for more redistributive measures. However, the executives of the country's powerful conglomerates are close presidential allies, and many now have positions within the state at the highest reaches of political power. They have enormous influence over policy and bolster the market predisposition of the administration.

Nor have the recently elected governments achieved much in the areas of poverty and inequality reduction, factors that contribute to criminal activity and violence, and threaten civil society autonomy and democratic legitimacy. The current government's commitment to the market model encourages it to adhere to an authoritarian, technocratic form of decision-making, unfriendly to civil society consultation and closed to those critical of neoliberalism. That commitment to the market also discourages active measures that might reduce poverty more effectively and would likely make inroads into inequality reduction. Regional inequality, with its important ethnic dimension, has long roots in Mexican history and continues unabated.

As this analysis has shown, a complex confluence of historical, political, social, and economic factors have contributed to the present challenges Mexico faces. After a long struggle, Mexico finally achieved electoral democracy, only to have this achievement placed in jeopardy. The country continues to confront its historical legacies of political exclusion, corruption, authoritarianism, widespread poverty, and high levels of inequality. All of these factors are heavily intertwined, and all have contributed to the weakening of the Mexican state.

NOTES

1 Poverty figures are passionately debated in Mexico. ECLAC puts Mexican poverty at 35.5 per cent in 2005, down from 46.9 per cent in 1998 (2007, 300). However, not only do some domestic observers list higher figures, but there is considerable dispute about the sources of poverty reduction where it has occurred. Critics claim that domestic policy has done nothing to reduce poverty, and that any decrease in poverty is a consequence of remittances sent home by Mexicans working outside of the country.

2 In 1990, during a debate with Mexican writer Octavio Paz, the Peruvian writer Mario Vargas Llosa described Mexico's political system as a "perfect dictatorship."

3 Both Obregón and Calles were lower middle-class mestizos who became large landowners in the north.

4 Pressure for nationalization from miners and electricity workers was also very strong, but Cárdenas resisted it.

5 The military also received sectoral representation within the PRI. It was eliminated in 1948.

6 Between 1940 and 1960, the state favored both big landed commercial and industrial interests, while after 1960 its support for commercial export agricultural interests diminished and it gave industry its undivided attention.

7 Such policies included tariff reductions on capital goods, and rebates and tax holidays on imported capital goods.

8 The proportional seats gave the opposition parties the opportunity to be represented in congress. However, the reform was a step backward, insofar as it stipulated that enough PR seats be given to the party with an overall plurality in the election (the PRI) to ensure that party a majority in the chamber of deputies.

9 Mexico's Gini coefficient stood at 0.53 in 2005 (ECLAC 2007, 299).

10 Labor flexibilization refers to changes in the labor laws that reduce the cost of labor by making it easier, among other things, to hire and fire.

REFERENCES

Bureau of Democracy, Human Rights and Labor, US Department of State. 2008. "Mexico. Country Reports on Human Rights Practices, 2007." March 11. July 7, 2008. www.state.gov/g/drl/rls/hrrpt/2007/100646.htm.

Cook, Colleen W. 2007. *CRS Report for Congress: Mexico's Drug Cartels.* Washington, DC: Congressional Research Service.

Corbacho, Ana, and Gerd Schwartz. 2002. "Mexico: Experiences with Pro-Poor Expenditure Policies." IMF Working Paper. Fiscal Affairs Department. Washington, DC: IMF.

De Navarette, Ifigenia M. 1967. "Income Distribution in Mexico." *Mexico's Recent Economic Growth.* Ed. Tom E. Davis. Austin: University of Texas Press. 133–99.

Díaz-Cayeros, Alberto. 2004. "Decentralization, Democratization and Federalism in Mexico." *Dilemmas of Political Change in Mexico.* Ed. Kevin J. Middlebrook. London: Institute of Latin American Studies. 197–234.

Díez, Jordi. 2006. *Political Change and Environmental Policymaking in Mexico.* New York: Routledge.

Dussell Peters, Enrique. 2000. *Polarizing Mexico. The Impact of Liberalization Strategy.* Boulder: Lynne Rienner Publishers.

ECLAC. 2007. *Social Panorama of Latin America*. Santiago: ECLAC, United Nations.

Economist, The. 2007. "Mexico. Reforms at Last. The President Shows Himself to be a Successful Dealmaker." July 7, 2008. www.hacer.org/current/Mex197.php.

Frenk, Julio, Miguel Angel González-Block, and Rafael Lozano. 2000. "Seis tesis equivocadas sobre las políticas de salud en el combate a la pobreza." *Familia, Género y Pobreza*. Ed. María de la Paz López and Vania Salles. Mexico City: Miguel Angel Porrúa. 339–65.

Gilbert, Denis. 2007. *Mexico's Middle Class in the Neoliberal Era*. Tucson: University of Arizona Press.

Guarneros-Meza, Valeria. 2007. "Urban Governance and Participation in Central Mexico." *Development* 50(1): 104–09.

Haber, Stephen H. 1989. *Industry and Underdevelopment: The Industrialization of Mexico, 1890–1940*. Stanford: Stanford University Press.

Harvey, Neil. 1998. *The Chiapas Rebellion: The Struggle for Land and Democracy*. Durham, NC: Duke University Press.

Hérnandez Navarro, Luis, and Laura Carlsen. 2004. "Indigenous Rights: The Battle for Constitutional Reform in Mexico." *Dilemmas of Political Change in Mexico*. Ed. Kevin J. Middlebrook. London: Institute for Latin American Studies. 440–65.

Hewitt de Alcántara, Cynthia. 1976. *Modernizing Mexican Agriculture: Socioeconomic Implications of Technological Change, 1940–1976*. Geneva: UN Institute for Social Development.

Human Rights Watch. 2005. "Mexico: Fox's Labor Reform Proposal would Deal Serious Blow to Workers' Rights. Letter to Mexico's Chamber of Deputies." July 15, 2008. hrw.org/english/docs/2005/02/09/mexico10156 txt.htm.

Inter-American Commission on Human Rights. 2007. *Annual Report of the Inter-American Commission on Human Rights, 2006*. Vol. 2. Washington, DC: General Secretariat, Organization of American States.

Klesner, Joseph L. 2001. "Legacies of Authoritarianism: Political Attitudes in Chile and Mexico." *Citizen Views of Democracy in Latin America*. Ed. Roderic Ai Camp. Pittsburgh: University of Pittsburgh Press. 118–38.

Lambert, Jacques. 1967. *Latin America: Social Structures and Political Institutions*. Berkeley: University of California Press.

Latin Business Chronicle. 2007. "Tax Reform: Mexico Marks the Path." January 8, 2009. www.latinbusinesschronicle.com/app/article.aspx?id=1687.

López Obrador, Andrés Manuel. 1999. *Fobaproa: Expediente Abierto, Reseña y archivo*. Mexico City: Editorial Grijalbo S.A.

Lustig, Nora. 1998. *Mexico: The Remaking of an Economy*. 2nd ed. Washington, DC: The Brookings Institution.

Miller, Michael. 2008. "The Age of Innocents." *Newsweek*. October 25. November 3, 2008. www.newsweek.com/2008/10/24/the-age-of-innocents.html.

Olvera, Alberto J. 2004. "Civil Society in Mexico at Century's End." *Dilemmas of Political Change in Mexico*. Ed. Kevin J. Middlebrook. London: Institute for Latin American Studies. 403–39.

Parkes, Henry Bamford. 1960. *A History of Mexico*. London: Eyre and Spotiswoode.

Rodríguez, Victoria E., and Peter M. Ward, eds. 1995. *Opposition Government in Mexico*. Albuquerque: University of New Mexico Press.

Schwartz, Jeremy. 2008. "Judges Latest Targets in Mexico Drug War." *Cox Newspapers*, Washington Bureau. February 2. July 7, 2008. www.coxwashington.com/reporters/content/reporters/stories/2008/02/02/MEXICO_JUDGES02_COX.html.

Tannenbaum, Frank. 1968. *Mexico: The Struggle for Peace and Bread*. New York: Alfred A. Knopf.

Teichman, Judith. 2009. "Competing Visions of Democracy and Development in the Era of Neoliberalism in Mexico and Chile." *International Political Science Review* 30(1): 67–87.

Tejera Gaona, Héctor. 2003. "Obstacles to Mexico City's Democratic Transition: Citizens, Culture and Political Relations." *Development* 46(1): 102–06.

Tello, Carlos. 1979. *La politica económica en México, 1970–1976*. Mexico City: Siglo XXI Editores.

Tobar, Héctor. 2007. "A Small Guerrilla Band is Waging War in Mexico." *Los Angeles Times/World*. September 20. September 8, 2008. http://articles.latimes.com/2007/sep/20/world/fg-guerrilla20.

Tobar, Héctor, and Cecilia Sánchez. 2007. "In Mexico's Drug Trade, No Glitter for Grunts." *Los Angeles Times*. December 2. August 15, 2008. www.latimes.com/news/nationworld/columnone/la-fg-hitmen6dec06,0,1399610.story.

Wilkie, James W. 1967. *The Mexican Revolution. Federal Expenditures and Social Change since 1910*. Berkeley: University of California Press.

E-RESOURCES

Historical Report to the Mexican Society [Informe Histórico a la Sociedad Mexicana]. 2006. Official Report on Mexico's Dirty War, 1960s–1980s (www.gwu.edu/~nsarchiv/NSAEBB/NSAEBB209/index.htm#informe). This is a report from the Office of the Special Prosecutor, appointed by President Vicente Fox, documenting the government's violent repression of its opponents.

Mexican government (English) (www.gob.mx/wb/egobierno/egob_General_Information). Official website of the Mexican government.

United Nations Development Report: Mexico 2002 (Spanish) (78.136.31.142/en/reports/nationalreports/latinamericathecaribbean/mexico/name,3210,en.html). The report documents socioeconomic and regional inequality in Mexico.

MEXICAN PRINTED MEDIA

El financiero (Spanish business newspaper) (www.elfinanciero.com.mx/ElFinanciero/Portal/). The major business newspaper in Mexico City.

La Jornada (Spanish) (www.jornada.unam.mx/2009/06/17/index.php). A newspaper that is often critical of the government.

Proceso (Spanish) (www.proceso.com.mx/). This is a left-wing weekly magazine that publishes articles highly critical of the government.

Reforma (Spanish) (www.reforma.com/). A major newspaper in Mexico City.

Zapatista Documents Collection (www.lib.utexas.edu/benson/zapatistas/index.html). University of Texas website with links to major Zapatista documents.

FIVE

Guatemala: Ethnicity and the Shadow State

KATHERINE ISBESTER

The most famous Guatemalan is undoubtedly Rigoberta Menchú, an ethnic Maya woman and 1992 Nobel Peace Prize recipient. She detailed her family's and her people's struggle against the Guatemalan military dictatorship in her autobiography, *I Rigoberta Menchú* (1984). Although it now appears that Menchú changed some facts to create a better narrative, it is undeniable that the military murdered her father, her mother, two brothers, her sister-in-law, as well as nieces, nephews, and neighbors. Some were killed because of their participation with the guerrilla movement or workers' union, some because they publicly protested the dictatorship, and some because they were born into a family who spoke a pre-Conquest language, wore handwoven woollen clothes, and lived in a non-Western culture. Because of her political activism, in 1981–82 when Menchú was 22 years old, she had to flee Guatemala for Mexico. Whenever she attempted to return to Guatemala, she received so many death threats that she had to flee again. In Mexico, she organized international resistance to the Guatemalan dictatorship. Menchú's efforts were one of the reasons for the international pressure that eventually democratized Guatemala and led to its UN-brokered Peace Accords. Few of the military have faced charges of human rights abuse despite a UN document detailing the extent of the murders. By the late 1990s, Menchú returned to Guatemala to sign and help implement the Peace Accords. Through her foundation, she continues to agitate for justice for the victims of the military's campaign against the Mayan people, as well as initiating a range of educational and cultural programs in her first language. In the 2007 presidential elections, Menchú created a new political party and ran as its candidate. Although half the population of Guatemala was indigenous and no other candidate was, and despite platforms that addressed the endemic poverty of the Mayan people, Menchú received only 3 per cent of the vote. Almost two-thirds of Mayan women had not voted in the previous election and little had changed in the interim. Some think that the reason for the low voter turn-out was that the Mayan people endorse collective rights and local politics, rather than individual rights and national politics. Others think that many Maya remain fearful of military retaliation and prefer to not destabilize their recently achieved peace. Still others think that it is because democracy is so minimal in Guatemala that few saw any reason why they should vote. Indeed, Guatemala has the lowest level of support for democracy in Latin America with a scant 32 per cent of the population in favor of it (Latinobarómetro 2008). Regardless of the reason, half the population of Guatemala is disengaged from the formal political process, calling into question the caliber of democracy in Guatemala, and the state's capacity to overcome the ethnic schism.

Guatemala is one of only two countries in Latin America where the indigenous people speaking a pre-Conquest language make up at least half of the population and most likely are in the majority (estimates range between 50 per cent and 80 per cent and the number chosen speaks to the political views of the writer). Until recently, the Maya, who speak 20-plus different languages, were settled in the Guatemalan Highlands. More recently, they were scattered by war and settled over most parts of Guatemala. They are among the poorest people in the Americas. People of mixed descent (white and indigenous) or indigenous people who live in a Westernized way in the cities or rural towns and who speak Spanish are called *ladinos*.[1] The *ladinos* control the economy and the political structure, although there are substantial numbers of poor *ladinos*. The *ladinos* are heavily influenced by large American-dominated businesses and by American foreign policy. Although the *ladinos* are the minority in Guatemala, they have not acted homogeneously, but instead have been divided about how best to develop Guatemala. This is especially evident in the military. This demographic and socioeconomic reality has divided Guatemala, producing appalling conflict, and hindering the emergence of anything beyond the most minimal of democracies.

THE LIBERAL REVOLUTION, 1871–1944

In the nineteenth century, the *ladinos* were divided between the conservatives and the liberals battling for control over the state. Liberal General Justo

Rufino Barrios (1871–85) modernized agriculture, especially the cultivation of coffee, to make it more productive. He encouraged private ownership and investment, and opened up "empty" lands to immigrants from Europe. This entailed removing traditional communal lands (*ejidos*) from the Maya and deeding them for private ownership, educating and Westernizing the Mayan people, and passing laws that ensured there would always be a cheap supply of agricultural laborers. The Maya became dispossessed and were forced to seek itinerant farm work, their lives became controlled by vagrancy laws, debt peonage, and lack of options. Rufino also built a national army to impose order in the countryside. Although the economy grew, it became dependent on its monocrop of coffee with land ownership concentrated in a few hands. Rufino built a railway, telegraph lines, and roads to get the coffee crop to ports for export. Because of this economic infrastructure, Guatemala was also able to grow bananas for export. In the early twentieth century, the United Fruit Company took control of the banana production and only port and came to own controlling shares in a public utility, the telegraph, and the railway. It later became the largest landowner in Guatemala, although it only utilized 15 per cent of its land. The extent of the company's control over the Guatemalan economy meant that the Guatemalan government had to negotiate with it over public policy (Schlesinger and Kinzer 2005).

As the Great Depression of the 1930s reduced exports to the United States, labor unrest in Guatemala grew. With the support of the United Fruit Company and the Guatemalan oligarchy, the dictator, liberal President Jorge Ubico y Casteñeda (1931–44), ruthlessly contained the discontent. Instead of accommodating dissent to a limited degree through political reforms and sharing of resources, Ubico suppressed the labor movement and political organizations, centralized power in the government, modernized the vagrancy laws to force Indians to work for the state, and confiscated German-owned properties (mostly coffee plantations). "This effectively converted the government into Guatemala's major labor contractor" (Booth and Walker 1993, 42). It also left Guatemala's middle classes frustrated and politicized.

The governments of Guatemala tied its elite to a repressive socioeconomic organization that was enforced by the military. The military became a social class with blood ties through marriage to the elite, rather than being an institution serving the government. The military was considered to be the most reasonable avenue open to ambitious and politically interested young men. This arrangement changed with World War II. Young soldiers were inspired by the speeches of Winston Churchill and Franklin Roosevelt and the fight against fascism in Europe. A student protest in June 1944 spiralled into multiple protests leading to a general strike by the middle classes and the popular sectors, and in July 1944, Ubico resigned from power. In October 1944, a group of young idealist soldiers, intellectuals, and dissidents took control of the government in the name of democracy. In the spring 1945, there was, for the first time in Guatemala's history, a free general election.

TEN YEARS IN SPRING OR THE OCTOBER REVOLUTION, 1944–1954

Dr. Juan José Arévalo Bermejo (1944–51), a university professor, was elected as president on a platform of "spiritual socialism," a quasi-mystical belief in the power of imagination, nationalism, and freedom. He did however have five concrete goals: democratic rights and freedoms, including elections; separation of power within all levels of governments; modernization of organs of mass mobilization such as education, political parties, and labor unions; redistribution of wealth through a minimum wage, collective bargaining, and social services; and economic development through manufacturing and land reform.

Arévalo reworked state–civil society relations. His reforms affected the political structure, shifting power relations from individuals such as the president to democratic institutions and civil society. These reforms broadened the franchise granting the fundamental rights and freedoms necessary for a democracy. He insisted that the state act with the capacity to intervene against entrenched interests. Political parties, peasant cooperatives, and labor unions formed during this period and the middle and popular classes mobilized. The reforms, however, affected the urban areas dominated by the *ladinos* and had little impact on the rural areas. Despite being much discussed, agrarian reform was never tabled, so the primary issue of the control of the economy was never dealt with. Significantly, Arévalo never institutionalized his reforms as a political party or even expressed a clear ideology that could be adapted by another political party. This weakened the ability of others to carry on his work after he left power. The transition to democracy occurred with some support of the elite (especially the military); however, democratization was not consolidated through multiple elections, an elite pact, or a democratic political culture. Guatemala's economy was not large enough to either cement loyalty through including malcontents in the economic system or to pay off dissent. Furthermore, the political administration was too inefficient and ineffectual to inspire support or to outperform alternative organizations of power. Instead, Arévalo survived 20 attempted coup d'etats and steadily lost legitimacy. What support Arévalo did have was split over the pace of the reforms.

In 1951, Colonel Jacobo Arbenz Guzmán (1951–54) was elected as president. Arbenz spoke with fiery rhetoric and sympathized with the communists, although he himself was not one. In fact, he spoke of the need to build a capitalist economy albeit one in which foreign investment abided by the rules of the nation. Arbenz had, however, several communists in his government. These communists were not taking instruction from the Soviet Union, which remained disinterested in them. In 1952, the Agrarian Reform Law was passed. It permitted the confiscation of unused land with compensation set at the value declared as taxable worth, which was almost certainly undervalued. Before the government fell, the government redistributed 1.5 million acres benefiting 100,000 families. The land reform, combined with Arévalo's reforms banning compulsory labor and permitting peasant co-ops and collective bargaining, threatened to undermine the elite's control of the economy.

At the time, the American government under President Dwight Eisenhower (1953–61) was worried that the Soviet Union would attempt to establish a presence in the Americas through the communists in the Arbenz government. Also, several members of Eisenhower's administration, including the Secretary of State and the director of the CIA, had close ties to the United Fruit Company. The United Fruit Company, having misstated the value of its land on tax returns and leaving much land untilled, was financially hit with the Agrarian Reform Program. In 1953, the OAS applied diplomatic pressure to the Arbenz government; the US imposed financial sanctions; and the CIA sponsored disinformation and covert actions to destabilize the government. The workers who had benefited from the reforms threatened to defend them with violence. The Arbenz government, witnessing the build-up for an American-backed invasion, attempted to buy weapons from Canada or Germany but was blocked by the US. Instead, Arbenz bought guns from Czechoslovakia. Although these guns were lightweight arms, they were enough for the Eisenhower government to declare that the Arbenz government posed a military threat and ordered the CIA to depose him. In June 1954, Colonel Carlos Castillo Armas and his private army, funded and supported by the CIA, invaded Guatemala from Honduras. The Guatemalan National Army could have resisted the invasion. But some officers did not support the Agrarian Reform Law for personal or ideological reasons or were worried about the inevitability of American reprisals, and so refused to defend the government. Arbenz resigned. Thousands were killed. Ironically, Arbenz's agrarian reform program was reworked in 1961 as the US Alliance for Progress and was exported back to Latin America as US foreign policy.

The coup in 1954 marked the end of one era and the beginning of another. Those 10 years in spring were "the only genuine democratic experience in

Guatemala's entire history" (Jonas 2006, 268). The failure of this democratic experience consolidated the role of the military as a protector of the elite's control of the economy. After the 1954 coup, "military rule, allied with commercial interests, became the primary mode of national politics" (Kumar 2005, 260).

INSURGENCY, COUNTERINSURGENCY, AND CIVIL WAR, 1954–1985

Castillo was declared president in September 1954. He ruled until his assassination in 1957. Operating with the support of an alliance of military, business elite, and landowners, the hierarchy of the Catholic Church, and the US, Castillo undid many of the reforms that Arévalo and Arbenz had initiated. He cancelled the 1955 presidential elections, made communism illegal, oppressed political parties, dismantled peasant organizations and unions, stopped literacy programs, rolled back civil liberties, removed the franchise from illiterates (i.e., 50 per cent of the adult population), returned confiscated land to its original owners, and revoked the Agrarian Reform Law and the labor protection laws. He was famously corrupt.

After Castillo's assassination, the military assumed more overt command of the political system and installed General Miguel Ydígoras Fuentes (1958–63) as president. Appalled at the increasing corruption under first Castillo and then Ydigoras, in addition to the president's unilateral decision made without consulting the military to allow the US to train troops in Guatemala for the 1961 Bay of Pigs Invasion of Cuba, young reformist officers attempted a military coup in 1960. The coup was unsuccessful and the reformists who survived fled into rural Guatemala and formed two guerrilla groups, the Rebel Armed Forces (FAR) and the 13 November Revolutionary Movement (MR-13). This marked the beginning of Guatemala's low-intensity civil war. Thus, the war did not begin as an ethnic genocide but rather as an intra-elite battle for power (Azpuru 2006).

From 1960 to 1970, Guatemala's economy prospered as a result of the Central American Common Market (CACM). Between 1961 and 1975, the average economic growth rate was 5.7 per cent per annum. However, manufacturing reached its greatest share of the GDP at 15 per cent in 1978; its rate of growth steadily declined throughout the 1970s as the oil shocks produced a global recession and raised the cost of manufacturing. The industrial workforce only ever reached a peak of 12 per cent of the total workforce and the middle class remained small. The populace had limited literacy (56 per cent) and a life expectancy of 56 years. There was an increasing concentration of landownership in fewer hands with the rural population's access to arable land falling from 1.71 hectares per capita in

1950 to 0.79 in 1980. The Maya were affected through these changes in the economy. By the end of the 1970s, USAID estimated that 90 per cent of those in the Highlands lacked sufficient land for subsistence farming and migrated to find seasonal labor on the farms or in the cities. This brought them into contact with *ladinos* and forced them to learn some Spanish. This contact had the unanticipated effect of raising the consciousness of their own cultural uniqueness, encouraging them to safeguard their own Mayan identity. Nonetheless, social indicators on the Mayan people were substantially worse during this period of economic growth as the indigenous people became increasingly dispossessed from their lands.

The diversification of the economy into new industries and non-traditional goods as well as public sector developments opened the possibility of an emerging entrepreneurial class. However, those able to take advantage of the new opportunities were either the elite or the military. As a result, the military acquired sources of income independent of the government and honed their business skills. As President Colonel Manuel Arana (1970–74) said: "If the military are to combat subversion, they don't have to be the employees of the rich, but their partners" (quoted in Dunkerley 1988, 467). Nonetheless, the coffee industry remained under the control of the same nineteenth-century oligarchy that had established it. Even fewer families controlled the newer agricultural industries of cotton and sugar, established in the 1960s and the 1970s under the CACM. The diversification of agricultural production into non-traditional goods such as flowers and cardamom in the postbellum era continued this pattern (Dunkerley 1988, chapter 5).

Arana's 1970 presidential victory was likely fixed. A ruthless military leader, he imposed a state of emergency to conduct the counterinsurgency campaign. He also targeted union groups, student organizations, and political opponents. Arana ushered in a decade and a half of government leaders who operated the same way. There seemed to be a tacitly agreed upon pact between the military and the elite over how to run the polity. First, capitalism, or to be more accurate, crony capitalism based on clientelism, corruption, and exploitation, was encouraged with few services for the poor. Second, although the military allowed a few political parties to compete for congressional seats, the military approved candidates from a list and controlled the executive. Thus, electoral politics became reduced to a competition among the elite, the military, and some of the middle class operating through ideologically narrow political parties. With blatantly fixed elections, hardly anyone bothered to vote. The real creation of public policy happened outside the legislature where business alliances competed with one another to influence the creation of public policy with the military coordinating and integrating competing agendas. This organization of the decision-making apparatus ensured that protests were directed into illegal channels such as unions, peasant organizations, or guerrilla groups. The third element of the pact was the military's freedom to pursue a counter-insurgency campaign. This campaign, which included right-wing civilian and paramilitary groups, grew increasingly brutal and oppressive as the decade wore on. As civil society protests met violent oppression and assassinations of community leaders and union organizers, more protests, organizing, and guerrilla action were spurred, which in turn spawned a more repressive military response. This violence was endemic and shifted terrain from urban to rural and back to urban giving both sides the impression, if only temporarily, of success. Extremely violent military action began in the Western Highlands, home to the Mayan people. Whole villages were wiped out and civilians of all ages from babies to the elderly were massacred in a brutal manner. By 1978, the human rights abuses had become so overt that the administration of US President Jimmy Carter (1976–80) cut foreign military aid, although it still sent $60 million in economic aid between 1979 and 1981.

By the early 1980s, there were 500,000 Maya peasants mobilized for protest, 250,000 to 500,000 collaborators and supporters, and 6,000 to 8,000 armed fighters. There was full-scale civil war between the business elite and the military versus the combined peasantry and guerrillas. Revolutionary overthrow of the government was entirely feasible. The elite and the military realized this and changed tactics.

In 1982, the peasantry and the guerrilla movement formally united as the Guatemalan National Revolutionary Unity (URNG). However, by 1981, the military had already begun an all-out effort to obliterate the Mayan people with a policy that has been called a genocide, a holocaust, and a scorched-earth tactic. It included not only murder on a mass scale but also the burning of crops and the land so that the people could not survive. The URNG did not anticipate these actions and had little effective response. In 1982, the military forced the population to murder one another through the civilian defense patrols (PACs), which conscripted close to one-quarter of the adult male population. This was the period when Rigoberta Menchú lost most of her family. Those who survived the military campaigns and the death squads were herded into resettlement camps, ostensibly for their own protection but actually to deprive the guerrillas of any support. These new model villages "served as rural concentration camps" (Chasten 2006, 298).

The Guatemalan economy was struggling as the cost of the war mounted, and both the business elite and junior officers were critical of the military's involvement in the economy, especially as it included corrupt business practices. Furthermore, there was increasing international criticism of the Guatemalan government. US President Ronald Reagan (1980–88), who was criticized internationally for undermining the socialist revolutionary government of Nicaragua, needed a better face for the Guatemalan government. This combination of international pressure, disgruntled members of the elite and reformist officers broke the pact that had governed the country for over a decade.

When the 1982 elections were again fraudulent, young officers overthrew the government and installed retired General Efraín Ríos Montt. He had an interest in political reform and a past of frustrated political efforts. Charismatic and devoutly Protestant, he became and remains a controversial figure in Guatemalan politics. He promised to democratize Guatemala. To fight the insurgency, Ríos Montt imposed a state of emergency, cancelling the promised elections. He oversaw the height of the genocidal campaign against the Mayan. According to the UN-sponsored Commission for Historical Clarification (CEH), there were 600 massacres during his 18 months in power, and rural deaths reached an estimated 150,000 between 1982 and 1985. The CEH wrote, "The massacres, scorched earth operations, forced disappearances and executions of Mayan authority figures and spiritual leaders were not only an attempt to destroy the social bases of the guerrillas, but above all, to destroy the cultural values that ensured cohesion and collective action in Mayan communities" (CEH 1999, section 31). The civil war had become an ethnic cleansing where every indigenous person was inherently guilty of collaborating and every Mayan child would inevitably grow up to become an insurgent. Ríos Montt was deposed after 18 months in power by junior officers frustrated by the absence of democracy. In 1984, Reagan reinstated military aid to Guatemala because of its commitment to democracy.

Throughout the 1970s and 1980s, civil society organizations in the form of social movements began to emerge. The lower order of the Roman Catholic Church as well as some bishops spurred the consciousness of the sinfulness of the situation and encouraged people to attempt to change it. The war was driving migration from the countryside into the cities, swelling the shantytowns and creating demands for government-supplied services such as potable water and sewage. Human rights groups and mothers groups protested and mobilized support both nationally and internationally. These groups, combined with the more established unions, prodded the government to democratize. As the economy suffered, the civil war shifted elite support from a military solution to a political one, realigning the balance of power.

DEMOCRATIZATION, 1984–1994

With the guerrilla movement defeated, some version of democracy became a possibility. The military wanted another pact but the business elite would not approve it. The 1985 Constitution established separation of powers and some civil liberties. In addition to fixed terms of office for the president and elected representatives, some seats were elected on the basis of proportional representation (PR). The president, elected by a runoff, appointed the governors of the provinces, some supreme court judges (some were elected), and a human rights ombudsman (PDH). This latter office was the first of its kind in Latin America and opened a space for human rights activists to become more visible and active. However, democratic power "was more apparent than real" (Williams and Seri 2003, 304) as the military and the elite warned that, regardless of who won the 1985 election, there would be little to no reform. Just before the elections, the last dictator passed an amnesty law protecting the military.

The most progressive party to run in the 1985 election, the Christian Democrats under Vinicio Cerezo Arévalo (1985–91), won with more than twice the votes for the presidency, taking the congress as well. Fifty-six per cent of eligible voters did not register, abstained, or cast invalid votes (Jonas 1995, 29). During his presidency, there was little economic growth, although Cerezo did liberalize some aspects of the economy. These reforms hit the poor especially hard. The media was submissive and uncritical, and a month after the election selective assassinations resumed. By 1987, the URNG had regrouped and begun guerrilla actions again, mostly so that they could negotiate peace from a position of strength. During Cerezo's term of office, there were several thousand killed or disappeared with the violence rising toward the end of his mandate. Although Cerezo and the URNG held peace talks in 1987, initiated a national dialogue on the war and its causes in 1989, and signed in 1990 "The Basic Agreement on the Quest for Peace through Political Means" (also known as the Oslo Agreement), peace talks stalled after 1992.

The Mayan activism that had supported the revolutionary movement in the 1970s and early 1980s shifted to autonomous and separate Mayan enclaves after the genocide. There was a range of voices representing the Mayan peoples, from traditional to activist. By the late 1980s, the Pan-Mayan movement emerged, bridging the 200 plus Mayan organizations. Deeply distrustful of the *ladino* progressive left and of each other, divided in its goals, and confused about the basics of democratic organizing, the Pan-Mayan movement remains politically ineffectual. Its focus is on forging a new Mayan identity through building language, religion, spirituality, schools, and traditional knowledge (such as calendars). This effort revitalizes and recreates a Mayan consciousness and community while subverting *ladino* culture. The Pan-Mayan movement created a sophisticated and inclusive network of activists and regular people, experts and diplomats, able to negotiate at the national and international level. More importantly, without a set political agenda, the Pan-Mayan movement has not alienated members of their own people or attracted repression from the government. This new Mayan identity, in theory, will organically produce a Mayan political consciousness and influence the organization of power (Montejo 2002).

The 1992 presidential election was won by the political moderate Jorge Serrano Elías (1992–93), although his party had to form an alliance to obtain a legislative majority. The number of eligible voters who did not register, abstained, or cast invalid votes rose to 70 per cent. This strongly suggests that the Guatemalan people perceived an exclusionary democracy in which there was freedom to vote, but not to choose (Jonas 1995, 32). There was widespread economic hardship as Guatemala struggled to regain its economic solvency. There were insufficient reserves in the Guatemalan treasury to pay the interest on its debts. Serrano managed to improve Guatemala's macroeconomic indicators, raised taxes on the wealthy, liberalized the labor code, and increased social spending. Nonetheless, there were increasing public protests against his neoliberal reforms and criticisms from the elite about his corruption. In 1992, Rigoberta Menchú won the Nobel Peace Prize. Serrano was unable to stop the military reprisals against her associates. In 1993, in response to student protests and with the support of the military, Serrano dissolved the congress and the supreme court, and announced he would rule by decree. Although he had some support from the military, this attempted *auto-golpe* united the country against him. Civil society organizations were already mobilized and experienced, and Menchú was able to get her people onto the streets. The business elite were worried that the coup would lose them access to US markets. Without elite or popular support, the military removed Serrano from power and the reinstated congress appointed the human rights ombudsman Ramiro de Léon Carpio as president, which lasted until 1996. This was the last coup in Guatemala and suggests that democracy has been consolidated as the only game in town. The military remains a powerful political actor but now shuns the limelight.

In 1993, Léon insisted on a constitutional reform to strengthen democracy (approved by a referendum in 1994). This Constitution still left much to desire. "[A]fter decades of naked military rule, the Guatemala military have crafted a unique Counterinsurgent Constitutional State in which State violence has been reincarnated as democracy" (Schirmer 1998, 258). In other words, the political became militarized and the military became politicized, and that form of power was codified. Thus, there were few real political options that the elected representatives could act on. Real political decision-making happened outside the formal political sphere or took the form of protest, violence, and counterviolence.

POSTBELLUM, 1994–2009

Under Léon's administration, peace talks were reactivated, this time brokered by the United Nations. They included a broadly convened Assembly of Civil Society (ASC), which allowed almost every civil society organization that wished to to join. "The assumption was that the peace building process itself should try to resolve the underlying political, social, and economic problems in order to avoid renewed violence" (Azpuru 2006, 103). As a result, it was an unusually broad and comprehensive process, and produced 300 sweeping but non-binding agreements (the Peace Accords) on practically every political issue imaginable. The Accords can be roughly grouped into two themes, one dealing with the war (e.g., disarmament) and the other dealing with peace (e.g., integration of ethnicity into the political process). The Peace Accords dominated the political agenda during the following decade, shaping idealized expectations of what a democracy would entail and producing unintended consequences, such as a depoliticized Mayan identity and a renovated military and elite.

Although a cease-fire had not yet been agreed upon, in 1994 the Peace Accords created the United Nations Mission for the Verification of Human Rights and of Compliance with the Commitments of the Comprehensive Agreement on Human Rights in Guatemala, later called the UN Verification Mission in Guatemala (MINUGUA). MINUGUA helped to disarm and demobilize URNG, implement the Peace Accords, demine areas, and reduce human rights abuses by opening up regional offices for the safe reporting of human rights abuses. Slowly, human rights improved, became a powerful discourse, and produced the 1994 Human Rights Accord.

The 1994 Historical Clarification Commission (CEH) Peace Accord produced a nine-volume investigation into the war. The military tried to limit the scope of the investigation prompting, in 1995, a network of Catholic clergy to do its own investigation. Headed by Bishop Gerardi Conedera, the Catholic report was released in 1998 with conclusions remarkably similar to the CEH's. Two days later, Bishop Gerardi was murdered. The men who killed him were brought to trial but those who ordered it were never charged.[2] The CEH found that 200,000 people were killed between 1960 and 1996 (2 per cent of the population), 83 per cent of whom were Mayan, creating 150,000 refugees in Mexico and 1.5 million internal displacements (over 10 per cent of the population). It further found that the military was responsible for over 80 per cent of the crimes with acts of genocide occurring between 1981 and 1983. With the release of both of these documents, and the murder of the bishop, "the Guatemalan political landscape was shaken" (Azpuru 2006, 119), strengthening human rights as a normative discourse. The CEH also found that US military assistance to the Guatemala military had significantly affected human rights violations. In 1999, US President Bill Clinton (1992–2000) publicly apologized for the role that the US had played in the genocide of the Mayan peoples.

The 1995 Accord on Identity and Rights of the Indigenous People entailed 30 changes to the Constitution. In 1996, the Guatemalan government passed a law that went further than the 1995 Accord. The government had to constitutionalize Guatemala as a multicultural, multiethnic, and multi-linguistic nation. It further constitutionalized indigenous rights to control over indigenous territory and communities and granted compensation for land that had already been expropriated. It also legalized indigenous rights to resources found on their land, to appropriate political organizations, to culturally affirming education, and to indigenous languages. These collective rights were given to the group, not the individual. So if a Mayan person chose not to dress in a culturally specific way, speak the Mayan language, or live as a Mayan, then that person ceded his or her rights. Collective rights imply that citizens are not individuals, and that they do not belong to an abstraction called "civil society" or the "nation" but to their community and its web of non-voluntary relationships, needs, and values. Democracy, however, is based on individual rights and freedoms, not collective rights, and further assumes that individuals can choose what is in their own best interests even if those interests clash. The democratic state and its institutions mediate between individuals and groups to resolve these clashes, rather than a culture or an authority figure doing the mediating. The 1996 law would erode deliberative democracy as it is classically understood, but only for the Maya; the rest of the population would abide by different rules. This prompted a national debate about the value and meaning of ethnicity and identity of both the *ladinos* and the Maya, and of the reality of fitting both identities into a modern nation-state[3] (Handy 2002).

In May 1999 a referendum decided cultural rights. It had 30 potential reforms and the voter could only answer yes or no. Of the 4 million eligible to vote, only 18 per cent did so, and the referendum was defeated. Because the Mayan identity is tied to the community and the reforms did not deal with local issues, there was the suggestion that the Mayan people were not as interested in it as one might have thought. Plus, Mayan intellectuals and leaders critiqued the constitutionalization of identity, language, customary law, and so on. Some Maya supported several but not all of the reforms, leading to confusion. There were significant problems reaching rural communities and poor publicity appropriate to the predominantly illiterate Maya. In addition, there was overt racist violence. Two days before the vote, two well-known activists for the "yes" side were assassinated in a clear message to the people that the reforms would not be tolerated. So Mayan collective rights have not been constitutionalized in Guatemala and, consequently, the judiciary has no basis to enforce implementation (Warren 2002).

The 1996 Accord on Socioeconomic Issues did not achieve a profound reworking of the economic order. It did, however, increase spending on education and healthcare and reformed the tax system so that by 2000 tax revenue would be 12 per cent of the GDP. At the time, it was 8 per cent and the average for Latin America was 13 per cent, the lowest regional level in the world (Sanchez 2009, 102). Finally, on December 29, 1996, peace was declared with the signing of the final peace accord that brought into force all the previous agreements. The 36-year civil war was over.[4]

The Peace Accords trained a generation on negotiation, compromise, and inclusion, developing new political actors and coalitions within the elite and civil society. These new players created strongly articulated democratic norms and promoted their ideas widely. However, the negotiations to forge the Peace Accords also sowed the seeds for Guatemala's future problems. First, the process trained a generation to bypass the legislature to obtain change. The lesson learned was that change happened through international pressure and actors.

Domestically, change was not perceived as feasible. Political actors based themselves in civil society and targeted international actors, rather than the government. This lack of participation and the fragile state–civil society relations weakened the democratic process. Because so many civil society organizations negotiated the agreements then retired from domestic politics, no one took responsibility for implementing the Peace Accords. Bypassing the legislature also ceded domestic governance to the traditional ruling elite. The elite unduly influenced the state through its own powerful civil society organization, the Co-ordinating Committee of Farmers, Business, Industry, and Finance Associations (CACIF), and as elected political representatives. With fragmented political parties, a divided and apolitical civil society, and an underfinanced state due to its inability to extract resources, there were few mechanisms to offset the power of the elite. Other factors assisted the elite in capturing the state: elite ownership of the bulk of the country's domestic capital, elite ownership of mass media, and elite non-democratic practices such as influence peddling, political party funding, and disinformation campaigns. Combined, there was the creation of a business/political ruling class. As a result, the state was unable to enact even the modest reforms called for in the socioeconomic accord. Successive presidents from 1999 up until today have attempted to increase state revenue through tax reform but all attempts so far have failed. Without adequate resources, the state cannot improve economic infrastructure, build human capital, or obtain its autonomy. "In its policy output, Guatemala differs little from a pure oligarchic democracy" (Sanchez 2009, 128).

Second, the Peace Accords were too ambitious, offering an idealized vision. They reorganized the economy to increase social justice in a time of neoliberalism. They established the principle of participation without dispersing power through the branches of government. They decentralized power but did not create effective local governments that were elected democratically and integrated into the national governing structure. They created two discourses of rights, one based on the uniqueness of Mayan difference and one based on citizens' inherent equality, but they never attempted to integrate the two political and legal modes. The sheer number of accords, plus the broad range of topics and the delightful, if unreasonable, picture of Guatemala that they painted, permitted groups to ignore those accords that they found to be problematic.

Third, the peace process did not sufficiently include the military. The military and the elite jointly and overtly controlled the state and had done so since the 1954 coup of the Arbenz government. The military was an extremely powerful political actor in its own right. As far as it was concerned, it had won the civil war and was voluntarily participating in power sharing. "With varying degrees of explicitness, the military perceives itself as a political actor and is recognized as such by wide sectors of civil society" (Serbin and Fontana 2005, 211). It is a measure of its continuing influence that those areas with which the military agreed were the ones that were implemented most successfully: the demobilization and reintegration of the guerrillas; the return of the refugees; and the incorporation of indigenous issues and concerns into the national agenda. There was limited progress in those areas they didn't agree with, such as socioeconomic reform, constitutional reform, and military depoliticization. During the negotiations, military participation was sidelined, its resources cut, and its authority partially removed. However, lacking a point of leverage, the Peace Accords were unable to fundamentally reform the military. Instead, the military learned how to become covert. To replace its smaller budget, the military expanded its sources of revenue to include legitimate businesses. This has made it a business elite comparable to any other.

The more lucrative business, however, appears to be narco-trafficking. Narco-traffickers shifted their transit route from the Caribbean to Central America in the 1980s in order to take advantage of the chaos and lack of state authority during Central America's political unrest. Guatemala, in particular, was attractive to narco-traffickers because corruption in its security forces had become entrenched over the extended length of its civil war (36 years). Furthermore, the extreme human rights abuses had brutalized a people, especially the children, who now seemed to lack reasonable boundaries on violence. The introduction of narco-traffickers opened the door to other forms of organized crime such as trafficking in firearms and people.

During the war and Guatemala's transition to democracy, the military built on its contacts and activities with members of organized crime. These included soldiers who—for a fee—did not "see" the activities of organized crime, or shared military intelligence on individuals from both the state and civil society (e.g., bureaucrats, human rights workers, and trade unionists). Regardless of the legality of its source, an independent financial base granted the military effective autonomy from governmental control as well as the ability to surreptitiously influence public policy through corruption, assassinations, influence peddling, clientelism, and crony capitalism (Keen 2003; UNODC 2007).

MINUGUA's ten-year mandate ended in 2004 and the UN left the country without having implemented many of the Peace Accords. "No substantial progress has been made in meeting the conditions of most of the substantive accords" (Handy 2002, 41). The window of opportunity to make profound changes to the organizational structures of power has probably now shut. This reality has been reinforced by the 2005 signing of the Dominican Republic–Central American Free Trade Agreement (DR-CAFTA), which came into force in 2006. With DR-CAFTA, landowners, agribusiness, and resource developers can challenge those Peace Accords that attempt land reform, tax reform, minimum wage increases, or improved working conditions (Shamsie 2007).

The presidential election of 1995 fielded for the first time candidates from the left-leaning New Guatemalan Democratic Front (FDNG), which won six seats in the congress and some mayoralties, and included some Mayan representatives. In January 1996 there was a runoff for president and the moderate conservative, Alvaro Arzú of the National Action Party (PAN), stood against Ríos Montt who was against the peace process. It was a narrow win by 2 per cent for Arzú, demonstrating how fragile the peace process was. Arzú privatized public utilities, liberalized and deregulated trade, and reduced the budget. Exports steadily increased but never overtook imports resulting in the Guatemalan state operating at a deficit. The insertion of the economy into globalized neoliberalism left the Guatemalan state reduced and weakened. As a result, poverty increased as did the division of wealth in the country.

In 1999, in a presidential runoff, Alfonso Portillo (1999–2003) of the Guatemalan Republican Front (FRG) won with a solid majority promising to introduce morality into politics and to reduce corruption. With the support of the US, he investigated dozens of former state officials. The US then linked Portillo and his associates to money laundering. Portillo is now in self-imposed exile in Mexico in order to escape charges of laundering $600,000 through four ghost companies in Panama. Given the pervasive corruption within the Guatemalan elite, Portillo demonstrated the cost of dealing with the issue and why it has not been addressed since. Oscar Berger (2004–08) of the business party, the Grand National Alliance (GANA), won power with 54 per cent of the vote in the 2003 election. Taking office in January 2004, Berger proved to be less corrupt than previous presidents. However, he lacked a congressional majority since GANA claimed only 47 of the 158 seats, and consequently was forced to make a series of alliances with other small parties.

Throughout the 1990s and continuing until today, crime and violence—including gangs, public lynchings, domestic violence, the state, and organized crime—have become endemic in many sectors of society. Some statistics exist for generalized crime. Of reported crimes, only 6 per cent are solved, and 42 per cent of Guatemalan businesses report a loss due to crime (versus 25 per cent as a global average). While generalized violence is difficult to measure, the number of homicides can be more easily counted.[5] There are approximately 59 murders per 100,000 inhabitants in Guatemala (the rest of Latin America is 27.5, the global rate is 5). A high level of generalized violence especially affects women. The 2008 Ombudsman Report showed that between 2001 and 2007 the number of homicides increased by 77 per cent, while in the same period homicides of women increased by 95 per cent.[6] Crime and violence account for annual material losses to the GNP of 6.8 per cent, as well as reduced foreign investment and tourism (Torres 2009; UNODC 2007).

High levels of crime and violence partially reflect Guatemala's endemic poverty. In the rural areas, 75 per cent to 85 per cent live in poverty with 67 per cent of indigenous children suffering from malnutrition. Between 1990 and 2000, the annual average growth rate of the GDP per capita was 1.4 per cent, which is insufficient to lift people out of poverty. Seligson (2005, 213) estimates that the annual growth rate per capita would have to be 6 per cent annually "for a long time," in other words, wealth would have to be redistributed in order to overcome poverty. With a Gini coefficient of 0.55, one of the highest in the world and growing, the income share of the poorest 20 per cent of the population fell from 2.7 per cent in 1989 to 1.7 per cent in 2002. Over 70 per cent of the population live in poverty or extreme poverty. Malnutrition and maternal and infant mortality are among the highest in the world. One-third of the populace is illiterate. While all these social indices are improving, they are doing so more slowly than in equally poor countries like Bolivia, Nicaragua, and Honduras (World Bank 2003).

But high levels of crime and violence also reflect the failure of the judicial system. Police corruption is so pervasive that the police are considered to be the most corrupt sector in Guatemalan society. Between 2005 and 2007, 20 per cent of the officers of the National Police were removed because they were corrupt. These included top heads of agencies dealing with intelligence and anti-narcotics, as well as elite squads accused of carrying out assassinations to cover up the extent of police involvement in crime. A similar situation exists for judges. A March 2007 UN Special Rapporteur on Summary Executions accused the judiciary of being corrupt and inefficient and found that less than 10 per cent of murders resulted in criminal convictions because of the weak rule of law. Elected representatives to oversee the judiciary were also sullied. For example, between 2000 and 2002, four ministers of government dealing with the law were implicated in corruption scandals. The muzzling of the media has limited free speech and journalists practice self-censorship to avoid retaliation. Citizens' responses have been to either hire private security firms for protection or to act collectively and publicly lynch known felons (Alston 2007; Handy 2004; UNODC 2007).

In response, the military has again emerged as a legitimate protector of the people. Arzú, claiming that the military has reformed itself, changed its mandate in the Peace Accords to include policing. However, the military is one of the reasons for the high levels of violence in the first place. The police and the military have been implicated in the torture and killings of gang members, criminal suspects, and social undesirables (i.e., the youth, the poor, union or neighborhood organizers, human rights workers, critics of the military). The military and police, with the tacit support of the government, have been allegedly organizing themselves into secret paramilitaries to commit political assassinations. The lack of impunity means that political assassinations are a routine part of the campaign trail. During the 2007 national and local elections, there were 55 attacks and threats against political candidates, 26 of whom died (Human Rights Watch 2008). Nonetheless, the military has learned not to be obvious in their murders, so "clandestine terror squads attack individuals in ways meant to look like common crimes" (Fischer and Benson 2006, 93).

Furthermore, the military has become a highly organized and efficient conduit for 400 metric tons of cocaine from South America to the US, in addition to the trafficking of humans to the US, and illegal small arms from Eastern Europe and the US en route to Latin America (US State Department 2009). Guatemala is the crossroads for the shipment of goods in both directions. In 2003, the US State Department added Guatemala to its list of countries considered to be uncooperative in the fight against drug trafficking (it was later taken off), and in 2006 it listed Guatemala as a "primary concern location" for money laundering. Money laundering, a key function in trafficking, has colonized a system created to process remittances. As much as 10 per cent of the Guatemalan population live in the US and remittances have become one of the pillars of the Guatemalan economy (Jonas 2006, 290). In 2008, Guatemala processed $4.8 billion in formal and informal remittances, a 4.7 per cent increase over 2007. Processing remittances has been supported by the neoliberal state, which lifted exchange controls on processing foreign currency, simplified obtaining dollar accounts, and limited regulation that oversees rapid financial transactions. These are also integral to the money laundering process. While the Guatemalan legislature has passed a series of laws to combat money laundering and has seized bank accounts of those found guilty of it, there is no tracking system for seized assets, even if they were deposited in a bank account. As a result, Guatemala has become the regional center for money laundering, one that is increasingly used by Mexican drug cartels. In eighteen months between 2007 and 2008, $60 million of drug-related proceeds were brought to or generated within Guatemala City (US State Department 2009; UNODC 2007).

The level of violence has meant that there is an effective restriction of citizens' movements and meetings in public spaces, and a reasonable fear of protest and activism. Distrust between citizens is prevalent. Civil society, therefore, cannot perform its democratic role of organizing, articulating, and persuading others of the value of its ideas or of creating democratic values of trust, tolerance, and mutuality. This seriously weakens democratic norms and processes. In an argument echoing Hobbes's *Leviathan*, Seligson (2005) suggests that Guatemala's high levels of violence have profound implications for the continuance of democracy. Because the state cannot protect its own citizens from one another and has no monopoly on authority and violence within its own territory, politics is reduced to a pre-democratic arbitrary existence. Under such circumstances, citizens more readily exchange democratic processes for security, even if that security is offered by authoritarian leaders.

That trade-off, however, may not happen. A weak neoliberalized state, incapable of supplying security for its citizens, is in the best interests of organized crime and a corrupt elite. Democracy, even a minimum democracy, acts as a cover. It gives the state an international stature and ensures that it will not be considered a "rogue" nation. Organized crime, a corrupt elite, and a weak democratic state operate in a mutually reinforcing dynamic. Crime cannot be seen as operating outside the state but within the state apparatus through the corruption of elected and non-elected officials. These include the judiciary, low and high-ranking bureaucrats, the police and military, government ministers, elected representatives, and presidents of republics. Within the state, there exists a parallel non-democratic organization of power acting through state institutions for its own ends. This "shadow state" has its own institutions that wield force (the military), collect rents and taxes (corruption), regulate the market (neoliberalism), and distribute resources (clientelism). People can act both legitimately and legally to fulfill their duties as elected representatives, bureaucrats, soldiers, or businesspersons but can also act illegally for the shadow state (Briscoe 2008).

In 2007, the government with the cooperation of the UN initiated a joint International Commission Against Impunity in Guatemala (CICIG) to investigate organized crime, despite considerable domestic resistance. The UN attempted to make the CICIG autonomous from the state, but the Guatemalan constitutional court forced the commission to work with the very institutions it was to investigate. The CICIG has been unable to force a prosecution of former attorney general Alvaro Matus for obstructing justice by not permitting the investigation into the murder of a government official working to halt impunity. In other words, the constitutional court protected the attorney general who was protecting a judge who was protecting organized crime. This is an example of the shadow state operating at its most blatant. If the UN-backed CICIG was unsuccessful at challenging the shadow state, there is little expectation that other international institutions would have more impact.

In the 2007 elections, Alvaro Colom Caballeros (2008–12) of the centrist National Unity for Hope Party (UNE) won with 52.8 per cent of the popular vote but received a minority in congress. While it was commonly understood that the Maya were too disinterested to vote, a study showed that insufficient identification, an incomplete voter's list, and the indigenous' extremely low levels of trust in the democratic system compounded their lack of electoral participation (Nevitte, Cruz, and Estok 2007). Despite international acclaim, Menchú alienated some Maya by not speaking to them in their own language. These factors combined can partially explain Menchú's poor showing of 3 per cent in the election.

Colom's administration intends to put a new income tax bill before congress and eject organized crime from the state. Since his election, he has replaced the attorney general, chief of police, two senior military leaders, and most senior police officers because of their connections to organized crime. However, Colom was implicated in 2008 in corruption scandals. In May 2009, he, his wife, and his chief of staff were implicated in the murder of a lawyer, a businessman, and the businessman's daughter. Given his declining legitimacy, UNE's minority in congress, and weak state institutions, it is unclear how he will accomplish his goals.

Indigenous people are still more likely to live in poverty than *ladinos* with the rural indigenous having five times the incidence of poverty of the average urban *ladino*.[7] Indigenous women have the highest levels of extreme poverty. In addition to being poorer, they have less access to education, healthcare, and basic utilities. Mayan employment is predominantly agricultural with 82 per cent of farmworkers paid less than minimum wage. The Maya face racism when job seeking and discriminatory practices from public officials when dealing with the government. The Pan-Mayan move-ment, seriously undermined after the loss of the 1999 referendum, has been experiencing internal conflicts over strategies, reduced negotiations with the state, and less international funding. More positively, it has been able to make alliances with the environmental movement and other NGOs. Furthermore, natural resources are frequently found on indigenous lands, which produce sustained protests and collective action. As well, the num-ber of Mayan mayors has increased from 18 per cent in 1985 to 36 per cent in 2002. In general, the Guatemalan public now sees more Maya individuals in the mass media carrying out legitimate political roles than it has in the past. In 2003, racism became criminalized for the first time. With Menchú again running for president in 2011, there will be a public platform to air indigenous views (World Bank 2003; UNDP 2005, 57–124; Caumartin 2007).

CONCLUSION

Guatemala has a democracy so weak that *The Economist* (2009, 53) wrote that, with the exception of Haiti, it is as close as any to a failed state in the Americas. At least half the population, the Maya, is effectively disen-franchised. Their poverty, isolation, illiteracy and lack of access to state resources diminish their ability to engage with the mechanisms of delibera-tive democracy. It appears that the Maya prefer local over national issues, cultural identity over public policy formation, and Mayan consensus over intra- or inter-ethnic conflict. As a result, their political participation does not reflect their demography.

Even if they did participate, they might well have a limited effect on the polity. The UN-brokered transition to democracy left fundamental aspects of the organization of Guatemala unreformed. These included its gross socioeconomic inequalities, military influence, and inadequate dispersion of power through the institutions of government.

This has produced a state with poorly functioning democratic processes ruled by an informal elite pact between the military, politicians and busi-ness class, which have divided power between them. Fragmented political parties, impunity, and renovated non-democratic practices have contrib-uted to this situation. A profound weakness is the apolitical civil society, in which the internationally-brokered transition to democracy created an odd dynamic. NGOs and INGOs have based civil society organizations on an ethos of human rights rather than on democratic rights (civil liberties, media, rule of law, etc.). While human rights has become the dominant discourse, without democratic rights it has no political power. As a result, there has been no societal creation of democratic norms to strengthen tendencies for reform. Furthermore, civil society has eschewed working through formal political structures to forge public policies. Political parties, therefore, are not grounded in the grass roots; the elected representatives and bureaucrats are not in a dialogue with civil society organizations; and the institutions of the state are not being held accountable. These factors have been interacting since 1994 and have slowly eroded the promise of a genuine democracy in Guatemala.

A weak state is always vulnerable to the forces of globalization. As a neoliberalized country, Guatemala was unable to negotiate DR-CAFTA's bilateral free trade deal to benefit Guatemalans (WOLA 2009). As well, Guatemala's weak state has always been vulnerable to capture by a business/military alliance. However, using neoliberal reforms and the cover offered by democratization and endemic violence, the military and political actors have colluded with organized crime to facilitate illicit activities. These activities have been institutionalized within the functioning of the state, producing a parallel governing regime or a shadow state. The legal operations of the neoliberal state with its limited citizen voting and nominal civil society participation are unable to adequately overcome Guatemala's deep divisions (ethnic, socioeconomic, illicit) to create even a minimum democracy. When combined with its shadow state, democracy is further undermined. That reality seriously mitigates any realistic expectation of reform.

NOTES

1 When quoting numbers of Maya people, Mayan languages, Mayan villages, and so on, it is best to be cautious and use categories as rough guidelines only. For example, if a person is born in an urban center because the family was fleeing oppression, can speak both Spanish and Quechua, works in Guatemala City as a bus driver while wearing Western clothes but returns to a highland village for festivals while wearing traditional clothing, is she or he Maya or ladino? What if the traditional clothes (which denote status and clans) are inappropriate, that is, wrong? What if the clothes, food, and cultural practices are traditional but she or he can no longer speak Quechua? The extent of the upheaval of the Maya people during the last 25 years and the complexity of their practices and lives are rarely reflected in the statistics. See Warren (2001).

2 For an excellent book on this murder, see Goldman (2008).

3 In Latin America, groups are frequently protected constitutionally, especially workers and children. However, the protection of the Mayan people would have been substantially more extensive. There are many democratic nations in the world that struggle with the same sort of issues. In Canada, for example, the Québécois have state recognition and support for their unique culture. In most democratic countries with an Aboriginal population, the institutionalization of their group rights has been extremely problematic.

4 For more on the Peace Accords, see Jonas (2000).

5 Homicide statistics are nonetheless more complex than one might think. See UNODC (2007, 52–53) for more on the difficulty of using these numbers.

6 Based on my own observations during the near collapse of the Nicaraguan state in 1994–96 and its concomitant high levels of generalized violence, this affects men, women, and children in varying ways, of which the number of women's homicides is the most accurate reflection. In other words, this statistic should be understood as indicative of the acute and pervasive violence that every person in Guatemala is vulnerable to.

7 Poverty between indigenous groups varies, and it is geographical. A poverty belt runs from the north to the northwest regions of Guatemala.

REFERENCES

Alston, Philip. 2007. "Civil and Political Rights, Including Questions of Disappearances and Summary Executions. Report to the Special Raporteur on Extrajudicial, Summary or Arbitrary Executions." United Nations, February 17.

Azpuru, Dinarah. 2006. "Strengthening Human Rights in Guatemala." *Promoting Democracy in PostConflict Societies*. Ed. Jeroen de Zeeuw and Krishna Kumar. Boulder: Lynne Rienner Press. 99–126.

Booth, John A., and Thomas W. Walker. 1993. *Understanding Central America*. 2nd ed. Boulder: Westview Press.

Briscoe, Ivan. 2008. "The Proliferation of the 'Parallel State.'" Working Paper No. 71. Madrid: Fundación para las Relaciones Internacionales y el Diálogo Exterior.

Caumartin, Corinne. 2007. "Emerging Ethnic Politics? Guatemalan Indigenous Movements and Participation." Paper presented at Central America's Challenged Transition Conference, Institute for the Study of the Americas, London, UK, June.

Chasten, John Charles. 2006. *Born in Blood and Fire: A Concise History of Latin America*. 2nd ed. New York: W.W. Norton.

Commission for Historical Clarification. 1999. *Guatemala: Memory of Silence: Report of the Commission of Historical Clarification Conclusions and Recommendations*. June 10, 2010. http://shr.aaas.org/guatemala/ceh/report/english/conc1.html.

Dunkerley, James. 1988. *Power in the Isthmus: A Political History of Modern Central America*. London: Verso.

Economist, The. 2009. "An Indictment from the Grave." May 23–29: 53–54.

Fischer, Edward F., and Peter Benson. 2006. *Broccoli and Desire: Global Connections and Mayan Struggles in Postwar Guatemala*. Stanford: Stanford University Press.

Goldman, Franscico. 2008. *The Art of Political Murder: Who Killed Bishop Gerardi?* London: Atlantic Books.

Handy, Jim. 2004. "Chicken Thieves, Witches, and Judges: Vigilante Justice and Customary Law in Guatemala." *Journal of Latin American Studies* 36: 533–36.

——. 2002. "Democratizing What? Some Reflections on Nation, State, Ethnicity, Modernity, Community and Democracy in Guatemala." *Canadian Journal of Latin American and Caribbean Studies* 27(53): 35–71.

Human Rights Watch. 2008. "Universal Periodic Review of Guatemala: Human Rights Watch's Submission to the Human Rights Council." May 4, 2008. June 10, 2010. www.hrw.org/en/news/2008/05/04/universal-periodic-review-guatemala.

Jonas, Suzanne. 1995. "Electoral Problems and the Democratic Project in Guatemala." *Elections and Democracy in Central America Revisited*. Ed. John A. Booth. Chapel Hill: University of North Carolina. 25–44.

——. 2006. "Guatemala." *The Politics of Latin America: The Power Game*. Ed. Harry E. Vanden and Gary Prevost. New York: Oxford University Press. 264–95.

——. 2000. *Of Centaurs and Doves: Guatemala's Peace Process*. Boulder: Westview Press.

Keen, David. 2003. "Demobilising Guatemala." Crisis States Programme Working Paper No. 37. London: Crisis States Programme, London School of Economics.

Kumar, Chetan. 2005. "The Role of the Military in Democratization and Peace Building: The Experiences of Haiti and Guatemala." *Security Sector Reform and Post-Conflict Peacebuilding*. Ed. Albrecht Schnabel and Hans-Georg Ehrhart. New York: United Nations University Press. 258–80.

Latinobarómetro 2008. Opinion Pública Latinoamericana. June 10, 2010. www.latinobarometro.org.

Menchú, Rigoberta. 1984. *I, Rigoberta Menchú*. Told to Elisabeth Burgos Debray. London: Verso Books.

Montejo, Victor. 2002. "The Multiplicity of Mayan Voices: Mayan Leadership and the Politics of Self-Representation." *Indigenous Movements, Self-Representation and the State in Latin America*. Ed. Kay B. Warren and Jean E. Jackson. Austin: University of Texas Press. 123–48.

Nevitte, Neil, Jose Cruz, and Melissa Estok (with the assistance of M. Painter-Main). 2007. *Barriers to Electoral Participation in Guatemala: Diagnostic of Four Municipalities*. Gautemala City: FLACSO-Guatemala and Mirador Electoral.

Sanchez, Omar. 2009. "Tax Reform Paralysis in Post-Conflict Guatemala." *New Political Economy* 14(1): 101–31.

Schirmer, Jennifer. 1998. "The Looting of Democratic Discourse by the Guatemalan Military: Implications for Human Rights." *Constructing Democracy: Human Rights, Citizenship, and Society in Latin America*. Ed. Elizabeth Jelin and Eric Herghberg. Boulder: Westview Press. 85–97.

Schlesinger, Stephen, and Stephen Kinzer. 2005. *Bitter Fruit: The Story of the American Coup in Guatemala*. 2nd ed. Boston: Harvard University Press.

Seligson, Mitchell A. 2005. "Democracy on Ice: The Multiple Challenges of Guatemala's Peace Process." *The Third Wave of Democratization in Latin America*. Ed. Frances Hagopian and Scott Mainwaring. Cambridge: Cambridge University Press. 202–31.

Serbin, Andres, and Andres Fontana. 2005. "Civil-Military Relations in Latin America: The Post-9/11 Scenario and the Civil Society Dimension." *Security Sector Reform and Post-Conflict Peacebuilding*. Ed. Albrecht Schnabel and Hans-Georg Ehrhart. New York: United Nations University Press. 207–24.

Shamsie, Yasmine. 2007. "The International Political Economy of Democracy Promotion: Lessons from Haiti and Guatemala." *Promoting Democracy in the Americas*. Ed. Thomas Legler, Sharon F. Lean, and Dexter Boniface. Baltimore: Johns Hopkins University Press. 249–69.

Torres Ruiz, Gladis. 2009. "Aún con Ley, en Guatemala feminicidio se volvió epidemia." *Cimacnoticias: periodismo con perspectiva de género*. May 19. June 10, 2010. www.cimacnoticias.com/site/09051905-Aun-con-Ley-en-Gua.37765.0.html.

United Nations Development Program (UNDP). 2005. *The 2005 Human Development Report*. New York: UNDP.

United Nations Office on Drugs and Crime (UNODC). 2007. *Crime and Development in Central America: Caught in the Cross-Fire*. New York: UNODC.

US State Department. 2009. *2009 International Narcotics Control Strategy Report*. Volume 1: *Drugs and Chemical Control*. Volume 2: *Money Laundering and Financial Crimes*. Washington, DC: US State Department.

Warren, Kay B. 2001. "Rethinking Bi-Polar Constructions of Ethnicity." *Journal of Latin American Anthropology* 6(2): 90–105.

———. 2002. "Voting Against Indigenous Rights in Guatemala: Lessons from the 1999 Referendum." *Indigenous Movements, Self-Representation and the State in Latin America*. Ed. Kay B. Warren and Jean E. Jackson. Austin: University of Texas Press. 149–80.

Washington Office on Latin America (WOLA). 2009. *DR-CAFTA and Workers Rights: Moving from Paper to Practice*. Washington, DC: WOLA.

Williams, Philip J., and Guillermina Seri. 2003. "The Limits of Reformism: The Rise and Fall of Christian Democracy in El Salvador and Guatemala." *Christian Democracy in Latin America: Electoral Competition and Regime Conflicts*. Ed. Scott Mainwaring and Timothy R. Scully. Stanford: Stanford University Press. 201–329.

World Bank. 2003. *Poverty in Guatemala*. New York: Poverty Reduction and Economic Management Unit.

E-RESOURCES

Acción Ciudadana (some English) (www.accionciudadana.org.gt). A civil society organization that promotes democracy through monitoring public institutions.

El Periódico (www.elperiodico.com.gt). An established and respected daily paper.

Foundation Rigoberta Menchú (www.frmt.org.es). A human rights foundation focused on education, civic participation, and political activism.

Guatemalan government website (www.guatemala.gob.gt). Gateway to the Guatemalan government.

Guatemala Times, The (www.guatemala-times.com). English-language daily newspaper.

International Commission Against Impunity (English) (www.cicig.org). A Guatemalan–UN commission that assists in strengthening the rule of law and combating organized crime.

SIX

Nicaragua:
Revolution and Betrayal

KATHERINE ISBESTER

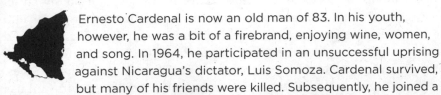 Ernesto Cardenal is now an old man of 83. In his youth, however, he was a bit of a firebrand, enjoying wine, women, and song. In 1964, he participated in an unsuccessful uprising against Nicaragua's dictator, Luis Somoza. Cardenal survived, but many of his friends were killed. Subsequently, he joined a Trappist monastery and ultimately was ordained a Catholic priest. His first congregation was located on the isolated poor islands of Solentiname, an archipelago in Lake Nicaragua. There he preached liberation theology, a belief system which taught that God does not want His people to live in virtual slavery; in order to achieve a state of grace with God, the structures that facilitate hunger, oppression, and exploitation first must be removed. In Solentiname, Cardenal wrote theology and poetry that garnered praise from around the world. He supported a nationalist socialist revolutionary group called the Sandinista Front for National Liberation (FSLN or the Sandinistas), which promised to create a more equitable society if it succeeded in overthrowing Somoza. Because of Cardenal's support for the FSLN, in 1977 Somoza's military police attacked Cardenal's island church and destroyed it. Cardenal fled to Costa Rica for his own safety.

In 1979, the FSLN successfully overthrew Somoza and installed its own leaders in power. The new government appointed Ernesto Cardenal as the minister of culture. As a revered priest and poet with an international following, Cardenal was instrumental in persuading both Nicaraguans and the international community to accept the FSLN as legitimate. However, in 1990 the FSLN was voted out of power, and by 1994 the party was divided, purging itself of its more critical members. Cardenal, disgusted at the process, left the country. After more than a decade of public acrimony, splintering, and constitutional reform, the FSLN regained power in 2006. In the summer of 2008, Cardenal was invited to Paraguay to celebrate the inauguration of its democratically elected, left-leaning president. There he publicly criticized the FSLN, accusing it of renovating the old Somoza elite through tactical alliances. In November 2008, a Nicaraguan judge, using the legal system speciously, froze Cardenal's bank account. Now, if Cardenal returns to Nicaragua, he will be jailed (Kinzer 2008; Lacey 2008). For Cardenal to go from respected Sandinista leader to vilified criminal is quite a reversal of fortune. But his story mirrors the story of the most dominant political party in Nicaragua, and its own reversals.

FROM LIBERATION TO DICTATORSHIP, 1821–1979

After achieving liberation from Spain in 1821, Central America formed a political union. Stressed by rivalries between its regions, a poorly structured regional state, and intra-elite competition, the union split in 1838 into the countries we know today. Independent for the first time, Nicaragua had its own government. However, it still had intra-elite conflict in the form of competition for power and resources between liberals and conservatives. Nicaragua's constitutional oligarchy resembled *caudillismo*, with militias deciding which political party held power. Intra-elite conflict and *caudillismo* describes Nicaraguan politics to this day, seriously weakening any authentic democratic structures, norms, or procedures.

The level of conflict between Nicaragua's elite groups left it vulnerable to outside interference. Nicaragua is strategically located. Before the opening of the Panama Canal in 1914, it was easier and cheaper to transport goods from the Atlantic to the Pacific through Nicaragua's lakes and rivers and across a short land bridge, rather than going around the tip of Chile and Argentina.[1] The Americans and the British competed for control over this transit route, with the Americans decisively winning in 1854 by shelling the British-controlled port of Greytown[2] on Nicaragua's Atlantic coast. In 1856, the American mercenary William Walker invaded Nicaragua at the request of the Nicaraguan Liberal Party and overthrew its conservative government. Walker then reneged on his promise to cede power to the Liberal Party and instead installed himself as president. The US government immediately recognized Walker's government, but Nicaraguans and militias from the rest of Central America united to overthrow him. In 1857 Walker fled from power and was executed by firing squad in Honduras. The conservative party ruled for the next 30 years, partially because of the debacle of William Walker.

For most of the nineteenth century, Nicaragua, with its abundant arable land and small population, had a free and large peasant population. However, by the 1870s the increasing importance of coffee exports meant that the elite needed large plantations and cheap labor to pick the coffee. Through legislation and violence, the elite were able to absorb small landholdings and dispossess the peasantry in the highlands of Nicaragua, thereby creating both the plantations and a cheap labor force. Exports (almost exclusively coffee) increased after World War I and Nicaragua became and remains heavily reliant on the American market for its economic survival.

Political conflict resulted in the rise of General José Santos Zelaya to power in 1893. He was a folk *caudillo* and a nationalist. When Zelaya entered into negotiations with Japan and Germany to build a canal in direct competition with the still incomplete Panama Canal, he alienated the Nicaraguan elite and the US. The US invaded in 1909, deposed Zelaya, then withdrew. The US invaded again in 1912 to protect American interests and occupied Nicaragua until 1932. Through dollar and gunboat diplomacy, the US government and Americans residing in Nicaragua were able to secure control over Nicaraguan finances, manage the economy, and choose presidential candidates. The elite benefited from this arrangement, so they were not opposed to it. The peasants, however, were not very satisfied with the new order. A nationalist guerrilla movement began in 1912. By 1927, Augusto Sandino, a charismatic and skilled strategist, forged the guerrillas who followed him into a small but unbeatable force. Since the Great Depression reduced American military spending, the American Marines trained a Nicaraguan National Guard and military to take their place, and left the country. The head of the National Guard was Anastasio Somoza. He arranged for the assassination of Sandino in 1934 during peace talks, and then deposed the president and installed himself in power in 1936. When complaints arose about Somoza's abuses of power, President Franklin D. Roosevelt (1933–45) is supposed to have replied, "Somoza may be a son of a bitch, but he's our son of a bitch." Until the 1979 revolution, Somoza or one of his two sons ruled Nicaragua, either overtly or through elected puppets.

The first Somoza was able to create alliances between the conservative and liberal elite through business partnerships and by sharing his wealth. He co-opted the tiny labor movement before repressing it, charmed the American government, and vigorously supported American foreign policy. He cemented his power using the National Guard, which became Nicaragua's organized crime syndicate in addition to being the oppressive arm of the dictatorship (Millet 1977).

After World War II, Somoza diversified the economy to keep the country from being completely dependent on coffee. There was a doubling of the land allocated to cattle farming and sugar cane. The need for more land to cultivate these new export crops pushed peasants off the lowlands and concentrated land ownership in fewer hands. Agriculture, with its clientelistic relations of power and its capital- and technology-intensive production, remained the dominant economic sector. By 1963, large farms constituted 2 per cent of the total number of farms but occupied 50 per cent of the land (Burns 1987, 3). Because farming was no longer used for domestic food consumption, food had to be imported at costs which were frequently too high for the poor.

From 1936, when Somoza took power, until 1950, the average growth rate of the GDP was 4.6 per cent, rising to 5.6 per cent in the 1950s and 7.5 per cent in the 1960s. This easily outstripped the population growth rate (Dunkerley 1988, 202). The modernization of agriculture and the industrialization of Nicaragua produced a small but growing middle class, concentrated in the urban areas. With the 1961 Alliance for Progress, an American strategy to reduce the chance of revolution through social and economic development, Nicaragua was given millions of dollars in aid. Using import substitution industrialization (ISI) strategies, internal tariffs between Central American nations were dropped, but were raised for imports from outside the region. Manufacturing increased, growing from 7 per cent of the region's exports in 1960 to 27 per cent in 1970. But manufacturing still remained small-scale, and consequently powerful unions never emerged to support populism and a redistribution of income. Wages rose for the working and middle class until the early 1970s, when ISI's exhaustion and inflation from the global oil crises eroded these gains. Because of the division of wealth, the benefits of the growing economy were concentrated in the hands of a few elite families, with some benefits going to the small middle and working classes. Poor people actually grew poorer.

Somoza was assassinated in 1956. His eldest son Luis took power after him, but died of natural causes in 1967. The presidency then passed to the younger son, also called Anastasio. Anastasio Junior shared less of the nation's wealth with the elite than his father and brother had done. By 1979, the Somoza family owned the vast majority of the nation's businesses and industries, and 20 per cent of the best land in the country. In an impoverished nation, the Somoza family fortune grew from $50 million in the 1950s to well over $500 million by 1979 (Booth and Walker 1993, 36). The unchecked greed of Somoza and his increasing control over the economy steadily resulted in the loss of the business class's allegiance. When US President Jimmy Carter (1976–80) began to withdraw support for Somoza because of his human rights abuses and corruption, elite support for the dictator all but vanished.

Without a genuine democracy and with little elite opposition, the only form of protest possible was armed insurrection. In 1961, three young men formed the Sandinista Front for National Liberation (FSLN). The movement was inspired by both the Cuban Revolution of 1959 and the Nicaraguan nationalist guerrilla fighter, Augusto Sandino. Its ideology was nationalist socialism achieved through armed peasant insurrection. The FSLN was remarkably unsuccessful in its confrontations with Somoza's National Guard, to the point of almost being obliterated. Still, the National Guard's repression, especially of the peasants, increased. In the long run, this strategy was unwise as it fueled anti-Somoza protests.

As the FSLN grew, it split into three distinct ideologies and approaches, called "tendencies," for fomenting revolution. One tendency was loyal to the successful Cuban model of revolution and based itself on mobilizing the peasants in the remote, mountainous regions of Nicaragua. This was the most famous tendency because it produced some fine popular books extolling the heroism and sacrifice of the young men and women who joined the movement.[3] The second was more traditionally Marxist and focused on mobilizing the working class in the poor urban centers. The third and final tendency focused on mobilizing everyone else, which included women, Christians, students, intellectuals, and disenchanted members of the elite. This last tendency was supported by the Ortega brothers, who foresaw that the Nicaraguan revolution could only be won in the urban centers with mass popular support. Mobilizing the populace required semi-autonomous, semi-secret civil society organizations where the connection to the FSLN was frequently downplayed or publicly denied.[4] These three tendencies supported each other and other autonomous groups in order to focus on the immediate goal of survival and overthrowing the dictator. This technique of semi-autonomous mass mobilizing within a broadly tolerant ideology focused on achieving short-term goals would become the modus operandi of the FSLN once it gained power.

Protests and disciplined armed uprisings increased until 1977, when the nation was swept with mass uprisings. Spearheaded by the FSLN, these were supported by a complex political alliance reflecting all classes and political leanings. In July 1979, Somoza fled the nation and the National Guard abandoned its posts. Somoza left Nicaragua bankrupt. He had emptied the treasury, leaving the nation $1.6 billion in debt to international financial institutions, banks, and countries. Property damage as a result of the 1977–79 armed insurrection amounted to $470 million. In a nation of 3 million, 600,000 people were left homeless, and 40,000 to 50,000 were dead (Black 1981). Somoza was later assassinated by Sandinista-hired mercenaries.

FSLN: THE SOCIAL DEMOCRACY VERSION, 1979–1990

The FSLN was better organized, better known, and had better connections to the grassroots than other organizations; therefore, it was in a good position to assume control of the government. The FSLN was a party, a mass movement, a government, and a state, all at the same time. Between 1979 and 1984, the country was led by the executive of the FSLN, the national directorate. It consisted of nine men who represented each ideological tendency equally. The national directorate controlled national security, set overarching policy, and controlled key ministerial posts and the bureaucracy. It appointed one of the nine men, Daniel Ortega, then just 34 years old, as president of the national directorate, the FSLN, and Nicaragua. At that point, Ortega was one of the lesser-known Sandinista commanders, and had a well-deserved reputation for lacking charisma (he learned on the job how to communicate, and his performance has improved over the years). By appointing Ortega, the national directorate was attempting to avoid the pitfall of the Cuban revolution, where the movement was personified in just one man, Fidel Castro.

The national directorate instructed the council of state, a legislative and representative body, which then drafted and passed legislation. The council of state had 47 seats (later 50) of which the FSLN controlled 27, as well as key posts. The council of state included representatives from all the major political parties, including Somoza's old Liberal Party, the Catholic Church, and the right-wing business alliance. The FSLN's seats were represented by mobilized Sandinista civil society groups, which included the women's movement, the peasants's organization, the labor union, the youth group, and so on. Civil society organizations were not fully autonomous from the state or the FSLN. Rather, these organizations were seen as vehicles for popular expression of the will of the people, and as such were obviously anti-Somoza and anti-elite, and pro-equality, freedom, and justice, and thereby inherently Sandinista. As popular representatives, civil society organizations could criticize aspects of individual policies and give feedback on how well they were implemented. In the early years of the 1980s, the leadership of these civil society organizations were appointed by the FSLN. However, toward the end of the 1980s, they increasingly democratized. With the legitimacy of being Sandinista, grassroots, and later democratic, these organizations walked a fine line of critique, support, and defense, and worked as an incubator of acceptable dissent of the FSLN.

The range of groups represented ensured that there was a governing ethos of social justice, inclusion, and dissent. To assist with the reconstruction of Nicaragua, the FSLN also recruited outsiders, including three Roman Catholic priests (one of whom was Ernesto Cardenal), poets and novelists (the vice president was a respected novelist), and women. Although it did have elements of a participatory democracy, the concentration of power in the national directorate and their non-elected positions meant that the new government was not as democratic as the FSLN claimed it was. Nonetheless, it was substantially more democratic than anything Nicaragua had experienced in the past. The council of state split Somoza's elite between those who supported the new direction and those who did not. The future Nicaraguan president, Violeta Chamorro, was one of those who resigned her seat on the council of state to protest the bias toward the FSLN in the organization of power, while one of her children, intellectual and journalist Fernando Chamorro, became an ardent supporter of the new government. Splitting the elite permitted the FSLN to consolidate power and legitimacy.

The new ideology which was to govern the FSLN and Nicaragua for the 1980s was liberation for everyone from all oppression. Dubbed Sandinismo, this obviously included socioeconomic oppression, and thus a strong criticism of capitalism and an enthusiastic espousal of socialist principles. However, the new government was not Marxist in its ideology or in its public policies, despite the number of self-proclaimed Marxists in the national directorate and council of state. The FSLN supported a mixed economy, embraced a foreign policy of non-alignment, and celebrated religiosity. It may not have had much option: the Soviet Union was in its death throes, and could not afford to support another small, poor, third world country as it had Cuba. Instead, Western Europe became Nicaragua's major source of aid.

The government's first major policies targeted social welfare, and included literacy and health campaigns. The Literacy Campaign reduced illiteracy to 12 per cent from 33 per cent, and won an award from the United Nations Educational, Scientific and Cultural Organization (UNESCO). The health campaign focused on inoculating children and on other preventative health measures, as well as ensuring greater access to primary healthcare. The World Health Organization (WHO) praised Nicaragua's health campaign in 1983 as a model for the rest of the developing world. Somoza's extensive properties were nationalized, his farms becoming state-owned farms or agricultural cooperatives. The agrarian reform program distributed land to peasants with a heavy emphasis on agricultural cooperatives, albeit at a pace too slow for some. By the mid-1980s, large farms had declined, only occupying 20 per cent of the total arable land. Land title was unclear, and frequently impossible to accurately determine. The issue of land title would confound Nicaraguan politics for years to come. Nonetheless, the revolutionary government began to rebuild Nicaragua through policies promoting social and economic equality, while widening rights for women and indigenous peoples.

The election of Ronald Reagan as president of the United States in 1980 signaled a decisive shift in international support. While former president Jimmy Carter had granted $8 million in emergency aid and a loan of $75 million in 1979 to the new government, Reagan and his administration were aggressively hostile to the FSLN. Sandinista rhetoric, its close connection to Cuba, and its refusal to stop shipping arms to El Salvadorean rebels made Reagan's cold war perspective more persuasive to members of congress. Starting in 1981, Reagan gave the CIA $20 million to fund and train Somoza's National Guard and other mercenaries, basing them in Honduras, and later in Costa Rica. Despite their superior military technology and financial support, they were never able to secure a base for themselves in Nicaragua from which to create an alternative government. This was either because of rank incompetence (Dickey 1987) or it was a strategy to whittle away Nicaraguan support for the FSLN.[5] Calling themselves counterrevolutionaries or contras, their numbers grew to 15,000 at the most.[6] They practiced terrorism, committing murders to instill fear. In an effort to discourage people from working with the new government, the contras tried to torture and assassinate those who were connected with it: teachers, nurses, water engineers, Sandinista mayors, et cetera. However, there was not a high degree of discrimination involved, and many ordinary people died, sometimes in the most horrific ways. These abuses were made public and eventually resulted in Reagan losing congressional financial support. In 1984 and 1985, to continue to supply the contras with supplies, Reagan's administration sold military arms to Iran—which was illegal—and gave the money to the contras. When the Iran–Contra Affair was uncovered in 1986, it provoked a constitutional crisis in the US. It is also probable that the US State Department made connections with Colombian cocaine traffickers to facilitate the sale of drugs in the US, and then funneled part of the proceeds to the contras. In addition to sponsoring a terrorist war, the United States set mines in Nicaraguan harbors in order to stop exports, imposed an economic blockade on Nicaragua, and blocked the FSLN from obtaining loans from international financial institutions. By 1989, legitimate US funds going to the 15,000 contras totalled at least $400 million (there is considerable evidence which suggests that the real amount is higher).[7]

As the costs of the counterrevolutionary war began to mount in 1982, half of the nation's budget was devoted to the Nicaraguan military. After the American invasion of Grenada in 1983, the Nicaraguans assumed they would be next. While the contra war barely affected the US, it seemed to be a battle for basic survival for many Nicaraguans. The FSLN's commitment to social justice was badly affected. So was its commitment to dissent. Violeta Chamorro ran the opposition newspaper *La Prensa*, which was shut down or censored many times during the 1980s. The FSLN created and/or controlled the military, the police, the bureaucracy, the unions, and most of the media. In 1984, to undercut their domestic opponents and to answer mounting international criticism of its increasing control over Nicaraguan society, the FSLN called an election. Right-wing parties supported by the US refused to participate, although independent right-wing parties did. The FSLN won with 63 per cent of the vote. Importantly, 93 per cent of those eligible to vote registered, and voter turnout was 75 per cent. Women won an astonishing 20 per cent of the seats. The election was denounced as a fraud by the governments of the United States and Britain but was more positively viewed by the governments of Western Europe and many in Latin America. Canada, then being led by Progressive Conservative Prime Minister Brian Mulroney (1984–93), refused to comment, although the Canadian Department of External Affairs made Sandinista Nicaragua its single largest recipient of foreign aid. To the FSLN and the Nicaraguan populace, the FSLN's electoral success legitimated its actions.

The competitive, transparent election of 1984 shifted the organization of power in Nicaragua from participatory democracy within a one-party state to a representative democracy. Yet the FSLN had never adapted itself to representative politics by becoming a modern political party. Instead, it remained a tightly controlled hierarchy, with party membership granted by invitation only and with individuals appointed to key roles. In time, this alienated the general populace and grassroots organizations, most of which became fully democratic. The primacy of Sandinista popular organizations to speak for the people was replaced with elected representatives speaking for a constituency. Many popular organizations that had mobilized support for the FSLN saw their influence wane. By the end of the 1980s, some Sandinista organizations were pushing for autonomy from the party, while others withered. Because power relations were being redefined through changing government practices, it was simply unclear how civil society organizations should organize themselves, and by what reasoning. The struggle for an autonomous—if usually government-friendly civil society—dominated activists into the 1990s. "In general, the more independent the organizations were of Sandinista domination, the stronger they were" (Stansifer 1998, 129).[8]

Representative democracy was reinforced by the new 1986 constitution (promulgated in 1987). Like many things Sandinista, there was much about it to celebrate, and yet deep, structural problems remained. The constitution enshrined civil liberties and democratic procedures. It was constructed through extensive public consultations that educated the people about constitutions and their rights. Yet, even by Latin American standards, it concentrated power in the president and made it easy to gridlock the political process. Additionally, the constitution had no mechanisms for making amendments, and poorly defined the role for the supreme court. While the FSLN was in power, this was not an issue, as the national assembly and the supreme court were acquiescent to the national directorate.

By 1988, the Nicaraguan economy was in free fall. Although the majority of the land remained in private hands, and the wealthy had been given incentives to stay in Nicaragua and produce, output continued to plummet. The contra war destroyed approximately $50 million per annum in economic infrastructure (Hoyt 1997, 110), interrupted farming, and conscripted young men to fight. Because of the decline in mining and industry, and the loss of their primary market from the economic blockade, agriculture had an increasing share of the GDP. Yet the harvest per acre of farmed land declined, despite the government putting more untilled land to use. The FSLN subsidized food, transport, and utilities in addition to its state-owned companies. Supply bottlenecks rapidly emerged, and soon after, the rationing was implemented. The FSLN also borrowed to finance the contra war. By 1989, the national debt stood at $9.7 billion, four times the GDP, and inflation stood at 43,000 per cent (Ocampo 1991, 331, 361). The FSLN was forced to engage in some modest structural adjustment and monetarist policies. These included a devaluing of the currency, a freeze on government hiring, a reduction in state support for industries, and improved tax collection. These structural adjustment policies did not accomplish much, except to confuse supporters of the FSLN. Many of the social justice benefits that had been evident in the early 1980s were lost.

In 1988, Costa Rican President Oscar Arias and Guatemalan President Vicente Cerezo brokered the Esquipulas Peace Treaty (also known as the Arias Peace Plan and the Central American Peace Treaty). The region had been destabilized by the Nicaraguan civil war, the El Salvadorean civil war, and the Guatemalan civil war. Honduras, Panama, and Costa Rica had been drawn into the political turmoil. While the US had supported these economies, governments were concerned that there was a limit to American generosity, but no limit to warfare. The treaty, combined with the Iran–Contra Affair and a change of American presidents from Reagan to George Bush Senior (1988–92), reduced contra actions to low-intensity warfare. Even so, the contras were not fully disbanded until the mid-1990s. Over 30,000 Nicaraguans out of a population of 3 million died in the contra war.

As Nicaragua approached its 1990 election, the US forged an opposition party, the National United Opposition (UNO), led by Violeta Chamorro, a coalition that spanned the political spectrum from left to right, and had as its unifying goal the defeat of the FSLN. It also had Bush's promise that the US would end the economic blockade, bring peace, and spur economic development. The FSLN had little to offer the country except more of the same: poverty, American hostility, and low-intensity warfare. The FSLN did not even promise to end the hugely unpopular conscription. UNO won 55 per cent of the vote and the FSLN won 41 per cent.

MULTIPLE PACTS, 1990–2006

After the FSLN lost power, no single party was able to control the National Assembly until the FSLN regained power in 2006. This was partially because no one had thought that the FSLN would lose the election, and hence no thought had been given to what a non-Sandinista state might look like. Nor had anyone considered how the UNO might govern, given its contradictory ideologies and goals. Consequently, temporary pacts to solve short-term political or economic problems were negotiated between the elite of the FSLN and the elite of the other parties. In the process of creating these pacts, all parties lost members and alienated their constituents, natural allies, and international supporters. More problematic for Nicaraguan citizens was the state's inability to address the fundamental problem of the economy. Legislative politics in the national assembly frequently ground to a halt, civil liberties and democratic procedures were reduced, and democratic norms and institutions undermined. The high point of Nicaragua's democracy was now over.

It appeared that Violeta Chamorro was not much interested in running the country. Instead, she appointed her son-in-law, Antonio Lacayo, to a specially created position of deputy president and for the six years of her term, the real president of Nicaragua was Lacayo. However, Chamorro did perform an important function. As the wife of a murdered anti-Somoza journalist, an anti-Sandinista editor, and a member of the elite family split between the pro-FSLN and anti-FSLN camps, she was able to represent the tensions that divided many Nicaraguan families. With her, the societal polarization of the revolution and counterrevolution dissipated to a large degree, permitting a dialogue within civil society about how to move forward.

Chamorro's UNO coalition quickly fell apart. The FSLN was still the largest political party in the national assembly, with 39 of the 92 seats. In order to maintain power, the FSLN and some UNO members negotiated an elite pact to decide political and economic issues. The pact determined that the military and police remained under Sandinista command, with its budget controlled by the legislature. The FSLN kept civil unrest to a minimum so that the government could enact neoliberal structural adjustments. In exchange, Chamorro did not overturn the two laws passed while the FSLN was a lame duck government that legalized all land title distributed during the agrarian reform, including those properties that passed to top-ranking Sandinistas. These laws were called "La Piñata" because they transferred wealth immediately and legally to the FSLN elite. Instead, she made land title a legal issue for the courts to decide. This pact gave the new government some stability for a few years, and Nicaraguans some peace. Peeler (2004, 67) suggests that without this elite pact, Nicaragua could easily have slid back into civil war.

Nicaragua was also stabilized by massive foreign aid infusions between 1991 and 1994. Between 1990 and 1992, the US transferred $541 million to Nicaragua, and by 1994 Nicaragua had received more aid than any other country in the developing world (Robinson 1994, 242). The economy however continued to be volatile. Inflation was at 13,492 per cent, debt was $10 billion, or four times the GDP, underemployment and unemployment stood at 45 per cent (Ocampo 1991, 331; Arana 1997, 86). The structural adjustments were harsh. The public workforce and military were reduced and credit was tightened, hurting a disproportionate number of small- and medium-sized businesses and farmers. The financial sector was deregulated, nationally owned companies were privatized, and in 1994 the Labor Code was reformed to "flexibilize" labor. Social welfare spending was cut. Maternal mortality (a key development indicator) rose 59 per cent between 1993 and 1998. Illiteracy, malnutrition, and deaths from preventable disease rose. The rule of law weakened as judicial funding declined, and corruption influenced rulings. By 1996, unemployment and underemployment had risen to 70 per cent, despite an increase in coffee exports in 1994 and 1995. By 1994, inflation was reduced to 12 per cent, although debt continued to grow. In 1998, Nicaragua's total external debt as a percentage of GDP was 336 per cent, compared to 39 per cent for other Latin American nations. By 1999 only 400 of the 3,800 agricultural co-operatives that had existed in 1990 remained as new plantations owned by the elite emerged. Meanwhile, both ex-FSLN soldiers and ex-contras, unable to find employment or land to farm, rearmed and pillaged the countryside, occasionally kidnapping deputies or occupying towns, which then had to be retaken by the military. Civil society organizations and unions went on strike or refused to engage with the political system (Stahler-Sholk 1997, 91; Babb 1996, 43; Spalding 1994, 166–69). By 1996, there was macroeconomic stability, controlled inflation, and modest economic growth. Nonetheless, "the Chamorro administration's naïve and uncritical faith in market forces and its general disregard for market imperfections injected a bias which—by default, if not by design—favoured large businesses and strengthened the positions of monopolies, oligopolies, and the business elite of the government" (Arana 1997, 84).

Respected Sandinista party members criticized the FSLN pact with Chamorro. In a bid to silence these criticisms, the FSLN held its first election with secret ballots for the national directorate in 1994. Fearful of disunity and without a strong grasp of the fundamentals of democracy, members of the upper echelon of the FSLN requested a ban on competition between candidates. After the old guard was easily reelected, their losing opponents were purged from the party, judged as being guilty for having challenged the party's authority figures. Ortega used his newly won position to concentrate power around him, steadily becoming less of an elected politician and more of a *caudillo*. The FSLN national directorate did not understand that a democracy is inherently competitive, a system in which everyone wins a little, including the losers, who win a little less. Instead, they perceived it as a zero-sum game, in which those who won, won everything, and those who lost, lost absolutely. Appalled at the vindictiveness of the purging and the lack of democratic values in the party, many high-ranking members of the FSLN quit, including Ernesto Cardenal. In 1995, a splinter party of the FSLN was formed. It took "the vast majority of the intellectual and leadership talent out of the FSLN" (Booth, Wade, and Walker 2006, 89), although it never was able to gain grassroots support.

The pact between the Chamorro administration and the FSLN ended in 1994. Technically, the pact ended over reforming the 1986 constitution. The constitutional reforms increased the power of the legislature and decreased the power of the presidency. The most important reforms reduced the president's term in office from six years to five, made it illegal for family members to inherit office (so Lacayo was automatically disbarred from running for the presidency, which had clearly been his intent), removed the president's ability to tax and spend by decree, and created instruments to increase oversight and control of governmental institutions which included the military and police. It gave each branch of the government economic independence, redesigned the supreme court, and legalized private property. As a result, democratic institutions were better balanced. Chamorro refused to promulgate them. Without the constitutional reforms, there was no means to break the political gridlock. Before the constitutional reforms were passed in 1996, two constitutions operated at the same time. Both the right wing of her party and the FSLN regularly boycotted the national assembly in protest, and the government between 1993 and 1995 was frequently unable to call a quorum (although it passed legislation anyway). The political crisis was so profound that it was unclear whether or not democratic politics would survive. Thanks to substantial international diplomacy led by Norway, the Chamorro administration and the FSLN were persuaded to continue to cooperate. In effect, what every political actor did was prepare for the 1996 elections.

Heading the Constitutionalist Liberal Party (PLC) was the mayor of Managua, Arnoldo Alemán. As mayor, he used aid money to build public works such as fountains. These projects proved to be remarkably popular and he campaigned on them, suggesting that he, unlike the gridlocked national assembly, was able to get things done. In the 1996 elections, he won 51 per cent of the presidential vote, versus 38 per cent for Ortega. The PLC won 42 of 93 seats in the national assembly while the FSLN won only 36. The PLC also won many municipalities, including Managua. The election was marred by accusations of irregularities.

In October 1998, Hurricane Mitch killed over 4,000 people, caused over $1 billion in damage, and wiped out the season's crops only one week before harvest. The loss of aid money resulting from fraud politicized the issue of corruption. In 1998 the national auditor (also known as the comptroller general) discovered that while Alemán had been mayor of Managua, his personal fortune had increased by 900 per cent. The national auditor criticized, among other acts, the 1999 national budget, because 20 per cent was given to the president and central bank for confidential expenses. In 2000, the Stockholm Consultancy Group, a committee set up by foreign donors and NGOs to help with the post-hurricane reconstruction, placed a moratorium on new aid because of widespread government corruption. In an impoverished nation reeling from the devastation of Hurricane Mitch, corruption became the primary political issue. Grassroots organizations mobilized against Alemán. Alemán's corruption alienated American support, and split the right. In 2000, Nicaraguans held their first municipal elections, and the FSLN swept the key cities with their track record of social justice and minimal corruption.

Economically, Alemán continued with Chamorro's neoliberal policies but augmented them by aggressively paying off the debt. Neoliberal policies included further reductions in export tariffs, and tax incentives to spur manufacturing for the export market, along with tourism and direct foreign investment. Banking was privatized, but several of these privatizations involved corruption, and those banks ultimately had to declare insolvency. Nicaragua's debt devoured 14 per cent of the country's GDP, while the rest of Latin America used only 7 per cent. "It is unlikely that any country can achieve sustainable economic growth while devoting so many resources to the service of their external debt" (Esquivel and Sachs 2001, 6). In December 2000, Nicaragua obtained 60 per cent debt forgiveness through the Highly Indebted Poor Countries Initiative (HIPC).

While the right was splitting up because of accusations of corruption, the FSLN was becoming increasingly divided. In 1998, Ortega's stepdaughter, Zoilamérica Narváez, accused Ortega of sexually abusing her when she was between the ages of 11 and 30. Ortega denied her accusations, but invoked parliamentary immunity to avoid criminal prosecution. His wife, Rosario Murillo who was Narváez's mother, supported Ortega and publicly turned on her daughter. Murillo's support increased her power and profile within the hierarchical and Ortega-controlled FSLN. Those Sandinistas who supported Narváez's demand for legal recourse were removed from positions of authority. Alemán, calling the issue "private," refused to make political gains from it. The success of the FSLN in winning the majority of the provinces and taking major cities in the 2000 municipal elections was widely interpreted as being a vindication of Ortega and of patriarchy.[9]

In 1999, after more than a year of negotiations, Ortega and Alemán agreed to again reform the constitution and electoral laws. The reforms came into effect after the 2001 election. Called "El Pacto," they weakened democratic institutions and governance by distributing key posts along partisan lines. The FSLN and the PLC could appoint their own people to the supreme court, the election oversight agency, and the National Auditor's Office. El Pacto also institutionalized a two-party system by making it more difficult for smaller parties to obtain legal standing. The National Auditor's powers were so substantially reduced that Nicaragua became one of the top ten locations for money laundering in the world (Chong and López 2005; IADB 2005, 243). Ex-presidents were given immunity for life from all criminal charges, freeing Ortega of concerns that he could face prosecution from his stepdaughter, and freeing Alemán from charges of corruption. Through weakening oversight mechanisms, horizontal and vertical accountability became harder to enforce. By concentrating power in two parties, the ability of the political system to respond in new ways and promote new political actors was diminished. By manipulating democratic procedures and making their power grab explicit, Ortega and Alemán ensured that any democratic ethos underlying governance was effectively abandoned. El Pacto also lowered the limit of popular vote needed to gain the presidency from 45 per cent to 35 per cent. It had become evident through polling and elections that approximately one-third of the population of Nicaragua would vote for the FSLN no matter what. It was equally evident that approximately half of the population would never vote for Ortega, under any circumstances. By lowering the threshold needed to secure the presidency, El Pacto offered Ortega the possibility of regaining power. Members from both the FSLN and the PLC criticized El Pacto, and some resigned in protest. Both parties continued to build support through clientelism. Despite the support given to the FSLN, the vast majority of Nicaraguan citizens did not think that El Pacto served democracy well (Close 2004; Nevitte, Cruz, and Estok 2007, 5).

In the 2001 presidential and legislative election, the PLC made Alemán's vice president, Enrique Bolaños, their candidate for president. He won the election with 56 per cent of the vote; Ortega received 42 per cent. In the national congress, the PLC won a small majority of 47 seats, versus 42 for the FSLN. When Bolaños took power, he was regarded as relatively weak because many PLC representatives owed their loyalty to Alemán, who was elected president of the national assembly. There were overt statements from Alemán himself that he intended to continue to govern through Bolaños.

Bolaños proved cannier than anyone expected. He adroitly used mass civil society protests against corruption (employing Transparency International's 2002 report on corruption in Nicaragua), and support from the US and the OAS to strip Alemán of his immunity. Alemán and 13 of his top governmental supporters were charged with embezzling, defrauding, stealing, and money laundering of up to $10 million.[10] Alemán was found guilty of these charges in 2003 and was sentenced to 20 years in jail. In protest, pro-Alemán supporters created a splinter right-wing party. Alemán used his connections with the FSLN to get parts of his sentence overturned on appeal, and the rest of the sentence commuted to house arrest. After Ortega regained power in 2006, the FSLN-controlled Nicaraguan supreme court overturned the sentence. However, Bolaños effectively removed a powerful *caudillo* and placed him under the control of the FSLN, further splitting the right.

In October 2005, the national assembly approved the Dominican Republic-Central American Free Trade Agreement (DR-CAFTA) to safeguard Nicaraguan exports from its export processing zones or *maquilas*. The FSLN voted against it. Up to 80 per cent of the population was dependent on agriculture, and it was the majority of its exports, yet agriculture suffered from declining terms of trade. Furthermore, since 1990, the liberalized economy had had a marked increase in imports and foreign services, leaving it with persistent trade and current account deficits. It was unlikely that DR-CAFTA would alter that economic reality. Bolaños obtained $4.5 billion in debt forgiveness from the World Bank and the IMF in 2004, and $700–$900 million from the IADB in 2006. He maintained macroeconomic stability with low inflation. However, economic performance was slow, increasing at only 3 per cent–4 per cent per annum from 1999 to 2006, with a high birth rate (over 3 per cent) so per capita income declined. Despite peace and the support from international financial institutions (IFIs) and the US, the right-wing governments of Chamorro, Alemán, and Bolaños have produced the second poorest country in Latin America after Haiti. Despite conditional cash transfers (begun in 1999) and remittances, the UN Human Development Report of 2003 reported that Nicaragua had the highest per cent of people living below the poverty line in Latin America. Approximately 82 per cent lived on less than $1 a day, and 92 per cent on less than $2 a day.

To remove Sandinista control over the judiciary and other state institutions, in 2004 Bolaños attempted to reform the constitution. To do this, he needed support from disaffected members of both the FSLN and PLC.

The national assembly, seeing an opportunity to increase its power, ratified constitutional changes in 2005 which increased the power of the legislature at the expense of the presidency. These changes made the judiciary autonomous, and removed presidential control over utilities by making them semiautonomous. Bolaños protested these changes, despite the fact that the Nicaraguan supreme court approved them. Bolaños used the police to stop executives of the utilities from entering their workplaces. Another political crisis emerged as the legislature pushed for impeachment, and Bolaños had several ministers critical of him arrested for corruption. As crises compounded over fiscal deficits, corruption, control of the legislature, and control of political parties, Nicaragua's political elite seemed barely in control of the state. Although Chamorro had professionalized and depersonalized the military, the commander in chief of the Nicaraguan army, Omar Halleslevens, gave this pointed warning, "Sometimes a country has political crises in the lower levels or on the first floor. Nicaragua's political crises have been making their way up the building and are now on the fifth floor or in the attic. The differing elements of political life must realize this and get their feet back on the ground" (Envío 2005). The crises were repoliticizing the military, and the US and OAS had to aggressively intervene to ensure that the Bolaños government was able to complete its last year in office.

The recurring political crises from 1990 to the 2006 election were intra-elite struggles for control for power. As a result, there was little to no governing. Due to the diplomatic interventions of the US, some European nations, and the OAS, in addition to their own experience with the futility of war, all the elite eschewed violent conflict. The battle split the right and the left, producing a four-way conflict. The struggle was between the Somoza elite (such as Alemán), who acted as if the state were a personal asset and democracy merely a fig leaf for authoritarianism (that is, bureaucratic patrimonialism), and the old elite (such as Chamorro and Bolaños), who preferred a more modernized economy. The Somoza elite was the weaker group. It could not defend itself in the new globalized political arena. On the left, there were the members of the new Sandinista elite who had benefited from their years in power and who attempted to maintain that position of privilege regardless of its legality. Paradoxically, the Sandinista splinter party did not weaken the FSLN because it allowed Ortega to reshape the party with less protest, turning it into his personal vehicle for self-enrichment and power. Opposing all of them were other members of the FSLN and political actors who worked to deepen democracy and equality, many through NGOs granting them some financial autonomy and international legitimacy. This four-way struggle does not accurately capture the considerable confusion of the political situation, as individuals changed sides, ideology played second to expediency, alliances formed or were broken, and key issues such as DR-CAFTA, child abuse, and constitutional reform distracted everyone, every organization, and every state institution.

The 16-year struggle reflected the primary importance in politics of organizing and uniting disparate aspects of the state, manipulating democratic structures, disciplining political parties, forging ad hoc pacts, as well as creating alliances and generating support from NGOs, the US government, and multinational institutions. In other words, those who were best at politics (not necessarily democratic politics) were better able to obtain power. In the process, the new values that underpinned the Nicaraguan governing system became clear. Political parties became fairly meaningless vehicles for stabilizing and deepening democratic politics, and instead became vehicles for clientelism and *caudillismo*. Political leaders used populist gestures to gain power, and then patrimonialism to distribute state goods. Civil society was not used democratically but instead was attacked by Alemán, ignored by Bolaños, and manipulated by the FSLN. Free speech and critical civil society organizations were legislatively curtailed and over-regulated. Those who embraced globalized power relations were more successful leaders, Bolaños in particular (Robinson 2003). The FSLN remained the power broker throughout this period because they were better able to maintain internal cohesiveness and a connection to the grassroots than their opponents, and they were willing to embrace neoliberalism.

Going into the November 2006 election, citizen confidence in key governmental institutions (political parties, the national assembly, the office of the president, and the electoral oversight agency) was low, with high levels of political cynicism (Nevitte, Cruz, and Estok 2007, 11, 21). Ortega refashioned himself as a neo-populist leader. Neopopulism is the result of the failure of state-led development and governance. Neopopulist leaders obtain power by appealing to the informal poor, and with their endorsement of neoliberalism, to the elite as well. Neopopulist governments are characterized by an anti-institutional bias, a weak party system, and a concentration of power in the executive (Cammack 2000). Ortega portrayed representative democracy during the period the FSLN was out of power (1990–2006) as a system that stole people's livelihood, and promised the return of participatory democracy.

To maintain support from the right, Ortega endorsed private property, and appointed Jaime Morales Carazo, a former contra leader, as his vice presidential running mate. More controversially, Ortega found God and remarried his wife in a church. In 2006, he supported and signed a law banning all abortions, including those to save a woman's life. Doctors who performed abortions could be criminally charged and ex-communicated. As a result, Ortega received the cautious endorsement of Cardinal Miguel

Obando y Bravo, the conservative and highly influential Catholic leader. The movement which emphasized Ortega as a man, rather than the FSLN's platforms, has been called Danielismo, as opposed to Sandinismo. Ortega's supporters became Danielistas instead of Sandinistas. The right fielded two parties, the PLC and a right-wing alliance, led by Eduardo Montealegre, the National Liberal Alliance (ALN). Montealegre had criticized El Pacto, and split from the PLC due to Alemán's continuing control of the PLC from inside jail. The US government endorsed Montealegre, and unwisely reminded voters of Ortega's communist past. According to a long-time analyst of Nicaraguan politics, this played into Ortega's populist rhetoric of equality and resistance, and further allowed Ortega to publicly align himself with Venezuela's anti-American and generous president, Hugo Chávez, who promised free energy supplies and medical support should Ortega win the election (Dixon 2006, 6). Abortion and poverty were the dominant issues during the election.

Ortega won with 39 per cent of the vote in 2006, with the FSLN winning 38 of the 92 deputies in the national assembly. Montealegre won 29 per cent of the vote, with 22 seats for the ALN. The PLC gained 25 seats, the splinter FSLN party gained 5, and an independent party won 1 seat. Voter turn-out was about 80 per cent of the electorate. A substantial part of the population who did not vote lacked the appropriate identification cards, which was required by a newly issued electoral ruling.

FSLN: THE NEOPOPULIST VERSION, 2006–

Reforging the state to enhance citizen participation started soon after the inauguration. An interparty committee was set up in 2007 to reform the constitution to create a participatory democracy. Local councils composed of people from grassroots organizations, places of work, schools, and neighborhoods were created to implement local policies. Thus, civil society became linked to the state. By 2008, it is estimated that there were more than 1 million people involved with 20,000 local councils. These councils elected 272 representatives to a newly created National Cabinet of Citizen Power (CPC) presided over by the president's wife, Murillo. Also on this board were appointed representatives of national groups such as women, youth, and children. The CPC was controlled by the government and subject to presidential decrees and guidelines. It was not autonomous from the state, political parties, or political leaders. The powers of the CPC expanded in 2007 to be an oversight mechanism of government officials, agencies, and departments, including state services such as healthcare and education. CPC's partisan control ensured that oversight would be political. This enhances the FSLN's control over the bureaucracy. Acting through the CPC, the state distributed subsidized beans and rice to poor neighborhoods, replacing the CCT program which was suspended in 2007. This food distribution program politicized poverty reduction by collapsing it into a political party distributing largesse in the name of the people. This was *caudillismo* refracted through a lens of participatory democracy. By the end of 2007, the CPC was constitutionalized by presidential decree, ensuring that the ability to reform this organization of state–civil society relations would be more difficult. "Thus the CPC looks like a parallel government centred in the office of the president" (Close 2009, 119).

Complaints against the new government were dealt with in a non-democratic fashion. Mob violence against dissenters and their organizations has emerged. Civil society organizations that refused to participate in the CPC have been investigated by the state. These autonomous civil society organizations and NGOs have had their offices broken into, their computers stolen, their members threatened and even beaten. Human rights organizations and the women's movement have been particularly harassed. Possibly these two groups have been targeted because they have united against the anti-abortion law. The Nicaraguan government has not released figures on the number of women who have died because they were denied therapeutic abortions. The illegality of abortions means that death from backstreet abortions also goes unreported. Citing her own sources, Sofia Montenegro, a leading intellectual, activist, and feminist, estimated that 110 women died in the first 18 months after the law came into effect (Inter Press Service News Agency 2008). In 2008, the famous ex-Sandinista journalist Fernando Chamorro and other critics of Ortega's government were arrested on spurious legal charges and released only after an international outcry. Ernesto Cardenal was charged soon after. "Ortega is using bogus lawsuits and is tightening control over the government bureaucracy to harass, marginalize, and discredit political opponents" (Simon 2009, 34).

The extent to which the FSLN controls the political sphere was brought into high relief during the municipal elections of November 2008. With decentralization, mayoralties have become powerful centers for the politically ambitious. Because they lack the oversight, both domestic and international, that national governments ensure, mayoralties are a means to create clientelistic relations. The FLSN rejected international observers for the 146 municipal elections. There were conflicting reports of wins and losses. The US State Department reported widespread irregularities. Montealegre ran for mayor of Managua. The supreme electoral council gave the FSLN candidate a 5 per cent greater win over Montealegre, with the FSLN winning 105 mayoralties and the ALN 37. Those who lost the municipal elections are said to be uniting against the FSLN, fomenting civil unrest, and attracting international support. It appears as if the FSLN was unprepared for an organized and united response to electoral fraud.

Neopopulist leaders are dependent to a large degree on the economy. The GDP annual growth rate had shrunk from 3.9 per cent in 2006 to 3.0 per cent in 2008, with per capita GDP shrinking from 2.5 per cent in 2006 to 1.7 per cent in 2008. Inflation is rising, although it is still within manageable levels, and the current deficit is still growing. Venezuela's economic cooperation with Nicaragua, estimated to be worth hundreds of millions of dollars, has never been disclosed. In 2009, Chávez announced that the two oil refineries he had promised, one in Ecuador and one in Nicaragua, would not be honored. It is unclear if Chávez can meet his other promises of support. With an economic contraction, declining remittances, lower prices for its exports, and cutbacks in foreign aid over fears of corruption, the Nicaraguan state will be seriously hampered in its ability to maintain its promises to its citizens. This will affect the persuasiveness of Ortega's neopopulism and its political viability (ECLAC 2009, 119).

Nonetheless, the FSLN and PLC are working together on more constitutional reforms to change the system of governing to a two-party parliamentary system with a reelected head of state and prime minister chosen from elected representatives. It is assumed that Ortega and Alemán will share or alternate presidency and prime ministership, tightening their control over the organization of power.

CONCLUSION

The 1979 Revolution ushered in a socialist participatory democracy. The roots of the revolution lay in the unequal distribution of wealth and power in Nicaragua, the intra-elite struggle for power, and the overt intervention of the US. This political pattern continues to this day.

Regardless of what one thinks of the FSLN now, it is undeniable that in the 1980s many elements of democracy were in place: the rule of law, clean elections, social and economic equality, civil liberties, democratic procedures, a strengthened bureaucracy, a strong civil society, a democratic ethos, and a state with capacity. While not all elements were fully implemented, and while not conforming to an ideal description of either representative democracy or participatory democracy, the system as a whole was able to engage with criticisms and reform itself during a time of war and economic devastation. Sadly, this was the most responsive, fair, and capable political system that the Nicaraguans have ever experienced. After the war ended and the FSLN was voted out of power, the political system has steadily been reformed, by democratic means, to make it less democratic. Elite pacts, always problematic, solved short-term problems but did not grant long-term stability. Instead, these pacts reconsolidated and renovated the elite, who now include ex-Marxists, committed supporters of Sandinismo liberation, and unrepentant Somocistas. United in the pursuit of power, elite pacts undermined any democratic or social justice ethos that might have protected democratic procedures and institutions. Civil society has been ignored or, mostly recently, co-opted through renovated, informal institutions. Neoliberalism stabilized the economy, but was unable to alleviate widespread poverty or the unequal distribution of income.

Since 1977, the right has been split between modernizing itself and traditional, oligarchic *caudillismo*. It has been unable to coalesce around a coherent strategy or individual. In comparison, the left has also been split, but the FSLN has consistently reinvented itself and coalesced power around Ortega, who has become a neopopulist leader. Since 1977, the FSLN has been the only disciplined party with widespread grassroots support and a clear message about social equality and economic development. The FSLN's superior organizing skills and strategic pacts meant that it was the dominant political actor even while out of power and was able to regain power in 2006. Since then, the FSLN has increasingly controlled both the state and civil society through a non-elected, non-accountable, non-transparent parallel government. This context of poverty, undemocratic political structures, controlled civil society, and neopopulism does not bode well for Nicaraguans.

NOTES

1 Plans and international negotiation continue to this day about building a transportation conduit between the Atlantic and Pacific. However, recent concerns over government corruption have temporarily put a stop to any projects.

2 In 2002 the name was officially changed to Graytown.

3 The most famous book was one by Cabezas (1985).

4 See Isbester (2001) in chapter 2 and the references below for an example.

5 Between 1993 and 1995 while doing field research, I interviewed a number of former contras who understandably supported the latter explanation of the contras' strategy. There was an emphatic consensus that by 1983–84, the contras were not attempting to gain control over territory. There was a further consensus that this strategy was CIA-driven and unnecessary, because they could have been more successful if they had been permitted to be.

6 After peace was negotiated in 1988, the contras recruited heavily and raised their numbers to 20,000. It is unclear whether this is because they expected a large payout from the US to demobilize and thus were easily able to attract recruits or whether they perceived peace as a strategy to regroup and expand.

7 The most detailed report on US illegal funding to the contras was made by the Tower Commission in 1994.

8 Brown (2003) offers a more charitable analysis of this period.
9 The women's rights community tried to use Narváez's accusations to show how artificial the separation of public and private was, and how patriarchy in the private sphere translated into autocracy in the public sphere. The issue of child abuse has been a dominant social issue since Narváez went public. According to private conversations that I have had with feminist scholars and activists in Nicaragua, it appears that the forces of patriarchy have won this battle.
10 By its very nature, money laundering is hard to track. Alemán is still wanted in Panama for allegedly using 60 bank accounts to launder a further $57 million in embezzled funds, and he is wanted in Miami to face a civil trial for allegedly buying bank certificates with embezzled funds. It has been estimated that he has stolen up to $100 million.

REFERENCES

Arana, Mario. 1997. "General Economic Policy," *Nicaragua without Illusions: Regime Transition and Structural Adjustment in the 1990s*. Ed. Thomas W. Walker. Wilmington, VA: Scholarly Resources Books. 81–96.

Babb, Florence. 1996. "After the Revolution: Neo-Liberal Policy and Gender in Nicaragua." *Latin American Perspectives* 23(1): 27–48.

Black, George. 1981. *Triumph of the People: The Sandinista Revolution in Nicaragua*. London: Zed Books.

Booth, John A., Christine J. Wade, and Thomas W. Walker. 2006. *Understanding Central America: Global Forces, Rebellion and Change*. 4th ed. Boulder: Westview Press.

Booth, John A., and Thomas W. Walker. 1993. *Understanding Central America*. 2nd ed. Boulder: Westview Press.

Brown, David. 2003. "The Sandinista Legacy in Nicaragua." *Latin American Perspectives* 30(3): 106–12.

Burns, Bradford E. 1987. *At War in Nicaragua: The Reagan Doctrine and the Politics of Nostalgia*. New York: Harper Row.

Cabezas, Omar. 1985. *Fire from the Mountains: The Making of a Sandinista*. Translated by Kathleen Weaver. New York: Crown Publishers.

Cammack, Paul. 2000. "The Resurgence of Populism in Latin America." *Bulletin of Latin American Research* 19(2): 149–61.

Chong, Alberto, and Florencio López. 2005. "El Lavado de Dinero en América Latina, ¿Qué Sabemos de Él?" In IPES Desencadenar el crédito, cómo ampliar y establizar la banca. Washington, DC: Interamerican Development Bank.

Close, David. 2004. "Undoing Democracy in Nicaragua." *Undoing Democracy: The Politics of Electoral Caudillismo*. Ed. David Close and Kalowatie Deonandan. Oxford: Lexington Press. 1–16.

———. 2009. "Nicaragua: The Return of Daniel Ortega." *Reclaiming Latin America: Experiments in Radical Democracy*. Ed. Geraldine Lievesley and Steve Ludlam. London: Zed Books. 109–22.

Dickey, Christopher. 1987. *With the Contra: A Reporter in the Wilds of Nicaragua*. New York: Simon and Schuster.

Dixon, Helen. 2006. "Women's Rights at Stake in Nicaraguan Elections." *A-Genda: Gender and Trade in Central America*. December: 6–8.

Dunkerley, James. 1988. *Power in the Isthmus: A Political History of Modern Central America*. London: Verso Books.

Economic Commission on Latin America and the Caribbean. 2009. *Preliminary Overview of the Economies of Latin America and the Caribbean 2008*. New York: ECLAC.

Envío. 2005. "A Divided, Divvied Up and Directionless Country," no. 287 (June). June 10, 2010. www.envio.org/ni/articulo/2970.

Esquivel, Felipe Larraín, and Jeffry D. Sachs. 2001. "Central America's Foreign Debt Burden and the HIPC Initiative." *Bulletin of Latin American Research* 20(1): 1–28.

Hoyt, Katherine. 1997. *The Many Faces of Sandinista Democracy*. Athens: University of Ohio Press.

Interamerican Development Bank. 2005. *Money Laundering: What Do We Know?* New York: IADB.

Inter Press Service New Agency. 2008. "The Women's Movement is in Opposition: Interview with Sofia Montenegro for the Nicaraguan Autonomous Women's Movement" (August 9, 2008). July 10, 2010. www.awid.org/eng/Issues-and-Analysis/Library/The-Women-s-Movement-Is-In-Opposition-Interview-With-Sofia-Montenegro.

Isbester, Katherine. 2001. *Still Fighting: The Nicaraguan Women's Movement, 1977–2000*. Pittsburgh: Pittsburgh University Press.

Kinzer, Stephen. 2008. "Contra Hero to Despot," *Los Angeles Times* September 3, 2008, A21.

Lacey, Marc. 2008. "Sandinista Fervor Turns Sour for Former Comrades of Nicaragua's President," *New York Times* November 23, 2008, A6.

Millet, Richard. 1977. *Guardians of a Dynasty*. Maryknoll, NY: Orbis Books.

Nevitte, Neil, José Cruz, and Melissa Estok. 2007. *Nicaraguan Democracy Survey 2007*. Guatemala City: National Democratic Institute for International Affairs and FLACSO.

Ocampo, Jose Nation. 1991. "Collapse and (Incomplete) Stabilization of the Nicaraguan Economy." *The MacroEconomics of Populism in Latin America*. Ed. Roger Dornbush and Sebastian Edwards. Chicago: University of Chicago Press. 331–68.

Peeler, John. 2004. *Building Democracy in Latin America*. 2nd ed. Boulder: Lynne Rienner Press.

Robinson, William I. 1994. *Promoting Patriarchy: Globalization, U.S. Intervention, and Hegemony*. Cambridge: Cambridge University Press.

——. 2003. *Transnational Conflict: Central America, Social Change and Globalization*. London: Verso Books.

Simon, Joel. 2009. "'Dictatorial Designs' in Nicaragua." *New York Review of Books*, January 15–February 11: 34.

Spalding, Rose. 1994. *Capitalists and Revolution in Nicaragua: Opposition and Accommodation 1979–1993*. Chapel Hill: University of North Carolina Press.

Stahler-Sholk, Richard. 1997. "Structural Adjustment and Resistance: The Political Economy of Nicaragua under Chamorro." *The Undermining of the Sandinista Revolution*. Ed. Gary Prevost and Harry E. Vanden. New York: St. Martin's Press. 74–113.

Stansifer, Charles L. 1998. "Elections and Democracy in Central America: The Cases of Costa Rica and Nicaragua." *Assessing Democracy in Latin America*. Ed. Philip Kelly. Boulder: Westview Press. 117–35.

E-RESOURCES

Confidencial (www.confidencial.com.ni). A Spanish-language newspaper edited by Fernando Chamorro, Nicaragua's leading dissident.

El Centro Humboldt (www.humboldt.org.ni). An environmental NGO that offers extensive information about Nicaragua.

El Observador Económico (www.elobservadoreconomico.com). A Spanish-language business newspaper and website.

Envío (www.envio.org.ni). An English-and-Spanish progressive magazine that appears monthly and is funded by the Jesuits.

Instituto para el Desarrollo y la Democracia (www.ipade.org.ni). An NGO devoted to promoting democracy especially among the indigenous peoples of Nicaragua, the Rama, the Suma, and the Miskito.

Nicanet (www.nicanet.org). An English website that discusses Nicaraguan politics. It is occasionally written in Spanish.

SEVEN

Costa Rica:
An Ethos and a Strong State

KATHERINE ISBESTER

Throughout the 1990s, there were a growing number of protests against neoliberalism in Costa Rica, particularly against the privatization of state agencies. As more and more people turned out for protests, attendance records were regularly broken. This famously peaceful and democratic nation was acting out of character. In 2003, the government of Costa Rica conducted negotiations with the US government over a bilateral preferential free trade agreement, the Dominican Republic-Central American Free Trade Agreement (DR-CAFTA).[1] This agreement would assist Costa Rican industries in competing against the imports of other countries to the US market (notably those from China), and consolidate its American market. As a result, DR-CAFTA would, in theory, increase direct foreign investment (DFI) and support non-traditional exports. The Costa Rican government negotiated 11 special dispensations—substantially more than any other Central American nation received—protecting Costa Rican agriculture and services. All the major parties of both the right and the left in the country broadly endorsed DR-CAFTA. However, the trade agreement also included the privatization of Costa Rican monopolistic agencies, such as telecommunications, social services, and electricity, all of which ran efficiently, cheaply, and profitably, and which paid for other state services that ran at a loss. It also locked in a neoliberal state, which ran contrary to Costa Rica's history of being a social justice democracy. Finally, criticism from respected economists and case studies of the detrimental effects preferential free trade agreements have had in other countries increased the apprehensions many felt about DR-CAFTA. It didn't help that previous privatizations of other state agencies had mired several past presidents in corruption charges, jaundicing the populace against the benefits of privatization. Street protests, constitutional impasses, and threatened strikes temporarily halted DR-CAFTA. While the elite and the government in Costa Rica supported DR-CAFTA, the Costa Rican citizenry did not. With social tensions rising, the government announced a referendum would be held in October 2007 over DR-CAFTA, the first referendum in Costa Rica's history. The agreement passed, with a narrow majority. The schism over how to organize the economy has roiled Costa Rica since the 1980s, because many citizens are increasingly discontent with their democracy, yet there are no new leaders with new ideas.

Costa Rica, with its quality democracy, is such an exception to the rest of Latin America that there are those who think its successes cannot be replicated elsewhere. It is possible to look at the history of Costa Rica and find evidence that Costa Rica's uniqueness is due solely to an accident of history. It follows that few lessons from Costa Rica can be applied to the rest of Latin America without first disregarding their own 500 years of history. But history is the study of past politics. And politics present people with choices within a context of constraints and opportunities. Throughout Costa Rican history, its people and its leaders have chosen to compromise and accommodate discontent, and have slowly built social services and a responsive government based on a belief in social justice. The state grew strong by negotiating between the classes, and engaging in socioeconomic development. It then used its strength when negotiating with powerful external forces, such as transnational corporations and free trade agreements, and as a result was able to incorporate the best aspects of globalization while protecting its citizens from the worst. The result is an economically robust, deep democracy in the middle of a war-torn, economically underdeveloped isthmus.

THE LIBERAL REPUBLIC, 1820S TO 1948

From the beginning, Costa Rica had a fortuitous balance of resources (land), population, and political self-determination. There were few indigenous people when the Spanish arrived, and the indigenous who were present suffered many losses from disease. Costa Rica did not have gold, silver, or other natural resources that the Spanish valued. Without mining or extensive pasture lands, there was no need to import slave laborers. Without resources, there were few Spanish colonizers. As a result, Costa Rica was sparsely populated, with most people of European descent and practicing

Catholics. Subsistence-level farming was widespread, with the Costa Rican elite performing the manual labor or running their own shops. In addition, the population was isolated on the central plateau, physically cut off from the Atlantic and Pacific Oceans and their trade routes, and from their northern and southern neighbors and their potential trade. So Costa Rica suffered from benign neglect during the Spanish colonization, which reduced Spanish influence. It was short on laborers, relatively impoverished, and had a homogenous population.

After Costa Rica declared its independence, it fulfilled many of the stereotypes of other Latin nations. Between 1824 and 1899, the military ruled almost half of the time, and one in five governments ended with a coup d'état. Regardless of who was in power, it was always an elite rule. The dominance of elite rule is true to this day. Nevertheless, because of the combination of land and population, social and economic equality were promoted for economic development. Unfarmed land was abundant, and the first dictator-president, Braulio Carrillo Colina (1835–37; 1838–42), divided up municipal land to farmers to create smallholdings. The number of small farms increased through the tilling of virgin land and the gradual privatization of church lands or communal property. The slow pace and the easy access to land allowed citizens to avoid class conflict or intra-elite conflict. These small farms were encouraged to be export-oriented. Coffee was a natural crop: it was easy to transport to the coast, slow to spoil, and the country faced little competition in its production. By 1829, coffee exports had overtaken cacao, tobacco, and sugar, increasing its export markets throughout the 1830s and entering into British and European markets in the 1840s. The distribution of profits and the size of the farms were more equitable than those in countries that started exporting coffee later or had larger farms. Because of the minimal profits from the farms, the elite was also involved in the processing of export crops or other commercial activities. From the beginning, therefore, there was no need for a coercive state to dispossess the indigenous of their land and then engage in repressive labor policies to produce export goods. Instead, the rural agrarian class consisted of numerous small landholders who had a degree of equality, with laborers receiving a relatively good wage due to the high demand for them, and the elite operating in diverse sectors of the economy.

From 1870 to 1882, dictator-president Tomás Guardia Gutiérrez modernized aspects of Costa Rica's economy and society. To safeguard himself, Guardia limited the constitutional use of the military, hindering the legality and hence the legitimacy of military-backed coup d'états. He also exiled some members of the elite, weakening elite opposition. The Catholic Church was already a comparatively weak force, mitigating liberal–conservative tensions. Without a powerful and organized elite opposition based in a moral authority like the Church, the political opposition party struggled to become potent. The lack of ideologically driven political fissures and their own common interests facilitated compromise between the elite groups and permitted peaceful conflict resolution within the political process. This led to the emergence of a generally modernizing Liberal Party and a generally opposing (yet still modernizing) opposition party, both of which were loosely organized coalitions built around a *patrón* or *caudillo*. Coffee exports allowed the Costa Rican economic elite and state to maintain a degree of autonomy from foreign capital, an unusual situation for a small, poor nation.

Guardia improved the infrastructure of the country, in particular the roads from the central plateau to the Atlantic coast. He also negotiated a deal with the United Fruit Company, the highly influential American company, to build a railroad from the central plateau to the Atlantic coast to facilitate exports. Because the state was stable and united, it was able to insist that the United Fruit Company fulfill its contract, which it had not done in Honduras. The company planted banana plantations on the Caribbean coast to fund the building of the railroad, altering the ethnic makeup of Costa Rica. Due to a banana disease and the lack of huge tracts of land, the United Fruit Company never acquired the dominance in Costa Rica that it had in other Central American nations. Nonetheless, bananas became the second most important export after coffee, and remained as such until the middle of the twentieth century.

A government-run literacy program helped to slowly democratize the nation. Mauro Fernández, a reformer and the minister of finance, education and commerce, initiated free public education for both boys and girls in 1885. The illiteracy rate stood at 90 per cent when the program began and, by the time he died in 1905, it had dropped to 40 per cent. Because education was one of the prerequisites to voting, literacy expanded the electoral franchise in a gradual and acceptable way. Education had the unanticipated effect of forging a new national approach to the ideas of citizenship, nationhood, and rights. It also gave the state and the economy knowledgeable workers, which improved efficiency and productivity.

In the 1880s, with increasing demand for labor for the new banana plantations and expanding coffee farms, there were fears that the white European ethnicity of Costa Rica would be diluted. Black and Chinese laborers imported to work on the banana plantations were forbidden to leave the region or travel to the central plateau. In an effort to reduce the need to import labor, the good health and longevity of the existing white workers was supported and improved through a public healthcare program. With public healthcare and education, and assisted by the ethnic homogeneity and physical proximity of differing classes to each other and to the institutions of the state, a concept of national unity and inclusiveness emerged. This contributed to trust and tolerance between classes, although that trust did not extend to the visible minorities living on the coasts. The electoral franchise slowly increased in the early years of the twentieth century. There were new rules to the game of democracy, and these new rules were established *before* the people in the process of being educated were able to take advantage of them. The slowly expanding franchise became the norm, but did not threaten to immediately alter elite control over government or the balance of power between the classes. This kept the conflict between the classes to a minimum.

There were democratic experiments and constitution-writing until 1889, when Costa Rica had its first fraud-free election and the opposition won power. But electoral competition was restricted to the literate (at that time, only 11 per cent of the population) and to property owners. Thus, the democracy in the last decade of the nineteenth century and the first few decades of the twentieth century must be seen as an organized, intra-elite constitutionalized competition to control the state for a defined period. Nonetheless, key democratic values were in place: popular and elite acceptance of a strong, centralized state, elite acceptance of increasingly autonomous and state-resourced political parties, and political rights and freedoms.

With the global depression of the 1930s and a resulting drop in the prices of Costa Rica's exports, the economy was put under enormous stress. The standard of living for the agricultural workers fell. Led by the newly formed Communist Party Union, labor organization increased, particularly on the banana plantations. The banana plantations were further affected by disease, causing the collapse of the plantations on the Atlantic coast. The price of coffee in 1935 was half of what it was in 1929, and it fell even further. There were 15 per cent wage cuts in public sector salaries. The average annual growth of the GDP between 1930 and 1934 was 0 per cent. The small coffee farmers organized themselves into the National Association of Coffee Producers, and demanded a floor on the price of coffee. Working through town hall meetings, lobbying legislators, and publicizing their perspective in the newspapers, they were able to overcome the resistance of the coffee processors and the agro-export elite. In 1933, the state, the elite, and the small producers negotiated a compromise, the Coffee Pact. This pact allowed the state to regulate the price of coffee and to create a system of arbitration between the coffee growers and the commercial processors. It also led to the development of coffee co-ops for production and credit. This had three major impacts on democratization. First, it strengthened and augmented the state as a mechanism for resolving conflict between the classes. Second, the Coffee Pact protected small producers from being driven into bankruptcy by larger producers, maintaining Costa Rica's balance between the classes. Third, it rewarded the small producers and unions for working through the democratic system (Dunkerley 1988, 91–103).

The advent of World War II did not improve Costa Rica's economic situation. Economic hardship continued with the Communist Party Union gaining adherents and political influence. In 1940, the coffee oligarchy elected a doctor, Rafael Angel Calderón Guardia, as president (1940–44). He became a populist leader with a following among the urban poor. He created the concept of social harmony through state intervention for the purpose of collective development. In 1942, he initiated social legislation to support the poor. With union, Church, and Communist Party Union approval, he established the eight-hour workday, the right to strike, minimum wage, low-cost housing, national healthcare, and an expanded pension plan. In 1943, Calderón made a controversial alliance with the Communist Party Union to build a power base outside the coffee elite. Calderón's candidate won the 1944 election, and Calderón again ran in the 1948 presidential elections. He won, although his victory was regarded suspiciously; Otilio Ulate Blanco (1949–53), a conservative, was considered the real winner. The legislative assembly refused to announce the results, annulling the election.

José (Pepe) Figueres Ferrer, a small-scale coffee grower and industrialist, anticipated that Calderón would obstruct democracy and had planned a response. Figueres had returned to Costa Rica after being educated in the US, where he was influenced by Roosevelt's New Deal. He wanted to impose democracy throughout Central America, starting with Costa Rica. To do this, he engaged in activities that can only be described as terrorism: bombing, mobilizing a private army of malcontents and ideologues, and making alliances with leaders of other countries to promote a coup d'état. He ran in the 1948 election without expecting to win. When Calderón stole the election, Figueres organized a protest, which became an insurrection spearheaded by his own private army.

The civil war of 1948 lasted five weeks and killed 2,000 people; the greatest casualties were among the banana plantation workers who had supported Calderón and his reforms. When it became obvious that Figueres would win, negotiations resulted in a peaceful end to the civil war. Those supporting Calderón's reforms wanted them protected, as did Figueres and his supporters. So there was a considerable overlap of agendas, the primary difference being a respect for democratic mechanisms. Thus, a pact was created between competing elite and conflicting social classes. The pact agreed to establish political stability by permitting Figueres to run Costa Rica for 18 months; when the time was up, he would turn the presidency over to Otilio Ulate and a newly elected legislative assembly.

In his 18 months as dictator, Figueres substantially changed the political and economic organization of Costa Rica, ending the liberal republic and beginning the era of social democracy.

DEVELOPMENTAL STATE, 1948–1980

The developmental state became the mediator in all aspects of society, negotiating conflict between sectors and insuring order. Improving social justice to protect citizens from economic inequalities was an integral part of preserving that order. This required that the state become highly active in both the economy and in social issues, strengthening the state and granting it legitimacy. There was a broad consensus between the political parties and actors to support this kind of regime. Costa Rica "remained *politically* stable for decades because [it] was structured to maintain *social* and *economic* stability" (Peeler 2004, 54; emphasis in original). Costa Rica's developmental state had limited commitment to the idea of backward linkages and economic autonomy, except during its participation in the Central American Common Market (CACM) 1964–70. Instead, Costa Rica's developmental state built public infrastructure to increase equality, deepen democracy, and promote exports.

In his 18 months as ruler of Costa Rica, Figueres nationalized the banks, breaking the power of private capital to block loans to small producers and entrepreneurs. In order to ensure free and fair elections, he created a new branch of government, the autonomous supreme electoral tribunal, thereby weakening the power of the executive. He gave citizenship to the black people of Costa Rica, and the vote to both blacks and women. He wrote an innovative constitution, parts of which became the founding constitution of 1949. He removed the press from the control of the political parties and made them private, commercial enterprises, strengthening free speech. However, control of the media was transferred into the hands of the conservative elite, where it remains to this day (Rockwell and Janus 2003, 123).

Figueres unexpectedly lost to the conservatives in the 1949 election. This was one of the crossroads in Costa Rican history. He chose to peacefully hand over the reins of power to his political opponents, and then ran in the next election of 1953, which he and his newly formed party, the National Liberation Party (PLN), won. Given Figueres's past record of operating outside the system, it would have been entirely possible for him to insist on remaining in power using his charisma, track record, and private army to create a personal power base. Yet Figueres's commitment to social democracy meant that he became its architect, although not its first president.

While in power, the conservatives under Ulate maintained and expanded Figueres's reforms. The conservatives amended the constitution that Figueres developed. This newest constitution dispersed power through institutions, creating the mechanisms for a deliberative democracy. The 1949 constitution created a unicameral legislative assembly elected on proportional representation, which is still in use today. As a result, the office of the president is a weak executive. He cannot veto a budget, use line-item or pocket veto, assume emergency powers without two-thirds of the vote of the legislature, rule by decree, or stand for reelection without sitting out a term. However, he can appoint and fire cabinet ministers, and call emergency sessions of the legislature to discuss his own bill. Party candidates are selected through party conventions rather than through appointment by party leaders, and since 1978, primaries choose presidential candidates. Until recently, presidents could not be reelected, and elected deputies who wished to run again had to wait four years. The constitution also strengthened the judiciary. It decentralized Costa Rica to a degree, by granting power to municipalities. The state also encouraged local projects and participation, albeit on a small scale. Until the economic crisis of the 1970s and 1980s, these disparate, ad hoc community organizations were politically docile; however, they served as incubators for more recent, aggressive public action.

Most famously, the constitution abolished the Costa Rican military, replacing it with a Home Guard. This was done not only to free up money for social spending but also to ensure that an opposition party would be unable to unseat the government. Nonetheless, the state was not entirely defenseless. From his seat of exile in Nicaragua, Calderón twice tried to invade and overturn the government, and both times was repulsed by the support from the Organization of American States (OAS) and the US government. Calderón eventually accepted the new democratic reality, and in 1958 joined an opposition coalition party and ran against the government. His reaction was an affirmation that Costa Rica's democracy was recognized as the only game in town. Both then and to this day, "the political culture overwhelmingly favours democracy" (Seligson 2001, 106).

The PLN emerged as the dominant political party in the second half of the twentieth century, with the opposition party consisting of a shifting coalition. The PLN is a social democratic party with a strong base in the rural poor and middle class, rather than with the working class and trade unions. The opposition coalition slowly coalesced, and by 1983 became the Social Christian Unity Party (PUSC), a right-of-center party. While the two-party system (the PLN and the opposition coalition) rotated power, each party was essentially centralist, with the political extremes marginalized and lacking influence. Since 1948, the left in Costa Rica has never received more than 5 per cent of the popular vote.

Figueres created new public sector companies operating autonomously from partisan politics, although they had a government-imposed mandate. Public sector enterprises were intended to stimulate economic production to reduce unemployment and poverty, and to promote job training and human capital. These enterprises meshed economic development with social development. The state created autonomous agencies to run the railways, to build subsidized houses for low and medium income families, and to supply utilities and telecommunications. Prices were set for grain and other staple foods, petroleum products, alcohol, and transportation. Profits were fixed. These autonomous public sector agencies compensated for the lack of investment capital that small third world nations tend to suffer from, as well as diluting the influence of foreign capital. This allowed the country to develop far beyond its Central American neighbors. For example, the Costa Rican Electricity Institute (ICE) incorporated in 1949, providing extensive coverage for companies and consumers with subsidized prices and services. Eventually, ICE controlled 90 per cent of the nation's electricity supply, and became a source of national pride. In time, it also offered a telecommunications system, wiring the nation (not just the rich in the urban centers) for telephones and then for the Internet. Because these agencies were socially and geographically inclusive, they promoted a sense of economic nationalism based around the developmental state. "Although these measures [the creation of public institutions] were focused primarily on regulating economic relations and did not strictly constitute social relations, they did set the foundations for a modernization and diversification of the economy, territorial integration, and mobility of social sectors and emerging production groups" (Barahona 2007, 329).

The public sector agencies increased the number of state employees. Between 1950 and 1980, public sector employment increased eightfold, while private sector employment increased by three. By 1978, public sector employment accounted for 19 per cent of the economically active population, and received 28 per cent of the national income. This made the state an employer of the middle classes, which in turn meant that they supported a developmental state. A well-educated, unionized, stable middle class reduced the disparity of wealth between the rich and the poor. Highly important to this economic plan was the building of human capital. The National Wage Council, a tripartite commission composed in equal parts of labor, employer, and government representatives, established minimum wages in each sector of the economy. Healthcare, education, and social programs increased to cover large segments of the population. By 1960, 90 per cent of school-aged children were in school.

Between 1948 and 1980, there were over 100 government-initiated, autonomous public sector institutes, with the ultimate goal of achieving economic and social development. As the agencies grew, they swallowed up smaller businesses in a variety of sectors, some government agencies competing with .other government agencies, or with capitalist production. For example, the Costa Rican Development Corporation (CODESA) established in 1972 was an autonomous agency, with subsidiaries that included transportation, petroleum refining, aluminum smelting, sugar refining, cotton production, fruit packing, fertilizer, and cement production. By 1979, Costa Rica's GDP per capita was $558, rising from $289 in 1949 (in constant 1950 dollars).[2] Between 1960 and 1980, the GDP per capita almost doubled, with the real wages of the working class steadily rising. Worker productivity increased on an annual average between 6 per cent and 7 per cent from 1950 to 1970 (Chamberlain 2007, 10). The quality of life that the Costa Ricans enjoyed produced considerable national pride, and became an integral part of the Costa Rican national identity (Booth and Walker 1993, 117).

In the 1970s the global economy experienced oil shocks that raised the price of petroleum, creating global inflation, a global recession, and a decline in the price of coffee. However banks, flush with oil dollars, made credit easy to obtain. Between 1974 and 1977, state investment in productive activities increased by 183 per cent, financed predominantly by borrowing heavily from abroad. Direct foreign investment declined in the 1970s, requiring more borrowing abroad to replace the missing capital. This borrowing maintained Costa Rica's impressive standard of living, but foreign debt as a share of the GDP increased from 12 per cent in 1970 to 147 per cent in 1982. Many of the public sector agencies and businesses which had developed Costa Rica so successfully for the previous 30 years were running deficits. Even if there had not been the oil shock, the economic model was producing a slowing average annual growth rate. Between 1965 and 1970, it was 7 per cent, between 1970 and 1975 it was 6 per cent, and between 1975 and 1980 it was 5 per cent (Booth, Walker, and Wade 2006, 61; Sandbrook, Edelman, Heller, and Teichman 2007, 103–04; Chamberlain 2007, 57).

Pepe Figueres, autonomous agencies, and the 1949 constitution created modern Costa Rica with its ethos of social justice and penchant for populist leaders; a country based on a strong party system and operating through democratic structures. To modernize an export-driven economy while supporting the middle and lower classes required a strong state with the capacity to build quality institutions (autonomous agencies, among others), economic infrastructure (rural and urban), and develop human capital. Political parties were institutionalized so that, when combined with state capacity, the democratic system could absorb, respond to, and dissipate new political mobilizations or discontent. However, it is unwise to idealize this system, as it was full of contradictions. It was "founded on military victory yet consolidated through the disestablishment of the army, social democratic in character yet initially little less anti-worker than it was anti-Communist, conducted through constitutional channels and parliamentary government yet sustained by *caudillismo"* (Dunkereley 1988, 594).

By 1980 two factors, one internal and one external, intersected to create a crisis. The first factor was the economy: the import substitution industrialization (ISI) model was exhausted, and foreign debt had become unsustainable. Costa Rica's financial crisis was compounded by a second factor: a revolution in Nicaragua, the country immediately to the north. Support from President Rodrigo Alberto Carazo Odio (1978–82), a PUSC president, for the new socialist revolutionary government of Nicaragua, the FSLN, threatened Costa Rica's traditional neutralism. In 1981, Jeane Kirkpatrick, the US ambassador to the United Nations, spoke of Nicaragua destabilizing Costa Rica, with the clear implication that Costa Rica had lost its traditional autonomy and was in need of American "security assistance." When Carazo declined this assistance, relations between the US and Costa Rica became strained. Costa Rica's successes appeared to be threatened by a regional war and an economic crisis.

NEOLIBERAL STATE, 1980–

The government of Costa Rica restructured the nation's economy, liberalizing and diversifying it. However, the country's citizens hardly embraced these changes enthusiastically. Due to extensive organizing within civil society and the interference of state institutions, Costa Rican politicians usually made only the minimum changes necessary, protecting social programs to the greatest possible extent. Nonetheless, the economic restructuring affected the organization of political power, increasing the divide between the rich and the poor, and alienating the citizenry from the political process. This restructuring and its impact on social spending, state organization, and social and economic equality have dominated the political agenda for almost three decades. The debate has yet to be resolved.

The economic collapse was sudden and profound. Costa Rica defaulted on its foreign debt payments in 1981, and between 1980 and 1983, the currency was devalued by 500 per cent. There was rising unemployment in the middle classes, and a reduction of state welfare. In 1982, Costa Ricans were one of the most indebted peoples per capita in the world, with foreign debt as a share of GDP rising from 12 per cent in 1970 to 147 per cent in 1982. Inflation rose from 9 per cent in 1979 to 90 per cent in 1982, with real wages contracting. Unemployment also rose, climbing from 5 per cent in 1979 to 10 per cent in 1982. In 1981, the government announced austerity measures which included a fuel price increase of 85 per cent (followed four months later by a further 27 per cent rise), an electricity price increase of 17 per cent, and a telephone service price increase of 30 per cent. In 1982, the government reduced its subsidies of food and water. These reforms were insufficient to meet the agreement signed with the IMF, and as a result, in 1980 and 1981 the IMF suspended its loans to the Costa Rican government.

The working classes were well organized, and in 1979 took strike action against the government's efforts to reduce public sector wages. There were 59 strikes in the first 10 months of 1980, versus 109 in the previous 7 years. When government repression resulted in several workers being killed by the police, and workers and the police exchanging fire, the government decided that repression was not politically realistic.

In 1985, the government of Luis Alberto Monge (PLN) (1982–86) imposed even more painful economic restructuring. CODESA was privatized, the currency was floated, private banks were permitted, private enterprises were allowed to compete with government agencies, public sector employment was reduced, and prices were raised, especially on utilities. In all, structural adjustment programs were initiated by the PLN governments of Monge (1985), Oscar Arias (1989), and José María Figueres Olsen (1995). All of these policies were heavily protested and negotiated. Because the PUSC never signed a structural adjustment policy, it was able to criticize them while abiding by them.

Despite representing a center-left party, Monge learned from Carazo's error of alienating the US. To remedy this, Monge appointed right-wing ministers and maintained positive relations with the United States. The American government wanted to isolate the revolutionary government of Nicaragua, and needed a base in Costa Rica from which the American-funded counterrevolutionary movement could deploy. The American government also pressured Costa Rica to expand and militarize its Home Guard, ostensibly for its own protection. In exchange, they offered over $1 billion in aid, the majority of it in the form of grants to assist the Costa Rican government with its balance of payment problems. Between 1983 and 1985, American aid made up 35 per cent of the budget, 10 per cent of the GDP, and one-fifth of Costa Rica's export earnings. In 1982, the IMF gave Costa Rica an emergency loan as well as stand-by loans. American largesse buffered the Costa Rican state from the worst impacts of economic restructuring, stabilizing it. The fiscal deficit declined, inflation declined, and the economy began to recover, although the country would not achieve the same standard of living its people once enjoyed until 1990. Mainly thanks to US aid, Costa Rica was nonetheless able to maintain most components of its health and education system (Hoffman 2007, 13).

Despite the unprecedented level of American aid, restructuring presented the Costa Rican democracy with a paradox. The developmental state needed to be dismantled to create a neoliberal state. Yet the retreat of the state jeopardized middle- and lower-class support, which would precipitate a fall from power for any government which attempted it. So while the elite coalesced around the need for extensive economic reform, it was much harder to achieve sweeping change within a democratic system. The viability of Costa Rica's democratic institutions was reflected in how the governing elite and the masses dealt with public protest: there was no breakdown of public order, or overturning of Costa Rica's democratic structures. There was little government repression; instead, the government chose to respond sympathetically to protests, initiating investigations into causes, promising to do more to protect those hurt by the economic crisis, and compromising when it was possible. The state was able to negotiate some relief from the rising prices, and to provide some protection from employee layoffs. The elite allowed their own standard of living to contract in favor of protecting the middle classes. As a result, the vast majority of the population remained loyal to traditional parties and the democratic political system despite the economic crisis. Thus the radical elements in society were not empowered or legitimated. Nonetheless, there was the inevitable change in social relations that accompanied structural adjustment: the rise of state technocrats, the decline in the trade union movement, the reduction of public employees, the privatization of state businesses and agencies, and the contraction of small and medium producers. This weakened the old political balance of elite, middle, and working classes, with a strong state acting as the negotiator and arbiter (Sánchez-Ancochea 2005, 717). What survived was "the overarching framework of the constitutional democratic regime established in the late 1940s and early 1950s" (Booth, Walker, and Wade 2006, 64).

American aid however was drawing Costa Rica into regional warfare. An American-funded Nicaraguan guerrilla fighter, Eden Pastora, established a base in northern Costa Rica from which he and his followers made military incursions into Nicaragua. The government worried that the Sandinista army might invade Costa Rica in order to remove this threat. Based on a publicly known American military plan, the Costa Rican government was worried that the American government would escalate regional warfare by attacking Nicaragua from their base inside Costa Rica. Costa Rica was also worried about absorbing the flood of Nicaraguan refugees fleeing the conflict. Monge attempted to maintain Costa Rica's neutrality, but in 1983 after the Sandinista Army and the Costa Rican Home Guard were involved in a border skirmish in which several Costa Ricans died, neutrality was no longer possible. In 1985, Monge agreed to allow the American military to train and equip the Costa Rican Home Guard so it could fight terrorism.

In 1986, Oscar Arias Sánchez (PLN) (1986–90) was elected president on a platform of restoring Costa Rica's neutrality. He ran against Rafael Angel Calderón Fournier, a PUSC member who had a pro-American platform.

Almost immediately upon winning, Arias initiated a series of meetings between all parties involved in every conflict, in an effort to create a regional peace treaty. The countries of Central America, under a previous initiative led by many nations, including Sweden, Colombia, Mexico, Venezuela, and Panama, had already begun negotiating in 1983 for peace in the region. They created the Contadora Peace Plan of 1984, which encouraged peace, democracy, and economic cooperation for all the nations of Central America. Neither Costa Rica nor Honduras accepted the plan. However, it served as an excellent starting point for Arias to reinitiate peace talks, because the Contadora Peace Plan linked economic development with the organization of the state, and both of those with civil strife. With Arias and the newly elected Guatemalan president, Vinicio Cerezo (1986–91) leading the peace process, there was a shift in the negotiations from an externally led process to a Central American-led process. This "CentralAmericanization" of the process vested more legitimacy in the negotiations. In addition, the situation had changed somewhat, with Ronald Reagan (1980–88) as a lame duck president, and the Nicaraguan economy straining from the cost of war. In 1987, the governments of Central America signed the Esquipulas Peace Plan, which contained the military conflict, pledged democratization, and decided upon a verification process. The American government refused to recognize this peace plan, and cut Costa Rica's aid package. Despite the American reaction, Arias was awarded the Nobel Peace Prize in 1987 for his efforts in securing regional peace.

With peace restored in the region, Arias turned his attention to domestic issues. He took a second risk for Costa Rica, altering its institutions and programs "into a laboratory for sustainable development" (Silva 2003, 93). He had an ambitious plan to base economic policy and social equity on sustainable development, redefining ecotourism as not only desirable for the country's natural resources but also for socioeconomic development. Costa Rica has 5 per cent of the world's biodiversity, and now national parks and reserves cover up to one-quarter of its territory. To give the new agenda political authority, a new Ministry of Natural Resources, Energy, and Mines was inaugurated in 1987, and was reorganized in 1996 as the Ministry of the Environment. However, the ministry was never well integrated into the rest of the government: its policies lacked coordination and bureaucratic expertise. Sustainable development was heavily supported by foreign aid, causing problems when foreign donors left. This lack of political sophistication, combined with neoliberalism, which reduced credit and sidelined government agencies, meant that in the long run ecotourism benefited private sector groups and environmental NGOs. Tourism, nonetheless, is the country's largest source of foreign exchange. Furthermore, ecotourism increased citizen participation, decreased the rate of deforestation, and trained a generation of Costa Ricans to value and expect sustainable development.

Rafael Angel Calderón (PUSC) (1990–94) ran for election on the promise of increasing social welfare and decreasing income inequalities, and this time won the 1990 election. It is a truism that in Costa Rica politicians who promise to protect and extend social justice programs are elected. Once in power, Calderón proved incapable of implementing his campaign platforms, and instead continued neoliberal policies. This provoked substantial protests from the populace. The PLN, however, was unable to take advantage of PUSC's weakness. Having signed all three structural adjustment policies, the party was weakened and divided by its actions. It had traditionally been a social democratic party, embracing redistributive and protectionist policies with a broad, inclusive appeal. But now its message had become confused. The party swerved increasingly to the right, and lost its middle- and working-class support as a result. Having dominated the Costa Rican political world since 1953, the PLN had a declining share of the presidential vote after 1986. In the 1990 election, it lost control of the legislative assembly. The views and policies of the PUSC and the PLN converged on the necessity for neoliberalism. This consensus meant that the traditional two-party system no longer offered any genuine opposition. The decline of the once-powerful PLN was also affected by the rise of internal technocrats at the expense of loyalists and activists, the adoption of presidential primaries open to non-PLN members, and the increasing role of personalistic politics during presidential campaigns, as ideology and grassroots organizations became sidelined. There have been increasing calls for the reform of the political party system to enhance transparency in its internal operations and in its campaign financing. The decline of the two main parties in the political system created space for new political parties with new platforms and strategies. In 1994, there were seven parties running for power. By the 2002 election, there were 15 parties and, by 2006, 14 remained (Lehoucq 2005).

A structural adjustment loan from the IADB in 1995 required that the state be reformed, which included the laying off of more than 25,000 state employees. In 1995 and 1996, there were month-long strikes and public protests, a rare phenomenon in Costa Rica. The government of José María Figueres Olsen (PLN) (1994–98) turned the IADB loan down. Eventually, the loan was granted with the requirement of layoffs removed. The state made limited reforms: some agencies and ministries were consolidated; some agencies, which ran at a loss, were privatized; and there was a freeze on hiring. The state, once a major employer, had a declining share of the total employment, falling from 19 per cent in 1985 to 14 per cent in 2005. While successive Costa Rican governments liberalized the market and reduced the size and influence of the state, they successfully resisted pressure to weaken the state as much as was demanded.

The government actively sought direct foreign investment for Costa Rica's economy and was able to attract INTEL, a computer firm, followed by other high tech firms. Industry and high tech companies were attracted by a high level of human capital, political stability, and the low cost of living. The economy shifted from being an agro-exporter to a diversified corporate importer. Nonetheless, "there are two key elements to Costa Rica's successful trade and investment strategy: free trade agreements and free trade zones" (Mirchandani and Condo 2005, 354). Textiles assembled in the *maquiladora* zones or export processing zones multiplied in the 1990s, with Costa Rican exports increasing by an annual average of 17 per cent., Costa Rica's *maquilas* generated almost $2 billion in exports and employed 30,000 people in 2007. These jobs were low-skilled and dominated by women. However, unions and the state regulation of labor meant that the abuses associated with these industries in other countries were less prevalent in Costa Rica. Some experts have even made the controversial suggestion that DR-CAFTA might strengthen labor laws in the *maquilas* (Abrahamson 2007, 351), although a recent study of its implementation in other countries in Central America strongly suggests the exact opposite (WOLA 2009). Despite this increase in industry, membership in trade unions declined. Unionization of the total labor force was 15 per cent in 1990 and only 10 per cent in 1999.

By 1993, the economy had recovered to the level that it had been at before the debt crisis of 1980. The gross domestic product per capita grew by nearly 25 per cent between 1990 and 2000, with inflation steadily dropping into the single digits. But the contradictions within the neoliberal model were becoming apparent. The indices for human development fell. The number of small- and medium-sized businesses also dropped and there was an increased concentration of capital in the private sector. The gap between the wealthy and the poor grew, although near universal social welfare programs were augmented by targeted social assistance to tackle poverty and inequality. By 1997, 90 per cent of the population had health coverage and 82 per cent of the elderly received pensions (Filgueira 2007, 145). Furthermore, the impetus of economic success was not the market and a flexibilized workforce but rather a strong and proactive state with an educated and regulated workforce (Sánchez 2008).

Although the economy grew by an average of 4 per cent during Rodríguez's mandate in power, civil society mobilized independent of the political parties to protest changes. Students and peasants, fearful of the effects neoliberal policies would have on their lives, took to the streets. The ombudswoman spoke against neoliberal policies on behalf of the "unorganized, silent majority." Starting in 2000 and continuing for years after, massive public protests took place against the privatization of the Costa Rican Electricity Institute (ICE), which had become a symbol of protest against the neoliberal direction of public policy. Business groups did not like the social unrest and encouraged the government to accommodate the demands from civil society organizations. In 2002, a new branch of the judiciary, the constitutional court or Sala IV, was created to adjudicate on constitutional issues. The court provided a judicial review of the constitutionalism of legislation, as well as government rules and procedures. This strengthened and clarified the branches of government. Sala IV ruled against the privatization of the ICE on procedural grounds. It also strengthened workers' rights, and upheld the state's role as a provider of welfare benefits, including healthcare (Wilson, Cordero, and Handberg 2004).

In the 2002 election, Costa Ricans expressed their disappointment with their political elite. The combined vote for the PLN and the PUSC was only 62 per cent, whereas in the previous five elections it had averaged 92 per cent. A new party, the Citizen Action Party (PAC) headed by Otton Solís, won 26 per cent of the vote. Abel Pacheco of PUSC (2002–06) won the presidency with 58 per cent of the vote, in the first runoff in Costa Rican history. In the legislative assembly, the PLN and the PUSC had to work together to hold their majority, reducing any remaining differences between them (Lehoucq 2005, 142). Pacheco introduced controversial legislation to tackle the fiscal deficit by increasing taxes and privatization. Taxes in Costa Rica made up only 13 per cent of the GDP in 2005; they were low for Latin America and about one-third of the amount levied in the first world. Meanwhile, debt servicing consumed 15 per cent of exports, and the debt itself was 60 per cent of the GDP or 250 per cent of exports. Fifty per cent of the government's public sector budget was funded through borrowing. The bill was debated for three years, before being declared unconstitutional by Sala IV in 2006. Public protests continued, with strikes by teachers and public sector workers (Sandbrook, Edelman, Heller, and Teichman 2007, 121). The limits of neoliberal policies were being decided on the streets and in the courts, rather than in the legislative assembly.

Between 2004 and 2006, corruption scandals involving four ex-presidents were brought to light. Calderón (1990–94), Figueres (1994–98), Rodríguez (1998–2002), and Pacheco (2002–06) were each accused of accepting "consultancy fees" from international firms and countries who wished to obtain contracts from the Costa Rican government, or of having irregularities in their campaign finances. Numerous high-ranking administrators from all governments were also implicated, or found guilty of bribery and corruption. These scandals embarrassed the nation, caused a decline in its Transparency International ranking, which affected Costa Rica's ability to attract direct foreign investment, and lost the country several high profile international seats, the head of the OAS being one example. They have also cast doubt on the governments' reasons for privatizing state agencies, and on the benefits of privatization. The government has also been accused of staffing the boards of state agencies with political appointees, a form of cronyism. This has brought more protesters out on the streets, demonstrating against political corruption. The Costa Rican legislature rapidly responded by passing its first law in 2004 to combat corruption. "This is a sign that Costa Rican politicians may be ready to demand nothing but the highest behaviour from each other" (Lehoucq 2005, 152). Costa Ricans, however, remain distrustful of their ruling class, even though individual Costa Ricans have rare personal experiences with corruption.

In 2003, the Pacheco government negotiated DR-CAFTA, signing it in 2004. Costa Rica had to open three sectors of the telecommunications market, its private network services, Internet services, and wireless services. These three sectors generate much of the revenue used to maintain other, less profitable government initiatives, such as extending services to the rural areas. Costa Rica also had to liberalize the insurance sector. Agriculture and some manufactured goods were partially exempted from liberalization in an effort to protect those industries. DR-CAFTA would ensure the continuation of the neoliberal economic model, locking in this organization of power relations (Sánchez 2008). Rather than a high level of openness to trade facilitated by state-owned agencies, Costa Rica's idiosyncratic political economy would be eroded for a more rationalized model.

The timing was bad. Corruption had tainted the privatization of public sector companies. DR-CAFTA had powerful and knowledgeable critics, able to use the experience of other countries with neoliberalism and free trade agreements to highlight potentially negative effects. Both the PUSC and the PLC supported it, as did the business sector. Solís of PAC favored renegotiating clauses within DR-CAFTA, and suggested alternative ways to improve economic development and engage with globalization. The bill was not passed in the legislative assembly. The issue of whether to accept DR-CAFTA dominated the election of 2006. Oscar Arias, again representing the PLN, won a second term as president with 40.9 per cent of the votes versus 39.8 per cent for Solís.[3] Fewer than 20,000 votes separated the two, showing a clearly divided country. The PUSC got just 3.5 per cent of the vote.

In February 2007, thousands marched in the streets of San José, protesting DR-CAFTA. By April 2007, PAC had the supreme electoral tribunal's approval to collect signatures of 5 per cent of the electorate (132,000 signatures in total) to hold a referendum on DR-CAFTA. PAC was successful in its campaign, and the referendum was held on October 2007. To promote the advantages of DR-CAFTA before the referendum was held, the government outspent the opposition, which included trade unions, intellectuals, and civil society organizations. The "yes" vote received 51.6 per cent of the vote, and the "no" vote received 48.4 per cent, with 60 per cent voter turn-out. To be ratified, the national assembly had to pass 13 implementing bills, which it did by the end of 2008. While this was widely interpreted as a win for the elite against the average citizen, the length and severity of the debate over economic restructuring (1982–2008) strengthened the public commitment to social democracy. This debate, mediated by the deliberative mechanisms of democracy, "permitted the survival of a reinvented welfare state and, moreover, has made a willingness to adapt, preserve, and extend the model an essential ingredient of political legitimacy for any government" (Sandbrook, Edelman, Heller, and Teichman 2007, 95).

CONCLUSION

There are three reasons why Costa Rica has been the exception to Latin America's minimum democracies. These reasons are Costa Rica's deliberative democracy, its strong state embedded in mutually supportive socioeconomic political structures, and its ethos of social justice. These three factors reinforce each other, giving Costa Rica's deep democracy an envious sustainability.

First, although the initial impetus behind Costa Rica's socioeconomic and political structure was an accident of history, the Costa Rican people and its state continued to make small reforms, gradually changing their country. Larger risks were occasionally taken, with the most obvious being the defiance of American foreign policy to negotiate regional peace during the presidency of Ronald Reagan. Nonetheless, the vast majority of change in Costa Rica was small, manageable, and continual. This is deliberative democracy, which prefers small changes and accommodation over exclusion and oppression. Small changes were built on the small changes that came before, an approach which became institutionalized until it seemed perfectly normal and the only way to do things. Costa Rica's gradualism found a way to slowly extend the franchise and deepen democracy without altering the balance of power or spreading radicalism from below. Gradualism was also the approach taken to implement structural adjustments, which had the potential to seriously disrupt the social fabric and political organization of the country. Instead, neoliberalism was slowly implemented piecemeal, with the maximum protection provided for social welfare. Gradualism promoted accommodation, peaceful social relations, and compromise. As a result, politics was not a zero-sum game but rather a system of give and take. Changes all happened through the normal channels of democratic politics, strengthening democratic norms and procedures.

Second, Costa Rica's political organization of government arose from its socioeconomic relations of equality and balanced classes. Economic production was dominated by a large number of small- and medium-sized producers, well-paid laborers, and a relatively poor elite. A strong state was needed to balance relations between the classes, because no one class was dominant. This was achieved through a series of informal, inter-class pacts or bipartisan agreements as a method of conflict resolution. The state acquired the role of neutral arbiter of competing needs, able to intervene with capacity against any one group, should broader needs require it. Political mechanisms rose from economic and social stability, to reinforce this stability. The mechanisms most conducive to maintaining stability were a slowly expanding franchise, quality institutions, and a balance of powers between the branches of government, especially the rule of law. With these mechanisms and no one group controlling the state, clientelism had less opportunity to become the dominant social relation, political parties could be autonomous and embedded in the grassroots, and an autonomous civil society could become vibrant and well organized. These practices strengthened democracy, equality, and the state. The strong state became a developmental state, creating agencies and institutions based on Costa Rica's own need to enhance development, exports, and social equality. This gave Costa Rica a degree of autonomy from international capital, so it could offset the penetration of globalization and elite capture of the state. The strong state was then able to negotiate with powerful business organizations such as the United Fruit Company, attract high tech businesses, defy American foreign policy and IFIs, and protect itself and its institutions. Costa Rica's successes in negotiating with international and globalized forces gave the state greater legitimacy and deepened its own power. Its successes also showed the limits of the power of globalization, which may constrain domestic political choices and public policies, but cannot always dictate them. These three relations of politics, economics, and society mutually reinforced each other in a constantly renegotiated whole, achieved through the mechanisms of a deliberative democracy and a strong state.

Finally, the Costa Rican people embraced an ethos of social justice as the principle underlying their democracy. Costa Rica's early commitment to social inclusion was due to the populace's close proximity, their relative social and economic equality, and ethnic homogeneity. These factors enhanced tolerance, inclusion, and trust, the social norms that support a deliberative democracy. Led by Pepe Figueres, these values became a commitment to democracy. These social norms were strengthened by the developmental state and national institutions, including social services and autonomous agencies. These institutions helped to integrate everyone in the country, creating a national identity of equality. Thus, an ethos of social justice supported equitable economic growth, which in turn deepened democracy.

Despite Costa Rica's remarkable achievement, deep-seated problems remain. First, it continues to be a very elitist country. The same names dominate politics and the media from one generation to the next. And the elite are frequently in agreement with each other, against the wishes of the masses. Corruption and cronyism among the elite are alienating the citizenry from its political leaders, and undermining support for democratic mechanisms. Second, despite strengthening the rule of law and social care, the institutions that helped to create Costa Rica's deep democracy have been weakened. Powerful political parties that helped to stabilize Costa Rica's political process and deepen its democracy over the decades have lost their core constituents and guiding ideology. The developmental agencies that have promoted national identity, integration, and economic equality have been privatized. Rising social and economic inequality, crime and violence, and climbing housing prices have produced a discontent that the state cannot easily resolve. Finally, Costa Rica continues to run a chronic fiscal deficit because it has a sophisticated social care program and a public sector which consumes 15 per cent of the GDP, while the state has only managed to capture between 12 per cent and 13 per cent of the GDP in tax revenue. Given the option between cutting public sector services (a highly unpopular approach) or borrowing abroad, the state opts for the latter option (Lehoucq 2005, 150). DR-CAFTA will not alter this arrangement. Unless a more substantial economic development program is adopted, the debt will inevitably become unsustainable.

The great unknowns in Costa Rican politics are whether the neoliberal state is strong enough to act with capacity to continue to develop Costa Rica, and whether Costa Rica's traditional norm of inclusion and accommodation is still an appropriate mechanism for socioeconomic reform.

NOTES

1 There is an unusual inconsistency with this acronym. It is also known as CAFTA-DR, or sometimes just CAFTA.
2 For the sake of comparison, Nicaragua's per capita GDP was $251 in 1979, Guatemala's was $377, and Honduras was $193. None of those nations qualified as democratic.
3 In 2003, Sala IV permitted former presidents to run again for office.

REFERENCES

Abrahamson, Peter. 2007. "Free trade and Social Citizenship: Prospects and Possibilities of the Central American Free trade Agreement." *Global Social Policy* 7(3): 339–57.

Barahona, Manuel, Ludwig Güendel, and Carlos Castro. 2007. "Social Policy and Social Reform 'Costa Rican Style': A Paradigmatic Case of Heterodoxy in the Context of a Peripheral Economy." *Latin America: A New Developmental Welfare State Model in the Making?* Ed. Manuel Riesco. New York: Palgrave MacMillan. 327–55.

Booth, John A., and Thomas W. Walker. 1993. *Understanding Central America*. 2nd ed. Boulder: Westview Press.

Booth, John A., Thomas W. Walker, and Christine J. Wade. 2006. *Understanding Central America: Global Forces, Rebellion, and Change*. Boulder: Westview Press.

Chamberlain, Anthony B. 2007. *Privatization in Costa Rica*. Lanham: University Press of America.

Dunkerley, James. 1988. *Power in the Isthmus: A Political History of Modern Central America*. London: Verso Books.

Filgueira, Fernando. 2007. "The Latin American Social States: Critical Junctures and Critical Choices." *Democracy and Social Policy*. Ed. Yusuf Bangura. New York: Palgrave MacMillan. 136–63.

Hoffman, Bert. 2007. "Why Reform Fails: The 'Politics of Policies' in Costa Rican Telecommunications Liberalization." Working Paper No. 47. German Institute of Global and Area Studies Research Unit: Institute of Latin American Studies.

Lehoucq, Fabrice. 2005. "Costa Rica: Paradise in Doubt." *Journal of Democracy* 16(3): 140–54.

Mirchandani, Silip, and Arturo Condo. 2005. "Doing Business in Costa Rica." *Thunderbird International Business Review* 47(3): 335–63.

Peeler, John. 2004. *Building Democracy in Latin America*. Boulder: Lynne Rienner Press.

Rockwell, Rick, and Noreene Janus. 2003. *Media Power in Central America*. Chicago: University of Illinois Press.

Sánchez-Ancochea, Diego. 2005. "Domestic Capital, Civil Servants and the State: Costa Rica and the Dominican Republic under Globalisation." *Journal of Latin American Studies* 37(4): 693–726.

———. 2008. "The Politics of DR-CAFTA in Costa Rica, Dominican Republic and El Salvador." *The Political Economy of Hemispheric Integration*. Ed. Diego Sánchez-Ancochea and Kenneth C. Shadlen. New York: Palgrave MacMillan. 171–200.

Sandbrook, Richard, Marc Edelman, Patrick Heller, and Judith Teichman. 2007. *Social Democracy in the Global Periphery: Origins, Challenges, and Prospects*. Cambridge: Cambridge University Press.

Seligson, Mitchell A. 2001. "Costa-Rican Exceptionalism: Why Ticos are Different." *Citizen Views of Democracy in Latin America*. Ed. Roderic Ai Camp. Pittsburgh: University of Pittsburgh Press. 90–106.

Silva, Eduardo. 2003. "Selling Sustainable Development and Shortchanging Social Ecology in Costa Rican Forest Policy." *Latin American Politics and Society* 45(3): 93–127.

Wilson, Bruce, Juan Carlos Rodríguez Cordero, and Roger Handberg. "The Best Laid Schemes ... Gang Aft Agley: Judicial Reform in Latin America—Evidence from Costa Rica." *Journal of Latin American Studies* 36(3): 507–31.

WOLA. 2009. *DR-CAFTA and Worker's Rights: Moving from Paper to Practice.* Washington, DC: WOLA.

E-RESOURCES

Actualidad Económica (www.actualidad-e.com). A website that provides financial and economic data about Costa Rica.

Costa Rican government (www.casapres.go.cr). This is the government's official website.

La Nación (www.nacion.com). The largest and highest-quality Spanish-language daily newspaper in Cost Rica.

Tico Times (www.ticotimes.net). An English-language newspaper.

EIGHT

Colombia: Violence, Drugs, and Democracy

ROBERTA RICE

The story of Colombia's "Black Vladimir," the guerrilla insurgent turned paramilitary counterinsurgent, perhaps best represents the many tragedies and travesties of justice that have long characterized this country. The son of a poor farmer, Vladimir was recruited into the country's principal guerrilla army at the age of 11. By 18, he had become so skilled in the art of combat that the FARC made him a war instructor. It was in the classroom that he met and fell in love with fellow rebel "Berta," which changed everything for him. When Berta gave birth to their daughter shortly thereafter, the two decided to desert the guerrilla army rather than being forced to send their child off to live with relatives, as was standard practice in the FARC. The trio ended up on the steps of the mayor's office, penniless and desperate in the town of Puerto Boyacá. In exchange for detailed information on the whereabouts and activities of the guerrillas, the couple was provided with housing and work, Berta as a maid in the mayor's house and Vladimir as a paramilitary. Vladimir quickly advanced through the paramilitary ranks, using the knowledge and training he gained as a guerrilla against the rebels he once served. His skill at disposing of the bodies of captured and interrogated guerrillas earned him the new nickname of "the doctor." Vladimir specialized in orchestrating and leading missions to destroy the guerrillas' political party, the Patriotic Union (UP), along with its supporters. Following his arrest in 1989, he admitted to killing over 800 people during his paramilitary career. This extraordinary level of violence, institutionalized in

207

both the government and among the drug-trafficking insurgents, seriously erodes Colombia's efforts at democratization.[1]

Colombia is known as a land of paradox. It is home to one of Latin America's oldest and most militarily powerful guerrilla movements as well as one of the region's longest lasting democracies. Labeled as the most violent place on the planet in the 1990s, it is also the country with the least experience of military rule in Latin America. Colombia is both admired for its sound economic planning and admonished for its levels of corruption and dependence on the drug trade.

And while its political system today enjoys improvements in democratic participation and contestation, it cannot guarantee basic civil rights and liberties. These seemingly contradictory tendencies point to the historic absence of a strong and centralized state, along with profound socioeconomic inequalities as possible reasons for its current predicament.

A HISTORY OF POLITICAL VIOLENCE, 1819–1902

Colombia is a country of incredible geographic diversity. Located in the northwestern corner of South America and connecting the continent with Central America, Colombia shares borders with Panama, Venezuela, Brazil, Ecuador, and Peru. Both the Caribbean Sea and the Pacific Ocean border it. Similar to its neighbors, the Andes mountain ranges are a defining feature of the Colombian landscape. In the case of Colombia, the Andes branch off into three separate ranges that run in parallel fashion, dividing the country into three major regions: east, west, and the Caribbean coast. In addition to making ground transportation a challenge, this topography has resulted in distinct regional identities and a heightened sense of localism. Historically, Colombia has been characterized as a collection of isolated city-states predicated on the dispersion of power as opposed to a modern nation-state with centralized power and a strong sense of nationalism (Rochlin 2003). In what was a bitter disappointment to legendary Andean independence leader Simón Bolívar, Colombia's political elite preferred to maintain control over their regional strongholds rather than become part of Bolívar's dream of a united Gran Colombia made up of the Andean nations.

Colombian independence from Spain in 1819 not only ushered in an era of political fragmentation but also one of political violence. By the 1840s, a system of two-party dominance based on a bitter rivalry between the Liberal Party and the Conservative Party had been established. The main point of contention between the two was the relationship between church and state, with the conservatives favoring a leading role for the Catholic

Church in state and society and the liberals supporting secularism. The conservatives also tended to promote economic protectionism and centralized political authority, while the liberals advocated for federalism and free trade (Dugas 2006). The two parties developed strong roots in society early on that they used to mobilize the populace in their struggle for control over the state. The masses became so deeply divided in their partisan identities and took party differences so seriously that one observer had suggested that Colombians came to be "'born with party identification cards attached to the umbilical cord'" (Santa 1964, cited in Kline and Gray 2007, 205). The powerful partisan loyalties that the liberals and conservatives cultivated in civil society in the nineteenth century still have meaning today. Colombia's Liberal and Conservative Parties are among the oldest functioning political parties in Latin America, with the constitution of 1886 being the oldest constitution in continuous use in the region (Archer 1995, 164).

Colombia's traditional parties established a disastrous political norm of zero-sum democracy, which continues to haunt the nation to this day. Throughout the nineteenth century, the party that came to power systematically attacked the basis of the opposition's support and excluded them from positions of power. In what amounted to a pendulum-like alternation in power, the liberals ruled under constitutions that were heavily decentralized, secular, and politically liberal in character, while the conservatives governed under constitutions that recentralized political authority and reestablished church and state relations (Skidmore and Smith 2005). With little to no compromise, continuity, or role for losing politicians, the zero-sum framework of governing heightened political tensions, and led to frequent civil wars between the parties and their supporters. Violence became normalized as a means of settling political scores. During the second half of the nineteenth century, at least seven major civil wars broke out as a result of partisan disputes. These civil wars largely consisted of party elites mobilizing the peasantry as their troops, with the elites reaping the benefits and the peasants paying the consequences. The inability of political contenders to act in the spirit of compromise and reconciliation, or to even achieve a lasting political hegemony, created a situation of chronic violence in the country.

Colombia's nineteenth-century partisan violence culminated in the War of a Thousand Days between 1899 and 1902 that left an estimated 100,000 dead and the country in ruins. According to Rochlin (2003), the conflict, which was triggered by a liberal party attempt to overthrow the governing Conservative Party, produced a number of important legacies for the country. First and foremost, the guerrilla armies formed by the liberals to challenge state power were thought to foreshadow the rise of the twentieth-century FARC, which began as a splinter of the party. Second, the weakening of the country as a result of the devastating toll of the war facilitated Colombia's loss of Panama in 1903 to secessionist leaders backed by the United States government, which had a vested interest in building the Panama Canal. Third, the conflict resulted in a push to bolster national security forces. Finally, the extent of the violence and damage inflicted appeared to have concluded a cycle of violence that had plagued the nation since independence, ushering in a unique, albeit transitory, period of relative peace in Colombia.

THE BOOM YEARS, 1903–1945

The early twentieth century was a period of conservative hegemony and of economic growth and modernization for Colombia, based on the booming international market for the country's main export crop of coffee. Coffee had become the country's leading export by 1898, accounting for nearly half of its export earnings. Prior to that point, gold had been the nation's main export-earner. By 1924, coffee accounted for almost 80 per cent of Colombia's export revenue, with bananas, petroleum, and light manufacturing making up much of the rest (Bushnell 1993, 169). Coffee production and export proved to have positive spin-off effects on the nation's development. Public works projects in the areas of railroad, transportation networks, and basic infrastructure laid the foundations for Colombia's economic expansion. US investment in Colombia also contributed to the country's growth. In what came to be known as the "Dance of the Millions," the US government paid Colombia an indemnity of $25 million in 1921 for its loss of Panama as Colombian territory, along with another $173 million in loans (Rochlin 2003, 92). Improved relations between the two countries paved the way for US oil companies to invest in Colombia's infant petroleum industry.

The fruits of Colombia's economic expansion, however, were not equitably distributed. Colombian elites showed little interest in investing in education and social welfare programs for the emerging urban working class. In the countryside, the large landowners blocked any attempts at land reform or efforts to address rural poverty (Palacios 2006). Throughout the 1920s, popular discontent and social tensions gave rise to a number of labor unions, peasant associations, and the Revolutionary Socialist Party (PSR). The banana workers' strike of 1928 over low wages and poor working conditions was harshly repressed by the governing Conservative Party, causing a backlash of resentment against the conservatives. In all, almost 75 workers lost their lives as soldiers opened fire on the mass of strikers. Public outrage over the banana workers massacre signaled the end of the conservative era and the rise of the liberal republic.

The election of liberal president Alfonso López Pumarejo (1934–38; 1942–45) marked the first time a Colombian leader sought to address the "social question" over the appropriate role of the working classes within the economic and political system of the country (Bushnell 1993). Adopting what he called "The Revolution on the March," López introduced a number of small reforms, including a moderate agrarian reform law, improved taxation, and extension of the suffrage. However, the rising expectations of the masses soon outpaced the willingness of his party to satisfy them, leading to frustration on the part of the working classes and unease among the ruling classes. López's political successor proved to be a moderate liberal with little interest in pursuing social reforms. By the time López himself returned to power in 1942, he had largely abandoned his progressive platform. The inability of the liberal republic of the 1930s and early 1940s to put into practice its rhetoric of greater socioeconomic inclusion led to growing discontent among the workers and peasantry with the Liberal Party.

LA VIOLENCIA, 1946–1958

The return to power of the Conservative Party in 1946, and its attempt to settle old scores with the liberals, was the spark that ignited a new round of violence. The civil war that broke out later that year between the liberals and the conservatives far exceeded any previous conflict between the two parties in its scope and intensity. The conflict, which lasted well into the establishment of the National Front power-sharing agreement in 1958 and resulted in at least 200,000 deaths, came to be called *La Violencia* (the Violence). The event that fanned the flames of the violence was the assassination of populist liberal leader and presidential hopeful Jorge Eliécer Gaitán on April 9, 1948, in the streets of the capital city of Bogotá by an unknown assassin. Unlike López who came before him, Gaitán was a self-made man of humble origins who identified with the plight of the working class and promised significant social reforms. The young and charismatic Gaitán rose to power by vehemently criticizing the ruling classes' inequitable concentration of power and resources, a discourse which garnered him support from the masses and many enemies among the oligarchic factions of both the Liberal and Conservative Parties (Hylton 2006). In the process of economic modernization, Colombia was witness to significant increases in the country's already inequitable distribution of wealth. During that era, its Gini coefficient rose from 0.45 in 1938 to 0.53 in 1951 (Rochlin 2003, 95). Following Gaitán's murder, Colombia exploded in a series of urban riots that quickly spread to the provinces and shook the very foundations of the country. While the initial uprising was soon quelled, it touched off a wave of partisan conflict that enveloped the country in an almost 20-year cycle of violence.

The violence of the era produced the only military dictatorship that Colombians have ever known—that of General Gustavo Rojas Pinilla (1953–57). Rojas Pinilla, who seized power with a military show of force, vowed to stem the tide of violence in the country and launched a nation-building effort. Initially, factions of both the Liberal and Conservative Parties lent their support to Rojas Pinilla, under the assumption that his regime would be transitory in nature. However, when it became apparent that the general was planning on remaining in power by consolidating his base of support through populist reforms, the two parties quickly joined forces to hasten a return to democratic rule (Dugas 2006). Having found common ground, the liberals and conservatives worked together to remove Rojas Pinilla from power. A series of top-secret discussions between party elites led to the adoption of a governing pact in 1958 called the National Front. The power-sharing agreement, which remained in place until 1978, terminated the historic rivalry between the liberals and conservatives, and drew to a close the country's period of partisan violence once and for all.

THE NATIONAL FRONT ERA, 1958–1978

A defining feature of the National Front governing pact between the Liberal and Conservative Parties was party parity. Among its various points, the presidency would alternate every four years between the liberals and conservatives, regardless of election outcomes. In addition, all legislative bodies and government positions would be equally shared between the two parties. This system of institutionalized bipartisanship served to deter partisan conflicts by providing the parties with mutual guarantees in the protection of their interests (Bushnell 1993; Dugas 2006). As a matter of course, new political parties were excluded from the polity. Consequently, while the rules of the political game may have changed, the system itself remained based on the old logic of political exclusion. Instead of working to exclude one another from power, the traditional parties now worked together to exclude all others from the political arena (Rochlin 2003). The parties justified these democratic restrictions as being necessary for bringing about a measure of political stability to a deeply divided nation.

The stability afforded by the National Front coalition translated into significant economic gains for Colombia in the second half of the twentieth century. The economy became more industrialized and diversified as the nation underwent a process of import-substitution industrialization (ISI), designed to replace manufactured goods previously imported with those made domestically. However, unlike much of Latin America, Colombian policymakers complemented their ISI strategy with export promotion (Hershberg 2006). The country's internationally renowned economists also avoided the high degree of state intervention that characterized many other economies. As a result, Colombia managed to sidestep the debt crisis of the 1980s that devastated many countries of the Global South. In fact, Colombia did not experience a single year of negative economic growth during that time period (Dugas 2006, 500). Colombia's combination of macroeconomic stability and low debt growth also allowed it to avoid having to implement harsh neoliberal economic policies, at least until the 1990s. By that time, the country's economy looked quite different from what it did at the start of the century. In the 1990s, coffee accounted for less than 10 per cent of Colombia's export earnings. This decline in importance was precipitated by the growth of non-traditional exports, including cut flowers, processed foods, and petroleum. The country's most lucrative export, however, was cocaine and other illegal narcotics, which by some estimates added $36 billion to the Colombian economy in the 1980 to 1994 period (Skidmore and Smith 2005, 234). However, this economic boost came with a high social cost.

The National Front may have succeeded in ending partisan conflicts and instituting the basis for economic development, but it produced a number of unanticipated consequences. Many scholars have suggested that the rigid and exclusionary logic of the power-sharing arrangement contributed to a new and distinct cycle of violence led by social actors denied access to political participation. Chief among those shut out of the system were the newly emerged middle class, intellectuals, the political left, and the poor (Rochlin 2003). According to Peeler (1976), the behavior of the traditional parties reflected perfectly the conservative strategy for preserving order and stability suggested by Samuel P. Huntington's influential thesis. Huntington (1972) argued that socioeconomic modernization tends to broaden popular participation and increase political demands on the state to remove obstacles which prevent the deepening of democracy and increase the standard of living of the people. The state, lacking autonomy from the elites and quality institutions, is unable to implement popular demands. Without state capacity, one of the top priorities of modernizing governments should be the strengthening of political institutions and the moderation or restriction of political involvement as a means of preventing instability. In Colombia, the process of modernization proved to be a gradual one, and the party system along with the weak state easily absorbed the inherent tensions and disruptions it produced. Nonetheless, the failure of the traditional parties to respond to the changing nature of Colombian society provided fertile ground for the rise of opposition movements. Without access to legitimate political avenues, opposition groups were left with no choice but to resort to extra-systemic means of fomenting change.

GUERRILLA MOVEMENTS AND THE STATE

The crescendo of partisan violence that culminated in the National Front gave way to a new assortment of belligerents in Colombia in the 1980s: left-wing guerrilla movements, right-wing paramilitary forces, and criminal-minded narco-traffickers. However, unlike the partisan violence of the previous era that originated from within the state, the latest cycle of violence that erupted with the rise of leftist guerrillas in the 1960s and 1970s was aimed at overthrowing the established political and socioeconomic order (Archer 1995). The explosive combination of profound socioeconomic inequalities and highly exclusionary political structures was one of the central contributing factors to the rise of guerrilla movements in Colombia in particular, and in Latin America in general. Early in the history of the republic, a decision was made on the part of Colombian elites to repress rather than address popular concerns. This well-established pattern of governing has resulted in seemingly endless cycles of violence, with the current conflict producing even more deaths than the War of a Thousand Days and *La Violencia* combined (Green 2005).

A central actor in the current crisis is the Revolutionary Armed Forces of Colombia (FARC), Latin America's most militarily powerful subversive group at the dawn of the current century. The FARC is made up of approximately 18,000 members led by a 12-person secretariat and operates with virtual impunity in almost half of Colombia's territory. The central leader and founder of the FARC, Manuel Marulanda Vélez (also known as "Tirofijo" or "Sure Shot"), originally took up arms as a liberal peasant during *La Violencia* (Kline and Gray 2007). Marulanda waged war against the Colombian state until his death in March 2008. The new FARC leader is the guerrilla hard-liner Alfonso Cano. The FARC, like many Latin American guerrilla movements, was formed in the post-Cuban revolutionary context of the 1960s. The revolutionary group was forged out of disgruntled members of the Communist Party, armed peasant groups, and other leftist forces. It espouses a dogmatic Marxist ideology. The cornerstone of the FARC's support base, then and now, is the Colombian peasantry. The situation of extreme rural poverty and unequal land distribution that characterizes the Colombian countryside has fueled support for the guerrillas and influenced their mandate. The FARC, along with other guerrilla groups operating in the country, call for a redistribution of power and resources away from foreign interests and national elites to the poor.

Colombia's other notable guerrilla groups include the National Liberation Army (ELN), the 19th of April Movement (M-19), Quintín Lame, and the Popular Liberation Army (EPL). With the exception of the FARC and the ELN, all of Colombia's other guerrilla groups demobilized and were reintegrated into society in the early 1990s. Colombia's second-largest guerrilla group, the ELN, is a Cuban-inspired guerrilla movement which was founded by radical priests, intellectuals, and university students in the mid-1960s. Its current membership stands at approximately 5,000 individuals. The ELN largely finances its activities by imposing a "tax" on multinational oil corporations operating in Colombia, and by kidnapping foreign oil workers for ransom. Relations between the FARC and the much weaker ELN have proven just as fractional and conflict-ridden as the rest of Colombian society. In 1987, the FARC, the ELN, and the EPL created an umbrella organization called the Simón Bolívar Guerrilla Coordinator (CGSB), in an effort to coordinate action among the guerrillas. The CGSB experiment fell apart after only a few years due to ideological differences and competition over resources. According to Rochlin (2003, 124), the various guerrilla movements have been more interested in maximizing their own power and territorial control than in working together toward a common revolutionary goal. Today, direct confrontations between the FARC and the ELN have become more common because the FARC is attempting to attain guerrilla hegemony.

Since the 1980s, the FARC has more than doubled in its size and strength, thanks in large part to its links with Colombia's illicit drug trade. The relationship between the FARC and the drug industry is a point of contention among analysts. It is widely acknowledged that the drug trade, particularly the coca (used for cocaine production) and poppy (used for heroin production) industries, accounts for at least half of the FARC's operating budget. The proceeds from the drug trade have funded the FARC's military expansion and enabled the group to become self-sufficient at a time when external support for revolutionary movements from the Soviet Union and China had disappeared. The FARC's main connection to the narcotics industry is in providing law, order, and protection to peasant populations involved in coca and poppy cultivation, processing, and distribution, in exchange for a 10 per cent "revolutionary tax" (Rochlin 2003). The FARC provides coca and poppy growers with protection from the state and its US-backed War on Drugs, and from the drug cartels that seek to take over their lands and maximize profits at the expense of the workers. As Seres points out (2000, 205), labeling the FARC as a criminal enterprise or its members as "narco-guerrillas" for their role in the drug trade only obscures the roots of the current crisis. The FARC and the revolutionary conditions in the Colombian countryside predate the drug boom of the 1980s.

In what ultimately amounted to a lost opportunity for social peace, the conservative government of Belisario Betancur (1982–86) sought an end to the current conflict by entering into peace negotiations with the guerrilla movements. Betancur passed an amnesty law in 1982 in an attempt to get the various guerrilla groups to lay down their arms. In 1984 the government signed peace accords with the FARC, the EPL, and the M-19. The ELN refused to participate. The peace process, however, faced a number of insurmountable obstacles, including resistance from congress and the military, criticism from the guerrillas for lack of action on pressing socioeconomic issues, and the inability of both sides to comply with the terms of the accords. Frustrated with the process, the EPL and the M-19 returned to their armed struggle against the state. The FARC, in a good faith gesture, maintained its tenuous cease-fire with the state and launched its own political party in 1985—the Patriotic Union (UP). The UP experiment represented the FARC's first attempt at a political strategy, as opposed to a military one. In the 1986 congressional elections, the UP won an impressive number of seats and had begun to build a support base. The government, for its part, turned a blind eye to the systematic slaughter of UP leaders and supporters that was carried out by paramilitaries such as the one led by Black Vladimir shortly thereafter. It is estimated that some 2,000 to 4,000 UP politicians and their supporters were murdered during the late 1980s and early 1990s, wiping the political party off the map (Dudley 2004). According to Dugas (2006, 511), "This systematic campaign against UP militants, which would continue for years, is one of the greatest human rights tragedies of recent Latin American history." The incident sent a powerful message to the FARC that no legitimate political avenue for socioeconomic reform exists in the country.

Beginning in the 1990s, the FARC focused its efforts on obtaining official control over a section of Colombian territory as a means of consolidating its presence and instituting its own system of governing. At the height of the conflict in 1998, the conservative government of President Andrés Pastrana (1998–2002) ceded control of five municipalities spanning 42,000 square kilometers (roughly the size of Switzerland) to the FARC in an effort to jump-start peace talks (Bejarano and Leongómez 2002, 19). The ceasefire zone was in the heart of the country's coca and poppy industries, an area long dominated by the FARC and in which the state had been historically absent. The new territorial focus of the FARC represented a narrowing in scope of its initial revolutionary objective of state takeover. It was increasingly clear to the rebels that they lacked the support of the general public needed for a successful revolution, and so they opted instead to carve out their own isolated city-state structure (Rochlin 2003). However, the Pastrana government's complaints over FARC abuses in the supposed demilitarized zone and the rebels' concerns over the increasingly hostile paramilitary forces soon jeopardized the peace process. Any hopes for a negotiated settlement to the conflict were dashed in 2002 when the military, backed by US support, was sent in to repossess the zone. The FARC retaliated with bombing attacks in the major urban centers, including firing mortar bombs at the presidential palace during the inauguration of the current president, Álvaro Uribe. The most devastating of these attacks was against the Nogal nightclub in Bogotá in February 2003, which resulted in the death of more than 30 civilians (Crandall 2005). This definitive break in peace talks marked the start of the latest government strategy toward the guerrillas based on the increasing use of force to secure victory via military defeat.

NARCO-TRAFFICKERS AND THE STATE

Smuggling has long been a mainstay of the Colombian economy. Since the colonial period, the country's geographical advantage, of being bordered by two seas with a dense network of tributaries serving as important transport systems, coupled with the historic absence of the state in these areas, have provided the ideal environment for the import and export of contraband (Vargas 2004). Over time, the consumption of illegally sold goods and services became a socially accepted practice in Colombia. The country's high import tariffs and tight foreign exchange controls which were in place from the 1930s until the neoliberal reforms of the 1990s translated into increasing reliance on black market items for much of the population (Thoumi 1995, 173). In addition to a flourishing market for import contraband, Colombia developed an export contraband tradition. The smuggling of a vast array of manufactured products, exotic species, coffee, emeralds, and even human beings put enterprising Colombians in contact with international black markets and underground networks. The combination of these factors produced an environment conducive to the growth of the illegal drug trade.

The drug trade has been a source of both direct and indirect violence in Colombia. Directly, the country's major drug cartels are responsible for the assassinations and kidnappings of numerous opposition politicians, judges, reporters, police officers, soldiers, and government functionaries. During the 1980s and early 1990s, the considerable power of the country's three main drug cartels, the Medellín, Cali, and Atlantic Coast cartels contributed to one of the highest murder rates in the world. Between 1982 and 1991, Colombia's homicide rate peaked at 86 per 100,000 inhabitants (Posada-Carbó 2004, 69). Leaders of the drug cartels have also sought to gain direct access to policy-making in the country by financing election campaigns and influencing local level election outcomes, as well as relying on bribery, corruption, threats, and the indiscriminate use of terror. The most notorious case of campaign finance was that of liberal President Ernesto Samper (1994–98) by the Cali cartel.

After the 1989 assassination of Senator Luis Carlos Galán, a presidential candidate promising to take a hard line on drugs, liberal President Virgilio

Barco (1986–90) declared an all-out war on drug traffickers, confiscating their properties and agreeing to extradite them to the United States to stand trial (Kline and Gray 2007). The cartels responded by declaring war against the Colombian state, and began a massive urban bombing campaign. Drug-related violence eased under the liberal administration of César Gaviria (1990–94) due to the president's plea bargain approach. Drug traffickers were given guarantees of non-extradition and a reduced sentence if they surrendered to authorities. The approach proved effective at bringing in the drug kingpin Pablo Escobar in 1991, and in the eventual dismantlement of the major cartels. However, Colombia's drug trade continues to thrive, as dozens of small- to medium-sized trafficking organizations took over the business of the big cartels, in effect decentralizing the industry.

Indirectly, proceeds from the drug industry have financed both the guerrillas and the paramilitaries, expanding their ranks and military capabilities relative to that of the state, and escalating the level of violence in the country. Initially during the 1980s, sections of the FARC served as armed security forces for the large drug traffickers, protecting their landing strips and processing plants for a percentage of the profits (Rochlin 2003). The ideological clash between the two groups, however, soon turned them into embattled enemies. The drug kingpins are known for being fiercely capitalistic, viewing themselves as Colombia's new elites. The cartels have also obtained vast amounts of land on which to build their estates and run their businesses, often by forcing peasants off their lands, resulting in a counteragrarian reform in the countryside (Dugas 2006). These actions alienated the socialist FARC, and pitted them against the cartels. The reaction of the narco-traffickers was to work together with other large landowners to create their own private security forces to combat the FARC and protect their investments in areas where state presence was especially weak (Kline 2008). For example, in 1981 the infamous Death to Kidnappers (MAS) organization arose to protect wealthy landowners and drug lords from a rash of kidnappings being carried out by the FARC and the ELN. These private armies gave rise to the right-wing paramilitary forces of today that are in open combat with the guerrillas. Thus, the original two-way conflict between the FARC and the state now involves two additional armed actors—the narco-traffickers and the paramilitaries. The drug trade has completely transformed Colombia's economic, social, and political landscape. The level and mode of violence that the industry has produced has little in common with the country's partisan conflicts of the last two centuries.

PARAMILITARIES AND THE STATE

The Colombian state's response to insurgent groups has been characterized by Mauceri (2004) as one of abdication and privatization. In other words, rather than strengthening the state's monopoly of force, governments have ceded control to private societal actors to deal with the guerrillas. The Colombian military has historically been weak. For example, while Latin American military forces on average consisted of 4.4 soldiers per 1,000 inhabitants in 1980, Colombia's average stood only at 2.3 soldiers (Rochlin 2003, 101). Since colonial times, regional elites in Colombia have relied on private militias to maintain their territorial strongholds. The rise of the FARC and other guerrilla movements in the 1960s met with renewed interest in the formation of self-defense groups or death squads on the part of the nation's elites. In 1968, the government promulgated legislation that permitted and encouraged the formation of armed civilian self-defense groups under the supervision of the armed forces. Over time, these private armies evolved into militarily sophisticated and well-financed paramilitary forces. While the paramilitaries and the Colombian government share a common enemy in the FARC and the ELN, the links between the two have never been clear. Many analysts have suggested that the brutal campaign conducted by the paramilitaries against the guerrillas allows the Colombian state to reap the benefits without having to pay the price of being associated with gross human rights violations.

The paramilitaries claim to be defending society from guerrillas and criminals, and view their role as one of establishing much-needed security. In 1997, the various paramilitary units operating throughout the country coalesced under an umbrella organization called the United Self-Defense Forces of Colombia (AUC). The AUC currently stands at approximately 14,000 members. Its forces target guerrillas as well as their suspected civilian supporters, including trade unionists, peasants, indigenous peoples, teachers, and journalists. As a result, the AUC has now become the major perpetrator of human rights abuses in the country. In 2000, it was estimated that the AUC committed 70 per cent of Colombia's political assassinations. It is also estimated that at least 70 per cent of its financing is derived from the drug trade (Rochlin 2003, 147). The AUC supports itself by collecting "rents" from wealthy landowners, narco-traffickers, and multinational corporations. In fact, in March 2007, the US government fined the Chiquita banana corporation for paying out $1.7 million to the AUC for protection of its properties and employees over the previous decade (Kline 2008, 214). The AUC is Colombia's fastest-growing illegal actor. The level of brutality of paramilitary-led massacres led President Barco in 1989 to publicly call the groups "criminals" and to declare them unconstitutional. Later that year, the supreme court overturned the 1968 authorizing law. However, little action has been taken on the part of the state to curtail paramilitary activities. In 2002, current President Álvaro Uribe (2002–10) signed a cease-fire agreement with the AUC, and a number of paramilitaries did demobilize, but many units continue to operate with impunity (Kline and Gray 2007). Instead of resolving Colombia's long-standing problem of violence, the paramilitaries are now part of the problem.

PLAN COLOMBIA

Since the 1990s, the United States has played an increasing role in the Colombian conflict by way of the US War on Drugs. President George Bush Sr.'s (1988–92) Andean Initiative, the precursor to Plan Colombia, poured over $2 billion in loans and aid into Colombia, Bolivia, and Peru, in an effort to stem the flow of drugs at the source (Avilés 2006, 390). At that time, Colombia's flagging military was falling back into a defensive position against the onslaught of the quick, mobile, and well-trained guerrilla forces. The goal of the US and Colombian governments was to bolster local anti-drug law enforcement and military units in order to dismantle drug-trafficking networks as well as to combat the FARC. The association between the FARC and the drug trade served as the pretext for the US counterinsurgency campaign in the country. In 2000, President Clinton (1992–2000) announced a massive $1.3 billion emergency aid package known as Plan Colombia. This comprehensive package was initially designed to eradicate illicit crops, support a negotiated settlement with the FARC and the ELN, revive the Colombian economy, provide support for human rights, strengthen the rule of law, and promote alternative development. In practice, however, Plan Colombia has served as a conduit for US military assistance. Under the plan, $519 million has been allocated for military assistance, while only $3 million has been earmarked for peace objectives (Rochlin 2003, 152). Colombia currently receives the third largest amount of US military aid in the world.

One of the repercussions of the September 11 terrorist attacks on the United States was that the George W. Bush administration officially dropped any pretense of supporting Colombia's security forces solely for the purpose of stamping out the drug trade. Under the new discourse of counter-terrorism, the FARC is now labeled a terrorist organization and is perceived as a threat to democracy and regional security (Dugas 2006). Many analysts take a different stance. For example, Youngers (2004) has argued that the US government's War on Drugs, as it is played out in Colombia, constitutes one of the largest obstacles to the strengthening and deepening of democracy in the country. The increase in the influence and role of security forces

relative to that of civilian institutions as a result of Plan Colombia undermines an already weak and delegitimized state. Furthermore, the merging
of counternarcotics and counterterrorism operations only increases the
level of political violence in the country and fosters even greater human
rights abuses. Finally, US military aid to Colombia has come at the expense
of development assistance, which remains woefully inadequate despite its
potential to address the real roots of the crisis.

DEMOCRACY UNDER SIEGE

There are a number of obvious threats to democracy in Colombia. In an
effort to bolster the country's political system and seek an end to the conflict, Colombian leaders have introduced an array of democratizing reforms
since the mid-1980s. While the reforms have managed to remove all vestiges
of the democratic restrictions from the National Front era, they have not
solved the crisis of Colombia's weakly institutionalized democracy. In fact,
some scholars have suggested that reforms such as political decentralization
have done more harm than good by further weakening and destabilizing
the central state (Bejarano and Pizarro 2002; Eaton 2006; Whitehead 2003).
Bejarano and Pizarro (2002) argue that the solution to Colombia's impasse
is to build a democratic state with strong central authority that is matched
by effective controls on abuses of that authority, or "authority without
authoritarianism." Avilés (2006) adds that in order to deepen democracy
in Colombia, political elites must combine political reforms with policies
aimed at reducing socioeconomic inequalities. Almost all analysts agree
that the current crisis cannot be resolved by bullets; instead, a concerted
effort to promote social justice, human rights, and democracy is necessary.

The idea of pacification through decentralization first gained prominence
under the administration of President Belisario Betancur in the early 1980s.
Betancur tied his proposal for direct mayoral elections to the peace process.
The successful 1988 mayoral race saw a number of new political parties
win seats in local office, including the FARC's Patriotic Union (UP). Three
years later the UP was on the brink of extinction, and the Colombian state
was suffering from a partial collapse due to the serious challenges posed by
the expansion of guerrilla warfare and drug-related violence (Bejarano and
Pizarro 2002). In an effort to salvage the state's legitimacy, newly elected
President César Gaviria called for a constituent assembly to redraft the
nation's Constitution. The new Constitution was meant to heal state–society relations, and to reincorporate guerrilla groups into civilian life. The
EPL, M-19, and Quintín Lame guerrilla movements all signed peace accords
with the government, demobilized, and became active participants in the
constitutional process (Dugas 2006). The 1991 constitution represented a

significant step toward democratization. It deepened the process of decentralization, introduced a bill of citizen rights, and provided for a variety of new participatory mechanisms. It also increased representation for ethnic minorities by establishing two reserved seats in the senate for indigenous representatives (Van Cott 2005). Perhaps most importantly, it promoted a political solution to Colombia's persistent problems.

The democratizing reforms of the 1990s produced a number of unexpected and unsavory consequences. It was hoped that political decentralization would open up spaces for meaningful participation in the formal political arena for excluded actors, and bring about a negotiated settlement with insurgents. Decentralization is frequently used in post-conflict settings as a means of increasing the various actors' stake in the political system. In the case of Colombia, however, decentralizing reforms were pursued during the height of the conflict in an effort to end hostilities. According to Eaton (2006), not only has this strategy failed, it has also destabilized the country. The devolution of greater power and resources to sub-national governments has led the FARC to refocus their efforts on the consolidation and expansion of its control over municipal governments rather than the central state. The number of municipalities recorded as either partially or completely beyond the control of locally elected officials due to the threat and practice of guerrilla violence rose from 173 in 1985 to 622 in 1995; more than half of all municipalities (Eaton 2006, 552). The high levels of electoral abstention that characterize these municipalities provide further evidence of the precariousness of democracy in the country.

The new rules of the political game have also altered the strategy of Colombia's paramilitary groups. Since the 1990s, paramilitaries have sought to legitimize themselves and attain direct political authority by making inroads into municipal and departmental governments. For example, in the municipal elections of 2003 in Medellín, Colombia's second-largest city, demobilized paramilitary soldiers managed to capture 30 out of 50 seats in the local governing body (Eaton 2006, 557). Along the Caribbean coast, a major paramilitary stronghold, all but one candidate withdrew his name from the race, the others citing threats made on their lives by the AUC as the reason. Guerrillas and paramilitary groups have, in effect, created parallel state structures that are polarized between the political left and right (Eaton 2006). This dynamic has also produced what can only be called an open season on mayors and mayoral candidates in Colombia. For instance, between the January 1998 and the October 2000 local and regional elections, 34 mayors were killed and over 100 were kidnapped (Caballero 2000). In the most recent campaign leading up to the October 2007 elections, 16 mayoral candidates and 70 of their supporters were killed as a result of armed clashes between guerrillas and paramilitaries over control of local governing bodies (Tocancip 2007). Analysts have found that Colombian mayors are 25 times more likely to be murdered than the average citizen in the country, which makes being a mayor in Colombia one of the most dangerous jobs in the world.

Public outrage over the levels of violence and corruption in Colombia has translated into growing support for politicians who promise to take a hardline against illegal actors. In 2002, liberal party defector Álvaro Uribe was elected president based on a get-tough platform. His policies have sought to reestablish state authority throughout Colombian territory by reinforcing the military and working closely with the US government. In his address to the UN General Assembly in 2002, President Uribe emphasized that every month in Colombia violence claims the lives of the same number of people who died in the September 11 terrorist attacks on the United States (Posada-Carbó 2004, 69). During his first four years in office, his government's military offensive succeeded in pushing the guerrillas out of the major urban centers. His administration also began the difficult process of paramilitary demobilization, resulting in 2,624 paramilitary soldiers surrendering their weapons in 2004. Overall, crime statistics reveal a downward trend during Uribe's administration, with murder rates in 2006 being the lowest reported in 20 years, and the number of kidnappings down to 621 from a record high of 3,572 set in the year 2000 (Kline 2008, 205). By mid-2004, President Uribe's efforts had led to the capture or killing of 10,000 guerrillas and operative paramilitaries, earning him an approval rating of nearly 80 per cent. Cresting on a wave of popularity, President Uribe was granted a constitutional amendment, allowing him to serve two consecutive terms as president. Uribe won the presidential race of 2006 in a landslide victory. Since that time, however, his administration has come under serious national and international scrutiny because at least 60 congressional representatives were arrested or placed under investigation by the supreme court for alleged links with paramilitary forces in mid-2008. The so-called parapolitical scandal, which primarily involved Uribe's political allies, cast a pall over his administration's reputation. More worryingly, it calls in question the ability of any government to separate itself from Colombia's broader context of violence and non-democratic processes.

CIVIL SOCIETY RESPONSES

Colombia's civil society is notoriously weak and fragmented. Marginalized social groups have been the main casualties of Colombia's never-ending war. In the countryside, threats and violence by paramilitary and guerrilla groups have forced millions to abandon their lands to travel to the relative safety of the major cities. The conflict has produced the world's second-largest internally displaced population, estimated at approximately 3.6 million people (Kline 2008). The majority of the displaced are Afro-Colombians and indigenous peoples. Colombia has the second-largest population of African descent in Latin America, an estimated 25 per cent of the Colombian population. The strong presence of paramilitary troops along the Caribbean coast, where the majority of the Afro-Colombian population resides, has resulted in forced migrations out of the region. Although the country's indigenous peoples represent only 2 per cent of the total population, their reserves, which make up almost 30 per cent of Colombian territory, have become battlegrounds between the guerrillas and the paramilitaries (Hylton 2006). In the cities, thousands of trade unionists, NGO workers, intellectuals, leftists, and anyone else who dared to speak out against the conflict have been murdered. Colombia is one of the most dangerous places in the world to be a trade unionist. Between 1986 and 2003, almost 4,000 union activists were assassinated (Avilés 2006, 403). The Colombian conflict has produced a humanitarian crisis of epic proportions.

One of the few positive developments in Colombia over the past decade has been the emergence of organized social actors promoting an agenda of peace. Mass peace rallies and marches began to occur with greater frequency in the nation's cities and provincial capitals during the 1990s. A number of peace communities also formed during this time period. Peace communities reject violence by refusing to take up arms or to support any armed actors, whether they be guerrillas, paramilitaries, or national security forces, using tactics that include denying them food, supplies, shelter, and information (Alther 2007). This grassroots peace initiative originated among war-torn Afro-Colombian, indigenous, and peasant communities. There are currently 50 officially declared peace communities in Colombia. Colombia's oldest and most well-known community is San José de Apartado in the department of Antioquia, which has received international recognition for its efforts to promote peace (Hylton 2006). The community employs a number of protection strategies, including traveling in groups, using whistles to alert members to the presence of armed actors, and relying on NGO accompaniment outside of their towns. Despite their best efforts, more than 100 members of San José de Apartado have been killed since it was first established as a peace community in 1997 (Alther 2007, 109). The community, however, remains firm in its commitment to not choose sides and to seek an alternative route out of the conflict.

CONCLUSION

Colombia's 1960-era guerrilla groups continue to fight long after their counterparts in neighboring countries have demobilized. What explains the persistence of the revolutionary path to social change in the country? The conditions that led poor peasants such as Black Vladimir to take up arms in the first place included a highly exclusionary socioeconomic and political order. While significant steps have been made since the mid-1980s to reform Colombia's political system to make it more open and representative, social and economic inequalities persist. Colombia is second only to Brazil in having Latin America's most unequal distribution of wealth. Its concentration of land and income in the hands of a small minority has worsened since the late 1980s. Colombia's Gini coefficient currently stands at 0.58, making it one of the most unequal countries in the world. Unless substantial efforts are made to address poverty and inequality in the country, protracted warfare seems the most likely scenario.

What might the future hold for the beleaguered nation of Colombia? The current administration of President Uribe is attempting to resolve the conflict by escalating it (Gallón 2007). In stark contrast to its Pink Tide neighbors, the public association of civil society actors ranging from human rights organizations to indigenous groups with insurgent movements reflects the intolerance of even the reformist political left among sectors of Colombian society. The redefinition of the problem as one of terrorism signals the end of a negotiated or political solution to the crisis. According to Rochlin (2003), Plan Colombia's introduction of advanced military technology and intelligence may be what ultimately derails the FARC by slowly eating away at its military power. The recent and highly publicized rescue in July 2008 of presidential candidate Ingrid Betancourt, who was kidnapped by the FARC in 2002 as a result of a carefully planned operation based on military intelligence, speaks to this trend. While this impressive victory for the Uribe government may have prompted some observers to sound the beginning of the end of the FARC, most scholars agree that Colombia's prospects for peace and security in the near future remain bleak.

NOTE

1 Adapted from Dudley (2004, 55–64).

REFERENCES

Alther, Gretchen. 2007. "Colombian Peace Communities: The Role of NGOs in Supporting Resistance to Violence." *Development and Humanitarianism: Practical Issues.* Ed. Deborah Eade and Tony Vaux. Bloomfield, CT: Kumarian Press. 101–21.

Archer, Ronald P. 1995. "Party Strength and Weakness in Colombia's Besieged Democracy." *Building Democratic Institutions: Party Systems in Latin America.* Ed. Scott Mainwaring and Timothy R. Scully. Stanford: Stanford University Press. 164–99.

Avilés, William. 2006. "Paramilitarism and Colombia's Low-Intensity Democracy." *Journal of Latin American Studies* 38: 379–408.

Bejarano, Ana María, and Eduardo Pizarro Leongómez. 2002. "From 'Restricted' to 'Besieged': The Changing Nature of the Limits to Democracy in Colombia." Working Paper No. 296. Notre Dame: Helen Kellogg Institute for International Studies.

Bushnell, David. 1993. *The Making of Modern Colombia: A Nation In Spite of Itself.* Berkeley: University of California Press.

Caballero, Maria Cristina. 2000. "Opinion: Colombia, the Nastiest Elections in the World" (October 27). June 2, 2010. http://archives.cnn.com/2000/WORLD/americas/10/27/colombia.opinion/index.html.

Crandall, Russell. 2005. "From Drugs to Security: A New US Policy toward Colombia." *The Andes in Focus: Security, Democracy and Economic Reform.* Ed. Russell Crandall, Guadalupe Paz, and Riordan Roett. Boulder: Lynne Rienner Press. 173–89.

Dudley, Steven. 2004. *Walking Ghosts: Murder and Guerrilla Politics in Colombia.* New York: Routledge Press.

Dugas, John C. 2006. "Colombia." *Politics of Latin America: The Power Game.* Ed. Harry E. Vanden and Gary Prevost. New York: Oxford University Press. 497–525.

Eaton, Kent. 2006. "The Downside of Decentralization: Armed Clientelism in Colombia." *Security Studies* 15(4): 533–62.

Gallón, Gustavo. 2007. "This War Cannot Be Won with Bullets." *Peace, Democracy, and Human Rights in Colombia.* Ed. Christopher Welna and Gustavo Gallón. Notre Dame: University of Notre Dame Press. 415–32.

Green, John W. 2005. "Guerrillas, Soldiers, Paramilitaries, Assassins, Narcos and Gringos: The Unhappy Prospects for Peace and Democracy in Colombia." *Latin American Research Review* 40(2): 137–65.

Hershberg, Eric. 2006. "Technocrats, Citizens, and Second-Generation Reforms: Colombia's Andean Malaise." *State and Society in Conflict: Comparative Perspectives on Andean Crises.* Ed. Paul W. Drake and Eric Hershberg. Pittsburgh: University of Pittsburgh Press. 134–56.

Huntington, Samuel P. 1972. *Political Order in Changing Societies.* New Haven: Yale University Press.

Hylton, Forrest. 2006. *Evil Hour in Colombia.* New York: Verso Books.

Kline, Harvey F. 2008. "Colombia." *Countries at Crossroads 2007: A Survey of Democratic Governance.* Ed. Sanja Kelly, Christopher Walker, and Jake Dizard. New York: Rowman and Littlefield. 197–220.

Kline, Harvey F., and Vanessa Joan Gray. 2007. "Colombia: A Resilient Political System with Intransigent Problems." *Latin American Politics and Development.* Ed. Howard J. Wiarda and Harvey F. Kline. Boulder: Westview Press. 199–233.

Mauceri, Philip. 2004. "State, Elites, and the Response to Insurgency: Some Preliminary Comparisons between Colombia and Peru." *Politics in the Andes: Identity, Conflict, Reform.* Ed. Jo-Marie Burt and Philip Mauceri. Pittsburgh: University of Pittsburgh Press. 146–63.

Palacios, Marco. 2006. *Between Legitimacy and Violence: A History of Colombia, 1875–2002.* Durham, NC: Duke University Press.

Peeler, John A. 1976. "Colombian Parties and Political Development." *Journal of Interamerican Studies and World Affairs* 18(2): 203–24.

Posada-Carbó, Eduardo. 2004. "Colombia's Resilient Democracy." *Current History* 103(670): 68–73.

Rochlin, James F. 2003. *Vanguard Revolutionaries in Latin America: Peru, Colombia, Mexico.* Boulder: Lynne Rienner Press.

Santa, Eduardo. 1964. *Sociología Política de Colombia.* Bogotá: Ediciones Tercer Mundo.

Seres, Philippe. 2000. "The FARC and Democracy in Colombia in the 1990s." *Democratization* 17(4): 191–218.

Skidmore, Thomas E., and Peter H. Smith. 2005. *Modern Latin America.* 6th ed. Oxford: Oxford University Press.

Thoumi, Francisco E. 1995. *Political Economy and Illegal Drugs in Colombia.* Boulder: Lynne Rienner Press.

Tocancip, Luz Stella. 2007. "Colombia: Assassinations Cast a Pall over Upcoming Elections" (October 18). June 2, 2010. www.highbeam.com/doc/1P1-145063840. html.

Van Cott, Donna Lee. 2005. *From Movements to Parties in Latin America: The Evolution of Ethnic Politics.* New York: Cambridge University Press.

Vargas, Ricardo 2004. "State, Esprit Mafioso, and Armed Conflict in Colombia." *Politics in the Andes: Identity, Conflict, Reform.* Ed. Jo-Marie Burt and Philip Mauceri. Pittsburgh: University of Pittsburgh Press. 107–25.

Whitehead, Laurence. 2003. "The Dark Side of Democratization: 'Dysfunctional' Democracies in South America?" *Colombia Internacional* 58: 8–35.

Youngers, Coletta A. 2004. "Collateral Damage: The US 'War on Drugs' and its Impact on Democracy in the Andes." *Politics in the Andes: Identity, Conflict, Reform.* Ed. Jo-Marie Burt and Philip Mauceri. Pittsburgh: University of Pittsburgh Press. 126–45.

E-RESOURCES

Amnesty International on Colombia (in English) (www.amnesty.org/en/region/colombia). This organization reports on news and campaigns concerning human rights violations in Colombia.

Center for International Policy: Colombia Program (in English) (www.ciponline.org/colombia/index.htm). A guide to US security policy in Colombia.

Government of Colombia Online (www.gobiernoenlinea.gov.co). This website provides access to the main branches of the Colombian government.

Indigenous Authorities of Colombia (www.aicocolombia.org). The website of Colombia's main indigenous organization.

National Department of Statistics (DANE) (www.dane.gov.co). Provides census data for Colombia.

UN Office of the High Commissioner for Human Rights in Colombia (in English) (www.ohchr.org). An international body dedicated to the promotion and protection of all human rights.

NINE

Venezuela: Pacts, Populism, and Poverty

ROBERTA RICE

Early in the morning on February 27, 1989, a group of university students formed a human chain across the entranceway to the intercity bus terminal in the capital city of Caracas, Venezuela. The students stood in resistance against the impending public transportation price hike as part of the conditions for an IMF loan. The protests against the fare increase were part of a larger struggle against the program of macroeconomic adjustment announced by the government of President Carlos Andrés Pérez earlier that month. When the transportation lines began to charge more than the scheduled 30 per cent fare increase, students and commuters in Caracas and the surrounding townships set buses on fire in retaliation against the government's actions. In the grips of a popular revolt, Caracas exploded in a series of riots. The event turned into one of the most violent episodes of the austerity protests in Latin America's "lost decade." Overwhelmed by the violence as the riots spread across the country, the government declared a state of emergency. State repression was particularly harsh in the poor neighborhoods of the capital. Thousands were injured and arrested, with the official death toll reaching 277, though unofficial estimates put the fatalities in the thousands. The "Caracazo," as it become known, left many observers wondering how such violent protests could occur in one of the region's most historically stable and democratic countries. However, the year 1989 marked the end of Venezuela's democratic exceptionalism. It exposed the depth of its institutional decline and the failure of the state to respond to public sector demands. The harsh socioeconomic impacts of market reforms in the 1980s produced a crisis in the party system and democratic institutions to the point that they were unable to respond to existing demands. This gave rise to an alternative political and economic project in the country. The unraveling of representative democracy in Venezuela and with it, the emergence of a political outsider and champion of the poor, President Hugo Chávez, has effectively addressed the needs and demands of the country's dispossessed, but it has done so at a high cost to democracy.[1]

OIL IN HISTORICAL AND POLITICAL PERSPECTIVES, 1819–1935

Venezuela is situated on the northern coast of South America, facing the Caribbean Sea. Colombia, Guyana, and Brazil are its neighbors. The third longest river in South America, the Orinoco, runs through the center of Venezuela and drains into the sea. Much of the country's small indigenous population lives along the Orinoco River in the Amazonian basin. The country's indigenous people make up less than 2 per cent of the total population, yet they have managed to secure a measure of representation in the political system since the late 1990s through electoral reforms and their own partisan organizing efforts (Rice and Van Cott 2006). Contemporary Venezuela is a predominantly mestizo society, with most people living in the coastal highland cities in the northwest. It is the wealthiest of the Andean nations, with a per capita gross national income (GNI) of $7,550 in 2007. The World Bank classifies Venezuela as an upper-middle-income economy. The country's wealth is derived almost exclusively from its massive oil deposits. It is currently the world's fifth largest oil exporter. Venezuelan politics and society revolve around oil production for export and the wealth that it generates. The country's dependence on oil has led to boom and bust cycles in the economy, based on fluctuating international prices for oil. Yet, at the same time, relatively easy access to a highly valued commodity has created the illusion of prosperity and great expectations among Venezuelans. The country's politicians have long bought political loyalty and civil peace through the distribution of oil revenue, or "rent." The artificial sense of stability and development that has flowed from oil production and export has led some scholars to label Venezuela a "subsidized democracy" (Collins 2005).

Prior to the twentieth century, Venezuela's main exports were coffee and cacao. A small Spanish elite established the country's export market for these goods during the colonial period. The leader of the Andean independence movement, Simón Bolívar, was born into this ruling class. Bolívar's successful campaign in the Andes shone a spotlight on the country for the first time. Venezuela gained its independence in 1819 after a grueling war with Spain that resulted in the loss of almost 40 per cent of its population and the near devastation of its social, political, and administrative institutions (Karl 1997, 74). The weakness of the country's governing apparatus in the aftermath of the Independence Wars led to a reliance on local militias and their leaders as the foundations of authority. These paramilitary groups formed the nation's local and regional governments. According to Karl (1997), *caudillismo*, or strongman rule, left an indelible mark on state formation in the country. It created a legacy of personalism and presidentialism in the conduct of politics. For almost a century after independence, contending regional *caudillos* vied for control of the state. The project of nation-building only began in earnest in 1908, when one of the strongest *caudillos*, Juan Vicente Gómez, seized control of Caracas.

The discovery of large oil deposits in Venezuela took place in the early 1920s. Much of the wealth that flowed from these finds went into the pockets of ruling *caudillo* Juan Vicente Gómez (1908–35) and his associates (Hellinger 2006). Gómez's first priority in office was to consolidate power in the central government in order to secure control over regional *caudillos* and later over the oil supply. His institutional innovations included the establishment of a professional national military and a Ministry of Finance to account for all public revenues. Between 1920 and 1925, oil's share of Venezuela's total exports increased from 1.9 per cent to 41.6 per cent, and by 1935 it accounted for 91 per cent of the country's exports. By 1928, Venezuela was the world's largest oil-exporting nation (Karl 1997, 80). By that time, civil society groups had begun to agitate for change. The growing movement to oust Gómez was led by the so-named Generation of 1928, made up of university students who had been arrested in that year following massive social protests. The students were eventually released and went into exile. A member of this group, Rómulo Bentancourt, would later found one of Venezuela's most historically important political parties, the Democratic Action (AD) party. The AD's mandate centered on standing up to the foreign-owned oil corporations operating in Venezuela and demanding a greater share of the profits. The party wanted to invest in economic and social programs and institute a broadly representative democratic regime. At that time, the common goal of Venezuelan society was to harness the potential of oil wealth to develop the country, or "sow the oil," as it became known (Kelly and Palma 2004).

PACTED TRANSITION TO DEMOCRACY, 1935–1958

The death of Juan Vicente Gómez in 1935 ushered in a period of political liberalization in Venezuela. This time period saw the emergence of the two main political parties that would come to dominate Venezuelan politics for more than half a century. The AD formed in 1941 under the leadership of Betancourt to represent the interests of workers and peasants, while the opposition Christian Democratic Party (COPEI) formed in 1946 under the leadership of Rafael Caldera to represent the interests of elite groups and the Church hierarchy. Thus, the two parties initially stood on opposite ends of the divide, labor and capital versus church and state (Molina 2004). A number of smaller parties also emerged in the post-Gómez period, including the leftist Democratic Republican Union (URD) and the Venezuelan Communist Party (PCV). The PCV and the AD became intense rivals, as both parties competed for union backing. In the end, the AD succeeded in not only gaining the support of organized labor but also of the peasantry and the middle class (Hellinger 2006).

Frustrated with the slow pace of the transition process, Betancourt and the AD sought out allies in the military to overthrow the interim military government of General Isaías Medina Angarita to move the country to full democracy. The successful coup of October 18, 1945, brought the AD to power. In the national elections that followed, the AD legitimized itself as a democratic force by winning overwhelming majorities. The AD-led government of 1945–48 marked Venezuela's first experience with democracy. However, the AD's far-reaching social reforms and massive popular support made conservative groups in the country nervous. Elite groups supported the overthrow of the fledgling democracy by conservative forces within the military in November 1948 (Roberts 2003). In 1952, General Marcos Pérez Jiménez seized power for himself and plunged the country into a dictatorship that would last six years. By 1958, the corruption and violence of the Pérez Jiménez regime had even alienated factions of the military. On January 23, 1958, a broad-based movement consisting of civilians and disgruntled members of the military ousted Pérez Jiménez (Myers 2004). The new civic–military provisional government scheduled elections for later that year.

In October 1958, the representatives of the major political parties, excluding the Venezuelan Communist Party (PCV), hammered out a series of formal and informal agreements over the ground rules for the new democracy. Desiring an end to the political and economic instability that had plagued the country for the past two decades, the AD and COPEI parties agreed to modify their stances. The AD agreed to share power, restrict its capacity for social mobilization, and limit the scope of its social reforms. The COPEI agreed to a state-led model of development that would respect private property while generously bestowing patronage payoffs from the oil industry to major organized interest groups. The result was an oil-fueled class compromise which reduced the sharp ideological divisions that previously existed within the party system (Roberts 2003). The power-sharing pact was signed at Rafael Caldera's estate in Caracas, called Punto Fijo. The pacted democracy that grew out of this agreement became known forever after in Venezuela as the Punto Fijo system.

PARTYARCHY AND THE PUNTO FIJO PERIOD, 1958–1983

Following the pacted transition to democracy in 1958, Venezuela became the model of democratic stability in Latin America. Its characteristic two-party system with high rates of political participation and sustained economic growth was the envy of the region. According to Levine (2002), Venezuelan democracy in the Punto Fijo era rested upon four main pillars. The first pillar was economic growth resulting from steadily rising oil revenues. This oil revenue was used to fund a large, centralized state and a vast system of clientelism. The second pillar was made up of the various pacts and arrangements negotiated by political elites for sharing the spoils of power and maintaining civil and political order. The third pillar was a depoliticized military that was contained, controlled, and paid off. The fourth and final pillar of the system consisted of the strong and well-institutionalized political parties that exercised hegemonic control over the entire system. Political parties became so effective at monopolizing access to resources and to the state that one scholar termed the Venezuelan democratic system in the post-1958 period as a "partyarchy," or a dictatorship of parties (Coppedge 1994).

In comparison to other presidential systems, the formal legislative powers of the Venezuelan president during this time period were somewhat curtailed. Presidents had virtually no veto power and limited decree authority. They were also barred from reelection until a mandatory 10-year period had passed. The constraints placed on Venezuelan presidents under the Punto Fijo system earned them the title of "lame ducks" (Coppedge 1994). Informally, however, the high level of party discipline in the legislature augmented presidential powers. Majority presidents could count on their party's support, while minority presidents were able to form stable party coalitions (Crisp 1997). Most presidents headed up their respective parties prior to receiving the presidential nomination. Venezuela's strong and well-institutionalized party system did not permit political outsiders, effectively insuring that the practice of democratic politics remained in the hands of the elite.

In the Punto Fijo period, civil society became permeated and controlled by political parties through vertical relations of power. Corporatism in Venezuela was characterized by the mobilization and organization of both the peasantry and the urban working class into a limited number of officially sanctioned, non-competitive, and state-supervised interest associations linked to the traditional parties (Collier and Collier 2002). A handful of peak organizations came to represent societal interests, including the Confederation of Venezuelan Workers (CTV), the Venezuelan Peasant Federation (FCV), and the Federation of Chambers of Commerce and Production of Venezuela (FEDECAMARAS), a business organization. Together, these organizations constituted the main social interlocutors with the state and political parties. They functioned to mediate as well as to contain civil society interests before the state (Salamanca 2004). Participation under this corporatist system stifled the growth of a vibrant civil society. Political parties dominated the peak organizations, subordinating their internal structures and activities to suit the interests of the parties. The problem of party infiltration of the major civil society organizations turned Venezuela's strong and effective political institutions from a blessing into a curse (Levine 2002). In the end, the country's pacted transition to democracy gave way to a restricted and unresponsive form of governance.

The pact of Punto Fijo not only limited popular input and participation but also actively excluded any political challengers, especially from the revolutionary left. In response, a faction of the alienated left formed the guerrilla organization, the Armed Forces of National Liberation (FALN), and waged a brief insurgency against the government in the 1960s. Continued government repression and the promise of amnesty for the guerrillas brought about the return to politics as usual by 1969 (Hellinger 2006). By that time, the Venezuelan party system had become, in effect, "frozen," and would later prove incapable of responding adequately to rapidly changing political and economic conditions. Perhaps Crisp and Levine (1998, 31) sum up the situation best, stating, "In a nutshell, Venezuelan society in the democratic years changed, while political institutions and the basic rules of the game did not." The partyarchy model centralized power and authority in itself. As is typical of a rentier state whose national income is derived almost exclusively from the sale of petroleum, Venezuela has historically lacked a capacity to extract revenue from its own population in the form of taxes. The state's economic independence from a domestic tax base has allowed it to become highly state-centered and unresponsive to public demands (Coronil and Skurski 2004). In fact, based on calculations of the difference between the percentage of governmental revenues controlled by the central government versus that of state and regional governments, Venezuela is Latin America's most centralized state.

When the oil crisis of the 1970s hit and the price of oil spiked significantly, Venezuela was turned upside down. State revenues quadrupled between the years 1974 and 1976 (Wilpert 2005). The country succumbed to what is known as "Dutch disease," in which a substantial increase in foreign exchange is accompanied by the overvaluing of the domestic currency. This makes a country's manufactured goods more expensive and therefore less competitive in the global marketplace, resulting in a process of deindustrialization. At the same time, out-of-control government spending soon outpaced the added oil revenue. Economic mismanagement and massive corruption sank the country deep into debt as the price of oil began its steady decline in the 1980s. On February 18, 1983, popularly known as "Black Friday," Venezuela's currency collapsed, leading to inflation and further economic decline. The state was no longer able to deliver on its promises. Once economic performance faltered and poverty levels began to increase dramatically, the flaws in Venezuela's political system were revealed.

REPRESENTATIVE DEMOCRACY UNRAVELED, 1980s–1990s

Venezuela's economic troubles in the 1980s quickly translated into political ones. The Punto Fijo system was predicated on continued economic growth and the capacity of the two main parties to contain conflict, control organizations, and mobilize votes through the use of patronage spending. In the absence of any significant ideological distinctions between the traditional parties, partisan support depended on its effective economic management. The waning of economic strength brought about the collapse of the entire system, as one by one the three remaining pillars fell over the course of the late 1980s and early 1990s (Crisp and Levine 1998). The IMF riot of 1989 discussed at the opening of the chapter undermined the political pacts that had long maintained order and civil peace. Two failed military coup attempts in 1992 revealed the extent to which the country's military had become politicized. Finally, Rafael Caldera, the founder of COPEI, abandoned his own party in the 1993 presidential elections, in favor of a new coalition. This act broke the hegemonic hold of the traditional parties over the system. Ironically, as the other countries in the region made their first tentative steps toward instituting democratic regimes, Venezuela's democracy was rapidly becoming unglued.

Austerity measures in the form of reduced government spending were first introduced in Venezuela in 1984 under the AD-led government of Jaime Lusinchi (1984–89). Drastic cuts in social services were accompanied by deteriorating living conditions and rising rates of hunger, malnutrition, and disease for large portions of the population. An empirical study on the socioeconomic impacts of structural adjustment programs in Venezuela by López Maya and Lander (2004, 212) revealed that between 1980 and 1997 the percentage of the country's households living in extreme poverty skyrocketed from 9 to 28 per cent. Neoliberal reforms were deepened under the presidency of Carlos Andrés Pérez (1989–93). The neoliberal reform package introduced by President Pérez in February 1989 constituted the first, and so far only, coherent attempt to restructure the economy using free market principles. The package known as *El Gran Viraje* (The Great Turnaround) was to be administered rapidly and in one dose. Almost overnight, subsidies for basic consumer goods were eliminated, price controls removed, currency and interest rates were allowed to fluctuate, import tariffs were lowered, and the price of government services were increased. The impact of the reforms was particularly devastating for the middle class, whose livelihoods had already been threatened by government downsizing. According to López Maya and Lander (2004, 211), the size of Venezuela's public sector was reduced from 23 to 16 per cent between the years 1983 and 1998. The announcement at the end of February 1989 of the impending oil price hike that would be accompanied by increased public transportation costs was the catalyst that sent working- and middle-class groups into the streets of Caracas and its surrounding townships to protest the austerity measures. The riots forced the government to postpone the implementation of its neoliberal package. Under the subsequent government of Rafael Caldera (1994–99), the reform process was slowed even further.

In an attempt to enhance the legitimacy of the democratic system, a series of electoral and political reforms were introduced beginning in 1989. The boldest of these reforms included political and administrative decentralization (Kornblith and Levine 1995). As mentioned, highly centralized power has long been the hallmark of Venezuelan politics. The country's dependence on oil has made access to and control over the state especially critical. Thus, the move to open up the political system with the direct election of local and regional political authorities was a watershed moment in Venezuelan democratic history, one that had major implications for the traditional parties. Lalander (2004) has suggested that the strongly centralized AD and COPEI parties had, in effect, committed political suicide in adopting decentralizing reforms by allowing opposition parties to gain a foothold in the political system. This, in turn, sped up the demise of the partyarchy model. The push for decentralization came from both without and within Venezuela. On the one hand, international development donors such as the World Bank and the United Nations Development Programme (UNDP) promoted decentralization within recipient nations as a tool for the provision of services and the consolidation of democracy. On the other hand, leftist opposition parties sought decentralization as a means of deepening democracy (Veltmeyer 2007). Important in this regard were the Radical Cause (Causa R) and the Movement Toward Socialism (MAS) left-wing parties, both splinters of the former Communist Party (PCV), which took up the mantle of decentralization and, in so doing, captured an important protest vote in sectors adversely affected by structural adjustment.

During the 1990s, Venezuela experienced one of the world's largest increases in inequality (Ellner 2003b, 19). The country's Gini coefficient jumped from 0.31 to 0.49 over this time period. As socioeconomic inequality increased, so too did the level of social conflict. The changes in the class structure and labor markets brought on by the implementation of neoliberal economic reforms had important consequences for social and political organizing in the country (Roberts 2003). Civil society became increasingly disjointed and fragmented as market reforms undercut traditional, class-based forms of organizing, such as labor unions and peasant associations, and contributed to the growing informalization of the workforce. Between 1983 and 1998, the percentage of the population employed in Venezuela's informal sector increased from 41 to 48 per cent (López Maya and Lander 2004, 211). As the capacity of the peak societal organizations to represent the diversity of civil society interests weakened, the main political parties hold on society grew even more tenuous. The effective exclusion of new social groups from the political system served to further delegitimize representative democracy in the eyes of the citizenry. The result was the crumbling of the old political order. According to Crisp and Levine (1998, 51), "The decay of parties sets groups free, but in the same measure sets them adrift, leaves them with dwindling resources, and makes them easy prey to manipulative leaders and personalist politics." The Venezuelan public was ready for change, and that change came in the form of Hugo Chávez and his Bolivarian alternative.

HUGO CHÁVEZ AND THE BOLIVARIAN REVOLUTION

Hugo Chávez, a former lieutenant colonel, first captured the public's attention when he led a group of young military officers in an attempted overthrow of the administration of President Carlos Andrés Pérez in February 1992. The coup attempt failed when Chávez was taken prisoner. In a brief, televised message by the would-be president that was intended to restore peace and order, Chávez took responsibility for his actions and suggested that his movement's objectives had failed, but only for the moment. The message served as a rallying cry for many Venezuelans. In the year that followed, the country was witness to almost daily street protests, a second failed coup attempt in November, and finally the impeachment of President Pérez on corruption charges in May 1993 (Hellinger 2006). The December 1993 presidential elections were also marred by controversy, as the candidate for the left-wing Radical Cause (Causa R) party claimed victory despite coming in third place in the official results. In the end, ex-COPEI leader Rafael Caldera was declared president. In an effort to promote national reconciliation, President Caldera freed Chávez and his officers upon taking office. Chávez then turned to the task of building an electoral movement to contest for national power using the mechanisms of democracy already in place.

Hugo Chávez and his newly formed Movement of the Fifth Republic (MVR) party won the December 1998 presidential elections with 56 per cent of the vote, ushering in Latin America's Pink Tide era. The backbone of his movement was made up of progressive sectors of the military, factions of the political left, and the largely unincorporated masses from the marginalized, all united in a multiclass alliance (Ellner 2003a). Chávez's fiery rhetoric and anti-elite discourse resonated well with those sectors of society that had been excluded under the Punto Fijo system, or what Chávez termed the "Fourth Republic." His humble origins as the son of two schoolteachers and his mixed indigenous, Afro-Venezuelan, and Spanish ancestry also found him favor with the country's popular sectors. The cornerstone of Chávez's plan for the country was his Bolivarian Project, named after Andean independence hero Simón Bolívar. Bolivarianism is essentially a state-led approach to development that emphasizes the redistribution of the country's oil wealth in favor of the poor through a variety of social programs. It is explicitly anti-neoliberal in character, opposing market-oriented reforms such as privatization and deregulation in favor of government-supported local businesses and co-operatives. Politically, the Bolivarian Revolution stresses participatory democracy and inclusion as important correctives to the elitist and exclusionary nature of representative democracy (Wilpert 2005). The result is an uneasy mix of statist and grassroots approaches. While broad agreement about overarching goals existed within the coalition, there were considerable differences over the specifics of policies.

Lastly, in keeping with Bolívar's vision of a united Latin America, Chávez's project calls for greater regional integration as a counterweight to US hegemony. In 2001, Chávez proposed the Bolivarian Alternative for the Americas (ALBA), a trading bloc based on the principles of cooperation, solidarity, and preferential treatment for poorer nations (Collins 2005). ALBA member states include Cuba, Bolivia, and most recently, Nicaragua and Dominica. The ALBA is Chávez's response to the US-sponsored Free Trade Areas of the Americas (FTAA) initiative. Since assuming the presidency, Chávez has advocated for a "multipolar world" and has sought to work together with other developing nations for their mutual benefit. One means of promoting South–South solidarity has been through oil diplomacy. For instance, in 2005, Venezuela, along with a number of Caribbean nations including Cuba, Jamaica, and the Dominican Republic, created the PetroCaribe program that allows for the sale of Venezuelan oil to signatory countries at below market values and at reasonable repayment rates (Ellner

2008). The increase in oil sales to the region has enabled Chávez to justify the agreement on both economic and humanitarian grounds. Most recently, Chávez has sought to develop an alternative market for its oil by striking a deal with the government of China. Venezuela has long been dependent on US markets and technology for refining the country's unusually heavy grade oil. As part of the agreement that was signed between the two countries in November 2007, China will fund the development of Venezuela's oil industry in exchange for a steady supply of oil for its industrialization plans (Miller Llana and Ford 2008). Although the high costs associated with oil transport to Asia may not make much economic sense, it does serve a strategic and geopolitical purpose for the Chávez administration.

CHÁVEZ IN POWER, 1998–

Since capturing the presidency in the December 1998 elections, Hugo Chávez's brand of populism has divided the country between supporters and opponents of his democratically elected government. Chávez's top-down policies and programs are specifically directed at marginalized sectors of the population, which have become his almost exclusive base of support (Buxton 2005; Ellner 2003a). In prioritizing the interests of the poor over those of previously privileged groups, Chávez has created a zero-sum framework for governing, meaning that one group's losses are the other's gains. As a result, capture and control of the state has become essential for contending social groups to ensure the protection of their interests. The extent to which the middle and upper classes are now pitted against the lower classes mitigates any possibility of negotiation and compromise. Growing class polarization has been evident in the voting patterns of Venezuelans since Chávez's rise to power (Heath 2009; Roberts 2003). As Ellner (2003a) points out, the high degree of polarization in the country acts as a double-edged sword for Chávez. While it generates intense loyalty to the president and his governing program, it also intensifies the opposition's rejection of his administration.

The initial years of Chávez's presidency were dominated by efforts to bring about political change in the country. One of his first orders of business was to call for a constituent assembly to redraft the country's constitution. The new constitution, which came into effect in 1999, instituted wide-ranging reforms. The country was officially renamed the Bolivarian Republic of Venezuela. The senate was dissolved in favor of a unicameral national assembly. Two new branches of government were created: the National Electoral Commission and the People's Branch, also called Citizen Power (Collins 2005). The new constitution underscored the participatory and protagonist nature of democracy and dramatically restricted the role of political parties in the system. Public funding for political parties was cut. The constitution provided for more direct democracy measures, such as the use of popular referenda that had the power to revoke legislation and recall politicians, including the president (McCoy 2004). The constitution also provided greater protection for human rights, including reserved seats for indigenous peoples in the national assembly.

Most controversially, the 1999 constitution reinforced the power and autonomy of the central government, the executive branch, and the military (Levine 2002). It increased presidential powers by lengthening the presidential term to six years and allowing for immediate reelection. It emphasized a stronger role for the central state in the economy. The military was also given a role in politics. The constitution gave the military the right to vote and removed the requirement of congressional approval for military promotions. Under the new rules, the military is subordinate only to the president (López Maya and Lander 2004). The new constitution completely transformed the Venezuelan political landscape.

Chávez's economic policies, at least in the early years of his presidency, were much more modest than his political reforms. His administration focused on ways to contain the country's economic recession, including standard austerity measures (McCoy 2004). Chávez also sought to reap more benefits from the oil industry to invest in social and economic development initiatives. The country's oil industry had already been nationalized in 1976, following a lengthy process of operations and technology transfers that began in 1960 when Venezuela became a founding member of the Organization of Petroleum Exporting Countries (OPEC) (Kelly and Palma 2004). In an effort to renationalize the industry, Chávez implemented a new hydrocarbons law requiring that foreign investment in the oil and gas sectors be made through majority partnerships with domestic private and state enterprises (Collins 2005). The royalties paid by oil corporations to the state were also raised from 16 to 30 per cent (Wilpert 2005). Perhaps most impressive, Chávez managed to convince the remaining OPEC countries as well as other major oil producers to agree to reduce their production levels in order to raise the international price for oil. The price of a barrel of oil, which stood at $16 in 1999, climbed to $27 in 2000 (McCoy 2004, 278). This had an immediate and positive impact on the Venezuelan economy. The newly generated wealth more than compensated for the loss in foreign investments and capital flight that resulted from his rise to power. The year 2000 marked the end of Venezuela's recession and the reversion of the previous negative trends in the country's basic social and economic indicators. It also marked the beginning of policy autonomy for the country, as the IMF agreement signed by the previous administration of Rafael Caldera expired in 1999. Chávez has successfully avoided signing a new one (López Maya and Lander 2004).

Once the country's economy was back on its feet, Chávez was able to turn his attention to social investment. Beginning in 2003, amidst the din of a vociferous and embittered opposition movement, Chávez developed a number of "mission" programs to alleviate poverty as well as cement support for his administration (Corrales and Penfold 2007). The Bolivarian Missions are a series of social, political, and economic programs in specific policy areas. Most well known in this regard is the Mission *Barrio Adentro* ("Inside the Neighborhood"), which provides comprehensive community healthcare services for poor neighborhoods. There are approximately 14 different missions dedicated to activities ranging from voter identification campaigns to restoring indigenous land titles. The missions have introduced innovative programs in the areas of literacy and adult education, healthcare, housing, employment training, agricultural production, and university scholarships for the poor. Not only did quality of life indicators rebound in this period, but support for democracy in Venezuela dramatically increased as well, with the country ranking second highest in the region at 74 per cent according to an annual study conducted by Latinobarometer (Wilpert 2005, 20). At the same time, however, Chávez was busy insulating his social programs from his opponents or anyone suspected of being an opponent for fear of having his Bolivarian project derailed. For example, the mission programs were run outside of the existing ministerial structures to prevent them from being tampered with by bureaucrats linked to opposition forces. The governing climate was such in Venezuela that for one to benefit from government programs, one had to be a Chavista, a loyal follower of the president. Another way of understanding this is to view it as clientelism, in which the state is the patron.

Chávez's distrust of the opposition was not unfounded. Although Chávez was democratically elected with a majority of votes in the 1998 presidential race, and was reelected in 2000 with an even greater majority, his opponents have refused to recognize his government as legitimate. The "authoritarian thesis" put forward by opposition groups suggested that despite being democratically elected, Chávez's government used authoritarian means to accomplish its goals. Either Chávez relied too heavily on presidential decrees or he abused his majority in the national assembly to pass new legislation without bothering to consult interest groups or opposition parties (Buxton 2005). More than anything, it was the new constitution promulgated by Chávez and the complete displacement of previously privileged groups from state power that angered the opposition (Wilpert 2007). In 2002, anti-Chavista groups formed an alliance known as the Democratic Coordinator (CD) for the purpose of ousting Chávez from power. Ironically, the CD's members included disaffected sectors of the middle and upper classes and the AD and COPEI parties, in other words, the very actors who had benefited under the previous Punto Fijo system and who had worked to exclude others from access to state power. For his part, Chávez has refused to negotiate with opponents who have openly declared their intention to remove him from office.

By 2002, tensions between the government and opposition forces reached the boiling point. On April 11, a joint civil–military coup temporarily removed Chávez from power. Pedro Carmona, president of the peak business organization FEDECAMARAS, replaced him. Perhaps as a hint of what may be to come, Carmona immediately dismissed all state authorities and appointed an interim government consisting overwhelmingly of conservative right-wing groups (Buxton 2005). Massive street demonstrations and a military revolt by pro-Chávez factions forced Carmona to flee the country after just 48 hours and returned Chávez to power. Refusing to admit defeat, the opposition then turned to economic sabotage and organized a two-month-long strike by anti-Chavista workers and managers at the main state-owned oil company Petroleum of Venezuela (PDVSA) beginning in December 2002. Chávez responded by firing more than half of PDVSA's employees and ordering the military to take over production. After nearly crippling the economy, the strikers finally backed down. In a last-ditch attempt to wrest control from Chávez, the opposition decided to use the recall referendum mechanism put in place in the 1999 constitution against the president himself (Corrales and Penfold 2007). By March 2004, the opposition had gathered enough signatures to force a referendum. The August 2004 referendum resulted in a landslide victory for Chávez, with 59 per cent of voters voting against the recall. Chávez further strengthened his grip on power in the December 2006 presidential elections, in which he walked away with 63 per cent of the vote.

What made the opposition forces think that they stood a chance at undermining popular support for Chávez? According to Buxton (2005), the tenacity of the opposition was not based on their views having any sort of widespread appeal within Venezuela, but rather on external factors. The CD membership received sizeable donations for its anti-government organizing efforts from the US National Endowment for Democracy (NED), an organization established by US President Ronald Reagan (1980–88) to support democratic movements in communist countries. Washington even appeared to endorse the 2002 coup against Chávez by promising to work with the newly installed Carmona government. It was only after Chávez was returned to power that the US government backtracked on its statements and adamantly denied any involvement in the coup (Williams 2005). Thus, the overt support that the opposition groups received from

President Bush's (2000–08) administration served to legitimize their cause both domestically and internationally, and allowed them to radicalize their tactics. The private news media in Venezuela also played a key role in spurring on the opposition through its harsh and relentless commentaries on the Chávez administration. Hellinger (2006) has suggested that perhaps the most vehement opposition to Chávez came not from political parties or interest groups, but from the media itself. Chávez's similar use of state-owned radio and television stations to advance his administration's causes only added to the openly hostile political climate in the country. In May 2007, Chávez silenced one of his harshest critics, the Radio Caracas International Television (RCTV) network, by refusing to renew its broadcast license. Now that the opposition has soundly been defeated, the door has been swung wide open for Chávez to proceed to the next stage of his revolutionary project.

PARTICIPATORY DEMOCRACY?

Hugo Chávez's Bolivarian Revolution is a quintessentially populist political experiment. Populism can be understood as a top-down process of mass political mobilization that is directed by a personalist leader who takes aim at a country's ruling class on behalf of "the people" (Roberts 2007, 5). Although Chávez describes his political model as a "participatory democracy," the pattern of mobilization and the logic of political representation in his Venezuela are those of radical populism. The new political order rests on the relationship between a dominant personality and an ill-defined or amorphous mass that designates him personally as its representative to carry out a radical agenda of socioeconomic and political change (Levine 2002). In other words, it is an unmediated form of interest representation. Under such a model, democratizing power becomes impossible. Decision-making is centralized in the executive branch. Political institutions are undermined. Civil society becomes even more dependent on a central leader. The opposition is overpowered, demoralized, and completely excluded. This scenario is the antithesis of democracy.

A central tactic of populist figures faced with a potential backlash by elite opponents is to promote popular organization as a counterweight to the economic and political power of elite groups. According to Roberts (2007, 7), the greater the challenge posed by a populist leader to elite sectors, the more extensive popular organization is likely to be. This dynamic can be witnessed in Chávez's promotion of a vast network of grassroots organizations in civil society, including neighborhood committees, missions, cooperatives, and community councils. These institutional innovations served to incorporate into the polity groups which were formerly unorganized and whose interests went unrepresented. However, many of these organizational experiments proved to be short-lived. For instance, Chávez initially promoted the formation of Bolivarian Circles, neighborhood committees made up of small groups of citizens engaged in political education and community works. Empirical studies found that individual Circle members supported highly democratic goals and methods, and represented, at least on the surface, a potentially radical transformation of civil society (Hawkins and Hansen 2006). The high degree of dependence of the Circles on the state and Chávez himself, however, ultimately undermined their capacity to make a lasting, positive contribution to democracy. Many of the Circles degenerated into loose associations of Chavistas tied to government social programs. The Bolivarian Circle experiment took on strong clientelist tones, as members campaigned for Chávez and served as an easily mobilized and loyal base of support for his administration in exchange for government favors. By 2004, the Circles had all but been abandoned as its members were drawn into new projects.

Since consolidating his support in the 2006 elections, Chávez's revolution has taken a radical turn. He celebrated his impressive presidential win by proclaiming, "Nothing can stop the revolution!" Chávez plans to implement what he calls "21st century socialism" or what his former vice president Jorge Rodríguez has called "a dictatorship of true democracy" (Corrales and Penfold 2007, 111). Specific measures include the use of enabling laws to enact legislation that will deepen the process; a constitutional amendment to abolish presidential term limits; the redrawing of political and administrative boundaries to further curb the influence of governors, mayors, and local officials; efforts to extend the Bolivarian ideology into the public school system; and the creation of communal assemblies as a form of "dual power" in society. Most notably, the establishment of communal power by way of the 2006 Law on Communal Councils promises a radical transformation of existing governing structures. The goal of the initiative is to gradually transfer power to organized communities, so that the state apparatus itself becomes unnecessary. In the short run, the councils are to dictate the will of "the people" directly to the government bureaucracy (Ciccariello-Maher 2007). The communal councils are intended to oversee the central government and serve as a democratic counterweight.

There are a number of flaws inherent to Chávez's vision of participatory democracy. First and foremost, participatory democracy is not something that can be legislated from above—it must come from below. As chapter 1 highlighted, participatory democracy requires citizens to be actively engaged with democratic practices at all levels of society. A strong and vibrant civil society is supposed to shape government policies and proposals, not the other way around. Second, for participatory democracy to function, citizens must be able to influence the upper reaches of government (Wilpert 2007). In Chávez's Venezuela, however, decision-making authority is concentrated in the executive branch. The absence of well-defined mechanisms for citizen input runs counter to the concept of participatory democracy. The third internal contradiction of the Chavista model is the lack of autonomy of civil society groups from the state. A defining characteristic of civil society is that it is made up of self-constituted groups representing distinct societal interests and identities. Civil society groups are further characterized by a "dual dynamic" in which they simultaneously resist subordination to the state while making demands on it (Oxhorn and Ducatenzeiler 1999, 36). By contrast, finding Venezuelan civil society deficient in many respects, Chávez has sought to remake it in his own image. Most dramatic in this regard was the effort by the Chávez administration to create a new national labor confederation following an oil workers' strike in October 2000 (McCoy 2004). After considerable national and international condemnation by labor rights organizations, the plan was ultimately defeated in a referendum held in October 2001. These developments have generated considerable confusion over which groups represent authentic civil society in contemporary Venezuela, with some scholars suggesting that it now consists of the middle- and upper-class sectors and business interest groups pressing for access to the state (Levine 2002). In sum, rather than an experiment in deepening democracy, the Bolivarian Revolution is perhaps best understood as radical populism masquerading as participatory democracy.

CONCLUSION

The shortcomings of the Punto Fijo system, in particular, and of representative democracy, in general, opened the door to a unique experiment in direct democracy in Venezuela. However, the zero-sum manner in which the poor have been incorporated into the political and economic life of the country has heightened class tensions and exacerbated social conflict. Instead of improving state–society relations in Venezuela, Chávez's regime has simply reversed the groups who are excluded from the system (Kornblith 2006). Buxton (2005) has suggested that there is a striking similarity in the way in which politics has been practiced in the so-called Fourth and Fifth Republics. The continuity between the Punto Fijo period and the current era lies in the hegemonic practice of the "politics of exclusion." According to Buxton (2005, 329), "There has been a revolutionary shift in the distribution of power, but a remarkable permanence in the art of its practice." In an effort to correct the many injustices and failures of representative government, Chávez has generated new ones. By governing in the interests of the marginalized sectors at the expense of all others, Chávez has created what Corrales and Penfold (2007) term a "quasi-tyranny of the majority." This dynamic constitutes a betrayal of the underlying assumption that democracy is the dispersal of power through transparent, efficient, and accountable institutions so that all can benefit. No tyranny, quasi or otherwise, disperses its power. It is unclear what direction the country will move in once President Chávez's term ends in 2012.

There are a number of impediments that Chávez must address if his revolution is to become consolidated. The first is the persistence of clientelism and corruption in Venezuela. Such practices undermine democratic legitimacy and the value of his political party. The second is the near total dependence of the Bolivarian Revolution on Chávez himself, such that it could not proceed in his absence. Chávez has failed to institutionalize his MVR party; in 2008 he abandoned it altogether when he formed the United Socialist Party of Venezuela (PSUV). While Chávez suggested that the PSUV was intended to merge all parties which support the Bolivarian Revolution, others have suggested it was a means of removing obstinate leaders within the MVR (Lalander 2008). As a result, this mechanism of democratic deliberation is lost. Again, democracy is weakened. Third, Chávez's top-down governing and centralized decision-making style ultimately undermines the transformative potential of his experiment in participatory democracy (Wilpert 2007). Lastly, Chávez's continued success is threatened by the growing number of citizens that are neither for nor against the president (known in Spanish as the *Ni-Nis*). Thus far, the strategy of the Chávez administration for winning over the *Ni-Nis* has been to condition government programs, jobs, and contracts on regime support. While effective in the short run, the Achilles' heel of the Chávez regime, much like that faced by previous administrations in Venezuela, is its reliance on continuing high international prices for oil.

In contrast to the trends outlined in the other country chapters of this volume, support for democracy is on the rise in Venezuela. Much of this support may be contingent on governmental performance and continued high levels of state spending. However, democracy is more than just service delivery. It embodies an ethos, an intrinsic valuing of democracy as meaningful in and of itself and worthy of struggle. What are the implications of Venezuela's political model for the future direction of democracy in Latin America? Wholesale disappointment in the quality and outcomes of representative democracy in Venezuela has led citizens to risk the unknown and lend their support to populist President Hugo Chávez rather than remain with the existing system. According to Mainwaring (2006, 18–19), "What starts out as plebiscitary representation easily slides into nondemocratic or even antidemocratic representation." This preferred way of doing politics might very well exacerbate the political crisis afflicting the region.

NOTE

1 Adapted from Margarita López Maya (2003, 117–37).

REFERENCES

Buxton, Julia. 2005. "Venezuela's Contemporary Political Crisis in Historical Context." *Bulletin of Latin American Research* 24(3): 328–47.

Ciccariello-Maher, George. 2007. "Dual Power in the Venezuelan Revolution." *Monthly Review* 59(4): 42–56.

Collier, Ruth Berins, and David Collier. 2002. *Shaping the Political Arena: Critical Junctures, the Labor Movement, and Regime Dynamics in Latin America.* Notre Dame: University of Notre Dame Press.

Collins, Sheila D. 2005. "Commentary: Breaking the Mold? Venezuela's Defiance of the Neoliberal Agenda." *New Political Science* 27(3): 367–95.

Coppedge, Michael. 1994. *Strong Parties and Lame Ducks: Presidential Partyarchy and Factionalism in Venezuela.* Stanford: Stanford University Press.

Coronil, Fernando, and Julie Skurski. 2004. "Dismembering and Remembering the Nation: The Semantics of Political Violence in Venezuela." *Politics in the Andes: Identity, Conflict, Reform.* Ed. Jo-Marie Burt and Philip Mauceri. Pittsburgh: University of Pittsburgh Press. 81–106.

Corrales, Javier, and Michael Penfold. 2007. "Venezuela: Crowding Out the Opposition." *Journal of Democracy* 18(2): 99–113.

Crisp, Brian F. 1997. "Presidential Behavior in a System with Strong Parties: Venezuela, 1958–1995." *Presidentialism and Democracy in Latin America.* Ed. Scott Mainwaring and Matthew Soberg Shugart. New York: Cambridge University Press. 160–98.

Crisp, Brian F., and Daniel H. Levine. 1998. "Democratizing the Democracy? Crisis and Reform in Venezuela." *Journal of Interamerican Studies and World Affairs* 40(2): 27–61.

Ellner, Stephen. 2003a. "The Contrasting Variants of Populism of Hugo Chávez and Alberto Fujimori." *Journal of Latin American Studies* 35: 139–62.

———. 2003b. "Introduction: The Search for Explanations." *Venezuelan Politics in the Chávez Era: Class, Polarization, and Conflict.* Ed. Steve Ellner and D. Hellinger. Boulder: Lynne Rienner Press. 7–26.

———. 2008. *Rethinking Venezuelan Politics: Class, Conflict, and the Chávez Phenomenon.* Boulder: Lynne Rienner Press.

Hawkins, Kirk A., and David R. Hansen. 2006. "Dependent Civil Society: The Círculos Bolivarianos in Venezuela." *Latin American Research Review* 41(1): 102–32.

Heath, Oliver. 2009. "Explaining the Rise of Class Politics in Venezuela." *Bulletin of Latin American Research* 28(2): 185–203.

Hellinger, Daniel. 2006. "Venezuela." *Politics of Latin America: The Power Game.* Ed. H.E. Vanden and G. Provost. New York: Oxford University Press. 469–95.

Karl, Terry Lynn. 1997. *The Paradox of Plenty: Oil Booms and Petro-States.* Berkeley: University of California Press.

Kelly, Janet, and Pedro A. Palma. 2004. "The Syndrome of Economic Decline and the Quest for Change." *The Unraveling of Representative Democracy in*

Venezuela. Ed. Jennifer L. McCoy and David J. Myers. Baltimore: Johns Hopkins University Press. 202–30.

Kornblith, Miriam. 2006. "Sowing Democracy in Venezuela: Advances and Challenges in a Time of Change." *State and Society in Conflict: Comparative Perspectives on Andean Crises.* Ed. Paul W. Drake and Eric Hershberg. Pittsburgh: University of Pittsburgh Press. 288–314.

Kornblith, Miriam, and Daniel H. Levine. 1995. "Venezuela: The Life and Times of the Party System." *Building Democratic Institutions: Party Systems in Latin America.* Ed. Scott Mainwaring and Timothy R. Scully. Stanford: Stanford University Press. 37–71.

Lalander, Rickard. 2004. *Suicide of the Elephants? Venezuelan Decentralization between Partyarchy and Chavismo.* Helsinki: Renvall Institute for Area and Cultural Studies, University of Helsinki.

———. 2008. "Venezuelan Leftist Parties in the Era of Hugo Chávez." *Stockholm Review of Latin American Studies* 3: 131–42.

Levine, Daniel H. 2002. "The Decline and Fall of Democracy in Venezuela: Ten Theses." *Bulletin of Latin American Research* 21(2): 248–69.

López Maya, Margarita. 2003. "The Venezuelan *Caracazo* of 1989: Popular Protest and Institutional Weakness." *Journal of Latin American Studies* 35: 117–37.

López Maya, Margarita, and Luis E. Lander. 2004. "The Struggle for Hegemony in Venezuela." *Politics in the Andes: Identity, Conflict, Reform.* Ed. Jo-Marie M. Burt and Philip Mauceri. Pittsburgh: University of Pittsburgh Press. 207–27.

Mainwaring, Scott. 2006. "The Crisis of Representation in the Andes." *Journal of Democracy* 17(3): 13–27.

McCoy, Jennifer L. 2004. "From Representative Democracy to Participatory Democracy? Regime Transformation in Venezuela." *The Unraveling of Representative Democracy in Venezuela.* Ed. Jennifer L. McCoy and David J. Myers. Baltimore: Johns Hopkins University Press. 263–95.

Miller Llana, Sara, and Peter Ford. 2008. "Chávez, China Cooperate on Oil, But for Different Reasons." *The Christian Science Monitor,* January 3, 2008. June 2, 2010. http://www.csmonitor.com/World/Americas/2008/0103/p06s01-woam.html.

Molina, José E. 2004. "The Unraveling of Venezuela's Party System: From Party Rule to Personalistic Politics and Deinstitutionalization." *The Unraveling of Representative Democracy in Venezuela.* Ed. Jennifer L. McCoy and David J. Myers. Baltimore: Johns Hopkins University Press. 152–78.

Myers, David. J. 2004. "The Normalization of Punto Fijo Democracy." *The Unraveling of Representative Democracy in Venezuela.* Ed. Jennifer L. McCoy and David J. Myers. Baltimore: Johns Hopkins University Press. 11–29.

Oxhorn, Philip, and Graciela Ducatenzeiler. 1999. "The Problematic Relationship Between Economic and Political Liberalization: Some Theoretical Considerations." *Markets and Democracy in Latin America: Conflict or Convergence?* Ed. Philip Oxhorn and Pamela K. Starr. Boulder: Lynne Rienner Press. 13–42.

Rice, Roberta, and Donna Lee Van Cott. 2006. "The Emergence and Performance of Indigenous Peoples' Parties in South America: A Sub-National Statistical Analysis." *Comparative Political Studies* 39(6): 709–32.

Roberts, Kenneth M. 2003. "Social Polarization and the Populist Resurgence in Venezuela." *Venezuelan Politics in the Chávez Era: Class, Polarization, and Conflict.* Ed. Steve Ellner and D. Hellinger. Boulder: Lynne Rienner Press. 55–72.

———. 2007. "Latin America's Populist Revival." *SAIS Review* 27(1): 3–15.

Salamanca, Luis. 2004. "Civil Society: Late Bloomers." *The Unraveling of Representative Democracy in Venezuela*. Ed. Jennifer L. McCoy and David J. Myers. Baltimore: Johns Hopkins University Press. 93–114.

Veltmeyer, Henry. 2007. *On the Move: The Politics of Social Change in Latin America*. Peterborough: Broadview Press.

Williams, Mark Eric. 2005. "US Policy in the Andes: Commitments and Commitment Traps." *The Andes in Focus: Security, Democracy and Economic Reform*. Ed. Russell Crandall, Guadaloupe Paz, and Riordan Roett. Boulder: Lynne Rienner Press. 151–72.

Wilpert, Gregory. 2005. "Venezuela: Participatory Democracy or Government as Usual?" *Socialism and Democracy* 19(1): 7–32.

———. 2007. *Changing Venezuela by Taking Power: The History and Policies of the Chávez Government*. London: Verso Books.

E-RESOURCES

Bolivarian Republic of Venezuela Online (www.gobiernoenlinea.ve). Provides access to the branches of the government in Venezuela.

National Electoral Council (CNE) (www.cne.gov.ve). Provides electoral data for Venezuela.

National Institute for Statistics (INE) (www.ine.gov.ve). Provides census data for Venezuela.

Venezuela Information Office (in English) (www.rethinkvenezuela.com). A public education website funded by the Government of Venezuela.

Venezuelan News, Views, and Analysis (in English) (www.venezuelanalysis.com). An alternative media website dedicated to disseminating news and analysis about current political events in Venezuela.

TEN

Brazil:
Constraints and Innovations

LAUREN PHILLIPS

Vadão Gomes is a 51-year-old member
of the Brazilian chamber of deputies,
the lower of Brazil's two houses of
congress. He is a deputy from the state of
São Paulo and has been in elected politics
throughout the majority of Brazil's history
as a new democracy. A question that in many
other cases would appear simple—what party does
he belong to?—is more complex with Mr. Gomes. The
answer, now, is that he is a member of the Popular Party (PP). But in the
course of Mr. Gomes's political career, he has also been a member of the
Liberal Front Party (PFL, a major center-right party which has recently
been renamed the Democrats), the National Reconstruction Party (PRN,
a center-oriented populist party which folded in 2000), and the Brazilian
Populist Party (PPB). In other words, he has been affiliated with four
political parties in 20 years, a circumstance that would seem absurd or be
impossible in many established democracies. But by Brazilian standards,
his case is not unusual: a random scroll through the biographies of several
Brazilian deputies would reveal that most have changed parties several
times throughout their careers, and in the more extreme cases, have even
changed parties several times during the same legislative season. As
many as 40–50 per cent of all deputies routinely switch parties at least
once during a four-year legislative period. This example is but one of the
problems that Brazil is experiencing with its organization of political power.

Rather than just being a strange eccentricity of Brazilian politics, the propensity of Brazilian deputies to change political party affiliation is symptomatic of an important flaw of Brazilian democracy: the weakness of the party system, what Scott Mainwaring has called the "weak institutionalization" of Brazilian political parties (Mainwaring 1999). Brazilian democracy, restored after several decades of military rule in 1985 and formalized by the constitution of 1988, is far from perfect. In addition to the weakness of its party system, it has a number of institutional shortcomings: it is both unwieldy and sclerotic. A book published in 2000 aimed at taking stock of Brazilian democracy in its first full decade argued that "many of the main national political institutions are dysfunctional: they have objective deficiencies that have been pointed out repeatedly not only by academic political scientists but also by the politicians who use and inhabit these institutions" (Power 2000, 32).

Given the negative picture painted above, it might be surprising to simultaneously characterize Brazilian democracy as both vibrant and experimental. But Brazilian democracy is also this: a laboratory in which some of Latin America's and indeed the developing world's most innovative public policy has been crafted and perfected. Brazil has a highly ineffective organization of the state at the national level, while the devolved structure of federalism has allowed political and economic innovations to strengthen democratic norms and processes at the local level.

HISTORICAL OVERVIEW OF BRAZIL

To understand the features of Brazil's young democracy (reestablished in 1989), it is useful to briefly examine the country's history, because the political and socioeconomic features of modern Brazil have been strongly determined by it. For example, the institutions, and in many cases the absence of institutions, developed during the colonial period continue to have important implications on features of the Brazilian political economy. As Skidmore (2004) argues, several features of Portuguese colonialism stand out vis-à-vis Spanish colonialism in Latin America and have served to create the base of income inequality in Brazil that persists to this day. He highlights four features. First, the relatively low level of political development in Portugal at the time it colonized Brazil meant that Portugal passed to its colony a political model based on hierarchy and paternalism, where personal networks and class status determined success. Second, slavery, a dominant institution in Brazil, was not abolished until 1888, resulting in the largest transfer of African slave labor in the hemisphere. Slavery formed the basis for discrimination and inequality on the basis of color. Third, Portuguese colonialists did not emphasize education: there were no universities in Brazil until the twentieth century, unlike Mexico and Peru where universities were set up in the seventeenth century. Furthermore, primary schools and other education systems were notoriously absent, resulting in persistently high levels of illiteracy in Brazil. Finally, and related to the previous point, the Portuguese crown prohibited the establishment of a printing press in Brazil, which meant that no books, newspapers, or magazines were printed in Brazil during the colonial period. This was unique among Latin American colonies and contributed to an anti-intellectual bias.

Brazil's history as an independent nation from 1822 onward has also had decisive effects on the shape of its modern political economy. Brazil's history as an early independent state is similar, yet different, from the rest of Latin America. While the Hispanic states of Latin America gained their independence in a series of wars taking place in the 20-year period between 1810 and 1830, Brazil's history of independence from the Portuguese crown was more complicated. Brazil served as the seat of the Portuguese crown for a number of years prior to 1821, while the monarchy was in exile from the Napoleonic occupation of their country. When King João VI returned to Lisbon in 1821, he left his heir-apparent, Pedro, to rule Brazil. An independence war ensued shortly thereafter, and Brazil gained its independence from Portugal in 1822 after a series of battles with the Portuguese navy. Unlike its neighbors in South and Central America, where tenuous democracies were put into place after independence, Brazil remained a monarchy ruled by Pedro, who later gave himself the title Pedro I, Emperor of Brazil. In 1889, the Brazilian republic was established concomitant with the abolition of slavery.

The early years of the Brazilian Republic might best be described as a "pacted democracy." The constitution of 1891 created a federal democracy where powerful governors checked presidential power. But the results of presidential elections (the presidency being the highest prize in the political system) were negotiated among governors of powerful states, the two most important and wealthy being São Paulo and Minas Gerais, with an informal switching system in place which ensured that political power was not captured by one party for too long. Electoral results were manipulated to ensure that the vote corresponded with these decisions, through the use of rural strongmen (a practice known in Portuguese as *coronelismo*) and direct electoral fraud. This system was disrupted by an armed rebellion organized by a radicalized opposition group in 1929–30, which led to the very brief imposition of rule by a military junta and followed by the assumption of power of one of Brazil's most important political figures, Getúlio Vargas (1930–45; 1951–54).

Vargas's presidency caused a major shift in the practice of Brazilian politics, introducing what became known as the *Estado Novo*, or new state.

"In the decade and a half after Vargas assumed power, nearly every feature of the political system and administrative structure was subjected to the zeal for reform. Many of these changes remained juridical fictions. Enough were implemented by 1945, however, to have transformed irrevocably the world of government and politics which had produced the revolutionaries of 1930" (Skidmore 1967, 7). The constitution of 1934 put in place a federal structure similar to that which existed under the 1891 constitution but which also ensured free elections, a more independent judiciary, and a state more active in managing pro-labor social and welfare policy (through the establishment of a minimum wage, for example). But the constitution was the result of a compromise between political actors who were already losing relevance in the political order created in the wake of the 1930 "revolution" (Skidmore 1967, 20), and was therefore bound to a short destiny as new political actors matured and strengthened their claim to power, for example, the Communist Party and the left generally.

In 1935, the communists had organized a failed coup, paving the way for a period of rule by emergency decree, and eventually for Vargas to suspend the planned 1938 elections through his own coup, installing himself as the head of an authoritarian Brazil, where he remained in power until 1945. Removed by the military, Vargas was able to recapture the presidency through the popular vote in 1950, albeit with some constraints on his power. In 1954, he resigned on the orders of the Brazilian military, and committed suicide on the same day.

Vargas's death resulted in a number of years of very fragile democracy, with an increasing rift between the military and the left of the political spectrum. President João Goluart's (1961–64) reformist policies, which included agrarian reform and nationalization of the key oil sector, convinced the military that a communist revolution was about to take place in Brazil. In 1964, the army seized power, installing a military dictatorship.

The Brazilian period of military authoritarianism shared some of the characteristics of the military regimes established elsewhere in the Southern Cone during this period. For example, between 1968 and 1974, the Brazilian government excessively oppressed the opposition, torturing political "subversives." Nonetheless, it maintained the core institutions and functions of democracy. This period of "relative democracy" had ongoing elections at state and local levels,[1] as well as congressional elections. Although the powers of congress were reduced, it continued to hold session, and the military regime created two political parties: the National Renewal Alliance (ARENA), which represented the interests of the military government, and an official opposition party, the Brazilian Democratic Movement (MDB).

An interesting feature of the Brazilian military rule was the degree to which successive presidents would swing between liberalizing the political sphere and maintaining a hard military rule.[2] President Ernesto Geisel (1974–79) preferred re-democratization on terms favorable to the military and the re-professionalization of the military. He also reduced censorship of one major newspaper. Skidmore notes that Geisel believed that the "Revolution of 1964 should, after a limited period of emergency government, lead to a prompt return to representative democracy.... Geisel promised 'sincere efforts toward a gradual but sure democratic improvement'" (Skidmore 1988, 163–64). He allowed for the most competitive elections since the establishment of military rule in 1974, giving opposition candidates from the MDB equal access to television advertising and refusing to use intimidation strategies to ensure a favorable vote. As a result, the MDB massively increased its representation in both houses of congress and in the state legislatures where, in some important states, they gained control.

But the progress toward democratization did not move in a straight line: during Geisel's presidency, several high-profile journalists and political activists were tortured to death by state officials, and more generally there was a careful balancing between hard-line elements of the military (who Geisel still relied on for support) and more liberalizing elements.

The authoritarian regimes began to unwind in the late 1970s and early 1980s, a period marked by economic upheaval and massive strikes. Both events pushed the state toward democratization and reinforced the extent to which the military government had to accept that some form of democratic opening was inevitable. In 1979, the military government deregulated the political party system, encouraging the official opposition party, the MDB, to splinter into more moderate and radical factions. The military government hoped that this splintering would help to prolong its rule. But by 1984, public pressure was mounting for a change in the electoral system, in particular, for the right to directly elect the president. While a law aimed at direct election proposed by the MDB failed to obtain a congressional majority, an opposition candidate, Tancredo Neves, gained enough support from members of the ruling military party to be elected as president on January 15, 1985. Unfortunately, Neves became very ill on the eve of his inauguration (March 15, 1985) and died just one month later. Vice presidential candidate, José Sarney (1985–89), a member of ARENA, became president instead, undermining the reformist credentials of the first elected government. Despite this unfortunate start, the democratic transition went forward, and Sarney formed a constitutional assembly to draft Brazil's new organization of power.

The process through which democracy replaced the autocratic regime left a number of lasting marks on the sort of democratic institutions to emerge, particularly in the scope and tone of the constitution. But in other ways, the military rule failed to make a permanent mark on Brazilian politics; the military's two-party system reverted back to a multiparty system as soon as the military loosened its grip on power, a feature which has persisted in Brazil up to the present day.

DEMOCRATIC BRAZIL AND THE 1989 CONSTITUTION

CONSTITUTIONALISM AND THE CONSTITUTIONAL ASSEMBLY

Unlike most constitutions, which are written by a select few, the drafting committee for the Brazilian constitution was composed of the entire congress.[3] While this structure was chosen to ensure that the constitution reflected the will of the people rather than that of the political elite, the reality fell short of this ideal. The assembly's work on the constitution quickly degraded into a battle between representatives' individual and parochial interests, and horse-trading for provisions aimed at placating special interest groups and lobbies bloomed. It was a long and relatively undisciplined process, resulting in the world's longest constitution. It contains very detailed articles protecting a variety of groups and also has an exceptionally large degree of detail about spending and policy priorities for the Brazilian state. For example, chapter 2 of the constitution sets out a number of social rights and in the process enshrines benefits for unemployment, minimum wage, pensions, and leave policy (including paternity and maternity leave). Enshrining social rights into the constitution was a positive step toward the idea of equality among all Brazilians, and it reflects the high levels of centralization of minority rights which had taken place under the more than 20 years of military dictatorship.

Overall, the constitution resulted in a weak party system, a malapportioned legislature, a presidential system where "ruling by decree" has become standard practice, budgetary inflexibility, and highly devolved federalism.[4] More specifically, it created a complex and highly decentralized set of institutions which "enshrined the existing institutional framework ... that was more oriented toward representation and protection of minority rights than toward the formation of stable ruling majorities" (Sousa 1999, 50–51). Thus, state capacity and democratic governance decreased. In a highly unusual mix of systems, electoral voting is based on an open-list proportional representation system (OLPR), which awards representation on the proportion of population each party wins but at the same time does not require parties to prioritize candidates. The natural inefficiencies of this system are further exacerbated by the fact that the constitution provided no incentives for a reduction in the unwieldy multiparty system, marked out exceptionally large electoral districts, and divested significant powers to a three-level federation. By opting for a two-round presidential voting system, the drafters of the constitution hoped that a strong president with a majority popular mandate would "make the whole system cohesive, counterbalancing the centrifugal forces at work elsewhere in the political system" (Sousa 1999, 51). To avoid a deadlock in the legislative branch on matters of critical importance, additional powers were given to the president to legislate by decree (with a law known as the *medida provisória*, or MP). In an effort to pass important laws without negotiating with unwieldy congressional coalitions, presidents have made liberal use of decree rule,[5] undermining congressional legitimacy.

Additionally, the constitution's provision of legal protection for social rights and the protection of economic minorities, such as regulation on the social security and pension systems, implied that later administrations would require constitutional amendments to make changes to large parts of the budget that were allocated in a non-discretionary manner. As Stepan notes, "Almost everything in Brazil is constitutionally embedded. In order to change the constitution, 60% of the members of both houses (both those present and those absent) must vote in favour of an amendment *twice*" (Stepan 1999, 29; emphasis in original). He calls Brazil one of the most "demos-constraining" political systems in the world. In periods of economic crisis, such as during the financial crises of the 1990s, this constitutionally mandated spending has presented serious challenges to the Brazilian government's ability to reallocate or decrease spending priorities. It is possible to analyze the difficulties in redistributing Brazil's budget or indeed reforming any aspect of the organization of the polity through two features of Brazilian democracy: the weak party system and the federalist structure of the Brazilian state.

THE PARTY SYSTEM

The Brazilian party system, which is in large part the result of the electoral system, has had a profound impact on the manner in which policy-making and politicking in the Brazilian government take place at the federal level, affecting the distribution of power among the executive, legislative, and judicial branches of government. The number of parties currently represented in the two houses of the Brazilian legislature (the *Câmara dos Deputados* or chamber of deputies and the *Senado* or senate), as well as their weak roots in Brazilian society, have made enacting reform legislation exceptionally difficult.

The party system has been one of the most frequently analyzed, and lamented, aspects of the post-authoritarian Brazilian state. The first noteworthy feature of Brazilian parties is their sheer number: as a result of the 2006 congressional elections, 21 parties had representatives in the lower house of the Brazilian legislature. Given the wide distribution of votes across numerous parties, presidents must rule through unwieldy coalitions of potentially disparate parties. In fact, Brazil has one of the highest levels of legislative fractionalization (a measure which looks at the distribution of power among different parties and groups) in the world: higher than notably unwieldy democracies such as those in Peru and Italy.

Their sheer abundance, however, is not the only notable feature of Brazilian parties. Historically, Brazilian parties have been weak. Mass constituency parties emerged only in 1945, much later than in surrounding Latin American states, and not a single party endured the military dictatorship which began in 1964 and lasted into the mid-1980s, despite 18 years of democratic governance during that period (Mainwaring 1995). Brazilian parties have routinely been called "weak and inchoate" by comparative political scientists (e.g., Mainwaring 1991; Mainwaring 1995; Power 2000; Ames 2001). "No other democracy grants politicians so much autonomy vis-à-vis their parties" (Mainwaring 1991, 21) and further, "[t]he most distinctive feature of Brazilian political parties are their fragility, their ephemeral character, their weak roots in society, and the autonomy politicians of the catch-all parties enjoy with respect to their parties" (Mainwaring 1995, 354). Party strength is undermined both by electoral laws, which favor the power and popularity of individual politicians over ideology, as well as laws governing the behavior of deputies within the legislature itself.

The open-list proportional representation system gives individual representatives an incentive to engage in anti-party behavior. Since candidates owe their seat to voters rather than to the party (as in a closed-list system where the voters select a party rather than a candidate), they often lack a strong tie to the party for whom they are running. Voters, in turn, have an incentive to choose politicians on an individual rather than a party basis. This problem is exacerbated by the proportional allocation of seats, providing power to ideologically weak parties, and by the provision in the constitution that allocates a high number of seats to smaller states, depriving large states from their "true" representative power.[6]

As ideology is seldom the unifying principle of Brazilian political parties, the electoral cost of switching between parties is low. Until the late 1990s, there were no laws preventing deputies from switching parties at will,[7] and, as mentioned in the introduction to this chapter, it is not at all unusual for a single politician to switch parties several times during the course of one legislature. Desposato (2004) estimates that "about a third of deputies and a fifth of senators will switch party during any four year period" (5). Given the low costs of party-switching, deputies do so for a variety of reasons. First, candidates in legislative elections often register themselves for parties in which they have the highest chance of winning (those in which individual politicians are not well known but proportional representation is likely to be high) rather than those in which they have long-standing political or ideological ties. A switch back to the candidate's "natural" party immediately after the election is routinely witnessed. This phenomenon is known as "parties for rent." Second, rather than voting along party lines, legislators sometimes prefer to switch parties, insuring that they maintain support from important constituents without experiencing backlash from party leaders and whips. There is no provision for party fidelity in Brazil, having been abolished in the first democratic reforms of 1985.[8] This subsequently undermines governing coalitions and makes it more difficult for governments to garner legislative majorities for their proposals.

While the above observations of a weak ideological base and little deputy loyalty are characteristic of the average Brazilian political party, there is some variation among parties regarding the extent to which this is true. Mainwaring has described three different types of Brazilian parties: disciplined and programmatic parties, generally of the left and typified by the Workers' Party (PT); moderately disciplined parties with moderate program commitments (centrist parties like the PSDB and PSB); and loosely organized parties with weak programmatic commitments which are used by individual candidates to forward their own agenda (Mainwaring 1995).[9] Thus, there is less party-switching among the parties of the left. This is true in particular for the PT, which has a low to zero rate of switching and a commitment to grassroots party democracy. Party-switching increases dramatically, however, for loosely organized parties, such as the Popular Party (PP), which had a switching rate of greater than 100 per cent in the first two years of the 52nd congress.

There are three broader impacts of party weakness on Brazilian democracy. First, fractionalization makes it difficult to pass key legislation as majorities are difficult to create, and super-majorities, required to amend the constitution, are nearly impossible to achieve. Second, party weakness has an impact on the ability of the president to generate "coattails," that is, a president's capacity to get party members elected into the legislature on the basis of his or her own popularity. Combined with few cohesive electoral coalitions between parties that transcend the national, state, and municipal levels, presidents are forced to cobble together multiparty coalitions. Many of these coalitions have no strongly developed policy ideology, and therefore participate in coalitions more to gain the spoils of leadership (e.g., ministries and state favor) rather than because of a commitment to implementing a legislative platform. In turn, coalitions are more likely to collapse, and corruption and pork-barrel politics are more common as votes must be "bought," legally or illegally. This instability leads to a high turnover rate in Brazilian ministries, as reshuffling to accommodate shifts in power occurs frequently. The average Brazilian minister serves just over 1.3 years, a much shorter tenure than ministers in countries such as Argentina, Mexico, or Italy.

Finally, the weakness of political parties makes electoral results more unpredictable (a phenomenon known as electoral volatility). Because voters are more likely to follow popular politicians rather than to adhere to well-established party loyalty, the distribution of votes among parties varies greatly from election to election. Brazil ranks very high in terms of average volatility using a metric called the Pedersen index,[10] with a legislative volatility score of 27.7 and a presidential score of 60.0, the highest in the Latin American region (Roberts and Wibbels 1999).

FEDERALISM

The Brazilian political system is further constrained by the delegation of power and authority to the state and municipal level, which undermines the ability of the president and legislature to make policy and generate change. Federalism presents both opportunities and challenges. On the one hand, because significant money is provided to state governors and city mayors, the central government has been less effective at maintaining fiscal discipline. On the other hand, federalism has provided space for state and local officials to conduct useful experiments in governing, which has been critical in creating successful social policy.

Federalism is not a new feature of the Brazilian political system. Powerful local and regional leaders have been a feature of the Brazilian political system since independence from the Portuguese crown, when a federal republic dominated by powerful governors in Minas Gerais and São Paulo was created. While the military government (1964 to the early 1980s) attempted to centralize political and economic power, states remained relatively strong throughout the period, and emerged strongly during the democratic transition.[11] Brazil's 27 states elect their own legislative and executive branches, and governors in particular are relatively autonomous from the central government. The political powers of the governors are strongly influenced by the weak and decentralized nature of the party system. This is because the distribution of intergovernmental resources and power tends to favor decentralized power bases when the federal party system is weak (Riker 1975).

There are four other sources of gubernatorial power. Foremost is the governor's role in the nomination of candidates for the legislature. In the absence of strong, cross-national political parties, Brazilian governors play a crucial role in selecting state representatives. Sub-national committees formally nominate candidates, but the personalistic nature of Brazilian elections ensures that the support of the governor for a candidacy bid is central to the selection process and ultimately, to electoral success (Garman, Haggard et al. 2001). Would-be representatives exchange political allegiance to the governor for access to financial resources and the contacts necessary to run successful campaigns (Abrucio 1998). This also implies that gubernatorial elections tend to set boundaries on electoral alliances in the legislature, and governors have greater "coattails" than presidential candidates (Samuels 2000). This trend is exacerbated by the fact that state and national elections are not on the same electoral cycle. Partially as a result of the above, governors also play a strong role in shaping the policy preferences of deputies and senators from their state once in office. There is a high level of crossover between senators and governors in Brazil, and the continued support of the governor is crucial to career advancement for a legislative politician as many Brazilian deputies serve only one or two terms in the congress.

The second source of state power is the misdistribution of representation to favor smaller and poorer states in the Brazilian congress. Brazil is the second most malapportioned democratic state in the world, after Argentina (Stepan 1999, 25), and is skewed both in the chamber of deputies and senate (as in the case of the US, where all states have two senators despite vast differences in population). Poor rural states, which have disproportionately high representation, are also the states in which there is a higher incidence of traditional, patronage cleavages—the head of which is almost always the governor (Ames 1995). This in turn means that state allegiance on policy priorities has tended to trump other potential alignments. The northeast is a particularly good example of this: one of the largest parties in the congress (the PFL or Democrats) has largely been a vehicle for northeastern interests, and northeastern governors meet with one another and their congressional counterparts (who hold important positions on committees dealing with tax, fiscal, and infrastructure committees) more frequently than other state representatives (Selcher 1998).

Third, in matters of national policy-making and priorities, governors tend to act on behalf of municipal leaders. Given the high distribution of the Brazilian population in urban centers (some 80 per cent of the country's population) and the allocation of resources to this third tier in Brazilian federalism, this becomes a substantial source of further power. State legislatures, given the power of Brazilian governors, are relatively weak and have little role in the policy-making process. As such, governors are extremely important political players ("little presidents," as one commentator called them), and securing their support for legislation and broader policy programs is a central feature of Brazilian presidential politics.

Finally, Brazil's delegation of economic power, or fiscal federalism, to mayoralties and state governments strengthens the tendencies that already accumulate power to the governors because it grants them access to revenue. The country has higher levels of tax autonomy, vertical imbalances, and expenditure share delegated to the states and municipalities of Brazil than most other large federal states. While on average, Latin American national governments give just 12.2 per cent of the budget to states, in Brazil, states control more than 34 per cent of the federal budget. This is also a greater allocation to states than is found in other large federations, such as the US and Canada. Similarly, Brazilian states have more tax authority than do other Latin American states (Afonso and de Mello 2000, 3).

Much like political parties, it is not only the sheer level of fiscal decentralization that is of interest, but the way in which that decentralization is provisioned. In Brazil, the majority of fiscal decentralization takes the form of revenue decentralization rather than transfers from the central government. Additionally, like provisions on social spending, a large percentage of Brazilian intergovernmental transfers are constitutionally mandated, and few are discretionary. This distribution ensures that there is a greater level of stability in the transfers from the federal government—especially given the legislative constraints discussed in the previous section with regards to amending the constitution.

This section has highlighted two features of Brazilian democracy, the party system and the federalist system, which in turn have provided insight into the electoral system, the structure and constraints of the chamber of deputies and the powers of the presidency, governors, and municipal leaders. What has emerged is a picture of a democracy constrained by its own institutions, and one in which legislating change is made difficult by the nature of the institutions governing it.

THE INNOVATIVE FACE OF BRAZILIAN DEMOCRACY

Despite the institutional constraints described above, Brazil is also the home of a number of innovative social and economic policies that have evolved during the past decade of Brazilian democracy. Many of the most notable policies have originated with state and municipal governments, where the federalist structure has been a blessing in terms of crafting feasible and functional policies to address the social inequities that are a major feature of Brazilian politics. This section addresses three policies that demonstrate how Brazil is attempting to overcome its institutional rigidities to make progress on social and economic issues: participatory budgeting; a social support system for poor families known as *Bolsa Família*; and macroeconomic management at the central government level.[12] These three policies are not only innovative but also have attracted the attention of international audiences ranging from NGOs to Wall Street analysts.

PARTICIPATORY BUDGETING

Participatory budgeting (PB), invented in the southern city of Porto Alegre immediately after the country's transition to democracy, is a process through which ordinary citizens determine the spending priorities and allocation of resources from municipal (or less frequently, state) governments. Participatory budgeting has several goals: to increase the participation of citizens in their government and to increase their knowledge about political processes and policies; to enhance social justice through distributing greater resources to lower-income areas and groups; to allow citizens to advance their own ideas about the development needs of their neighborhood or region; and to reform budgetary and other administrative aspects of governance in order to prioritize transparency and accountability.

Mayors control large budgets for local spending on public works and other social services. In 1989, the Workers' Party was elected to the municipal government of Porto Alegre with an ideological commitment to increase equality among Porto Alegre's residents through the provision of social services to traditionally overlooked groups and neighborhoods. With this goal in mind, the municipal government designed several flagship policies aimed at making their ideological goals concrete, measurable, and accountable. Participatory budgeting, a policy which allows citizen councils to determine how social spending in their neighborhoods should be allocated, became the cornerstone of these policies. All citizens were invited to meetings (held several times a year) to debate and decide the manner in which funds for public works would be spent. Keen to ensure that the meetings were not overlooked by the general population or captured by an elite group, the government also actively encouraged citizen participation. New community leaders were recruited and employed as municipal officials, and these officials toured neighborhoods to explain the PB process, enumerate its benefits, encourage participation, and look for members of the communities with sufficient standing or interest to act as community representatives. Those representatives would be in charge of putting forward spending proposals at meetings, which citizens then debated and voted on. The government's role at the meeting was to act as a mediator, and to provide additional details or clarifications when required to improve the debate. Later meetings were organized to give oversight into the spending of funds and to check on the government's progress in fulfilling the spending priorities set by the neighborhoods.

Over time, the PB process in Porto Alegre moved from a sole focus on infrastructure and public works to larger discussions about economic development and city planning in thematic forums. In the process, PB helped to strengthen civil society in Porto Alegre, contrary to expectations. As Abers documents, "In countries like Brazil, state efforts to influence civic organizing have usually been geared toward weakening rather than strengthening civic groups representing the poor.... The participatory budget forums were created from the 'top down,' largely in the absence of strong pressure from autonomously organized civic groups. And yet ... that policy promoted the empowerment of organized civil society to such a degree that new civic groups were increasingly able to challenge the very state that helped them organize" (Abers 2000, 222). Thus, among the PB program's successes in Porto Alegre were citizen empowerment, growth of civil society, increased transparency over budgetary allocation, and increased allocation of budgetary funds to low-income areas. These successes led municipal governments throughout Brazil to adopt PB: in particular, participatory budgeting became a major part of the Workers' Party's political platform when running for municipal elections. Between 1990 and 2004, 250 Brazilian municipalities had adopted participatory budgeting at some point, spreading out from the Workers' Party to other parties. In fact, Wampler reports that only half of the cities with PB programs in 2004 were run by the PT. The success of the program has made it of high interest to development banks and nongovernmental organizations, which have helped to replicate the program in more than 40 countries.

Participatory budgeting's achievement in Brazil, however, has not been as uniformly successful as it is in Porto Alegre. Wampler (2007) undertook an in-depth study of eight different cities in which participatory budgeting was utilized and found a highly mixed record of success. Of the eight cities, only two were unequivocal successes, two were failures, and the final four cases were intermediate, with some successes and some failures. Wampler argues that there are a number of shortcomings in participatory budgeting. First, the focus on individual public works often means that citizens organize to achieve one project and then disband, with little positive spillover. Second, the process is highly dependent on the mayor's office, and therefore the quality of municipal government, making it susceptible to manipulation or corruption. Third, there is a weak track record of using PB to achieve longer-term planning, which means that strategic long-term initiatives can be overlooked in favor of public works. Finally, the focus on the local level prevents people from organizing on a regional or national level. Additionally, he found evidence that PB was more successful in cities, where initial levels of civic organization were higher. Many of these potential pitfalls have been overlooked by the development community advocating the adoption of PB in other cities and countries.

Nonetheless, there is little doubt that participatory budgeting is an innovative way to increase citizen participation in Brazilian democracy, achieve elusive social goals, and encourage transparency. The failure of PB to function in other cities as well as it did in Porto Alegre does not mean that the idea should be abandoned, just that both politicians and citizens should be aware that PB is not a "magic bullet" for either democracy or social equity. It requires dedication and ongoing investment to function well.

THE CONDITIONAL CASH TRANSFER PROGRAM (CCT)

Brazil spends a relatively high percentage of its gross domestic product (GDP) on social programs, comparing relatively favorably with developed countries. However, this spending has traditionally been heavily weighted toward payment of state pensions (provisioned in the constitution), which tend to benefit relatively rich members of society. In the past decade, however, the portion of social spending which has been allocated to assistance programs for low-income Brazilians has increased: it accounts for 6.5 per cent of social spending, a 60 per cent increase during the most recent Lula administration (2002–11) (Hall 2006, 691). This increase in spending has been fueled by the expansion of the *Bolsa Família* (or Family Grant) program. *Bolsa Família* is better described as a series of conditional cash transfer (CCT) programs, almost all of which began before the Lula administration, enhanced and unified to form a large social safety net for poorer families.

The central idea behind Brazil's CCT programs is to provide cash to poor Brazilians to increase their well-being, conditional on some criteria. For example, the *Bolsa Escola* program, which began in 1995 in Brasilia and was adopted nationally in 2001, provides a monthly cash stipend to parents if their children attend school 85 per cent of the time. Social support varies, depending on how poor the family in question is, how many children they have, and other criteria (e.g., whether there are pregnant or lactating female members of the household). Thus, the overall approach is to provide "cash grants ... conditional upon proof of regular presence at school, children's vaccination, attendance at health clinics, and, where relevant, participation in nutrition and vocational training courses" (Hall 2006, 698). It is known as a "conditional cash transfer" program, a social policy technique that was pioneered in 1992 by Mexico through a program originally known as PROGRESA (Programa de Educación, Salud y Alimentación) and which is now called *Oportunidades*. CCT programs are becoming increasingly popular both in Latin America and in other parts of the developing world (e.g., Bangladesh). Brazil's CCT program is the largest in the world, and has been enthusiastically supported both financially and otherwise by the World Bank, the Inter-American Development Bank (IADB), and other aid agencies and international NGOs. As Anthony Hall (2007, 698) notes, the World Bank and IADB have provided one-quarter of the funding for Brazil's CCT program through loans, and "the [World] Bank has been very generous in its public praise for *Bolsa Família*, whose instruments are seen as having an applicability beyond Brazil itself to other countries implanting CCT schemes."

While the CCT program is run by the central government through the social development ministry, local government played a central role both in the program's creation and in its ongoing administration. Local governments implement the program, collect data, register beneficiaries, and monitor compliance with conditions. The program therefore represents another example of how the federalist structure in Brazil allowed local governments to become innovators and implementers of social policy, albeit with central government buy-in and funding.

The World Bank estimates that 10.3 million families in December 2004 were registered to participate in the program (the central government maintains a unified register, and allocates spaces in the program based on need and municipal availability), and 6.57 million families were benefiting from it. A major assessment of the impact of CCT programs on Brazilian poverty was completed in December 2007 by Brazil's International Poverty Centre (Soares et al. 2007). The findings are striking: the Gini coefficient (a measure of financial inequality) fell by 4.7 per cent between 1995 and 2004, and *Bolsa Família* was responsible for 21 per cent of that decrease in inequality, second only to increases in wages. This is despite the fact that *Bolsa* only accounts for 0.5 per cent of Brazilian GDP. It has also had powerful impacts on the poorest 5 per cent of Brazilian society who derive 10 per cent of their income on average from CCTs. There have also been positive impacts on the distribution of household consumption, school attendance, and malnutrition levels. Negative outcomes include no increase in child immunization levels, despite the program being explicitly conditioned on this, and the failure of students to advance a grade level, despite enrolment. Overall, the program has been less efficient in choosing households to target than comparable programs in Mexico (creating some wasted spending), but has reached a higher percentage of poor households. Critics have argued that the program provides a disincentive to work, but the authors of the evaluation found that recipients of the Brazilian CCT program had higher rates of labor participation than non-participants.

Given the generally positive results as well as the widespread international acclaim for the CCT program, the Brazilian government has continued to increase spending on it, and political commitment to it is high.

CCT has become a major cornerstone of the government's social spending policy, and a means through which the Workers' Party demonstrates its commitment to a pragmatic version of democratic socialism. This commitment has often been questioned by critics of the government's economic policy choices, which have been solidly neoliberal.

MACROECONOMIC STABILITY

Despite the constraints created by the democratic constitution of 1989, Brazil has managed to consolidate its role as a major economic and political power in the past decade, and is viewed by some as a leader among developing countries on a number of diverse issues, including agricultural trade, the environment, and health policy. It has done this by consolidating a neoliberal macroeconomic policy framework, and by emphasizing Brazil's role as an important global power in the context of its foreign policy.

In the 1980s, Brazil suffered through what has come to be known as the "lost decade" of economic crisis and stagnation that plagued most of Latin America and a large part of the developing world. Having defaulted on their massive foreign debts and suffering from recession, Brazil experimented with a number of economic policy platforms under various governments. Some of these reflected the recommendations of the IMF and World Bank. Others were "heterodox" plans to solve the crisis through increased government spending and other means. However, neither of these approaches eradicated inflation, which by the early 1990s peaked at 2,000 per cent a year. In 1993, then finance minister Fernando Henrique Cardoso devised a plan to introduce a new currency (the real) and end hyperinflation through orthodox neoliberalism. The Real Plan, as it was known, had a surprisingly quick impact, and riding on a wave of popularity based on his skills in economic management, Cardoso was elected president in 1994.

After his election, Cardoso continued to pursue neoliberal economic policies, including the privatization of many state enterprises and the reform of constitutionally mandated spending priorities. But the Real Plan failed to insulate the Brazilian economy entirely from crisis. In 1999, in the aftermath of the massive financial crisis in East Asia and a similar crisis in Russia, Brazil was forced to devalue its currency and allow it to float freely on the international markets. Cardoso worked hard to maintain fiscal discipline, both at the central government and state government levels, and to help the economy recover quickly from the crisis during his second term in office. While never growing as quickly as the dynamic economies of Asia, Brazil's economic management continued to improve after the crisis of 1999.

New challenges arose in 2002, however. Presidential elections were to take place in October 2002, and Luiz Inácio Lula da Silva (known universally as "Lula"), founder of the Workers' Party and previous presidential candidate in three elections, was leading in the polls. International investors viewed the likelihood of Lula's win in the 2002 presidential elections as a threat to neoliberal macroeconomic management because in previous elections, the Workers' Party had espoused a strongly socialist economic doctrine and emphasized their distaste for Brazil's reliance on international financing. Given these perceived risks, international markets reacted strongly to each poll showing Lula in the lead, and the country was forced to the brink of default as international creditors showed decreasing willingness to lend to Brazil. This instability lead to Lula and the other presidential candidates pre-committing to a rescue package from the IMF, which had as conditions some tenants of economic management. After his election in October 2002, Lula immediately put in place measures and advisors aimed at underlining his commitment to orthodox economic management and Brazil's continued insertion into the globalized economy.

To the surprise of many economic analysts, macroeconomic policy under the Lula administration has been equally if not more conservative than it was under Cardoso. Lula's government has paid back loans to the IMF and World Bank on time or ahead of schedule and has announced that Brazil was no longer interested in borrowing from these funds, which just years earlier had acted as lifelines. At the same time, Brazilian growth has increased, and the government's trade balance is in surplus, as is its primary fiscal balance. Given these positive trends, credit rating agencies have upgraded Brazil to "investor-grade," which essentially means that the price Brazil pays to borrow money from international banks has decreased to be more in line with the price paid by developed countries.

Interestingly, Brazil has been able to improve its economic situation without addressing the massive spending challenges presented by the constitution—a result of the hard constraints of Brazilian democracy described in the previous section. While both the Cardoso and Lula administrations have, on numerous occasions, facilitated the introduction of legislation into the congress to tackle the constitutionally mandated spending and tax provisions, the party structure and electoral system have made it impossible to make any significant reforms. In contrast, in the wake of the crisis of 1999, the government was able to pass a "fiscal responsibility law," which forced the Brazilian states into limiting their indebtedness and improving their fiscal balances. Thus, while the party system has continued to play a role in hampering efforts at economic management, challenges presented by the federalist structure are being overcome.

The ability of the Lula government to achieve such positive economic results was, in no small part, the result of favorable international economic conditions which dominated until 2008—prices for goods that Brazil exports (e.g., agricultural products) were high, international interest rates were low, and until recently, there was limited international market volatility. Fortunes were looking particularly positive when the country discovered massive stores of oil while prices were at historic highs, though with the recent crashes in prices, the future of Brazil as an oil exporter is uncertain. The volatility in international capital markets has, perhaps inevitably (considering the extent to which Brazil relies on foreign capital as well as its integration with the global economy), spread to Brazil. The stock exchange has suffered major losses, and Brazil was identified by the IMF in 2008 as one of several countries for which emergency lines of credit would be open. The long-term economic and political implications of this downturn are unknown. But it is clear the solid macroeconomic program pursued by the Cardoso administration and strengthened by the Lula government will help Brazil to weather the current storm much better than it could have just 10 years ago.

But even before the current economic downturn, praise for the government's economic management was not universal. Reid (2007) notes that among economists, the government has been criticized for failing to reduce debt, for increasing the tax burden to pay for social spending rather than reducing wasteful constitutionally mandated spending, and for making few improvements on public investment. Domestically, the pursuit of macroeconomic stability as defined by a neoliberal economic paradigm has generated ferocious criticism from the more radical left within and outside Lula's Workers' Party. Internal divisions in the once strong party have appeared, despite Lula's second electoral victory in 2006. These criticisms reflect the fact that the persistence of exceptionally high levels of income inequality in Brazil is a major challenge, and one which undermines democratic institutions. The vast gap between Brazil's richest and poorest has given rise to characterizations of the country as "Belindia," a combination of the prosperity of Belgium and the deprivation of India. This presents great challenges for insuring that democratic institutions are not captured by the elite and that the poorest have adequate representation and vehicles for interest aggregation so that their votes, and voices, are not co-opted.

FOREIGN POLICY

As the economic fortunes of Brazil have been transformed over the course of the decade, the perception of Brazil's political importance has also been transformed. The watershed moment for this took place in 2003, when two events called attention to the foreign policy that the new Lula government was pursuing; a foreign policy aimed much more explicitly at positioning Brazil as a major power through its development aid policy and other foreign policies.[13] The first was the collapse of the Cancun Ministerial of the World Trade Organization (WTO), held in September 2003. The ministerial drew international attention to large developing countries involved in the so-called G22, a group of developing countries led by Brazil and India who had forged a common position on agriculture and used their joint strength to negotiate with larger countries such as the US and the EU trading block. The ministerial collapsed in no small part because the G22 blocked further discussion on the inclusion in the WTO of the "Singapore Issues" (investment, competition, procurement, and trade facilitation) if discussion on agriculture did not move forward. Brazil has continued to consolidate its central role in the progress of the WTO's Doha Round, becoming one of five major negotiating parties in the wake of the Cancun Ministerial.

The second was the publication of a relatively simple piece of research in October 2003 by two analysts at the global investment bank Goldman Sachs. Entitled "Dreaming with BRICs: The Path to 2050," the report argued that the world economy would be dramatically transformed in the coming 50 years by the growth of four emerging market economies—Brazil, Russia, India, and China (Wilson and Purushothaman 2003). The authors forecasted that of the current "G6" (the US, Japan, Germany, France, Italy, and the UK) only two would still be on the list in 2050—the US and Japan. Brazil, Russia, India, and China (collectively, the BRICs) would take the other four slots. Increased attention to the rising power of large developing countries began after this time, both in academic journals and in the press. Academics were interested in understanding how developing countries had overcome previous collective action problems to maintain a cohesive voting stance within the WTO (Narlikar and Tussie 2004; Narlikar and Wilkinson 2004). In comparison, the press began to focus on this story as part of a broader narrative of the rise of developing countries, especially China and India and, to a lesser extent, Brazil. This increased attention on the policies being pursued by Brazil in a number of fields, particularly international development aid and trade, but also trilateral cooperation with India and South Africa (the "IBSA" initiative), support for humanitarian interventions in Haiti, and Brazil's advocacy for reform of the United Nations Security Council.

This attention dovetailed with a number of reform processes in international institutions intended to increase the power and voice of Brazil and other large developing countries. In 1999, an institution called the G20, a body of finance ministers composed of the G7 countries and a number of large developing states, was formed in acknowledgment of the large role that developing countries played in the international economic system. The G20 has increasingly been the forum for discussing major issues in the international economy, such as the global response to the recent financial turmoil. The G20 has also played a leading role in forging agreements between developed and developing countries on reforming the governance structure of the International Monetary Fund, a reform pursued by the United States to increase representation for large developing countries in order to preserve the relevance of the institution.

Brazil has benefited from the international recognition increasingly given to large developing countries and to the growing consensus about the importance of incorporating these countries into the global governance system on more equitable terms. By using its foreign policy to showcase Brazil's potential as a "great power," the Lula administration has managed to get Brazil firmly established in the discussions about the increasing importance of large developing countries, insuring that the country's voice is heard more strongly in an array of international institutions. Yet the transition to great power status is hardly complete: significant challenges to macroeconomic stability have been highlighted by the international financial distress of 2007–08, and its lobbying for a place at the table with big powers in institutions such as the United Nations, for example, has had little effect.

CONCLUSION

This chapter started by presenting two different "faces" of Brazilian government. On the one hand, the government is characterized by less than ideal democratic institutions, which cause problems in efficiency and accountability across the three branches of government. But on the other, Brazil has become a "laboratory" of social and economic policy, with major innovations in the ways in which the government interacts with the society as a whole, and especially the poor. What has hopefully emerged is a better understanding of how Brazilian politicians and policymakers have sought to work around problematic institutions to make good policy—and, in the case of federalism, how the "problem" (a) has been used positively to encourage social policy experimentation at the local level and (b) has been minimized in the realm of national economic policy. Making similar progress in minimizing the impact of the fractionalized party system would require major electoral reform, something which has not been seriously pursued by recent governments because of the built-in opposition to such reforms (Power 2000).

In recent years, the view of Brazil from abroad has increasingly focused on the successful, innovative side of its democracy, while acknowledging its ongoing constraints. The Workers' Party government has found unlikely supporters: viewed in the context of a Latin American region, which some argue is drifting increasingly "leftwards" as a number of countries have elected left-leaning or populist presidents, the liberal economic establishment has praised Brazil for finding a middle ground between macroeconomic orthodoxy and interventionist economic and social policy. Javier Santiso, director of the OECD Development Centre, characterizes Brazil as the "political economy of the possible," a post-utopian world of pragmatic democratic politics (Santiso 2006). Changes and reforms do not happen at a revolutionary pace because of the compromises inherent to democracy, and some changes never happen at all. But "what made Brazil's progress look all the more remarkable was that it was the fruit of the patient construction of democratic consensus" (Reid 2007, 198).

NOTES

1 Governors and in some cases mayors were not directly elected, which prevented the opposition party from controlling any state or important city.
2 For a thorough overview of the transition from military to civilian rule, see Kinzo (2001).
3 It was called the National Constituent Assembly (ANC).
4 Brazilian federalism is similar to systems in Canada and the US in that authority and expenditure power is shared between state (provincial) and national governments. Brazil also has strong local governments, creating a three-tier power-sharing system.
5 Sousa (1999) reports that Collor used nearly 100 MPs during the course of his truncated administration. By October 1998, Cardoso had issued 135 MPs and had reissued 2,179 older MPs.
6 Power (2000) estimates, for example, that in 2000, São Paulo was underrepresented by some 40 seats; making an individual from a small rural state like Roraima "worth" 33 times that of a Paulista (27).
7 A law was introduced in 1998 that prevented deputies and senators from changing parties in the three months prior to elections.
8 The Workers' Party (PT) is the only Brazilian party that practices party fidelity on a voluntary basis, as noted in Keck (1992).
9 There is some disagreement about the relevance of this distinction. Samuels, for example, questions whether party discipline is related to ideology or, what he calls, "structural features" such as the party's alliance strategy and candidate access to funding (Samuels 2000).
10 The Pedersen index calculates the net shift in voting percentages by dividing the sum of individual party gains and losses by two. The index is scaled from 0 to 100, with a score of 0 corresponding to no gains or losses in votes for parties, and a 100 indicating that every vote went to a new party.
11 Kingstone and Power (2000, 83) report that the segment of the fiscal budget controlled by the central government was 59.5 per cent in 1960, 60.8 per cent in 1970, slightly higher at 68.2 per cent in 1980, and 58.9 per cent in 1990.

Municipal governments lost more fiscal powers under the military regime than states did.
12 There are many examples of good governance and good policy-making in Brazil, a sampling of which are documented in an excellent book by Judith Tendler (1997).
13 This section is largely taken from a previous publication: see Phillips (2008).

REFERENCES

Abers Neaera, Rebecca. 2000. *Inventing Local Democracy: Grassroots Politics in Brazil*. Boulder: Lynne Rienner Press.
Abrucio, Fernando Luiz. 1998. *Os Barões da Federação: os Governadores e a Redemocratização Brasileira*. São Paulo: Universita de São Paulo Hucitec Press.
Afonso, José Roberto, and Luiz de Mello. 2000. "Brazil: An Evolving Federation." IMF/FAD Seminar on Decentralization. June 10, 2010. www.imf.org/external/pubs/ft/seminar/2000/fiscal/afonso.pdf.
Ames, Barry. 1995. "Electoral Rules, Constituency Pressures, and Pork Barrel: Bases of Voting in the Brazilian Congress." *The Journal of Politics* 57(2): 324–43.
———. 2001. *The Deadlock of Democracy in Brazil*. Ann Arbor: University of Michigan Press.
Desposato, Scott. 2004. "The Impact of Party-Switching on Legislative Behaviour in Brazil." Working Paper. June 10, 2010. http://dss.ucsd.edu/~sdesposa/ps2.pdf.
Garman, Christopher, Stephen Haggard, et al. 2001. "Fiscal Decentralization: A Political Theory with Latin American Cases." *World Politics* 53(2): 205–36.
Hall, Anthony. 2006. "From Zero to Bolsa Família: Social Policies and Poverty Alleviation under Lula." *Journal of Latin American Studies* 38(4): 689–709.
Keck, Margaret E. 1992. *The Workers' Party and Democratization in Brazil*. New Haven: Yale University Press.
Kingstone, Peter R., and Timothy Power, eds. 2000. *Democratic Brazil: Actors, Institutions and Processes*. Pittsburgh: University of Pittsburgh Press.
Kinzo, Maria. 2001. "Transitions: Brazil." *Democracy in Latin America: (Re) constructing Political Society*. Ed. Manuel A. Garretón and Edward Newman. Tokyo: United Nations University Press. 19–45.
Mainwaring, Scott. 1991. "Politicians, Parties and Electoral Systems: Brazil in Comparative Perspective." *Comparative Politics* 24(1): 21–43.
———. 1995. "Brazil: Weak Parties, Feckless Democracy." *Building Democratic Institutions: Parties and Party Systems in Latin America*. Ed. Scott Mainwaring and Timothy Scully. Palo Alto: Stanford University Press. 354–98.
———. 1999. *Rethinking Party Systems in the Third Wave of Democratization*. Palo Alto: Stanford University Press.
Narlikar, Amrita, and Diana Tussie. 2004. "The G20 at the Cancun Ministerial: Developing Countries and their Evolving Coalitions in the WTO." *The World Economy* 27(7): 947–66.
Narlikar, Amrita, and Rorden Wilkinson. 2004. "Collapse at the WTO: a Cancun Post-Mortem." *Third World Quarterly* 25(3): 447–60.
Phillips, Lauren. 2008. "International Relations in 2030: The Transformative Power of Developing Countries." Discussion Paper, No. 3/2008. Bonn: German Development Institute.

Power, Timothy. 2000. "Political Institutions in Democratic Brazil: Politics as a Permanent Constitutional Convention." *Democratic Brazil: Actors, Institutions and Processes.* Ed. Peter R. Kingstone and Timothy Power. Pittsburgh: University of Pittsburgh Press.

Reid, Michael. 2007. *Forgotten Continent: The Battle for Latin America's Soul.* New Haven: Yale University Press.

Riker, William. 1975. "Federalism." *Handbook of Political Science.* Ed. Fred Greenstein and Nelson Polsby. Reading, MA: Addison-Wesley.

Roberts, Kenneth M., and Erik Wibbels. 1999. "Party Systems and Electoral Volatility in Latin America: A Test of Economic, Institutional and Structural Explanation." *The American Political Science Review* 93(3): 575–90.

Samuels, David J. 2000. "The Gubernatorial Coattails Effect: Federalism and Congressional Elections in Brazil." *The Journal of Politics* 62(1): 240–53.

Santiso, Javier, and Andrés Velasco. 2006. *Latin America's Political Economy of the Possible: Beyond Good Revolutionaries and Free-Marketeers.* Cambridge, MA: MIT Press.

Selcher, Wayne. 1998. "The Politics of Decentralized Federalism, National Diversification and Regionalism in Brazil." *Journal of Interamerican Studies and World Affairs* 40(4): 25–50.

Skidmore, Thomas. 1967. *Politics in Brazil 1930–1964.* Oxford: Oxford University Press.

———. 1988. *The Politics of Military Rule in Brazil: 1964–85.* Oxford: Oxford University Press.

———. 2004. "Brazil's Persistent Income Inequality: Lessons from History." *Latin American Politics and Society* 46(2): 133–50.

Soares, Fabio, et al. 2007. "Evaluating the Impact of Brazil's *Bolsa Família:* Cash Transfer Programmes in Comparative Perspective." IPC Evaluation Note No. 1. December. Brasília, Brazil: International Poverty Centre.

Sousa, Amaury de. 1999. "Cardoso and the Struggle for Reform in Brazil." *Journal of Democracy* 10(3): 49–63.

Stepan, Alfred. 1999. "Federalism and Democracy: Beyond the US Model." *Journal of Democracy* 10(4): 19–34.

Tendler, Judith. 1997. *Good Government in the Tropics.* Baltimore: Johns Hopkins University Press.

Wampler, Brian. 2007. *Participatory Budgeting in Brazil.* University Park: Pennsylvania State University Press.

Wilson, Dominic, and Roopa Purushothaman. 2003. "Dreaming with BRICs: The Path to 2050." Goldman Sachs Global Economics Papers 99. October. New York: Goldman Sachs.

E-RESOURCES

Brazil's federal government website (English) (www.brasil.gov.br/ingles/). A comprehensive website with access to many aspects of policy-making at the level of the Brazilian national government. There are links to information about economic policies and outcomes, social programs, and tourism. Links are also available to the website of the president and the Ministry of External Affairs (often referred to as *Itamaraty,* or the foreign ministry).

Brazilian chamber of deputies (some English) (www2.camara.gov.br/). The official website of the lower house of the Brazilian congress, the chamber of deputies. Information in English includes the composition of current and past legislatures, as well as an introduction to the Brazilian legislative process. More detailed information about approved and pending laws are available in Portuguese, as well as detailed biographies of current legislative members.

Folha de São Paulo (major newspaper) (www.folha.uol.com.br). The largest business daily from the city of São Paulo. The online version provides domestic and international news of all sorts.

Landless Movement (MST) (www.mst.org.br). MST is a civil society group fighting for the rights of landless rural workers in Brazil. The MST website provides a large amount of information about the movement, the status of various groups of Brazilian citizens (including women, indigenous peoples, etc.), the political goals of the group, and a library of related resources.

Veja (weekly news magazine) (www.veja.abril.com.br). *Veja* is one of the most widely read weekly news magazines in Brazil. Topics of all sorts are covered, including economics, politics, sports, and cultural issues.

Workers' Party (www.pt.org.br). The website of one of Brazil's largest political parties, the Workers' Party (PT), the party of the current president. There is a great deal of information in Portuguese about the party's policies and priorities, both for national and international issues. There is also excellent access to relevant news and opinions related to Brazilian politics, and information about upcoming elections.

World Social Forum (English) (www.forumsocialmundial.org.br/). The website of the World Social Forum, which was established in 2001 as an alternative gathering to the annual World Economic Forum in Davos, Switzerland. Although the first social forum was held in Porto Alegre, Brazil, it is now held in other developing countries as well. The website contains information about the organization of the forum, past forums, its principles, and ways to get involved with the WSF, including a schedule of events the WSF is affiliated with.

ELEVEN
Bolivia: Ethnicity and Power

ROBERTA RICE

On January 22, 2006, Bolivian President Evo Morales of the Movement Toward Socialism party (MAS) made history when he became the country's first indigenous head of state. Born in 1959 in the highland department of Oruro to Aymara parents, Morales grew up in abject poverty. Only two of his six siblings survived past childhood. As a child, Morales worked in the agricultural fields alongside his family and herded llamas to pay for school. He was unable to complete his secondary education. In 1982, after a devastating drought in the highlands, he and his family relocated to the Quechua-speaking valley region of Cochabamba where they began to cultivate coca, the principal ingredient used in the production of cocaine. Confronted with US enforced eradication programs, the growers (predominantly indigenous) defended coca production as part of indigenous culture and traditions. Morales soon joined a union of coca growers and worked his way up the ranks. By the 1990s, he had become the undisputed leader of the coca growers' movement. Following the general trend in Latin America, indigenous movements in Bolivia have played a central role in recent social upheavals in the country. Through the use of parallel or solidarity protest events, indigenous and popular groups are able to effectively shut down the entire country until their demands are met. In 1999, Morales and his supporters formed the MAS and successfully contested municipal elections. In 2002, Morales narrowly missed winning the first round of the presidential elections. The ultimate victory for the MAS occurred during the December 2005 elections when the party captured 54 per cent of the total national vote, the only party to win an absolute majority since the country's transition to democracy in 1982.

In December 2009, Morales was reelected for a second term in another landslide victory. As a result of the MAS's stunning electoral success, the current Bolivian legislature is the most ethnically and socioeconomically diverse in the nation's history and indeed in all of Latin America's history as well. But Bolivia's democratization produced a weak state and a strong and well-organized civil society with racial divisions corresponding to the wide gap between the rich and poor. The central challenge for MAS is how to govern in that context.[1]

REVOLUTIONARY HISTORY, 1825–1952

Bolivia is a landlocked country in the heart of South America. The Andean mountain range dominates the Bolivian landscape, dividing the country into the windswept highlands or *altiplano* and the tropical lowlands. The highland city of La Paz is located at the dizzying height of 3,640 meters above sea level, making it the world's highest capital. In addition to its incredible geographic variation, Bolivia is also one of the most ethnically diverse countries in the Western Hemisphere. Indigenous peoples constitute a majority of the total population, estimated at 50.5 per cent of the country's inhabitants. The country's principal indigenous groups are the Aymara peoples of the highland plateau region and the Quechua peoples of the highland valley region. In the Bolivian lowlands there are over 30 ethnic groups, including the Guaraní, Chiquitano, and Moxeño peoples. Bolivia is also one of Latin America's poorest and most underdeveloped countries. With a per capita gross national income (GNI) of just $1,260 US in 2007, the World Bank classifies Bolivia as a low-middle-income country. It is a country rich in mineral resources that has gone through a number of boom-and-bust cycles, beginning with silver and later tin. The poverty-stricken city of Potosí is but one example of the process of underdevelopment in the country. During the colonial era Potosí was a city of wealth and opulence due to the massive Cerro Rico ("Rich Hill") silver mine. According to Benjamin Dangl (2007, 15), "Residents of the city say the silver taken from Cerro Rico could have built a bridge all the way to Spain. Others say such a bridge could be made out of bones: an estimated eight million people died in the bowels of the mountain." By the time Bolivia gained independence from Spain in 1825, its silver mines were exhausted.

Organized resistance by the populace has long been a part of Bolivian politics. Throughout much of the twentieth century, the militant labor union movement that grew out of Bolivia's mineral export economy was a major actor in the political life of the nation. As a result, leftist political parties developed early in the country, drawing most of their support from the mining sector (Rueschemeyer, Stephens, and Stephens 1992). In the late 1930s, numerous parties of the political left began to emerge onto the Bolivian political scene, including the Trotskyist Revolutionary Workers' Party (POR) and the Stalinist Revolutionary Left Party (PIR). This time period also witnessed the emergence of the uniquely Bolivian National Revolutionary Movement (MNR), historically the nation's most influential political party. The MNR reflected populist, nationalist, and anti-oligarchic sentiments (Rivera 1987). The party sought to establish an alliance of the middle-class, workers, and peasants as the base of support for its plans to dismantle the traditional oligarchic or elitist society. In the 1951 presidential elections, the platform of the MNR's candidate, Víctor Paz Estenssoro (1952–56; 1960–64; 1985–89), was based on three major policy initiatives: universal suffrage, nationalization of the tin mines, and agrarian reform. When the regime in power refused to cede the presidency to Paz Estenssoro, who had clearly won the elections, the MNR called for a revolution on the part of the populace. The indigenous peasantry had already begun to mobilize at that time as a result of their involvement in the devastating Chaco War (1932–35) with Paraguay. After just three days of fighting, the masses defeated the army of the oligarchy on April 9, 1952, bringing the MNR party to power.

POPULAR POLITICAL INCORPORATION, 1952–1978

The MNR-led revolution of 1952 introduced profound changes to Bolivian society. The immediate agenda of the MNR government was to ensure greater state control over the economy, to end feudalistic labor relations in the countryside, and to incorporate increasingly radicalized peasant and indigenous communities into the formal political system. The MNR sought to channel the people's energies into support for the new regime through an elaborate system of state corporatism. Government-sponsored peasant and labor union movements effectively bound the populace to the party and the state. Initially, the MNR allied itself with the powerful Bolivian Workers' Central (COB), the country's largest union, as a means of incorporating newly enfranchised workers. During the heyday of the revolutionary period, the MNR government granted co-governing status to the COB. However, increasing tensions between the governing regime and the COB as a result of the growing militancy and autonomy of the union organization led the MNR to rely more heavily on force to maintain control, thereby alienating the labor movement (Van Cott 2008a).

By 1964 Paz Estenssoro, who was serving his second presidential term, faced severe economic difficulties and internal party divisions. With his governing alliance split, the military were able to gain power. In November of that year, a military coup led by General René Barrientos (1964–69) plunged the country into 18 years of almost uninterrupted military rule. In an effort to sever a potential alliance between the well-organized workers' movement and the peasant movement, Barrientos imposed direct military control over rural union organizing, institutionalized by the Military-Peasant Pact of 1964. Instead of the union-party-state organizational structure of the MNR period, the Military-Peasant Pact of the Barrientos regime linked the peasant union apparatus directly to the state via the military. Attempts at independent organizing by the peasantry were further hampered in 1971 when General Hugo Banzer (1971–78; 1997–2001) seized power in a bloody coup. The Banzer regime sought to reduce the role of the peasantry in national politics by repressing their organizational efforts.

During this time period, an important new Indianist ideology known as Katarismo became a key sociopolitical force in Bolivia. Although indigenous peoples were incorporated into the political system through universal suffrage after the 1952 revolution, they continued to suffer from ethnic discrimination and political manipulation (Ticona and Albó 1997). Feeling like strangers in their own country, a new generation of Aymara leaders studying in La Paz in the late 1960s began to call attention to issues of cultural oppression. Inspired by the writings of Bolivia's premier Indianist thinker Fausto Reinaga, Aymara intellectuals founded the Cultural Center of November 15, named after the date of execution of the legendary Inca revolutionary Túpaj Katari in 1781 at the hands of Spanish colonizers. The Katarista ideology that developed out of this period of ethnic consciousness blended Marxist analysis with indigenous rights claims. Katarista followers within government-sponsored peasant unions were the first to push for union autonomy. It was not until the formation of the independent United Peasant Workers Confederation of Bolivia (CSUTCB) in 1979 by dissident leaders within the peasant movement that the hold of the state over the peasantry was finally broken (Ticona 2000). The emergence of the CSUTCB marked the end of the Military-Peasant Pact era and the search for new forms of interest representation.

TUMULTUOUS TRANSITION TO DEMOCRACY, 1978–1982

Bolivians emerged from their arduous experience with military rule to face an equally difficult transition to democracy. Between July 1978 and July 1980, the country experienced four successive military coups. Within that time period, five different presidents held office amidst the constant circulation of coup rumors and threats. Of all of Bolivia's coups, that of General Luís García Meza (1980–81) in July 1980 is considered the most bloodthirsty and corrupt in the nation's history (Mayorga 1997). The coup, which was supported by the Argentine military government of General Jorge Rafael Videla (1976–81), overthrew the interim constitutional government of Lydia Gueiler Tejada (1979–80). The García Meza regime unleashed an unprecedented reign of state terror.

García Meza represented the most reactionary sector of the military opposed to the country's redemocratization. The military's anti-democratic sentiment was echoed in the apprehension and distrust felt by the private sector and right-wing political parties, which feared that a return to democracy would strengthen the country's leftist and unionist tradition. The human rights abuses that occurred under García Meza included the destruction of media and labor union headquarters, the suppression of all union and political activities, the prohibition of the constitutionally guaranteed rights to free speech and association, and the use of arbitrary detentions, torture, and disappearances. The indiscriminate violence of paramilitary groups terrorized the population and converted the country into a military zone.

The García Meza regime was also one of the most corrupt in Bolivia's history. The dictator's primary interest in keeping the armed forces in power was to use the resources of the state for personal gain. His regime was the first Bolivian government to be openly associated with the drug trade. The so-called narco-military regime transformed the state apparatus into a support network for drug trafficking and the illegal acquisition of wealth (Gamarra 1991). The criminal nature of the dictatorship resulted in the temporary suspension of US–Bolivian relations and in the alienation of nearly every political and social group in the country.

Popular resistance, growing anti-militaristic sentiment, and the downward spiral of the economy brought about the downfall of the García Meza regime. Throughout the dictatorship, the country's leading social and political organizations mobilized to demand a return to democracy. Civil society forces essentially determined the principal character of Bolivia's transition to democracy, that is, a transition through rupture or total collapse of the military. Bolivia's democratic transition thus contrasts sharply with the transition process in most other Latin American countries that took place through negotiations or elite pacts between military and political forces under conditions established by the military government. An important aspect of the Bolivian transition process was the resultant loss by the military of the ability to negotiate the terms of its withdrawal from power and thus its capacity to maintain an influential position in the newly established democratic order.

Democracy officially returned to Bolivia in October 1982 when Hernán Siles Zuazo was named president of the republic based on the June 1980 election results that were interrupted by the García Meza coup. One of the dilemmas faced by the nation was whether to ignore the criminal conduct of the García Meza dictatorship or to confront the regime's serious human rights violations and its usurpation of power. The political conditions for a trial of García Meza were favorable given the precarious state of the Bolivian military and the widely perceived and deeply felt need on the part of all Bolivians to bring those responsible to justice. After considerable debate and delay owing to procedural difficulties, legal questions, and the growing economic crisis, the Bolivian congress submitted a formal indictment against García Meza and 55 of his collaborators to the supreme court in February 1986 to have the defendants prosecuted in an accountability trial.

On April 21, 1993, after seven years of judicial proceedings, the supreme court's historic guilty verdict and sentence were read into the record. The occasion was marked by the declaration of a Day of National Dignity by the government. The court sentenced García Meza and his notorious minister of the interior, Luís Arce Gómez, to 30 years in prison without parole, the most severe punishment afforded under the constitution. The remaining defendants included the ministers of peasant affairs and of planning who received six years, the chief of the air force who received a five-year sentence, and 11 paramilitary agents implicated in assassinations who were sentenced to between 20 and 30 years in prison without possibility of parole (Mayorga 1997). The García Meza trial represented a truly momentous event in the democratic history of Bolivia and of Latin America in general. Bolivia's accountability trial was the first successful attempt in the region to settle accounts with a military dictatorship.

NEOLIBERALISM'S POSTER CHILD, 1980S–1990S

Bolivia's military governments of the 1960s and 1970s were all marked by heightened state involvement in the economy. Despite their varying stances toward organized labor and the peasantry, they were united by their conception of an activist state, backed by the military playing a leading role in the process of economic development (Conaghan and Malloy 1994). Substantial increases in world prices for Bolivia's main mineral exports in the 1970s in conjunction with an agro-export boom in the eastern lowland region of the country laid the basis for state-led development efforts. However, the economic success of the period was built on a unique set of transitory circumstances that included easy access to foreign credit and a short-term improvement in the country's trading position. When the debt crisis hit Bolivia in the early 1980s, its economic boom years were over.

By the time civilian president Siles Zuazo (1956–60; 1982–85) came to power in 1982, the Bolivian economy was on the brink of disaster. The collapse in commodity prices and the halt in the flow of foreign capital had set an economic crisis in motion. The administration of Siles Zuazo inherited an economic situation in which there was a 300 per cent annual inflation rate; a shortage of food, medicines, and imported parts for industrial production; mounting foreign debt; and a political situation characterized by intense social unrest. Between 1982 and 1985, Zuazo proposed six different stabilization packages, all of which were blocked by opposition parties in congress and by affected interest groups. Because the state lacked capacity and autonomy from vested interests, the failure of these initiatives served to magnify the severity of the crisis and paved the way for the drastic measures that were to come. Inflation under Zuazo rose to an annualized rate of well over 10,000 per cent by 1985, with some estimates ranging up to 26,000 per cent (Cariaga 1990). The situation had become so untenable by 1985 that Zuazo was forced to agree to shorten his term in office and called for an early election.

Neoliberalism officially arrived in Bolivia on August 29, 1985, when newly elected President Víctor Paz Estenssoro of the MNR party launched Supreme Decree 21060, otherwise known as the New Economic Policy (NEP). Ironically, Paz Estenssoro, whose party had led a leftish revolution of the masses 33 years earlier, implemented one of the most draconian neoliberal economic programs in the history of Latin America. The emergency economic team assembled under Paz Estenssoro included Gonzalo Sánchez de Lozada, leader of the Confederation of Private Entrepreneurs (CEPB), and influential Harvard economist Jeffrey D. Sachs, the principal architect of the NEP. The consensus among Paz Estenssoro and his advisors was that the government's response to the crisis had to be swift and dramatic. The objectives of the NEP were threefold: the liberalization of the economy; the promotion of the private sector as the central actor in economic development; and the reestablishment of control over key state enterprises that had been captured by labor organizations (Gamarra 1994). Expecting protest, the Paz Estenssoro government declared a state of siege following the announcement of the NEP and arrested hundreds of peasant and labor leaders. The impact of the NEP on hyperinflation was immediate, bringing down the rate of inflation to near price stability within weeks. Between 1986 and 1987, the average annual inflation rate was only 10 to 15 per cent, one of the lowest in the region (Morales and Sachs 1989). The model was hailed as a success.

Bolivia's new economic policy, rather than being strictly economic, also had the political aim of restoring the state's control over mobilized sectors of society. What happened instead was that mobilization shifted to new actors within new social movements. For instance, the privatization of state-owned mining enterprises in 1985, long a bastion of support for the Bolivian Workers' Central (COB), resulted in the loss of 23,000 jobs, leaving in place a workforce of only 7,000 unionized miners (Farthing and Kohl 2001). Consequently, economic restructuring broke up the strategic position that organized labor once held over the national economy. The massive layoffs in the mining sector, however, resulted in an influx of ex-miners into the Chapare valley region of the department of Cochabamba to cultivate coca. The organizational skills acquired through the tin miners' labor radicalism quickly took hold with the coca growers, producing a strong, politically savvy, and well-organized movement. The growers' defense of coca production as part of indigenous culture and tradition garnered the movement national and international appeal (Yashar 2005). The growing of coca plants is a centuries-old tradition in Bolivia. The coca leaf is considered sacred by indigenous peoples and used for rituals; it is also consumed on a daily basis as a means of suppressing hunger and easing altitude sickness. By the 1990s, the undisputed leader of the coca growers' movement was long-time union activist and indigenous leader, and who is now the president of Bolivia, Evo Morales.

PARTY POLITICS IN THE POST-STABILIZATION PERIOD

Bolivia possesses a weakly institutionalized multiparty system. Political parties in the country have generally served more as vehicles for the capture and circulation of state patronage among political elites than as organizations expressing the interests of society (Gamarra and Malloy 1995). The most important distinction between the Bolivian party system and other Latin American presidential systems lies in the selection of the president. According to Article 90 of the 1967 constitution, when no candidate achieves an absolute majority, congress must elect the executive from among the top three finishers (currently from among the top two since the constitutional reform of 1994). Thus, Bolivia's variant of the majority system is a hybrid that combines features of both presidentialism and parliamentarianism (Gamarra 1997). This particular election method has been argued to have a coalition-inducing effect as parties negotiate over candidate selection and patronage distribution. Empirical studies have found support for the hypothesis that the unique attribute of the Bolivian system works to reduce executive-legislative conflict (Jones 1995). This particular feature of the Bolivian party system has enabled presidents to manufacture working majorities in congress in support of their policy initiatives.

The political capacity of the Paz Estenssoro government to impose and sustain a draconian structural adjustment program was facilitated by a pact between the ruling MNR party and its main opposition, the National Democratic Action (ADN) party led by former dictator Hugo Banzer. Shortly after launching the NEP, Paz Estenssoro negotiated the so-called Pact for Democracy which provided legislative support for his policy in exchange for a share of state patronage for the ADN and a mechanism to ensure the rotation of the presidency between the two parties (Gamarra 1994). The fact that the MNR had placed second, behind the ADN, in the first round of the elections was an important consideration in Paz Estenssoro's decision to enter into a pact with Banzer's party. Defenders of the pact argued that since the arrangement was between the first and second place finishers, then approximately 55 per cent of the electorate was duly represented. However, the opposition, headed by Jaime Paz Zamora of the Revolutionary Movement of the Left (MIR) party charged the two leaders with attempting to establish a hegemonic party. In a round of political bartering, the MIR's electoral reform proposal favoring minority parties was accepted in exchange for the official opposition party's mild resistance to the NEP. Thus, the Pact for Democracy played a key role in the consolidation of neoliberal economic reforms. However, the Pact for Democracy and neoliberalism were so unpopular that they also helped to erode support for the existing system of governance.

Together, the MNR, ADN, and MIR coalitions came to dominate elections throughout the 1990s, rotating in and out of power. In 1989, the Pact for Democracy officially ruptured because of an interparty dispute. The ADN and MIR established an alliance known as the Patriotic Accord, shifting the balance of power between the MNR on the one hand and the ADN with the MIR on the other. This configuration of political power lasted until the elections of 2002, when a number of new and successful indigenous-based parties emerged onto the national political scene (Mayorga 2005). The recurring need to form governing coalitions is both the strength and the weakness of the Bolivian party system. While the ability to form coalitions has given the system a measure of stability, these same coalitions have also served to effectively shut out the non-coalition political parties from access to patronage and the decision-making process. As a result, there is always the potential for frustrated opposition groups to resort to extrasystemic means of affecting change.

In an attempt to draw in excluded sectors of the polity, the government undertook a number of crucial electoral reforms in the mid-1990s. A key reform initiative was the 1994 Law of Popular Participation (LPP), which was one of several new pieces of legislation designed to incorporate indigenous peoples into the legal, political, and economic life of the country. The LPP was the cornerstone of the brand of multicultural statecraft introduced by the coalition government of President Gonzalo Sánchez de Lozada of the MNR party (1993–97; 2002–03) and Vice President Víctor Hugo Cárdenas of the much smaller Tupaj Katari Revolutionary Movement of Liberation (MRTKL) party (Postero 2007). The LPP instituted the first-ever direct municipal elections and significantly strengthened local governments. The decentralizing reforms served the dual goals of cutting back on the central government's expenses and responsibilities by downloading them to the local level while co-opting resistance to neoliberalism by shifting the focus of popular struggles to local issues rather than national ones. While initially dampening resistance efforts through the creation of new institutional channels of social representation, decentralization and municipal reforms aided in the development of new local leaders and movements. Their strategies for working within the system changed, and some acquired the necessary political experience to move beyond local issues. Some movements managed to project themselves onto the national political stage during the country's most recent round of protests by moving the focus of resistance beyond the local level to a national critique of the neoliberal economic model. For example, the coordinator of water and life in Cochabamba managed to build a national awareness of the privatization of water in that region.

NEOLIBERALISM UNRAVELED, 2000–2005

It is notoriously difficult to establish a causal relationship between economic policies and societal outcomes. However, a number of recent empirical studies have discovered an association between neoliberalism and higher levels of inequality (Huber and Solt 2004; Portes and Hoffman 2003; Wade 2004). More precisely, Huber and Solt (2004) suggest that countries that have undergone drastic reform episodes, such as Bolivia, have incurred the greatest socioeconomic costs. In Bolivia, many of these costs have been borne by the nation's poor indigenous majority. A 2004 World Bank report on indigenous peoples and human development in Latin America revealed that the indigenous poverty gap increased in Bolivia between 1997 and 2002, despite the fact that the national poverty rate declined slightly (Hall and Patrinos 2004). This dynamic has produced a growing grassroots perception in Bolivia that it is the economically and politically powerful non-indigenous minority that is benefiting from the policies of economic liberalization. As the 1990s wore on, the crisis-induced policy consensus around neoliberalism began to unravel.

Social protests in Bolivia have increased in frequency and intensity since the late 1990s. Bolivia's latest protest cycle, which began with the Water War of Cochabamba in 2000 and culminated in the Gas Wars of La Paz in 2003 and 2005, is widely believed to mark the exhaustion of the neoliberal economic model in the country (Crabtree 2005; Kohl and Farthing 2006). Traditionally, social protests in Bolivia had been led by affected sectors of society, such as miners, teachers or retired workers, seeking to remedy a specific situation. In contrast, the most recent round of protests joined together a diverse array of actors, including indigenous peoples, students, workers, neighborhood associations, and sectors of the middle-class united through a common frustration with the promises and failures of neoliberalism (Arce and Rice 2009). While these popular coalitions are susceptible to the government's strategy of divide and conquer, the ability of movement organizers to link the claims of disparate groups into a coherent critique with the power to convoke the masses has proven to be a highly effective tool in the struggle against neoliberalism.

The victorious Water War of 2000 marked the first in a series of massive civic uprisings that led to a rupture in the national political system, which ultimately opened the door to the election of the country's first indigenous president. The epicenter of the dispute was the city of Cochabamba where a cycle of protest activities was incited by the sale of the area's water supply to Aguas del Tunari, a multinational consortium controlled by the Bechtel Corporation, a California engineering giant. Within weeks of the privatization, water rates in Cochabamba had increased by as much as 300 per cent (Schultz 2000). Public outrage against the blatantly unreasonable terms of the privatization deal quickly spread to other parts of the country. Civil society groups throughout Bolivia began to protest not only the issue of water rights but also the general direction of the government's economic policies. Faced with a massive civic revolt, the government of Hugo Banzer terminated the contract with Aguas del Tunari in April 2000. Bechtel subsequently filed a $50 million lawsuit against Bolivia with the World Bank's trade court. Intense international pressure, however, forced Bechtel to drop the case. The re-nationalization of Cochabamba's water system marked a key moment in the evolution of popular protest in the country. The Bolivian Water War demonstrated the weakness of the apparatus of the state in the face of organized civil society.

Following the civil society victory of April 2000, indigenous and peasants groups in the highland region of Achacachi, led by the head of the CSUTCB, Felipe Quispe, and in the Chapare region, led by Evo Morales, began to mobilize in September 2000 around a number of different issues. The conflict became known as Black September. In the Chapare region, peasant unions blockaded the main highway between Cochabamba and the wealthy eastern city of Santa Cruz to protest the increasing militarization of coca growing zones. In the highlands, indigenous men, women, and children demonstrated against continuing ethnic and cultural discrimination and deepening rural poverty. The Black September protests concluded with the signing of a lengthy accord between the government and the protest organizers covering more than 50 points, varying from the modification of specific laws to the implementation of infrastructural projects (Laserna 2002). Left out of the agreement was the controversial topic of forced coca eradication programs, leaving the door open to future uprisings.

The period of social mobilization reached its peak with the Gas War in the capital city of La Paz in October 2003 that led to the ouster of President Gonzalo Sánchez de Lozada. The nearly six-week-long social convulsion, which resulted in the deaths of over 70 civilians at the hands of military forces, was triggered by the government's decision to sell gas to the United States via Chile. Both countries hold negative associations for most Bolivians—the US for its imperialist intervention and Chile for annexing the Bolivian coastline during the War of the Pacific (1879–80). While the theme of gas may have been the rallying cry for the uprising, the underlying factors in the massive mobilization included the social costs of economic restructuring, the control of strategic sectors of the economy by transnational capital, and the loss of legitimacy of the nation's democratic political institutions. The crisis highlighted the complete disconnection between political and civil society. Their general disinterest and inability to attend to pressing national demands irreparably tarnished the reputations of Bolivia's long-dominant political parties, the MNR, the ADN, and the MIR.

In the aftermath of the October 2003 civic revolt, Vice President Carlos Mesa (2003–05) assumed the presidency. The three major policy initiatives of his government included a referendum on the sale of gas, revision of the Law of Hydrocarbons, and the call for a constituent assembly to redraft the country's constitution. The gas issue was put to a referendum in July 2004. However, the referendum questions deliberately sidestepped the issue of nationalization and referred instead to repealing the law on hydrocarbons enacted by President Sánchez de Lozada. The failure of Mesa's interim government to keep its policy promises produced a new round of gas protests in early 2005. By March 2005, President Mesa was threatening to resign his post, calling the country ungovernable (Hylton and Sinclair 2007). When the Bolivian congress enacted a new hydrocarbons law in May 2005 that increased the state's royalties from natural gas sales rather than nationalizing the country's reserves, the second Gas War broke out. On June 6, 2005, President Mesa tendered his resignation as close to half a million residents participated in demonstrations and blockades that brought the capital city and the country to a standstill.

The central lesson of Bolivia's latest protest cycle is that national policy decisions can no longer be made exclusively by the legislative and executive branches of government supported by elite pacts, but must be done in consultation with civil society. The Gas Wars were an open expression of the failure of the democratic institutions of the state to adequately represent the peoples' interests. The uprisings reflected a questioning of the effectiveness of political parties as the only mediator between the state and society, of liberal democracy in general, of pacted governments, and of the legitimacy of a mono-cultural state in the face of a multicultural society.

INDIGENOUS POLITICS AND THE ASCENDANCY OF EVO MORALES

A major dilemma for Bolivian social movements is whether or not to seek change through participating in existing democratic processes or to limit themselves to applying pressure on the political system from the outside. There are a number of disadvantages associated with the electoral path to social change. For instance, cooperation with mainstream political actors and reformist policies can undermine and demobilize once-vibrant social struggles, whose real strength lies in their capacity to disrupt rather than elect officials (Pallares 2002). Social movements may end up "selling out" or being co-opted by the system as a result. Partisan politics are also expected to pull activists from the social sphere to electoral campaigns, thereby subordinating the movements' objectives to parties' electoral goals. In comparison, a major advantage of participating in electoral politics for marginalized social actors includes greater access to state resources and policy-making venues. Social movements along with parties may also serve as a potential solution to the crisis of representation that plagues much of the region (Mainwaring, Bejarano, and Pizarro 2006). The creation of social-movement-based parties represents a critical step toward bridging the current gap in political representation by potentially linking long-excluded segments of the population to the formal political system.

The political unrest during the 2000–05 revolutionary period helped to launch a new generation of indigenous peoples' parties into the national spotlight. The country's first indigenous-based parties were inspired by the Katarista ideology that was in vogue in the 1970s. As a corollary to Katarismo, a more radical ethnicist ideology known as Indianismo also emerged in this time period. In contrast to Katarismo, which called for the reconstruction of the Bolivian state along ethnic criteria and stressed alliances with other marginalized actors, Indianismo was overtly anti-Western, stressed separation from non-indigenous elements, and called for the reconstruction of pre-Conquest Bolivia or Kollasuyo (Albó 1996). While the

Indianists formed the Tupaj Katari Indian Movement (MITKA) in 1978 to compete in the transitional elections, the more moderate Katarista faction formed the Tupaj Katari Revolutionary Movement (MRTK). Both parties experienced very limited electoral success. By 1980, MITKA and MRTK had already broken into a number of competing factions over personal rivalries between leaders. Although Katarismo was successful in introducing ethno-cultural themes into the mainstream political agenda, in the absence of a unified and consolidated indigenous movement, the initial experiment in indigenous party formation failed.

By the 1990s, Bolivia's indigenous movements had begun to emphasize autonomous social movement development, shying away from partisan politics. However, the electoral reforms of the mid-1990s created a more favorable set of institutional opportunities. In particular, the 1994 Law of Popular Participation (LPP) and its promotion of municipal decentralization prompted Bolivian indigenous leaders to reconsider the possibility of launching their own electoral vehicles. One of the first groups to take advantage of the new electoral opening was the coca growers' movement of the Chapare region led by Evo Morales. In 1995, the movement decided to launch its own political instrument to compete in the upcoming municipal elections—the Assembly for the Sovereignty of the People (ASP). The ASP won an impressive number of mayoral races and council seats in the Chapare in the 1995 municipal elections and earned 4 per cent of the total national vote in the 1997 general elections (Van Cott 2005).

In 1999, Evo Morales and his supporters left the ASP to form a new and ultimately more successful party—the Movement Toward Socialism (MAS)—because of tensions with rival party members. Now over 10 years old, the MAS serves as a political instrument of social movement organizations as opposed to a conventional, vertically oriented political party. The MAS emphasizes both worker and indigenous-based concerns, basing its ideology on a blend of Andean cosmology, Marxism, and liberation theology. Among its list of policy proposals, the MAS calls for the nationalization of industry, the implementation of a new economic model based on worker participation and administration, the end of forced coca eradication programs, and the redistribution of land in favor of indigenous and peasant communities (MAS 2001). The MAS is considered a part of the Pink Tide movement. In its first electoral outing in the 1999 municipal elections, the MAS captured 11 mayoral victories, 8 of which were in the department of Cochabamba. By the national elections of 2002, the MAS had greatly increased its support base, garnering 21 per cent of the national vote and winning 27 seats in the legislature and 8 seats in the senate (Van Cott 2005, 86). In 2005, the MAS took many political analysts by surprise when it captured a majority share of the presidential vote. Following that election, the MAS held a majority of seats in the legislature, with 72 out of 130 lower-house seats going to the party. However, the MAS narrowly missed winning a majority in the senate in 2005 when it secured only 12 out of its 27 seats. The opposition-controlled senate became the focus of much controversy as opposition parties used it to attempt to block government-sponsored legislation and curtail the growing power of the MAS.

Evo Morales and the MAS won another convincing victory in the most recent presidential elections of December 2009, garnering 64 per cent of the national vote. The MAS also won a two-thirds majority in both the national legislature and the senate. However, the MAS continues to face virulent opposition from the department prefects of the eastern lowlands. Since the 2005 election, the opposition-elected prefects of the departments of Beni, Pando, Santa Cruz, and Tarija have vocally represented the political right. In the past, prefects were appointed by the president and represented the central government at the departmental level. Direct elections for departmental prefects were introduced as part of the reforms carried out under the interim administration of Carlos Mesa (2003–05). After its 2005 presidential win, the MAS found itself in the difficult position of having opposition parties in control of six of the country's nine departments (Domingo 2009).

Bolivia's other contemporary indigenous-based party, the Indigenous Pachakuti Movement (MIP), also emerged during the 2000–05 period. MIP party leader Felipe Quispe, popularly known as "El Mallku" (the condor), has been one of the country's most active adherents of Indianismo. Quispe served as permanent secretary for the Indianista party MITKA in the late 1970s. With the collapse of the party, Quispe dedicated himself to armed resistance and formed the Tupaj Katari Guerrilla Movement (EGTK) in 1989, for which he was arrested and spent five years in jail (Rice 2006). In 1998, Quispe was elected executive secretary of the CSUTCB, a position he used to affirm his leadership and steer the organization in a more radical direction. After the Black September protests of 2000, in which the CSUTCB played a major role, Quispe announced the formation of the MIP party to exclusively represent the interests of the nation's indigenous peoples. The MIP is one of the few indigenous-based parties to call for the creation of a separate state for indigenous peoples. The party's political proposal is based on the restoration of the original authority and governing structures of pre-Conquest Bolivia. In its first attempt at electoral competition in the 2002 national elections, the MIP captured 6 per cent of the vote and won six seats in the legislature. Although the MIP fared poorly in comparison to the MAS, the party's 2002 results were impressive considering that its total votes were higher than that achieved by all the Indianista parties in previous elections combined. In the elections of December 2005, however, the MIP managed to garner only 2.2 per cent of the vote, leaving the party's future in question.

The 2002 and 2005 national elections showcased the ethno-cultural tensions in Bolivian society that had remained more or less dormant since the return of democracy. The MAS and the MIP parties not only represented the ethnic division between indigenous versus white and mestizo, they also divided the electorate between those sectors opposed to the model of the neoliberal state and those in support of it. The strong national performance of the MAS in the 2005 election reconfigured the country's electoral geography. The once dominant MNR, ADN, and MIR parties have all but disappeared. For the first time in decades, politicians are directly linked to social movement organizations. MAS party officials were and are union leaders who continue to be involved in strikes, blockades, and marches. In the case of the MIP, all of its party leaders are traditional authorities within their communities. Prior to the MAS's presidential win, indigenous party officials had in effect introduced social movement tactics and logics into congress by participating in hunger strikes and calling for demonstrations in order to force a seat at the negotiating table with the government when their political proposals were voted down. Now that the MAS is the government, an unprecedented window of opportunity has been opened to advance popular sector interests in the country.

THE MAS IN POWER, 2006–

The 2005 presidential victory of Evo Morales and the MAS marked not only the rejection of the neoliberal economic policies of the past two decades and the governments that imposed them but also the beginning of an alternative political and economic project for the country. One of the first actions of the Morales administration as part of the October Agenda, so named for the Gas War of 2003, was to reestablish state control over the country's oil and gas reserves. This mandate was all but dictated to Morales by the overwhelming support for nationalization expressed in the July 2004 gas referendum. Decree 28701 was announced by Morales in May 2006 and called for the partial nationalization of the oil and gas industry. The decree did not expropriate foreign holdings or ban foreign corporations. However, all 12 transnational gas corporations operating in the country were required to sign new contracts. The move increased Bolivia's share of the profits from the country's two major gas fields (San Antonio and San Alberto) from approximately 50 per cent to 82 per cent (Dangl 2007, 201). The two gas fields account for half of Bolivia's production and 70 per cent of its exports. The new controls are expected to increase the country's gas revenues from $608 million US in 2005 and $1,261 million US in 2006 to over $6 billion US in the next four years (Fuentes 2007, 105). Morales's success in "national-izing" gas within his first 100 days in office generated a surge of approval for his government.

Cresting on the tide of popularity, Morales then tackled the controversial issue of land reform. Despite the agrarian reform that occurred under the revolutionary government of the MNR in the 1950s, Bolivia continues to have one of the most unequal distributions of land in Latin America. It is estimated that 90 per cent of small agricultural producers rely on only 10 per cent of Bolivia's arable land, with large and medium landholdings accounting for the rest (Hylton and Sinclair 2007, 137). The country's Gini coefficient for land inequality stands at 0.82. A more equitable distribution of land is a key ingredient for the country's development. However, most of the large landholdings that are suited for expropriation are located in the elite-dominated eastern lowland region, an area the agrarian reform program never reached. Bolivia's wealthy crescent-shaped territory is popularly known as the "half moon." The profitable agribusiness devel-opments in the region were founded on immense concentrations of land. Following Morales's announcement of his government's new agrarian reform law in August 2006, the lowland elite began to increase pressure for regional autonomy. Despite denouncements by civic committees in the half moon region of the MAS's alleged disregard for its opponents, the agrarian reform does not pose a threat to legitimately acquired and titled properties. Instead, the reform enacts an existing provision in the constitution that states that all land must serve a social function. In other words, land that is used for speculative rather than productive purposes is now subject to confiscation by the state with compensation.

The move that has incited the most heated debates and confrontations during Morales's term in office thus far has been the constituent assembly. The call to redraft the country's constitution was initially made by the interim government of Carlos Mesa after the October 2003 uprising. In March 2006, Morales approved the law to convoke the assembly as a means of refounding the nation on the principles of democratization and social inclusion (Hylton and Sinclair 2007). In the assembly elections of July 2006, the MAS elected 137 out of 255 delegates. While the MAS won a slight major-ity of delegates, it failed to meet the two-thirds threshold needed to approve a new constitution. When the governing party suggested that a majority of 50 per cent plus one should be sufficient to pass each article following the opening of the assembly on August 6, 2006, the opposition responded by launching hunger strikes and protests. Thousands of MAS supporters then followed suit, grounding the entire process to a halt. Finally, in February 2007, a delicate accord on the voting issue was reached. Some issues were to be decided by absolute majority, while others would pass with a two-thirds majority (Van Cott 2008a).

In December 2007, after months of political unrest that resulted in several civilian deaths, the completed draft was presented to congress. The new constitution, which was put to a national referendum in January 2009, passed with just over 60 per cent of the vote. In addition to ensuring a stronger role for the state in the economy, the constitution provides for a whole host of rights for the nation's indigenous peoples. It combines elements of representative democracy with the recognition of communal structures of authority (Domingo 2009). The new constitution changed the country's name from the "Republic of Bolivia" to the "Pluri-National State of Bolivia," thereby reaffirming the existence of distinct sociopolitical and cultural groups. The successful passage of the new constitution reaffirmed Morales's political legitimacy and opened the door to his 2009 reelection.

CONCLUSION

The racially exclusive and impoverishing policy of neoliberalism provided fertile terrain for the rise of a pro-poor indigenous movement with alternative economic and political strategies. This was a result of the upheaval between 2000 and 2005 that provoked a crisis within the state and its political system. Mass protests explicitly expressed a strong rejection of certain actors in the democratic process as well as the desire to reconstruct the relationship between state and society. The validity of representative democracy itself came under increasing scrutiny. This can be seen in the muted support of 49 per cent for democracy in 2005. In the midst of this political instability and social unrest, the rise of indigenous leader Evo Morales represented a potential solution to the crisis of political representation that plagued the country. Indigenous and popular movements have opted to work within the democratic institutions of the state rather than continue to pressure for change solely through extrasystemic means. The inclusion of marginalized social actors in the formal political system has improved the quality of political representation for the masses. Support for democracy has dramatically improved while Morales and the MAS have been in power, reaching 68 per cent in 2008 (Latinobarómetro).

Bolivia's economic indicators have also improved markedly since 2005, due in part to the continuing high international price for the country's main exports as well as the increased revenue from the newly overhauled oil and gas industries. In March 2006, the government allowed its final agreement with the IMF to expire (Lucero 2009). By the end of 2006, Bolivia had a budget surplus and the country's public and foreign debts were substantially reduced. The GDP growth rate has since reached a respectable

4.5 per cent, a massive improvement over the low levels experienced under the neoliberal establishment of the past two decades. The country's unemployment rate has also dropped significantly, from 9.4 per cent in 2005 to 7.6 per cent in 2006 (Gamarra 2008, 131). Socioeconomic and political inclusion has improved considerably under the Morales administration. At the same time, however, the majority government of the MAS has produced something of a reversal of fortune for the country's political and economic elite, who now find themselves shut out from the state. Although there is a certain amount of delicious irony to the current situation, this dynamic mirrors the hegemonic and exclusionary governing practices that have long dominated Bolivian politics. In the words of Donna Lee Van Cott (2008b, 211), "Clearly Bolivia's indigenous people had mastered the science of politics. It remains to be seen whether they have mastered the art of democracy."

We are currently witnessing in Bolivia a resurgent right-wing political force and conservative civic committees claiming that the MAS, in general, and the new constitution in particular, discriminate against mestizo and white populations by only representing the interests of indigenous and popular groups. In response, opposition groups in the four eastern lowland departments have resolved not to recognize the new constitution and instead continue to agitate for regional autonomy. Political violence in the country has begun to escalate as MAS supporters clash with opposition groups who feel threatened by the former's political dominance. Eastern lowland business associations, grouped together as the Pro-Santa Cruz Committee (CPSC), are at odds with the redistributive and anti-market sentiments expressed by the highland indigenous and popular movements that are the backbone of Morales's administration. Having lost their voice in the political system, the economic elite are now looking for an exit (Eaton 2007). If President Morales is unable to ease the growing class and ethnic tensions in the country, then the most recent round of protests may only appear as a footnote in future chapters on Bolivia's history.

NOTE

1 Adapted from the Republic of Bolivia's presidential profile. 4 June 2010. www.presidencia.gob.bo/perfil.htm.

REFERENCES

Albó, Xavier. 1996. "Nación de Muchas Naciones: Nuevas Corrientes Políticas en Bolivia." *Democracia y Estado Multiétnico en América Latina*. Ed. Pablo González Casanova, Xavier Albó, and Marcos Roitman Rosenmann. Mexico City: UNAM. 321–66.

Arce, Moisés, and Roberta Rice. 2009. "Societal Protest in Post-Stabilization Bolivia." *Latin American Research Review* 44(1): 88–101.

Cariaga, Juan L. 1990. "Three Policy Experiments: The Case of Bolivia." *Latin American Adjustment: How Much Has Happened*. Ed. John Williamson. Washington, DC: Institute for International Economics. 41–53.

Conaghan, Catherine M., and James M. Malloy. 1994. *Unsettling Statecraft: Democracy and Neoliberalism in the Central Andes*. Pittsburgh: University of Pittsburgh Press.

Crabtree, John. 2005. *Patterns of Protest: Politics and Social Movements in Bolivia*. London: Latin America Bureau.

Dangl, Benjamin. 2007. *The Price of Fire: Resource Wars and Social Movements in Bolivia*. Edinburgh: AK Press.

Domingo, Pilar. 2009. "Evo Morales, the MAS, and a Revolution in the Making." *Governance after Neoliberalism in Latin America*. Ed. Jean Grugel and Pía Riggirozzi. New York: Palgrave Macmillan. 113–45.

Eaton, Kent. 2007. "Backlash in Bolivia: Regional Autonomy as a Reaction against Indigenous Mobilization." *Politics & Society* 35(1): 71–102.

Farthing, Linda, and Ben Kohl. 2001. "Bolivia's New Wave of Protest." *NACLA Report on the Americas* 34(5): 8–11.

Fuentes, Federico. 2007. "The Struggle for Bolivia's Future." *Monthly Review* 59(3): 95–109.

Gamarra, Eduardo A. 1991. *The System of Justice in Bolivia: An Institutional Analysis*. Miami: Florida International University.

——. 1994. "Crafting Political Support for Stabilization: Political Pacts and the New Economic Policy in Bolivia." *Democracy, Markets, and Structural Reform in Latin America*. Ed. William C. Smith, Carlos H. Acuña, and Eduardo A. Gamarra. Miami: University of Miami, North-South Center. 105–27.

——. 1997. "Hybrid Presidentialism and Democratization: The Case of Bolivia." *Presidentialism and Democracy in Latin America*. Ed. Scott Mainwaring and Matthew S. Shugart. New York: Cambridge University Press. 363–93.

——. 2008. "Bolivia: Evo Morales and Democracy." *Constructing Democratic Governance in Latin America*. Ed. Jorge I. Domínguez and Michael Shifter. Baltimore: Johns Hopkins University Press. 124–51.

Gamarra, Eduardo A., and James M. Malloy. 1995. "The Patrimonial Dynamics of Party Politics in Bolivia." *Building Democratic Institutions: Party Systems in Latin America*. Ed. Scott Mainwaring and Timothy R. Scully. Stanford: Stanford University Press. 399–433.

Hall, Gillette, and Harry Anthony Patrinos. 2004. *Indigenous Peoples, Poverty and Human Development in Latin America: 1994–2004*. Washington, DC: World Bank.

Huber, Evelyne, and Fred Solt. 2004. "Successes and Failures of Neoliberalism." *Latin American Research Review* 39(3): 150–64.

Hylton, Forrest, and Sinclair Thomson. 2007. *Revolutionary Horizons: Past and Present in Bolivian Politics*. London: Verso Books.

Jones, Mark P. 1995. *Electoral Laws and the Survival of Presidential Democracies*. Notre Dame: University of Notre Dame Press.

Kohl, Benjamin, and Linda Farthing. 2006. *Impasse in Bolivia: Neoliberal Hegemony and Popular Resistance*. London: Zed Books.

Laserna, Roberto. 2002. "Conflictos Sociales y Movimientos Políticos en Bolivia." *Las Piedras en el Camino: Movimientos Sociales del 2000 en Bolivia*. Ed. Maria Lujan Veneros. La Paz: Ministerio de Desarrollo Sostenible y Planificación. 7–38.

Lucero, José Antonio. 2009. "Decades Lost and Won: Indigenous Movements and Multicultural Neoliberalism in the Andes." *Beyond Neoliberalism in Latin America?* Ed. John Burdick, Philip Oxhorn, and Kenneth M. Roberts. New York: Palgrave Macmillan. 63–81.

Mainwaring, Scott, Ana María Bejarano, and Eduardo Pizarro Leongómez, eds. 2006. *The Crisis of Democratic Representation in the Andes.* Stanford: Stanford University Press.

MAS. 2001. *MAS Congreso Nacional: Programa de Gobierno.* La Paz: Movimiento al Socialismo.

Mayorga, René Antonio. 1997. "Democracy Dignified and an End to Impunity: Bolivia's Military Dictatorship on Trial." *Transitional Justice and the Rule of Law in New Democracies.* Ed. James McAdams. Notre Dame: University of Notre Dame Press. 61–92.

———. 2005. "La Crisis del Sistema de Partidos Políticos en Bolivia: Causas y Consecuencias." *Canadian Journal of Latin American and Caribbean Studies* 30(59): 55–92.

Morales, Juan Antonio, and Jeffrey D. Sachs. 1989. "Bolivia's Economic Crisis." *Developing Country Debt and the World Economy.* Ed. Jeffrey D. Sachs. Chicago: University of Chicago Press. 57–79.

Pallares, Amalia. 2002. *From Peasant Struggles to Indian Resistance: The Ecuadorian Andes in the Late Twentieth Century.* Norman: University of Oklahoma Press.

Portes, Alejandro, and Kelly Hoffman. 2003. "Latin American Class Structures: Their Composition and Change during the Neoliberal Era." *Latin American Research Review* 38(1): 41–77.

Postero, Nancy Grey. 2007. *Now We Are Citizens: Indigenous Politics in Postmulticultural Bolivia.* Stanford: Stanford University Press.

Rice, Roberta L. 2006. "From Peasants to Politicians: The Politicization of Ethnic Cleavages in Latin America." Ph.D. dissertation, Department of Political Science, University of New Mexico.

Rivera Cusicanqui, Silvia. 1987. *Oppressed But Not Defeated: Peasant Struggles Among the Aymara and Qhechwa in Bolivia, 1900–1980.* Geneva: United Nations Research Institute for Social Development.

Rueschemeyer, Dietrich, Evelyne Huber Stephens, and John D. Stephens. 1992. *Capitalist Development and Democracy.* Chicago: University of Chicago Press.

Schultz, Jim. 2000. "Bolivians Win Anti-Privatization Battle." *NACLA Report on the Americas* 33(6): 44–46.

Ticona Alejo, Esteban. 2000. *Organización y Liderazgo Aymara: La Experiencia Indígena en la Política Boliviana, 1979–1996.* La Paz: Universidad de la Cordillera.

Ticona Alejo, Esteban, and Xavier Albó Corrons. 1997. *Jesús de Machaqa: La Marka Rebelde.* La Paz: CIPCA-CEDOIN.

Van Cott, Donna Lee. 2005. *From Movements to Parties in Latin America: The Evolution of Ethnic Politics.* New York: Cambridge University Press.

———. 2008a. "Bolivia." *Countries at the Crossroads: A Survey of Democratic Governance 2007.* Ed. Sanha Kelly, Christopher Walker, and Jake Dizard. New York: Freedom House. 111–34.

———. 2008b. *Radical Democracy in the Andes.* Cambridge: Cambridge University Press.

Wade, Robert Hunter. 2004. "Is Globalization Reducing Poverty and Inequality?" *World Development* 32(4): 567–89.

Yashar, Deborah J. 2005. *Contesting Citizenship in Latin America: The Rise of Indigenous Movements and the Postliberal Challenge*. New York: Cambridge University Press.

E-RESOURCES

Andean Information Network (http://ain-bolivia.org). A scholar-activist website focused on contemporary issues in Bolivia.

Government of Bolivia Online (www.bolivia.gov.bo). The gateway to government branches in Bolivia.

Indymedia Bolivia (http://bolivia.indymedia.org). An alternative media source on current events in Bolivia.

National Electoral Court of Bolivia (CNE) (www.cne.org.bo). Provides election results for Bolivia.

National Institute of Statistics (INE) (www.ine.gov.bo). Provides census data for Bolivia.

TWELVE
Chile: Democracy in a Divided Polity

JUDITH TEICHMAN

Sandro Imacache works as a concierge for an apartment building in the upper-class neighborhood of Las Condes, in Santiago. On the $208 per month he makes, he can barely support his family and cover expenses. He could not afford to join the massive protests against the government of President Michelle Bachelet (elected in 2006). Transportation, he claims, is outrageously expensive, and it takes him at least an hour-and-a-half to get to work each day. The prices of basic necessities, such as food and healthcare, continue to go up. He is angry because he feels he has not shared in Chile's prosperity (Schweimler 2007). Mr. Imacache's difficulties might seem odd to many observers. With steady economic growth, substantial poverty reduction, political stability, and relatively little corruption, Chile is Latin America's success story.[1] Recently, Chile removed almost all of the vestiges of its authoritarian past. Moreover, compared to other countries in the region, the Chilean state appears to be relatively strong, and is capable of pursuing effective macroeconomic policies. However, shades of the past continue to haunt the present. The state is weak in a number of important respects. It has not been able to reduce the country's high level of socioeconomic inequality nor make much improvement in unequal public services.[2] For many observers (and citizens), Chile's democracy is still only skin deep: political and economic power continues to be highly concentrated, public authorities resist civil society consultation, civil society remains relatively weak, and labor rights are still limited. The country's high level of inequality has deep historical roots that were exacerbated by subsequent political events, particularly by the period of military dictatorship (1973–89). Searing disagreements over public issues related to social and economic equality endure, and continue to create difficulties for Chilean democracy. These disagreements will persist in the face of the reversal of the Pink Tide in Chile, which saw the election of right-wing candidate Sebastían Piñera in January 2010, ending 20 years of left-center Concertación rule.[3]

CHILEAN OLIGARCHY, LABOR MILITANCY, AND CONTROL THROUGH COMPETITIVE ELECTIONS

Chile's relatively stronger political institutional features, compared with other countries in the region, particularly its long history of electoral processes and a relatively stronger state, are a product of history. An atypical set of geographic and demographic features made the early establishment of a centralized national authority possible, which allowed the country to consequently avoid the general nineteenth-century dislocation and anarchy described in chapter 2. Chile's effective national territory was a small compact area, with most of the population concentrated in the Central Valley. To the north lay a barren and uninhabited desert, while the south, with the exception of a few Hispanic settlements, was the domain of the Araucanian Indians, who had been defeated and confined to reserves by 1883. With the indigenous population pushed to the frontier, Chile's population, composed largely of a mass of peasant mestizos and a *criollo* landed class, was socially homogeneous by Latin American standards. As mining and commerce developed in the nineteenth century, the country's social, economic, and political elite became highly integrated, and came to share common social values.

A brief period of internal post-independence strife in Chile ended in 1830 under the leadership of Diego Portales, who brought together a conservative coalition of businessmen, landowners, and clergy. As unofficial dictator and then minister of the interior during the 1830s, Portales's rule ushered in a 60-year period of remarkable political stability characterized by four elected presidents, each with two consecutive terms in office. Portales established a centralized autocratic regime and embarked on a program of modernization involving impressive infrastructural development (particularly railways), the introduction of income and property taxes, and tariff protection for agricultural products. Meanwhile, the 1833 constitution, with its heavy property and literacy restrictions on voting, offered a democratic facade but ensured that power rested in the hands of the traditional landed oligarchy. As the nineteenth century progressed, the country's landed oligarchy, increasingly integrated with capitalist business and financial interests, remained firmly entrenched.

Over time, Chilean elites opened the electoral system to opposition groups, creating a liberal pluralist political environment. However, the country remained classically Latin American in the persistence of profound inequalities. With the increase in cereal production between 1850 and 1880, the hacienda or *fundo* (large landholdings) expanded and the conditions of rural labor worsened. *Fundo* owners preferred to meet the growing international demand for their products through expanding the land under cultivation and by squeezing rural labor, rather than through investment in capital improvements to improve labor productivity (Bauer 1975, 70). In exchange for ever-smaller land allotments, big landowners required *fundo* workers, known as *inquilinos*, to work more days and demanded work from family members as well. Despite harsh conditions, rural rebellions were relatively rare and large-scale mobilizations practically non-existent. The large landholdings were isolated, workers seldom left, and the landlord was all-powerful. The fact that the *inquilino* was entirely dependent on the landlord for survival and lived in mortal fear of being cast off the land (the landlord provided both food and housing in exchange for labor) conferred tight control to landowners over rural workers. This highly dependent relationship ensured a quiescent labor force and guaranteed landowner control of the rural vote. Hence, the period of the parliamentary republic (1891–1924) was one during which a weak presidency and rural overrepresentation in congress allowed the landed and business oligarchy, through an alliance of the liberal and conservative parties in congress, to retain political control.

But if the countryside was relatively quiet, the mines and factories were not. Chile's major foreign exchange earning commodity was nitrate, the international demand for which tended to fluctuate substantially, producing frequent recessions and layoffs between 1896 and 1927. The conditions in northern mining communities—their isolation and the common experiences of exploitation and oppression faced by workers—rendered them open to radical left-wing political appeal. By the early 1890s, labor strife was beginning to emerge in the country's northern nitrate mines and in the coal mines of the south. As workers migrated from their communities in search of employment, they spread the ideology of worker militancy among factory workers. A militantly anti-capitalist labor federation, based on the support of coal, copper, nitrate, and railway workers, the Chilean Labor Federation (FOCH) was established in 1909. Its founder, Luis Emilio Recabarren, established the Workers Socialist Party in 1912, a revolutionary Marxist party.

When the nitrate industry fell into a sharp recession in 1919, union organizing and strikes rose. The plight of workers, framed as the "social question," now became a concern to the political parties. In 1920, presidential candidate Arturo Alessandri, supported by an alliance of the radical and democratic parties, called for a labor code, a social security system, and cheap housing. However, due to tight liberal and conservative control of congress, he was unable to get his social welfare legislation passed. Direct military intervention finally forced congress to pass the country's first social welfare legislation providing social security to the middle class and the most organized sectors of the working class. This event marked the demise of the parliamentary republic and resulted in a new constitution in 1925, which strengthened the power of the presidency.

Although the Chilean trade union movement was militant, it was organizationally weak. Labor legislation, which prohibited the formation of nationwide labor federations for the purpose of collective bargaining, kept the movement dispersed. Therefore trade unions sought support from political parties, while the left-wing parties, particularly the socialist and communist parties, competed for trade union support, especially in the mines and factories. In this way, trade unions became highly politicized and party activists developed a strong sense of solidarity with union goals. As worker strife increased through the 1930s, oligarchic control weakened. As we see below, a new political settlement eventually emerged. This settlement continued to protect the vested interests of large landholders, although it did make concessions to organized working-class demands.

THE BREAKDOWN OF ELECTORAL DEMOCRACY AND POLITICAL POLARIZATION, 1930–1973

The Great Depression, which hit Chile harder than any other Latin American country, momentarily shattered the country's elite cohesion and briefly shook its stable institutional framework. The resignation of President Carlos Ibañez in 1931 was followed by a succession of military coups over the next 17 months, until new elections allowed for the return of civilian government. Exports of copper and nitrate plummeted by 88 per cent, the steepest decline in the world, and over 50,000 workers lost their jobs (Roxborough, O'Brien, and Roddick 1977, 11; Loveman 1988, 230). This shock ushered in a new development model supportive of industrialization and selective redistributive measures. However, economic difficulties including a chronic balance of payments problem, large public deficits, and inflation continued through the 1940s, 1950s, and 1960s. Inadequate public policies, including the neglect of agriculture, excessive industrial protection, and a rapid rise of government expenditure, contributed to the country's economic woes. Particularly after 1953, the state's solution to its chronic revenue shortfall became the printing press, a measure that contributed to increasing problems with inflation, which hit a high of 80 per cent by 1955 (Aguilara Reyes 1994, 13). Inflation increased the country's political difficulties, as competing groups sought to recoup their lost share of income. Presidents Ibañez (1952–58) and Alessandri (1958–64) both attempted and failed to implement economic stabilization.

Meanwhile, wealth remained highly concentrated and the propertied classes became ever more cohesive as new members of the industrial and commercial financial elite bought large landed estates. Land ownership was highly concentrated, and an estimated 40 per cent of the agricultural workforce was landless (Petras 1970, 259). By the late 1960s, five economic groups controlled 36 per cent of the 250 largest enterprises in the country (Dahse 1979, 146). However, even in the face of income and asset concentration and economic stagnation, the social welfare of much of the population did steadily improve. Employment expansion provided families with an income and, as time went on, allowed more and more members of the organized working and middle classes to obtain social security protection. The fact that political contestation was channeled through electoral institutions allowed organized labor to make steady gains. However, poverty remained widespread in the countryside and the gains of the business elites were disproportionately high.

In 1938, the growth in support for the left brought about the victory of the Popular Front, a coalition led by the Radical Party and supported by the socialists and communists. It defeated the right-wing alliance of conservatives and liberals that had governed the country for over a century. While the Front was backed by the radical left, unlike other populist movements of the period, it did little to improve the lives of the rural and urban poor. Given its heterogeneous support base, the coalition did not last long. By 1941, the socialists had abandoned it and in 1946, the communists were expelled. The Radical Party continued to control the government until 1952. The failure of the Front government to meet popular expectations for reform, combined with growing political repression, especially of the Communist Party, fed leftist party solidarity, worker militancy, and social unrest. Nevertheless, in its short life, the Front was able to broker a deal that won the support of the political right and the landed interests it represented. The right agreed to allow the political incorporation of new actors (organized labor, the middle class), deeper social reform in the cities, and state-led industrialization. In return, the landed elite retained its most important privilege—tight control of rural labor. Under this arrangement, the government repressed rural labor and outlawed peasant unions on paper until 1947 and in practice until 1967. By 1952, the wages of agricultural workers, who constituted about 30 per cent of the economically active population, were 300 per cent below industrial wages (Mamalakis 1976, 102).

Worker mobilization continued to occur in the mines and the cities in response to the hardship caused by the volatility of international commodity prices. Faced with a sharp decline in the international copper market and labor unrest, President Ibañez repressed workers. In doing so, he consolidated labor solidarity and leftist party unity. In 1953, labor came together to form a nationwide organization, the CUT (Single Workers' Central). By 1958, the leftist parties, now united to form the FRAP (Popular Action Front), ran in the 1958 election with Salvador Allende as their presidential candidate. Meanwhile, the Christian Democrats and Radicals began to move leftward to expand their electoral bases. Attention now turned to the countryside, where the FRAP and the Christian Democrats campaigned among organized rural workers and made important inroads into the Conservative and Liberal Parties' rural bases of support. Even the Radical Party began to talk about the need for agrarian reform. But it was replaced by the Christian Democratic Party as the important centrist party.

A number of interrelated factors were contributing to the declining clientelist grip of the landed elites and their parties on the rural poor. Stagnation in the agricultural sector, in part a reflection of the heavy emphasis of public policy on industry and the urban sector, had stimulated increased migration to the cities. In addition, the expansion of communications into the countryside, the growth of the monetary economy into remote rural areas, growing corporate ownership of agricultural enterprises, and an increase in the numbers of landless workers reduced the dependency of peasants on landlords. The electoral law of 1958 increased the penalties for electoral fraud and bribery, thereby making it increasingly difficult for landlords to control the votes of peasants. The socialist and communist parties also spread their ideology into the countryside, where they competed for votes with the Christian Democratic Party. By early 1961, the parties of the old elite (the liberals and conservatives) began to see a drop in their seats in congress. The country's political center had begun to crumble as the Christian Democrats and Radicals moved leftward and the economic elite became increasingly fearful of threats to property interests.

The 1964 election featured a marked upsurge in rural political organizing. The Christian Democratic government of Eduardo Frei Montalva, backed by the parties of the political right, won the 1964 presidential election with 41.3 per cent of the popular vote. However, the Christian Democrats had promised a variety of measures—agrarian reform, rural unionization, and the enforcement of labor laws—that were intolerable not only to their right-wing party backers but also to many of their party members. As the number of strikes in the rural areas increased along with the takeover of large landholdings by peasants and of factories by workers, propertied interests became more and more fearful. Meanwhile, the MIR (Movement of the Revolutionary Left), a left-wing group formerly within the FRAP coalition, began to operate clandestinely, inciting subversion. In 1970, Salvador Allende, leader of a coalition of socialists and communists known as Popular Unity (UP), won the presidential election with 36.2 per cent of the popular vote. This event sent even louder alarm signals throughout the private sector. Once Allende assumed power, he pursued policies such as nationalization that were terrifying to the private sector. Lacking sufficient support from congress for the passage of major changes, the president used constitutionally conferred presidential decree powers that allowed him to bypass congress. The political right saw the regime as bent on the eradication of capitalism. Meanwhile, the government lost control of the upsurge in popular activism it had encouraged. Spontaneous takeovers of landed estates and factories accelerated.

The 1964 to 1973 period marked the years of the greatest economic redistribution in the country's history. In fact, Chile stands out from the rest of Latin America because of the extent of this radical redistributive experiment. While organized workers continued to obtain better wages and benefits, many new programs targeted those groups—the urban poor and peasants—who had hitherto been excluded from social improvement. Spending increased in health and education. Between 1964 and 1968, the government almost doubled the amount of milk distributed to children under six, a measure believed to be responsible for the improvement of health statistics (Borzutsky 2002, 105). Under Allende, asset redistribution, through the massive expropriation of industrial enterprises and large landholdings, was a key part of the strategy to improve living standards. Wages increased in both the urban and rural sectors, and employment expanded rapidly in the new land reform sector and in newly acquired state companies. The government also reduced taxes on the lowest income groups.

Between 1970 and 1973, fear, violence, and a rapidly deteriorating economic situation set the stage for the military coup of 1973. Expanded social programs occurring simultaneously with a marked slowdown in economic growth and a decline in copper exports caused the public deficit to skyrocket. An alienated private sector began to reduce investment, causing production and capital flight to accelerate. Widespread shortages of basic goods ensued. In the absence of sufficient resources, the government again resorted to the printing press. By 1973, the country was experiencing the highest rate of inflation in the world at over 500 per cent (Sigmund 1977, 368).

External factors played no small role in the growing economic and political difficulties leading to the overthrow of the Allende regime. The fall of copper prices on the international market reduced government revenue and access to foreign exchange. The nationalization of the American-owned copper companies Anaconda and Kennecott by the Popular Unity government prompted the companies' owners to take legal action against the Chilean government. With legal proceedings underway that contested the legality of Chilean government ownership of the mines, Chile found it increasingly difficult to market its copper. At the same time, the country's access to international credit faced a US-sponsored credit blockade. The US Central Intelligence Agency (CIA) aided the political right, supporting the truckers' strike, the right-wing media, and the assassination of the constitutionalist commander in chief of the Chilean armed forces, René Schneider (Kornbluh 2003). All of these actions contributed to the growing political destabilization leading to the overthrow of the government.

MILITARY RULE, REPRESSION, AND THE NEW ECONOMIC MODEL, 1973–1989

The 1973 military coup was enthusiastically supported by the country's most powerful industrial, financial, and landed interests. Chilean democratic political institutions could no longer contain the sharp redistributive conflict that stemmed from the country's searing socioeconomic inequalities. The two most powerful executives opposed to Allende were conglomerate owners who had had their firms expropriated by the government when they refused to sell to the state (Silva 1996, 105). The military takeover was also supported by small and medium businesses, where conflicts over wages and working conditions had become especially acute, and by members of the middle class concerned with the recent economic deterioration. The military had a generally low opinion of politicians and saw Marxism as a threat. However, it was a core of military men clustered around General Augusto Pinochet, strong adherents to what was known as the National Security doctrine, who formed the core of the coup's military conspirators. The National Security doctrine held that the country was fighting a war against an internal enemy (communism), which was intent upon eliminating Chile's Western Christian civilization.

Upon seizing power, the military closed congress, declared the political parties of the Popular Unity illegal, and proclaimed all other political parties in recess. According to the Report of the Chilean National Commission on Truth and Reconciliation (1993), repression changed character during the regime and occurred in phases. During the first few months following the coup, repression was directed at all people believed to be left sympathizers: political activists, peasants involved in agrarian reform, and youth in urban squatter settlements. Executions occurred after trials by "war councils." Then, between 1974 and 1977, the regime pursued a more targeted program of repression, involving the much more extensive use of disappearances. This phase was directed by DINA (Directorate of National Intelligence), the security organization created specifically for that purpose. DINA took those it detained to one of its numerous clandestine centers where agents engaged in the interrogation and torture of inmates. Many were tortured to death or eventually executed, and every effort was made to ensure that bodies would never be found. DINA was also involved in a number of assassinations on foreign territories, including those of Orlando Letelier, Allende's ex-foreign minister in Washington, and General Prats, Allende's vice president and commander in chief of the army in Buenos Aires. Between 1977 and 1983, there was initially a brief decline in repression due to international censure. It resumed after protests against the regime in 1983. In 1978, the military passed an Amnesty Law granting amnesty to all of those who had committed acts of violence between 1973 and 1978.

Much of the repression was directed against workers, peasants, and their organizations. The government suspended the right to strike and to bargain collectively. Unions were closed and their property confiscated. The government withdrew legal recognition from the national labor confederation (CUT), confiscated the CUT's property, and prohibited union elections and meetings except for informational purposes. Repression and the disappearance of union activists and leaders were frequent, and resulted in a dramatic drop in union membership from 41 per cent of the work force in 1973 to 9 per cent by 1981 (Oppenheim 2007). The 1979 labor code allowed bargaining at the factory level, but severely restricted union activities and left workers with almost no recourse against arbitrary and numerous layoffs and unsafe and unhealthy working conditions. The government was also committed to the demobilization and depoliticization of the rural lower classes. The partial reversal of land reform, through the return of expropriated land to some former owners and its sale to new owners, was a key component of this process. More importantly, however, was the fact that the military regime excluded all those who had participated in land invasions from the opportunity of purchasing land, and assigned land only to "apolitical" peasants (Kurtz 2004, 84).

As General Pinochet consolidated his power, those able to influence policy became an ever more restricted group of military leaders, conglomerate executives, and radical market reform technocrats known as the "Chicago Boys."[4] As the economy continued to deteriorate through 1974, these technocrats were able to get presidential backing for a radical market reform program known as "the shock treatment." It involved a drastic cutback in government expenditures and investment, sweeping trade liberalization, financial liberalization, and privatization. The debt crisis of the early 1980s meant a temporary setback for this market reform agenda because of the collapse of the country's banks. However, by 1985 the market reform program was back on track, as was the new emphasis on export-led growth.

The worsening of economic conditions for both urban and rural labor was a direct consequence of both the new economic model and the explicit policy to dismantle popular organizations and eliminate their leaderships. Although non-traditional agricultural exports such as fruit and vegetables expanded with the new economic strategy, trade liberalization also produced high levels of bankruptcy, and therefore unemployment, in sectors that had been highly protected such as textiles and leather goods. In addition, privatization of the social security system (healthcare and pensions) and the educational system resulted in sharp inequalities and contributed to deteriorating social welfare conditions. In 1981, the government established a two-tier system of healthcare that included a private system for the wealthy and a public system for the remaining 85 per cent of the population. This new arrangement produced a pronounced deterioration in the quality of health services for the majority of the population as both government and upper-class financial contributions to public healthcare dropped. New inequalities emerged when healthcare companies discriminated against women and the elderly. Pension reform meant that workers paid into new privately-run pension funds, and both employers and the state were no longer required to make any financial contribution, an arrangement that ultimately failed to produce adequate pensions. The privatization of the education system also contributed to a rise in inequality in education between the publicly subsidized schools attended by the lower classes, which did not charge tuition, and the higher-quality private schools used by the upper classes, which did charge tuition.

Both poverty and inequality increased drastically during the period of military rule. While the percentage of poor families stood at 28.5 per cent in 1970, that figure reached 48.7 per cent by 1987 (Montecinos 1997, 225). Income distribution also became more unequal and private consumption dropped. It is particularly important to recognize that the richest 10 per cent of families increased their income by 85 per cent during this period (Délano and Traslaviña 1989). Poverty was especially prevalent in some rural areas because of the move toward fruit and vegetable production; as a result, the rural labor force became overwhelmingly seasonal and strongly segmented by gender. Everywhere, wages declined sharply and unemployment rose to record levels. In 1982, unemployment stood at 22 per cent. However, the military was not completely oblivious to the rising level of poverty. The regime established temporary work programs to address unemployment and its social policy targeted the most desperately poor by implementing a means-tested mother–infant program. As export-led economic growth picked up after 1985, aided in no small measure by the increase in copper prices, employment gains began to contribute to poverty reduction. This economic recovery gave increased credibility to the market model—particularly among leaders of the political left.

The military regime took great care to ensure that no future regime would be able to tamper with the neoliberal economic model it had established by institutionalizing its reforms. Backed by the political right, the regime devised a new constitution (1980) for this purpose and, in so doing, established a set of institutional impediments that would hamper the operation of democracy for years to come. One of the most important provisions established nine appointed senators, all of whom were handpicked by Pinochet. The National Security Council, dominated by military appointees, gave the political right representation at the executive level, especially since presidential consultation of the council was mandatory. The binomial electoral system, which allocated two congressional seats per district, allowed the party or coalition with the most votes to gain the second seat only if it obtained twice as many votes as its opponent. This stipulation, in combination with the appointed senators, would become instrumental in maintaining right-wing strength in congress. A 1975 law gave the finance ministry, overwhelmingly populated by especially strong free marketers, ultimate authority over all policy decisions. This law reduced the power of other cabinet ministers and made any substantive change in policy direction unlikely. During the last few months it was in power, the military reinforced the conservative tendency of the state bureaucracy by instituting a series of laws to prevent the incoming president from replacing most of the federal bureaucracy (Oppenheim 2007, 223). Under growing pressure from the pro-democracy movement for a return to civilian rule, Pinochet called a plebiscite in 1988 in which the public was asked to grant him an additional eight years in office. The resulting victory for the "no" side opened the way for democratic elections in 1990.

Progress toward democracy after the return to civilian rule in 1990 would be blocked by a variety of non-institutional realities created by the military regime. One of the most important of these was the fact that the military government had granted the private sector privileged access to the state while other societal groups had been completely excluded. In the years before the economic crisis of the early 1980s, a small number of business conglomerate executives had direct access to the most powerful members of the cabinet. While the financial collapse of the early 1980s resulted in a diminishment in power of some of these powerful interests, economic influence remained heavily concentrated and business interests were still strongly favored. During the Pinochet years, the private sector became accustomed to limited labor rights, a quiescent labor movement, and an inside track to the highest reaches of political power. As we will see in the next section, it would prove extremely difficult for the civilian government to alter this strong sense of entitlement. The brutal repression of the military regime also had lingering consequences on the future willingness of much of the public to engage in politics and demand change after the return to civilian rule. Repression had produced a "culture of fear" on the part of those who had been its victims, especially the trade unionists and the left (Politzer 2001). Gradually, however, links between labor and political parties reemerged during the 1990s. When the military finally left power, both the left rank and file and the trade union movement expected a return of some of the basic labor rights they had lost under the military regime, and an improvement in wages and working conditions. Public pressure would also demand redress for the poverty and inequality created by the military's economic model.

DILEMMAS OF DEMOCRACY UNDER THE CONCERTACIÓN

Between 1990 and 2006, four civilian Concertación governments were elected: these were led by Presidents Patricio Alywin (1990–96), Eduardo Frei Ruiz-Tagle (1996–2000),[5] Ricardo Lagos (2000–06), and Michelle Bachelet (2006–10). The Concertación is an alliance of left-center parties that includes the Christian Democratic Party (PDC), the left-leaning Socialist Party (PS), and the Popular Party for Democracy (PPD). All of the Concertación governments have grappled with the social and political legacies of military rule. The Concertación's struggle for a return to democracy and its initial electoral campaign involved a promise—"growth with equity"—that imbued its democratic project with an important moral content. From 1990 onwards, the Concertación has endeavored to make good on this commitment with a substantial increase in social spending and an economic growth strategy conducive to poverty reduction. Through a series of incremental steps, these governments removed almost all of the institutional impediments to democracy and dealt with the military regime's culpability for human rights violations. The Concertación also made important progress on the social front with a substantial increase in social spending and an economic growth strategy conducive to poverty reduction. In all of this, the Concertación faced stiff resistance from the political right.

At the same time, the Concertación has not only accepted but in many respects has also deepened the neoliberal economic model inherited from the military period. Between 1990 and 2006, the country's rulers liberalized trade, privatized airlines, mining, electricity, and ports, sought new export markets, and kept a careful watch over government expenditures. Their administrations also added a number of new ingredients to the model. In addition to increased social spending, they pursued labor law reform, introduced measures to equalize healthcare, and improved pensions. In seeking these social improvements, the Concertación leadership has faced an uphill battle to achieve consensus. Indeed, it has failed to find one on some of the most pressing issues. As in the past, the country continues to be pulled in opposite directions by powerful pressures from the political right and the political left. While the Concertación's commitment to the neoliberal model might cause one to question just how "pink" its leadership actually is, the following analysis demonstrates an ongoing commitment to equity and social justice concerns—concerns that have been reinforced by social protest under President Bachelet.

Resistance from the political right was also evident in the issue of human rights. Those who had been victimized by the military regime demanded that the truth be told about the human rights violations that had occurred under military rule and insisted that those responsible be brought to justice. The military and the political right, on the other hand, called for an end to investigations into human rights violations. President Alywin appointed the National Commission on Truth and Reconciliation, which was chaired by renowned jurist Raúl Rettig. The publication of the commission's findings, however, prompted even more passionate demands by the families of victims that justice be done, including the demand that the 1978 Amnesty be abolished. Meanwhile, the military engaged in saber-rattling, and demanded that the Amnesty Law be extended to 1990. Prosecution of those responsible was briefly blocked when the supreme court declared the 1978 Amnesty Law legal, a decision flatly rejected by President Alywin, however, and later reversed.

Progress in addressing the human rights issue was extremely difficult, largely because Pinochet remained an important political force long after Chile's return to civilian rule. He remained commander of the armed forces and, later, became senator-for-life, a constitutional privilege accorded to any ex-president who has served in office for six years. It would require Pinochet's arrest in 1998 in London and revelations about the involvement of his family in a financial scandal before his reputation was damaged enough to make change possible. Two bills proposed by President Alywin to reduce the power of the National Security Council and another to return to the president the power to promote and retire military officers were blocked by congress. The military successfully resisted early efforts to prosecute DINA agents who had been involved in human rights violations. Even though the former head of DINA, Manuel Contreras, had been convicted of the 1976 murder of Orlando Letelier—a prosecution made possible because the crime had occurred outside of Chile—the military brazenly ensured that for many years he was able to avoid serving his seven-year sentence (Oppenheim 2007, 230).

Presidents Alywin and Frei made only limited progress in institutional reform with the establishment of local elections and regional government and, in 1997, with the reform of the judiciary, an institution widely recognized as corrupt and subservient to the dictatorship. Reform of the supreme court, which expanded its membership from 17 to 21 and instituted mandatory retirement at the age of 75, immediately altered the nature of the court, making progress possible on the human rights issue. This reform made the court's 1999 decision that the Amnesty Law could not be applied to cases where the bodies of victims have not been recovered a reality. These cases would henceforth be considered open cases of "kidnapping" and could be prosecuted. But the major impediments to democratic governance (the designated senators, the binomial electoral system, and the National Security Council) remained firmly in place by the end of the Frei administration. The binomial electoral system guaranteed the underrepresentation of the Concertación, even though the coalition had more votes than the opposition. The law stipulated that the party with the most votes in the district would have to win twice as many votes as the opposition to gain both seats in the constituency. It allowed the right-wing coalition to win legislative seats even in districts where its candidates did not have more votes than the second Concertación candidates. In conjunction with the nine appointed right-wing senators, this law ensured that the Concertación would have to negotiate its bills with the political right.

The arrest of Pinochet in London, as a consequence of charges brought against him by Judge Baltasar Garzón for the torture of Spanish citizens increased the weight of those Chilean voices demanding the prosecution of human rights violators and helped to push democratization forward. The Spanish charges and the international furor they created began to erode the myth of military impunity and damaged Pinochet's reputation, giving the Concertación government the backing to move more concertedly in prosecuting both Pinochet and other human rights violators. Although the British House of Lords had ruled in favor of Pinochet's extradition to Spain, the British defense secretary allowed him to return to Chile on humanitarian and medical grounds. President Frei had asked for Pinochet's return but, under pressure from Chile's own human rights organizations, was also forced to make the public pronouncement that the issue of Pinochet's culpability would be handled in Chile. As a result, upon Pinochet's return to the country in 2000, the government brought an increasing number of charges against the former general, some of which were later dismissed. The final nail in the coffin of Pinochet's reputation was hammered in during 2004, with revelations that Pinochet and his family had been hiding more than $27 million US in secret bank accounts. The government charged Pinochet with tax evasion and fraud. Then, in 2004, the report of the Valech Commission (the National Commission on Political Imprisonment and Torture) ended any lingering doubt about the institutionalized nature of repression under Pinochet. Established by President Lagos to investigate cases of torture that occurred between 1973 and 1990, it reported 28,000 confirmed cases. In that same year, the military reversed its past position that the repression had not been systemic when General Juan Emilio Cheyre, the commander of the army, publicly acknowledged the institutional responsibility of the military for these "punishable and morally unacceptable acts" (Rohter 2004, n.p.). Although the supreme court would eventually rule that Pinochet was unfit to stand trial, these developments were important in creating a new environment that encouraged the increased prosecution of human rights violations.[6]

The changed environment also allowed the state to begin making important constitutional reforms that removed all but one of the remaining impediments to formal democracy. The 2005 constitutional reform, involving more than 50 changes to the 1980 constitution, eliminated appointed senators and the right of former presidents to a seat in the senate. It also ended military control of the National Security Council and reduced the council's power to one of a purely advisory capacity. Another reform restored the presidential power to appoint heads of the four branches of the armed forces and the national police. The only formal institutional impediment to democracy is the binomial electoral system. In May 2008, a constitutional reform to change this system failed to muster a sufficient number of votes in congress.

The country had clearly made important progress. The institutional impediments removed by the 2005 constitutional reform had once allowed the political right to block important policy changes, particularly those aimed at social justice. As Boylan explains in her 1996 study of the Chilean tax reform, the control of congress by the political right meant that Concertación had to negotiate its bill increasing taxes to fund new social programs with the congressional political right. In doing so, it had to be satisfied with a lower increase than originally proposed. However, while the 2005 constitutional reforms are important, continuing institutional arrangements maintain a closed policy process and a heavy concentration of power in the executive, particularly in the presidency and ministry of finance. Presidentialism is a feature of the Chilean political system, particularly in fiscal matters. The Chilean congress is generally weak—it can, for example, only approve or reduce expenditures, not increase or redistribute them. The 1975 law granting control over all financial matters to the minister of finance remains in place and supports an insulated policy process, even excluding other ministries. Indeed, the finance ministry officials play a leading role in virtually all policy areas, including the development of social policy. They, more than other ministry officials, are fiercely resistant to public consultation.

As the Concertación's tenure in office wore on, more and more members of the public began to see it as governing in a closed manner and as resistant to public consultation. Despite its achievements, the Concertación had failed to meet the expectations of many of those who had voted for it. While the formal constraints bequeathed by the military regime are important explanatory variables, non-institutional factors may well play an equally important role in understanding this disjuncture between the Concertación leadership and many among its support base.

The commitment of the political elite to the neoliberal economic model is a major component of the political transition and has shaped the leadership's reaction to popular political pressures. Chile's political transition to democracy, like other transitions in the region, was a pacted transition, involving an implicit agreement between the new political leaders and the outgoing military regime to keep the neoliberal model firmly in place. While civil society mobilization played an important role in exerting pressure for a return to civilian rule, it was the center-left opposition party leaders who negotiated the transition. These political leaders were pragmatic. They understood that a commitment to the neoliberal model would assuage the fears of the country's powerful, propertied interests. At the same time, they themselves had become converts to the neoliberal model, although unlike the military they also embraced social welfare concerns. A variety of factors had produced this frame of mind. Some had spent time in exile in Eastern Europe, where the problems of centrally planned economies had become abundantly apparent. Others, having obtained advanced degrees in the US, began to understand the operation of the economy differently. In general, no such conversion occurred among the popular supporters of the left parties within the Concertación. Fearing that "populist" pressures could easily undermine the economic model, the Concertación leaders were predisposed to a closed policy process that would insulate them from public demands. The experience of the Popular Unity years (1970–73) shaped the belief that high levels of political mobilization were harmful to both economic growth and poverty reduction because they contributed to inflation and created both political and economic instability. On top of this, the political leadership shares a common set of characteristics (all were highly trained in the social sciences) with a common source of recruitment, largely drawn from the think tank CIEPLAN (Corporation for Economic Research on Latin America) (Silva 1991). Concerned about business confidence, the Concertación afforded the private sector privileged access to the policy process through both institutionalized and personalized channels. Working commissions on economic policy, a yearly conference during which ideas on economic policy are exchanged, and monthly meetings with the head of the central bank all provided the private sector with regular opportunities to press its point of view. Direct, personal access to the president and cabinet ministers continued to be important as well.

The generally skewed access to the highest reaches of political power has angered those who believe themselves to be excluded from the political process. Labor, the rank and file of the Concertación, and civil society leaders have complained bitterly of their exclusion from policy development. Labor has been particularly restive, given its exclusion from policy access and the failure of government to, in its view, reform the labor code sufficiently. Labor leaders have argued that the restrictive labor code, inherited from the military period, has contributed to labors' organizational weakness, undermining its ability to improve the living standards of workers, especially in the rural sector. Labor leaders regard the 1991 reform to the labor code, which removed the 60-day limit on strikes (among other things), as woefully insufficient. Their main criticism has been the fact that collective bargaining above the firm level is only possible if management agrees. Another labor reform bill was proposed in 1995, but was blocked by opposition from both the business community and the political right in the senate, including opposition from the appointed senators. Strikes and demonstrations continued through the 1990s, with growing criticism coming from rank-and-file members of the Concertación, particularly members of the Socialist Party. A third attempt to reform the labor code was made in 1999, and again it failed in the face of stiff opposition from business and the political right. President Lagos's attempt to arrive at a consensus on a new labor law through a tripartite commission involving representatives of labor, business, and government was also unsuccessful. Proposals for change seesawed between those that failed to satisfy labor but that reassured business and those that had labor support but angered business. It was only in 2004, as economic growth returned and business profits shot up, that the government introduced a new labor bill, which, it claimed, would distribute the benefits of economic growth more equitably by reducing the hours of the workday and regulating overtime pay. It was rejected by business. Labor unrest in Chile is ongoing; protests link the labor reform issue to a rejection of neoliberalism and to charges that the political system is undemocratic. In 2007, at a nationwide demonstration organized by the CUT, its secretary general called for greater equality, an "end to neoliberal practices," "true representation" and "no more exclusion" (*Santiago Times* August 30, 2007).

The consequence of the government's failure to reform labor law has been that Chile's labor relations remain unfair and, some might argue, undemocratic. Labor union membership has declined since a brief upsurge following the return to civilian rule. Union weakness stems, to a considerable extent, from the great inequality of power between capital and labor that not only inhibits the reform of labor law but also makes possible various business tactics that keep labor membership and activism in check. Some firms, for example, grant higher wage increases to workers who refuse to participate in unions. One recent study shows how the existing labor system encourages a business strategy that attempts to strengthen competitiveness through constraining wage growth for the weakest, most vulnerable (temporary) workers (Berg 2004). One of the most important provisions of the 1979 labor code that has not changed is the legal provision outlawing collective bargaining and the prohibition of strikes by temporary workers. In the fruit and vegetable sector, one of the success stories of Chile's export-led economic growth, 70 per cent of jobs are filled by low-skilled female temporary workers. Today, employers in the fruit and vegetable industries only offer temporary contracts, even when companies are able to provide year-round employment. Indeed, more and more employers fire workers and rehire them on temporary contracts.

This allows employers to avoid paying benefits (vacation, severance) and removes collective bargaining that would involve troublesome negotiations and the possibility of strikes; it also keeps wages at the minimum. Wages for low-skilled workers have crept up, but only as a consequence of government-legislated minimum wage increases. According to Kurtz (2004), the very process of market economics in the Chilean countryside has created almost insurmountable obstacles to collective action. Rural communities have become fragmented as individuals migrate to take jobs which are temporary and without benefits. These jobs in the rural export sector create high levels of dependence and economic vulnerability, features that reduce the likelihood of collective action. Hence, Kurtz concludes, Chilean democracy rests on the quiescence and political exclusion of the rural poor.

High levels of socioeconomic inequality have remained a persistent feature of the economic model, as have inequality in services such as in healthcare, education, and pensions. Like the labor issue, these issues tended to produce polarized positions, and the state, despite its best efforts, has found it extremely difficult to orchestrate a societal consensus on social reform. The first civilian government of Eduardo Frei established the National Foundation for Overcoming Poverty for the explicit purpose of building a society-wide consensus on how best to reduce poverty and inequality. Originally comprised of representatives from a cross section of society (labor, poverty organizations, government, and the private sector), private sector representatives have since exited the organization in opposition to increased labor protection and measures to reduce inequality.

Although the Concertación had consistently increased spending on public healthcare, the extent of the deterioration in infrastructure during the period of military rule means that inadequacies in public healthcare persist. In addition, the private system is a drain on the public one, because individuals enrolled in the private system often use the public one if their private insurance does not cover a particular treatment or if there is no service close by. Additional pressure on the public system also occurs because it continues to provide care for the elderly. In an attempt to equalize the quality of healthcare, the Lagos government introduced AUGE (the Guaranteed Universal Health Access Plan), a plan that aimed to ensure that all those suffering from a particular disease receive the same standard of care. The bill received final approval in 2005. The original scheme involved guaranteed comprehensive and rapid treatment for 56 diseases by public and private providers. In order to bolster the financial base of the public system, the plan called for the establishment of a Solidarity Fund, to be financed by contributions from both the public and private healthcare systems. However, because this plan entailed a reduction in the flow of funds to private healthcare providers, it incurred the wrath not only of the private healthcare companies but also of the private sector. Business and the political right eventually succeeded in having the Solidarity Fund removed from the legislation, while the socialist parties continued to campaign for its reinsertion. The defeat of the Solidarity Fund eliminated the redistributive component of the plan and as a result jeopardized its integrity by removing an important source of increased funding. Given the absence of adequate funding, one observer has suggested that the plan will probably introduce a new set of inequalities, with an underfunded system providing privileged care in accordance with particular diseases (Borzutksy 2006, 161).

President Bachelet introduced new initiatives in the areas of pensions and educational policy. She faced growing pressure from below (in the form of protests) to do so, but has also been fortunate to have the fiscal resources for these new initiatives because of the rising price of copper on the international market. In addition, with a strong showing in the 2006 elections and with the termination of the appointed senators, the new government briefly held a majority in both the senate and chamber of deputies. The pension system has suffered from a variety of inadequacies believed to be contributing to poverty. For one, its coverage has been declining since 1989 because of a drop in formal, permanent, full-time employment. At 53 per cent coverage of the economically active population, the coverage provided by the pension system is well below pre-1980 levels of about 70 per cent. In addition, the values of pensions have not increased, and marked gender inequality is apparent because pensions in the private system are based on employee wages and years of contribution, which tend to be less for women. When women do not qualify for private pensions, they opt for the state pension (since the state pays for a minimum pension when private pensions are insufficient), but these pensions are extremely low.

Soon after assuming power, the Bachelet government provided a 10 per cent increase for those receiving the minimum pension. She also set up a Presidential Advisory Council to study the private pension system and suggest changes. The consequence was the 2008 pension program, which provides a basic pension equivalent to $120 per month for all citizens over the age of 65 with no pension contributions. In addition, a pension supplement will be paid to those over 65 who only receive low private pension payments. Both of these categories of pensions require a means test. Critics claim that although the new pension program will undoubtedly improve the lives of many of Chile's elderly poor, the reform leaves the privatized pension system intact. That system, so the argument goes, is very costly and inefficient; private pensions are uncertain by nature, and when they are accessed by former employees the amounts paid out are extremely low, only a fraction of those still offered by the public system. Women in the private system continue to receive much lower pensions than men, and the new program does not reinstate employer contributions. Furthermore, regulation of pension providers has been reduced (CENDA 2008, 4).

The first three Concertación presidents had attempted to improve education largely through increased spending and increased regulation. However, these policies did not reduce the major inequalities in the system. In 2006, the government was faced with over one million protesting high school students, engaged in street mobilizations, sit-ins, and school takeovers. The focus of the unrest was the country's educational law, passed during the military dictatorship. That law shifted the responsibility for education from the national to the municipal level and had privatized the system by allowing individual private companies to run schools alongside municipalities. The system created marked inequalities, especially in poor neighborhoods where resources were limited. In addition, many schools demand high monthly payments from students' families, a requirement that limits their intake of students from the lower social classes. Students also wanted the government to provide free transportation and to pay for college entrance exams, because these costs are a financial burden for poor families. After three weeks of protests, the government responded with a bill requiring the government to pay for 80 per cent of the cost of college entrance exams in addition to transportation costs. President Bachelet also set up a special advisory committee to review the entire educational system that included student representation. The new educational reform bill, which keeps the basic features of the educational system intact, seeks to stamp out some of the worst features of the old system. It prohibits discrimination in student selection (although it does so only up to the ninth grade), a feature of the old system that discriminated against lower-class applicants. The new law also provides a four-year deadline for schools to become non-profit, sets up a new education superintendent in charge of the distribution of funds to public schools, creates an agency for monitoring student performance, and sets higher standards for new schools.

The various measures taken by the current Concertación government to address some of the country's long-standing concerns about inequality have, however, weakened the Concertación alliance. For some of its supporters, these measures have not gone far enough; for others, they have gone too far. Defections from the Concertación began to occur in 2006. Today, the Concertación has lost its majority in both houses. Members of the right wing of the alliance, increasingly distressed by what they see as an overly activist state, oppose the expansion of social policy because they regard such a measure as the cause of undesirable fiscal pressures. In 2007, five right-wing Christian Democratic congressional members, including a former president of the Christian Democratic Party, left the Concertación. In early 2008, four more Christian Democrats exited, this time from the political left of the Christian Democratic Party. The latter group was critical of the timid nature of the government's new pension program, and the failure of the government to do enough to rectify the high concentration of wealth in the country. Members of the other Concertación parties have also left. One of these was former Socialist Party member, Marco Enrique Ominami, who ran as an independent in the 2009-10 election, garnering 19 per cent of the popular vote in the first round of the balloting.

There is also a rising tide of criticism from civil society organizations about the perceived closed nature of the Concertación leadership. As it is elsewhere in Latin America, civil society has been weak in Chile following the return to democratic rule. This weakness stems from a variety of factors, including the fact that the party leaders took over the leadership of the transition process from civil society leaders, the "culture of fear," and the transformation of many popular organizations into service organizations carrying out government-funded programs. The Concertación did provide some improved channels of access for its citizenry, but these were generally afforded to groups who did not challenge the major precepts of the neoliberal paradigm and whose demands were not likely to create inordinate budget burdens. The administration became more open to a gendered policy agenda through the establishment of the National Service for Women (SERNAM). However, critics (Richards 2006; Franceschet 2005) have argued that organizations representing middle-class women have been much more successful at gaining access to SERNAM than have those representing poor and indigenous women whose demands incorporate the particular social dimensions of their inequality (class and race). Indigenous women argue that the state's neoliberal project shapes its desire to allow the continued exploitation of resources in Mapuche territory, while the poor women's demand for state-supported redistributive measures confronts a neoliberal imperative that rejects the high degree of state intervention necessary to address the problem.

The complaints about the Concertación leadership's closed policy style gave rise to an initial commitment on the part of Concertación President Ricardo Lagos (2000–06) to a more participatory political process. With funding from the Inter-American Development Bank, he established a new civil society consultative mechanism, the Citizens' Council, as part of his Program for Strengthening the Alliances between Civil Society and the State. By 2003, however, the work of the Citizens' Council had ground to a halt because its recommendations for measures to strengthen civil society went unheeded and it had failed to receive most of the funds that had been promised. Despite this initial foray into public consultation, the Lagos administration tended to avoid the process. His administration rejected civil society involvement in the development of his program to alleviate extreme poverty, Chile Solidario, even though World Bank funding for such consultations appeared to be forthcoming. In addition, he cut short the process of consultation on his new health program, AUGE, causing considerable disillusionment among civil society groups. As a result, civil society leaders claim to be virtually excluded from social policy.

Great hopes were pinned on President Michelle Bachelet (2006–10), who promised not only to address the social question more forcefully but also committed herself to participatory democracy. On a number of major policy initiatives, she struck advisory groups. Although these groups took petitions from civil society, civil society representatives were not appointed to them. Her advisory council for pension reform, for example, consisted of economists, including one member of the political right who had served under Pinochet, while her transport reform plan came from a neoliberal think tank headed up by her finance minister. Given that the latter proposed cutting the number of buses in half, the director of the country's oldest poverty organization (Hogar de Cristo) declared the transportation plan to be "the worst humiliation of the poor in a long time" (Vogler 2007, n.p.). Civil society organizations' rejection of self-financing for the city's transportation system and their insistence on a return to a state-funded redistributive pension system were demands the administration was unwilling to accommodate.

President Bachelet set up an advisory commission for educational reform as well. This body comprised some 81 members including students, teachers, and parents, along with government, political party, and other educational representatives. However, the group could not reach a consensus; teachers and students resigned and rejected the final report. Among their demands was an end to the decentralization of education and for schools to become non-profit sooner than stipulated in the new law. They returned to the streets to protest. Civil society is becoming increasingly restive and has been pushing the administration toward measures to address inequality in services.

CONCLUSION

Chileans are deeply divided on a variety of public policy issues that pertain to inequality. This is not new. Polarization on social justice has a long-standing history in Chile. It places strain on a country's political institutions, as illustrated by the fact that it brought about the downfall of the country's electoral democracy in 1973. Today, public pressure has ensured that poverty, socioeconomic inequality, and the disparity in government services (health, education and labor laws) are all firmly on the political agenda. The political leadership has been struggling to find consensual solutions. This fact alone speaks to the vigorousness of Chile's electoral democracy and the strength of the country's institutions. Public pressure, most recently in the form of protests, has been instrumental in pushing the administration to live up to its moral commitment to equity.

The accomplishments of the Concertación leadership in removing all but one of the formal authoritarian restrictions handed down by the 1980 constitution, the progress in human rights prosecutions, and the success in poverty reduction (a long-standing public concern) justifiably makes Chile Latin America's success story. Nevertheless, however successful Chile might look from the outside, it is undeniable that many Chileans, like Sandro Imacache, are deeply disillusioned. One of the consequences has been public pressure demanding change. While the Chilean state has been highly effective in maintaining macroeconomic stability and in providing incentives for export-led growth, it has not been able to orchestrate, from the viewpoint of its citizens, sufficiently effective redistributive measures. We saw this in the failure to reform the labor code and in measures for reform of the healthcare and educational systems. For a significant portion of Chileans, democracy is not about formal political process, but about whether policy outcome actually improves their daily lives (Klesner 2001). Many of the demands that labor and civil society organizations are making involve policies perceived as threatening to the neoliberal model. Furthermore, democracy for many Chileans is also about being involved in policy development to shape its outcome. Policy elites (including many leaders of the Concertación) and business are extremely uncomfortable with these redistributive and participatory pressures. Undoubtedly, some form of accommodation will have to be found because, over the long term, the disillusionment of those who feel excluded from both prosperity and politics could well erode the legitimacy of the country's formal democratic institutions.

NOTES

1 With economic growth rates averaging 7 per cent annually since the late 1980s, poverty fell to 18.4 per cent of all households by 2003 from 38.9 per cent in 1990 (ECLAC 2007, 299).
2 The standard measure of inequality, the Gini coefficient, has remained steady since 1990 at 0.55 (ECLAC 2007, 319).
3 Piñera's win (with 51.6 per cent of the popular vote) is widely attributed to divisions in the left-center coalition, which will be discussed later in this chapter.
4 The Chicago Boys were named for their education in economics at the University of Chicago.
5 He is the son of Eduardo Frei Montalva, who was president of Chile from 1964 to 1970.
6 Pinochet died of heart failure in 2006 at the age of 91 without having been convicted of any charges.

REFERENCES

Aguilera Reyes, Máximo. 1994. "La economía chilena en el período 1974–1993." Documentos Docentes. Santiago: Universidad Central, Facultad de Ciencias Económicas.

Bauer, Arnold J. 1975. *Chilean Rural Society from the Spanish Conquest to 1930.* Cambridge: Cambridge University Press.

Berg, Janine. 2004. *Miracle for Whom? Chilean Workers under Free Trade.* New York: Routledge.

Borzutsky, Silvia. 2002. *Vital Connections: Politics, Social Security and Inequality in Chile.* Notre Dame: University of Notre Dame Press.

———. 2006. "Cooperation or Confrontation between the State and the Market. Social Security and Health Policy." *After Pinochet: The Chilean Road to Democracy and the Market.* Ed. Silvia Borzutsky and Lois Hecht Oppenheim. Gainesville: University of Florida Press. 142–66.

CENDA (Centro de Estudios Nacionales de Desarrollo Alternativo). 2008. "Reforma previsional: Solución fiscal para las pensiones más bajas. Las demás siguen a merced de las AFP y los mercados financieros." July 10, 2008. www.cendachile.cl/ley_pensiones.

Dahse, Fernando. 1979. *Mapa de la extrema riqueza.* Santiago: Editorial Aconcagua.

Délano, Manuel, and Hugo Traslaviña. 1989. *La herencia de los Chicago Boys.* Santiago: Las Ediciones del Ornitorrinco.

ECLAC. 2007. *Social Panorama of Latin America.* Santiago: ECLAC, United Nations.

Franceschet, Susan. 2005. *Women and Politics in Chile.* Boulder: Lynne Rienner Press.

Klesner, J.L. 2001. "Political Legacies of Authoritarianism: Political Attitudes in Chile and Mexico." *Citizen Views of Democracy in Latin America*. Ed. Roderic Ai Camp. Pittsburgh: University of Pittsburgh Press. 118–38.

Kornbluh, Peter. 2003. *The Pinochet File: A Declassified Dossier on Atrocity and Accountability*. New York: New Press.

Kurtz, Marcus J. 2004. *Free Market Democracy and the Chilean and Mexican Countryside*. Cambridge: Cambridge University Press.

Loveman, Brian. 1988. *The Legacy of Hispanic Capitalism*. 2nd ed. Oxford: Oxford University Press.

Mamalakis, Markos J. 1976. *The Growth and Structure of the Chilean Economy: From Independence to Allende*. New Haven: Yale University Press.

Montecinos, Veronica. 1997. "Economic Policy, Social Policy and Family Economy in Chile." *Review of Social Economy* 55(2): 224–33.

Oppenheim, Lois Hecht. 2007. *Politics in Chile: Democracy, Authoritarianism and the Search for Development*. 3rd ed. Boulder: Westview Press.

Petras, James. 1970. *Politics and Social Forces in Chilean Development*. Berkeley: University of California Press.

Politzer, Patricia. 2001. *Fear in Chile: Lives under Pinochet*. New York: New Press.

Report of the Chilean National Commission on Truth and Reconciliation (the Retigg Commission). 1993. "Truth Collections, Digital Collection, Reports: Chile." Notre Dame: University of Notre Dame Press. September 9, 2008. www.usip.org/library/tc/doc/reports/chile/chile_1993_foreward.html.

Richards, Patricia. 2006. "The Politics of Difference and Women's Rights: Lessons from Pobladoras and Mapuche Women in Chile." *Social Politics, International Studies in Gender, State and Society* 13(1): 1–29.

Rohter, Larry. 2004. "A Torture Report Compels Chile to Reassess its Past." *New York Times*. November 28. September 8, 2008. www.nytimes.com/2004/11/28/international/americas/28chile.html?_r=1&pagewanted=print&position=&oref=slogin.

Roxborough, Ian, Philip O'Brien, and Jackie Roddick. 1977. *Chile: The State and Revolution*. London: Macmillan Press.

Santiago Times. 2007. "Chile's Largest Labor Union calls for Solidarity with Colombia." August 3. July 3, 2008. www.santiagotimes.cl.

Schweimler, Daniel. 2007. "Inequality Remains in Prosperous Chile." 23 September. September 9, 2008. news.bbc.co.uk/2/hi/business/7006120.stm.

Sigmund, Paul E. 1977. *The Overthrow of Allende and the Politics of Chile, 1964–1976*. Pittsburgh: University of Pittsburgh Press.

Silva, Eduardo. 1996. *The State and Capital in Chile: Business Elites, Technocrats and Market Economics*. Boulder: Westview Press.

Silva, Patricio. 1991. "Technocrats and Politics in Chile: From the Chicago Boys to the CIEPLAN Monks." *Journal of Latin American Studies* 23: 385–410.

Vogler, Justin. 2007. "Pinochet's Ghost, Bachelet's Swamp." March 2008. www.opendemocracy.net/?q=article/chile_pinochet_s_ghost_bachclet_s_swamp.

E-RESOURCES

Chilean Government (English) (www.chileangovernment.cl/). The official website of the Chilean government.

Estrategia. Santiago business newspaper (Spanish) (www.estrategia.cl/). This is the country's major business newspaper.

Gateway for NGOs in Chile [El Portal de las ONGs] (Spanish) (www.ong.cl/). This website leads to the web pages of Chile's NGO community.

La Segunda. Santiago (Spanish) (www.lasegunda.com/). A major Chilean newspaper.

National Commission for Truth and Reconciliation (1990) and National Commission on Political Imprisonment and Torture (2003) (English summaries) (www.usip.org/countries-continents/south-america/chile). These reports document the nature and extent of repression under President Pinochet.

The Santiago Times (English) (www.santiagotimes.cl/santiagotimes/). Chile's only English-language newspaper.

United Nations Development Report [Programa de las Naciones Unidadas para el Desarrollo]. Chile (2009) (Spanish) (www.desarrollohumano.cl/). The report documents the rise in human development indicators in the last decade and perceptions of the Chilean population about the future.

THIRTEEN

Argentina: Clientelism, Corporatism, and Democracy

VIVIANA PATRONI

Neka became a supporter of the *piqueteros*, or movement of the unemployed, while working as part of the health team in a hospital in the Buenos Aires province. She had known the *piquetero* community from its beginnings, when local people first started to reclaim land and build precarious homes there. With growing unemployment in the 1990s, several of those who lost their jobs came together to seek ways of organizing against the situation. It was only natural for Neka to provide her support to their struggle. It was even more straightforward for her to commit her participation to the demands of the Movement of Unemployed Workers (MTD) when she herself lost her job. Like many other *piqueteros*, she sees unemployment only as the most obvious manifestation of everything that is wrong with Argentina in the neoliberal age. Organizations within the MTD have been able to offer a space for unemployed workers to build a new sense of identity and solidarity as they faced mounting difficulties in their lives. Neka is aware that for many, necessity is a primary motivation to join an organization like the MTD. In many cases, *piquetero* organizations have become the administrators of short-term employment programs that are one of the only ways the unemployed can claim official assistance. The administration of other community projects is another benefit of belonging to an organization like the MTD. However, Neka recognizes that the challenge is to go beyond simple assistance

325

while safeguarding against the dangers of clientelism. She insists instead on the protection of the organization as a space for struggle and for the discovery of new ways of organizing society. Such change is possible, Neka is convinced, but can only happen through a long process of collective learning.[1]

The downfall of the last dictatorship in Argentina in 1983 initiated a new political cycle that was unique in at least two respects. The first and most obvious feature of politics in the country has been the continuity of civilian governments: a total of five presidents have been elected since 1983. Notwithstanding threats of military rebellions, major economic and political crises, and mass uprisings forcing civilian governments out of office, the fact still remains that for the first time in the contemporary history of the country, democratic rule has been consolidated. The second fundamental trend in the period has been the significant deterioration in living standards. Falling wages, rising unemployment and poverty, and an ever more unequal distribution of income have accompanied the process of democratic consolidation. While growing poverty has been a common trend in Latin America since the 1980s, the magnitude of the downturn in Argentina has been unparalleled from a sociological perspective. Thus, in a country that had been considered to be better off than its neighbors, by 2002 almost 54 per cent of the population lived below the poverty line. While conditions have recently improved, the material gains might only be temporary and the possibilities of democracy are still limited by embedded clientelism.

This chapter pays particular attention to the working class as a political actor in order to emphasize its role in the struggles for redistribution that have been central in determining the political trajectory of the country over the last century. These struggles stand at the core of the processes that define not only democracy but also the pattern of socioeconomic development. Democracy can be understood as a system that has made demands for a fairer redistribution of the gains of economic growth less costly in terms of repression. In turn, a better redistribution of income and the incorporation of workers as consumers are key factors to explain the dynamic nature that capitalism has acquired in today's advanced countries. That these countries are more stable and have enjoyed more effective liberal democracies is a fact that cannot be underestimated. In Argentina today, democracy has not adequately addressed the concerns and demands over income redistribution in order to ensure a stable and effective liberal democracy.

THE PATH OF NATIONAL INTEGRATION

The first Spanish settlement in Argentina dates back to 1526, with Argentina's main port and capital city, Buenos Aires, founded in 1536. The city was reestablished later in 1580, after it had been abandoned due to repeated attacks by the indigenous population. Overall, the territory was of only secondary importance for the Spanish. The relatively small indigenous population obstructed the development of any activity requiring a large labor force.

Full independence from Spain in 1816 initiated a period characterized by civil wars, economic decline, atomization of the colonial political unit, weakening central authority, and civil strife. Resolution of the conflicts finally came through the unification of the country under the constitution of 1853 and its amendment in 1860, incorporating the province of Buenos Aires. The enactment of the federalist constitution coincided with the expansion of economic activity, particularly in cattle and cereal production, in the fertile *pampas* (plains) that surround the city of Buenos Aires, the undisputed political center of the country since that time. The focus on agriculture was to secure the dynamic participation of the country in the expanding world economy of the second half of the nineteenth century.

The constitution of Argentina, last modified in 1994, establishes a republican, representative, and federal form of government with a clear division of power among the executive, legislature, and judiciary. The legislative power at the federal level resides in the national congress, a bicameral body composed of the chamber of national deputies and the senate, which contains representatives from the provinces as well as the city of Buenos Aires, the national capital. Deputies are elected directly, according to a system of proportional representation. Provinces also elect three senators, which implies the overrepresentation of smaller, less populated provincial territories. Some of the consequences of malapportioned legislatures have been addressed in chapter 3.

Between 1860 and 1914, Argentina experienced one of the most rapid processes of economic growth in the world (Rock 1987, 172).[2] This long growth period prompted a number of structural changes, in particular, immigration. A small national population and the lack of a sizeable peasantry made immigration a key variable in the economic boom. Between 1880 and 1930, 5.9 million immigrants entered Argentina, with over half of them staying permanently in the country (3.2 million). In 1914, 30 per cent of the Argentine population was foreign-born. Because most immigrants settled in the city of Buenos Aires or other urban centers, the ratio of immigrants versus indigenous population was even higher in these centers. Approximately half of the immigrants were Italians and one-third were Spaniards. The rest came mostly from other European countries (Waisman 1987, 54–57).

Until early in the twentieth century, there was a large gap between the intent of the law and the actual practices that ruled the political life of the country. Thus, while universal suffrage for all Argentine males over 16 had been in existence at the federal level since 1856, elections and voter registrations were marked by fraud and manipulation. Nonetheless, national elections played a not inconsequential role in prompting some civic engagement. Moreover, between 1862 and 1930, national elections were held at the intervals set out by the constitution, becoming for all purposes the accepted route to the acquisition of political power (Alonso 2000, 144–45).

Although many immigrants to Argentina had supported radical political options, they gradually sought mechanisms that could guarantee them some degree of social mobility and at least a partial realization of the dream of improved living conditions that had brought them to the country in the first place (Torre 1990, 40). This attempt changed the character of the labor movement—which up until then was heavily influenced by anarchism and socialism—and gave impetus to more pragmatic forms of unionism. The tempering of working-class politics was strengthened by another important political change. The electoral law was reformed in 1912 to make voting for all males over 18 years of age secret and compulsory, a change that made universal male suffrage potentially effective for the first time. In 1916, the electoral victory of the progressive Radical Party (UCR) under the leadership of Hipólito Yrigoyen (1916–22; 1928–30) reflected the effective broadening of the electorate in the country, and the capacity of the party to expand its basis of support to include a growing sector of the working class.

The 1930s were difficult times everywhere, and Argentina was no exception. Argentina also had a military coup in 1930 that deposed Yrigoyen during his second term in office. During the decade, a series of right-wing governments, elected through fraud, held power. The General Confederation of Labor (CGT), an organization that would play a central role in Juan Perón's rise to power, was also founded in 1930.

With economic reactivation by the mid-1930s, unions could once again press for some improvements. The growth of labor conflicts after 1935 provides a good indication of the increasing strength of working-class organizations. This new surge in the capabilities of labor was determined, in large part, by the significant economic transformation underway during this period. The recovery of the external sector made possible the implementation of a project of limited industrialization supported by the traditional elite. Based on an economic strategy called import-substitution industrialization (ISI), the number of workers in industrial plants had doubled by the mid-1940s and, for the first time, the manufacturing sector contributed a larger share to the GDP than agriculture.

Workers in the 1940s had developed a common identity connected to their economic exclusion and political marginality (Murmis and Portantiero 1971, 76). Thus, regardless of whether some sectors had a longer or shorter insertion in the working class, they were unified as social actors by their experience of exploitation and unfulfilled demands. After almost a decade of not very fruitful struggles, the rise of Perón on the public scene and his actions (particularly between 1944 and 1946) offered labor unions the opportunity to align themselves with a powerful political actor who would help them attain a larger share of the national income.

THE TRANSFORMATION UNDER PERÓN, 1943–1955

In June 1943 a new, more reformist military coup ended the period of conservative rule initiated after the overthrow of Yrigoyen in 1930. As one of the leaders within the new ruling military regime, Juan Domingo Perón was first appointed as head of the National Department of Labor in October of 1943. The exercise of this office, transformed a few months later into the Secretariat of Labor and Social Welfare, set him in a privileged position to support the growth of unions, intervene in the resolution of labor conflicts, and promote and enact social legislation. The support Perón gained from the working class during this very short period shielded him from the political setbacks he faced by 1945, and also secured his electoral victory in 1946.

But the close connection between government and unions and the political support Perón had from the working class were both the cause and the manifestation of a profound transformation of politics in Argentina. Peronism (as the movement became known) allowed the working class to develop a new political identity that transformed it into a key social and political player, defining a new political era in the country.

This labor–government alliance facilitated the emergence of populism in Argentina. Following Laclau (2008), new political identities were constituted through a process in which the working class and other sectors of "the people" gained consciousness of their role as political and social actors. In doing so, they defined their position as different from and in opposition to those who had access to power and who used it to benefit themselves economically. The shared experience of unmet demands, diverse as they might have been, gave the mobilization of these actors a particularly powerful meaning. In Argentina, workers and their demands for social justice and inclusion came to encapsulate the demands of a much larger segment of the population. It was Peronism that channeled successfully those demands and gave them political significance, although in the long run this seriously weakened the autonomy of working-class organizations. Finally, whether through its growing consumption, or as newly dignified agents of transformation, Peronism provided a political coherence to the working class that allowed it to withstand the several challenges it faced over the following decades. However, just as Peronism created a new political identity among large sectors of Argentine society, it generated an equally strong anti-Peronist identity.

There were several policies that fostered very high levels of support for Perón and his administration. Perón's commitment to altering the pattern of income distribution in favor of those marginalized by economic growth, to improving labor legislation, to promoting industrialization and the growth of the domestic market, to developing a system for the provision of basic welfare and, fundamentally, to acting as the catalyst for the political participation of very large sectors of the population were, without doubt, key factors in this respect. However, the state also acquired the capacity to shape labor unions and to extend benefits and protectionism to those loyal to the government. Enacting the Law of Professional Associations transferred to the state the right to recognize the legality of unions. This was an important instrument in permitting the state to shape and co-opt civil society organizations.

Either through these formal legal means or through coercion and repression, Perón secured his control over the organizations of the working class, whose backing was fundamental in providing political support. This is important too, because the serious democratic deficit in unions can be traced, at least in part, to this pivotal period in their history. Unfortunately, the undemocratic tendencies in unions have remained a constant until today and became yet another component in the predicament the country confronted in embarking on its path toward democracy.

Although populism encompassed the establishment of a more inclusionary political sphere, it took form under the tutelage of a state whose main concern was to control the way in which emerging social actors participated in the process. "Corporatism" is the concept used to study the process through which the state organized and then controlled various sectors of society, labor in particular. While labor was central in the strategy to structure society, the efforts of the government did not stop with it. Toward the end of Perón's second term in office (1952–55), the principle of an "organized community" encapsulated the corporatist pattern being promoted by government. As opposition increased, the government attempted to bring more sectors under its control by organizing them, sanctioning the expression of their demands, and limiting the scope for dissent within their ranks. Organizations representing owners of small- and medium-sized enterprises, professionals, government employees, and university and high school students were among the corporations created by Perón. These organizations never developed to the same extent as the labor sector, but they became nonetheless important conduits of the propaganda machine established by Perón (Rock 1987, 313–14).

Although one of the objectives of corporatism was to curtail opposition, repression became more overt as political and economic conditions deteriorated. In this regard, the populist government of Perón in Argentina illustrates the authoritarian nature of this kind of regime, as discussed in chapter 2. After 1949, a much heavier hand was used against the press, and this tendency only worsened over the last years of Peron's government. Even labor, the close ally of Perón since 1945, started to distance itself from the economic course taken by the government in the 1950s, as expressed by the increasing number of participants in strikes after 1952 (McGuire 1997, 69). The last presidency of Perón (1952–55) marked the growing polarization of politics in Argentina.

The rise and fall of Perón (1945–55), and the radical transformation of politics in Argentina during this period, constituted a watershed in the country's contemporary history. The military coup that deposed Perón in September 1955 ("The Liberating Revolution") initiated a new phase in this transformation which was characterized not just by political impasse but also by the relentless deepening of political conflict.

POST-PERONIST ARGENTINA, 1955–1976

After the 1955 coup, the military banned Perón's party from running in presidential elections. Because Peronism was a loosely organized movement, the only remaining sector with real organizational strength was labor, which also gave it the capability to broker the Peronist vote. As a result, some key unions became central players within the Peronist movement and thereby one of the most important political actors in Argentina. Labor's powerful role in politics was also a measure of its capacity to paralyze economic production nationally through general strikes.

Starting in the 1950s, a complex combination of political and economic factors set Argentina's long economic decline in motion. The most salient characteristic of Argentina during the 20 critical years between Perón's downfall and the military coup of 1976 were "stop-and-go" cycles of economic expansion and contraction. The cycles were accompanied by very high levels of political instability that were both the expression and also the cause of economic turbulence in the country. Between 1955 and 1976 there were three military dictatorships (1955–58; 1962–64; and 1966–73) and three civilian governments, including the last presidency of Perón (1958–62; 1964–66; and 1973–76). These recurrent crises framed the increasing polarization and violence that by the 1960s became the central element in Argentine politics.

The "stop-and-go" cycles were the expression of the alliances and counter-alliances that the political and economic trajectory of the country until then made possible. Without doubt, the increasing capacity of the working class, or more precisely the unions that represented it, was a pivotal determinant in the process. The power these labor unions had acquired as major players within the Peronist movement and, through it, within society as a whole, allowed them to effectively contest access to state power. Moreover, Peronism provided the terms around which the notion of a more socially just capitalist development found political expression. Nationalism, manifested in the consensus regarding the central role the state should play in the protection of the national economy, was also a key component of this alternative. Thus, Peronism was also able to represent in important ways the interests of a sizeable portion of industrialists who sought in the state an instrument to fend off the growing involvement of transnational companies in the economy. During key political moments, Peronism thus facilitated a powerful political alliance between the working class and other sectors within the middle classes and a critical sector among industrial employers.

Other powerful economic groups during this period, fundamentally the agro-exporting elite and those firms within the industrial sector more connected to international markets and capital and less dependent on protectionism, converged periodically in a second alliance. The availability of a stable source of hard currency was particularly important for the larger industrial firms connected to international networks, since it was required to guarantee access to imported inputs, secure profit remittance, and ease access to external financial markets (Smith 1991, 36).

These two sets of alliances collided around the difficulty of how to overcome the problems generated by the recurrent balance of payment crises that is a permanent problem for developing countries. However, these alliances were only sporadically operative, since there were also important cleavages within each that could not be concealed indefinitely (O'Donnell 1978, 13). Their internal coherence tended to buckle under the pressure exercised by the opposing alliance, and in so doing propelled a new alignment of forces that pushed for different policy responses.

Consistent with the power that Peronism retained as the main political referent of organizations of the working class, at no point during this period were the capitalist parameters of development in Argentina challenged. Similarly, the conservative governments did not undermine the corporatist power of unions since, ultimately, they were a means for the state to control worker opposition. However, after the late 1960s, Peronism became a much more fragmented force, encompassing a growing number of more radical voices. Moreover, some working-class organizations became more radicalized and questioned the authoritarianism and lack of democracy prevalent in the official labor unions. A similar process of radicalization took place among the middle class with the result that, by the late 1960s, the political forces on the left had considerably strengthened their presence in society.

Increasingly, the conflict over both the distribution of the costs and gains from development acquired a much more violent nature. Throughout this process, the fragile pillars that had been supporting sporadic manifestations of democracy became even weaker. Part of the explanation lies in the narrowing of the political space within which protest and dissent could find channels of expression and legitimization. As in the rest of Latin America, this radicalization of social conflict was shaped by the politics of the Cold War and, more specifically, the doctrine of national security that reduced the expression of dissent and demands for change to a perceived communist threat. The military dictatorship of 1966–73 was the clearest expression of the power of such a perspective (Altamirano 2001, 80–81). However, it was the military coup in 1976 that took anti-communism to its next catastrophic stage.

Two other factors contributed to narrowing the space for the search for a democratic alternative to the cyclical political crisis Argentina experienced during this period. One was the political inability of any party on the right to shape the interests of the economic elite of the country into a viable electoral option. Given this critical political obstacle, the elite relied on the military to put forth its interests against those of the popular sector (McGuire 1997, 5). For its part, labor, the other key political player, framed its demands around issues of social justice. It saw the struggles for these demands in relation to its own mobilization and political capabilities and not necessarily as a reflection of the survival of democratic governments. It was, in fact, only when elected governments appeared as the most expedient channel to address working-class demands that organized labor provided its support. However, when constitutional governments could not be counted on as allies, labor opposition possessed a de facto veto power. In the midst of this conflict, support for democracy as a key component of a process of development remained essential only within a small fraction of the political forces.

The electoral triumph of Peronism in 1973, notwithstanding its historical significance, could do little to turn the tide in favor of democracy. On the contrary, far from providing an alternative to the increasing polarization and violence that characterized politics in Argentina, particularly since the 1960s, the conflict permeated the Peronist party itself. Thus, Peronism became the central stage for the unfolding of the war that was to encompass the whole of society. To complicate matters, the economy suffered a serious downturn in 1975, itself the expression of the inability of the Peronist administration to provide an alternative. By the time of the military coup of 1976, Argentina was immersed in an unprecedented crisis. To observers at the time, the country was essentially an ungovernable society.

THE REIGN OF TERROR, 1976–1983

The military proposed to solve the problems that so deeply affected society by first eliminating all left-wing opposition. In the view of the military, "subversion" was an enemy like no other and thus the war against it justified the use of all means at the disposal of the state. Those means greatly surpassed any legal limits to the use of force. State terror became the main instrument to control the opposition. Disappearances, torture, imprisonment, and executions were widely used by the state in order to create the degree of terror necessary to eliminate and thwart opposition.

As had happened during the previous military dictatorship (1966–73), the military junta bypassed the constitution altogether, giving itself its own legal framework. The use of terror for the suppression of opposition was accompanied by the curtailment of all civil and political rights. While the left-wing opposition was what the military considered to be the root of the chaos that had made Argentina a "sick" society in need of a major reordering, all forms of collective action were the target of repression. The enemy could hide anywhere and "subversive" demands could take any form. Thus, not only was the CGT abolished, but a number of civil society organizations were brought under military control. Equally important, political parties were prohibited from carrying on their normal activities. In short, any avenue of potential resistance was eliminated.

If terror was important as a form of political control, it was also essential to secure the economic restructuring the military considered necessary. To the military, the pattern of development followed until then had made possible the power of the sectors that attempted to bring about revolutionary change. In this sense, ISI, and more specifically the protectionism that had made it possible, was at the center of the dispute. In insulating the national economy from international competition, protectionism had also given labor the power to struggle successfully for higher wages (Canitrot 1981, 133). Equally important, the form that labor struggles took in Argentina gave a much greater scope for the radicalization of the labor movement. Thus, opening up the economy to the discipline of international markets would weaken the labor movement, particularly its most radical organizational expressions. It is probable, then, that ISI did not simply become "exhausted" but rather was brought to a violent end along with the attacks on the interventionist state. Argentina illustrates the reality of politics underlying economic transitions.

Congruent with this diagnosis, the military attempted to implement Argentina's first neoliberal program of reforms, setting as its goals trade liberalization, the deregulation of capital markets, privatization, and fiscal discipline. Although the military regime could not escape an economic crisis of monumental proportions, it did certainly produce a major economic transformation. Labor was the sector most negatively affected by the changes. Between 1976 and 1981, real wages declined approximately 40 per cent. Repression made it very difficult for labor to protect wage levels, but the restructuring of the economy was equally important. The effect of the policies implemented by the military in the area of trade liberalization and exchange rate overvaluation resulted in a momentous decline in the sectoral weight of manufacturing, from 28.2 per cent of the GDP in 1974 to only 22.4 per cent in 1982.

Notwithstanding the power the military had in controlling the path of economic reforms and any opposition to it, they were unable to overcome the stubborn problem of inflation. The failure this time came with the very high price tag in massive foreign debt, up from approximately $8 billion US in 1976 to $43 billion US in 1982. Up to 44 per cent of these resources helped to finance capital flight, 33 per cent were used to pay interest on the debt, and 23 per cent covered the bill for imports, mostly of military equipment (Calcagno and Calcagno 2000, 2). But this was not all. During the period of military control, and as the ultimate sign of the failure of the economic program, the economy shrank by 13 per cent.

It is in this context of an economic crisis that the military sought a conflict with Great Britain over the Islas Malvinas (Falkland Islands) in 1982 as a political way out of the conundrum. Argentina's defeat, with its heavy death toll, removed any remaining vestige of legitimacy that the military had. Unable to sustain power any longer, members of the military regime were forced to call an election in 1983. The various defeats that resulted in their exit from power did not allow them to either negotiate their institutional position under the new democratic government or to control the conditions under which the transition was to take place. However, the profound transformation that had taken place in Argentina since the mid-1970s had weakened the power of labor and the political viability of those groups connected to redistributive concerns in fundamental ways. The political vacuum left by these actors was to mark the period of democratic government initiated in 1983.

TRANSITION TO DEMOCRACY, 1983–1989

The severe wounds the military inflicted upon Argentine society healed in different ways and at their own pace. The full unfolding of the extent of human rights abuses, the practically non-existent limits with which the military had been able to operate during this time, and the impunity that protected them were all historical lessons that a large sector of the population felt they could never forget. Decisively, the military also lost the trust that important sectors of the population had once so often placed in it. The economic quagmire the country faced by 1982 was the most tangible proof of the military's inability to govern effectively, even when exercising unrestricted power. Regardless of the depth and scope of the crises that have plagued the country since 1983, a military solution has not been among the options considered by key political actors. This does not mean, though, that the transition away from military power was easy. In fact, the military remained a challenge and, although without much apparent power, they did manage to secure important concessions.

The elections of 1983 were momentous for the Peronist party and the labor movement it had represented since the 1940s. In fact, these were the first free and unrestricted elections that the Peronist party had ever lost. The defeat was particularly costly for the Peronist labor leaders, since they had been the central figures in the reorganization of the party. Nonetheless, the elected president, Raúl Alfonsín (1983–89) from the Radical Party, was well aware of the political cost the Peronist labor movement could inflict on his government. It is not surprising then that one of Alfonsín's first acts of government was to submit to congress a bill aimed at facilitating the democratization of the labor movement and, indirectly, at weakening the basis of power of the traditional labor bureaucracy (Buchanan 1995, 136–37). This offensive on Alfonsín's part set the tone for the relationship between labor and the radical government for the rest of the presidential term. Unable to gain congressional support for the original bill and thus incapacitated as far as resolving the key issue of how to neutralize the power of labor, Alfonsín resorted to the strategy most governments since the 1950s have followed: he guaranteed protection to the CGT leadership in the form of the preservation of its corporatist power.

To understand why the relationship with the CGT was so central for the radical administration, one only needs to remember the profound economic crisis during which the democratic transition was undertaken in Argentina. Faced with the daunting task of balancing international pressure for structural reforms and the opposition of powerful political forces internally, the government attempted to secure some breathing space by including key social actors in a process of negotiation. The failure of the various plans through which Alfonsín attempted to take Argentina out of the crisis provided a strong indication of the political difficulties faced by his government. These were challenges that would prove, ultimately, to be insurmountable.

To add to the difficulties, the military remained a constant problem for Alfonsín. Although in retreat, the military still retained sufficient influence to limit the power of the courts to sanction human rights crimes. In 1986, the congress approved a law that set a final deadline—thus the name of the law, Full Stop—for the filing of legal cases against those suspected of human rights violations. After a military revolt in 1987, the government then passed a new law of Due Obedience through which all military personnel, except for those with the highest rank, were exempted from legal prosecution. There were three more military uprisings, two in 1988 and another in 1990. The few officers who previously had been sentenced for human rights violations soon became the beneficiaries of the Amnesty Laws passed by the second democratic president, Carlos Menem (1989–99), in 1989 and 1990. It was only in 2005 that these laws were declared unconstitutional by the supreme court of justice, allowing for a reopening of cases against those responsible for crimes against humanity.

As the economic crisis worsened and stabilization policies faltered, the political liabilities of the radical government increased. At the end of Alfonsín's term in office, the climate of economic crisis was accompanied by the military uprisings mentioned above and, in 1989, by a guerrilla attack against a military base. The 13 general strikes called by the CGT contributed one more element to the perception of widespread political instability that permeated the transitional period.

Early in 1989, the country fell into the most serious economic crisis any government in the history of the country had faced until then. After February of that year, inflation accelerated to reach an annualized rate of almost 5,000 per cent (Damill and Frenkel 1992, 63). Hyperinflation, declining wages and employment, and the fall in the rate of economic activity define the arena wherein the government tried to overcome the political crisis that the dismal economic performance had unleashed. Looting and other forms of violent social mobilization became common during this period. Under these conditions, Carlos Menem achieved an important electoral victory for the Peronist party in the elections of May 1989. Although Menem's inauguration was scheduled for December, Alfonsín agreed—as a last attempt to limit the political and economic chaos Argentina faced at the time—to relinquish power almost six months before his mandate officially expired.

The return of Peronism under Menem was, however, marked by the limitations the unprecedented crisis imposed on the new government. But the very same limitations also allowed the government to exercise a high degree of autonomy from its traditional basis of support in the search for a way out of the conundrum. This was particularly so because the acceptance of restructuring reforms in the manner proposed by the IMF and the World Bank appeared to be unavoidable (Palermo and Novaro 1996,

115). Thus, while Menem's electoral platform had rallied supporters around traditionally Peronist demands related to social justice and redistribution, his government oversaw one of the most extensive and rapid market reform programs in the region.

THE APOTHEOSIS OF NEOLIBERALISM, 1991–2003

Although the direction of Menem's economic plan was clear from the very beginning, inflation continued to be a major impediment to the implementation of structural reforms. It was only with the introduction of the Convertibility Law in 1991 that inflation was finally curbed. Although it came with a heavy social cost, controlling inflation nonetheless provided Menem with a level of political support that would have been impossible to anticipate given the about-face his policies represented from his electoral promises. In what was to become an outstanding example of presidential power, as explained in chapter 3, the political clout that Menem acquired was critical in moving ahead with structural reforms.

The Convertibility Law was the central piece in the anti-inflationary plan designed by Menem's economy minister, Domingo Cavallo. The law established a fixed exchange rate between Argentine currency and the dollar, set originally at $1 US for 1 Argentine peso.[3] The plan garnered a very high rate of approval and cemented a broad consensus around the primacy of stability as a target in economic policy-making. This is not surprising within a population that had seen their incomes erode through periods of very high inflation and bouts of hyperinflation. Thus, as the inflation rate fell from 1,344 per cent in 1990 to 84 per cent in 1991 and continued to decline during the decade to reach 0.1 per cent in 1996 (ECLAC 2000, 94–95), Menem's economic program enjoyed enormous popularity. Moreover, the guarantee of a fixed exchange rate as a safeguard against a possible devaluation was essential for foreign investors in order to secure the value of profit remittances. Convertibility was important for new investors in all sectors of the economy, but was particularly enticing to financial speculators (Ale 2001).

The Convertibility Law was much more than a stabilization program. In fact, during the ten years of its existence, the convertibility scheme became the central pillar in promoting the process of structural reforms—trade and financial liberalization, privatization, and the reorientation in the regulatory functions of the state over the economy—known as the Washington Consensus. However, beyond stability and the support it generated, Menem's economic plan was not based on solid ground. First, convertibility was heavily reliant on the inflow of foreign capital, either through investment or loans. As the domestic currency became overvalued during the decade, imports became increasingly cheap. The cost of imports in the current account reached extremely high levels during the 1990s. Exports, for its part, could not provide the kind of external resources to finance the high import bill. Besides trade deficits, though, Argentina also faced growing difficulties connected with the remittance of profits and interest payments on its foreign debt. Moreover, the major international financial upheavals of the 1990s (most notably the Mexican crisis in 1995 and the Asian crisis in 1997) increased investors' concerns and thus raised the premium they were willing to accept in exchange for more funds.

Second, although there were periods of economic growth in Argentina, the main characteristic of the economy during the 1990s was its propensity toward crisis and stagnation. Without the capacity to depreciate the currency to balance the current account, recession was the main mechanism to curtail the demand for imports. Foreign loans could also have solved the problem, but as Argentina became a higher risk in the eyes of investors, it became almost impossible for the country to secure new loans. Since 1998 the IMF became a major source of funds that were the only safeguard against default. It was, in fact, the rising perception that the IMF was unwilling to continue to finance the mounting foreign deficit that prompted the final collapse of the convertibility plan in early 2002. By that time, Argentina's foreign debt, both private and public, was $155 billion US, up almost threefold since 1991, the beginning of convertibility, when it had been $58.5 billion US. By March of 2002 also, the GDP per capita was almost a quarter smaller than it had been in 1976 (Lozano 2002).

Third, the social cost of structural reforms in Argentina was staggering, particularly in terms of the transformation of labor markets. Changes in the structure of firms—for example, the adoption of new imported technology and the introduction of new forms of work organization that increased work intensity—reduced the demand for workers even during periods of growth. The structural transformation of the country prompted by trade liberalization under an overvalued currency resulted in the destruction of large sectors of industry with a consequent loss in employment. Finally, the serious economic recessions the country faced during the decade generated ever higher levels of unemployment. Unemployment, however, was not the only negative transformation in the labor markets. The changes in the 1990s were also characterized by the continuous growth of precarious forms of employment, including jobs that did not offer any form of social security or formal contract (Beccaria 2001, 60). By October 2001, just a few months before the final collapse of the convertibility plan, unemployment and underemployment combined affected 34.6 per cent of the workforce (*Página 12*, December 14, 2001, 6–7). Moreover, in the metropolitan area of Buenos Aires, 40 per cent of those who were working were doing so under precarious conditions.

Conditions in labor markets continued to deteriorate until 2003, when some economic reactivation took place. By then, growing unemployment and underemployment, in combination with declining wages, explain why more than half of the population of Argentina lived below the poverty line. Falling wages and worsening conditions in labor markets also explain the momentous redistribution of income in favor of the better-off sectors of the population that accompanied restructuring in Argentina. The national income accruing to the poorest 20 per cent of the population fell from 4.55 per cent in 1990 to 3.8 per cent in 1998, while the income of the highest 20 per cent increased from 50.6 per cent to 54.25 per cent during the same period.

Growing inequality, poverty, unemployment, and precariousness in the labor markets provide a synopsis of the social cost of restructuring in Argentina. The question is not so much *why* this growing immiseration happened during a period of democracy, but rather *how* it did, considering the history of the country and the power the organizations of the working class had demonstrated in mobilizing in defense of their gains. Part of the answer can be found in the capacity of the Peronist administration to control the response from a key sector among the organizations of the working class. Another part of the puzzle was the development of important patronage networks through which the Peronist party controlled and mobilized those who depended on the state's dispensation to secure a living.

How to respond to the severe deterioration in labor markets was a particularly complex issue for the CGT. The core of the dilemma for the organization was the fact that it was a Peronist government, labor's historical ally, which was responsible for the reforms. The inclination of the party to undertake such a radical process of structural reforms was in part the result of the changes that had been implemented from within, fundamentally the displacement of labor from the position it had previously occupied (Gutierrez 2001). Thus, the CGT faced very concrete impediments limiting its ability to influence decision-making, and thus it presented only a very measured resistance to the policies that so clearly undermined labor achievements in the area of working conditions, wages, and protection against unemployment. Nonetheless, there were sectors within the CGT that actually opposed the Menem government and that became increasingly disassociated with its failing project as the decade went on. In this respect, it is worth mentioning the role of Hugo Moyano, the leader of a dissident faction within the CGT. Moyano remained an important oppositional figure against Menem's reform and this stance thus allowed him to regain, in the post-2001 period, some of the political territory the CGT had lost in the previous decade.

The ability of the Menem administration to neutralize labor's mobilization against his reforms solved one of the key challenges all governments since the 1950s had faced. Ultimately, the government could count on the political significance of Peronism for most workers in Argentina. However, political identity is itself a relationship that needs to be nurtured. If the Peronist party had traditionally supported and advanced policies that responded to deeply felt demands for social justice, it was clear that those options were limited during the 1990s. Instead, the party developed new bases of support through the extension of patronage networks that facilitated the party's ties to the most impoverished sectors, to those most affected by growing unemployment and underemployment, and to the self-employed (Levitsky 2005).

Political clientelism encountered a new, fertile space to grow in Argentina in the 1990s given the momentous growth of poverty, the limited scope of democratic practices, and the rather shallow reality of citizenship rights. In fact, these are the conditions that accentuate the unequal distribution of power that are the core of clientelistic relationships, as discussed in chapter 2. While seemingly a relationship of exchange, the link between those with access to state resources (patrons) and the loyalty and votes of those without the right to those resources (clients) is based on domination. But this reality does not always appear as such because the participation of a third agent, the intermediary, masks it. It is to this person that "clients" usually owe their loyalty. The intermediary is the person who knows the difficulties of their lives, and also the person who, like them, identifies with the goals of the political party they all support. One should also think of clientelism as existing in a direct and inverse relationship with citizenship rights: the more consolidated the exercise of rights, the smaller the space available for clientelistic domination (Torres 2002, 50). The mobilization of votes through these clientelistic networks became a fundamental element in securing electoral success for Menem. In fact, the relevance of patronage politics has become central in Argentina from the 1990s onward.

There was an extensive array of publicly funded, specially targeted programs that the party used to build support among the poor, as was particularly the case with programs that provided some relief for those unemployed. The programs were, and have remained, intended to provide some relief to unemployed workers by offering short-term, temporary contracts for community and public works projects. The point, though, is that they also have become crucial in the extension and consolidation of patronage. Sometimes their allocation has been undertaken through organizations of the unemployed and, in this case, the government has been able to gain an important source of power over these organizations.

The ability of the government to neutralize a response from the CGT and to control those sectors most affected by reforms through the development of a clientelistic relationship does not mean that it was able to suppress all opposition. It came as no surprise that the emergence of actors outside the CGT was pivotal in articulating some resistance to the devastating impact of neoliberalism in Argentina. One such actor was the Central of Argentine Workers (CTA) whose growth since its foundation in the early 1990s was mainly the result of its capacity to organize the sectors most affected by restructuring: the unemployed, the underemployed, and the precariously employed.

The other sector that has presented a major challenge to neoliberalism in Argentina was the movement of the unemployed, the *piqueteros*. The *piquetero* movement is composed of numerous smaller organizations. As a result, it was and continues to be a highly heterogeneous movement, marked by sharp political and organizational differences, and divided into factions (Svampa and Pereyra 2003). However, despite these divisions, there has been among *piquetero* members a common set of demands, and similar strategies in the form of protest, particularly the use of roadblocks. Although the *piquetero* movement gained prominence during the mid-1990s and increased its legitimacy as an oppositional force to Menem, some obstacles remained substantial. One clear divide among *piquetero* organizations has been the extent of their relative propensity and degree of willingness to maintain open communication with governments (Epstein 2003, 20–21). The movement also has differences regarding the role to be played by their organizations in the distribution of work programs among their members.

Although only a small proportion of work plans have been distributed through *piquetero* organizations, their role as agents in the implementation of government social policy affected in important ways their own dynamics as political organizations and has given their leadership a new element of power over the rank and file. Moreover, the government has also used its power to allocate work plans through various organizations of the unemployed as a way to discriminate among them. In practice, there has been an added premium to an organization's capacity to maintain a position of dialogue with the government. For instance, the Federation of Land, Housing and Habitat (FTV), the organization of the unemployed connected to the CTA, and the Combative Class Current (CCC), the two *piquetero* organizations more inclined toward negotiations with the government, were selected in 2002 to integrate the national body that advises the government on the implementation and performance of the program (Epstein 2003, 26). Proximity to the government also meant that the FTV and the CCC have been able to capture a proportionally large number of work plans.

The growing economic uncertainties faced by Argentina by the end of the 1990s, the increasing concerns over corruption, and rising awareness over the costs of restructuring provided the opportunity for the Front for a Country in Solidarity (FrePaSo), an alliance of center-left parties, to win the presidential election in 1999. Fernando de la Rúa (1999–2001) became the president under conditions that can only be described as critical. Although his government created expectations for change, the general orientation of economic policy remained unchanged. Moreover, a recession had begun in 1998 and had worsened, along with deepening fears about the future of convertibility. By November 2001, the solvency of the banks was in question. In response, the de la Rúa administration imposed limits on the amount of money people could withdraw from the banks. Although only a small portion of the population was directly affected by this policy, the social implications were devastating.

By mid-December of 2001, as had happened during Alfonsín's presidency, the government faced problems of increased looting and food riots. These mass actions clearly expressed the dissatisfaction that existed in Argentina and the rather broad range of demands against the government. The outcome of the massive uprising during those days was the resignation of de la Rúa. To the cry of "out with all of them," Argentines found, if only for a brief period, the strength to stop a situation that appeared unacceptable to most of them.

Two points are important to note. First, what could have become a major constitutional crisis remained confined to changes in government only. Three successive transitional governments failed to mitigate the crisis, until finally Eduardo Duhalde—the Peronist candidate who had lost the elections to de la Rúa in 1999—was successful in securing sufficient power to fulfill the mandate granted by the legislative assembly to complete de la Rúa's term. Second, although the outpouring of discontent was directed to the whole of the "political class," the Peronist party managed not only to navigate through it but to cement its power as well.

Significant new forms of popular organization emerged during this period, most notably Neighborhood Assemblies. Others, like the organizations of the unemployed, became even more vocal in their demands. Importantly too, the months immediately after the uprising of December 2001 brought these organizations close together in their demand for change. However, the alliance was to be short-lived.

A POST-NEOLIBERAL ARGENTINA? 2003–

The electoral victory of Néstor Kirchner (2003–07) opened a new chapter in Argentina's deeply troubled experience with democracy. Originally elected with only 22 per cent of the total vote, Kirchner managed to increase his popularity at an astonishing pace. Part of his success lay in his ability to interpret demands for change, particularly from within the middle classes. His attack on some of the institutions most connected to Menem's terms in office was a key component of Kirchner's strategy. Central in this respect was the renewal of the composition of the supreme court, in which judges closely connected to Menem were replaced. Another important initiative was Kirchner's new, stronger stance regarding human rights abuses during the last dictatorship; Kirchner requested a congressional annulment of the laws passed at the end of the 1980s that had made it impossible to prosecute many of those responsible for committing the crimes. These reforms have been crucial in responding to long-standing demands from human rights organizations, an influential social movement in Argentina. The presidential position in the renegotiation of Argentina's foreign debt and, more importantly, the decision not to subject the country to the stringent demands of the IMF, were also fundamental in securing political support for his government (Castorina 2009). Thus, as with other leaders riding the so-called Pink Tide, to the eyes of many at the time, Kirchner represented a significant departure from neoliberalism.

The strong economic reactivation Argentina has experienced since 2003 was also a major factor in securing support for the Kirchner administration. While there were some indications of an official questioning of the pattern of economic change under neoliberalism, in practice very little changed in broad economic trends for the country (Svampa 2008). Nonetheless, economic growth provided some relief to those who were unemployed and underemployed. According to official figures, by the last quarter of 2004 unemployment had been reduced to 12.1 per cent of the economically active population, and dropped further to 10.4 per cent in 2006. However, these figures have been calculated, rather controversially, by including as employed Argentines those who participated in government-sponsored employment programs. When beneficiaries of these programs are excluded from the calculations, the unemployment rate rises to 12.8 per cent (Lozano, Rameri, and Raffo 2006, 2). Most of the jobs created during the first few years of economic recovery continued to be contractually precarious or informal (Lozano 2005, 6). The persistently high rates of unemployment and underemployment certainly strengthened the negative conditions under which workers eventually have reentered work. But the lack of decisive initiatives on the part of the government to transform the conditions faced by most workers has also been an important variable. Growing employment and some gains in wages (although this should be taken with caution, given the fact that there is controversy over the way in which inflation is measured) have resulted in a reduction in the levels of poverty. According to official figures, poverty affected 15.3 per cent of the population in 2008, and 4.4 per cent of Argentines were below the line of extreme poverty (*Página 12,* March 21, 2009).

These trends reflect a number of important political and economic changes in Argentina. Yet, a number of variables have remained surprisingly unchanged. In particular, the continuing reliance on clientelism to secure political support and to neutralize the opposition, as well as the impact of anti-poverty policies on the *piquetero* movement have created winners and losers. As a wide range of *piquetero* organizations have faced increasing isolation from other political and social forces, the conflict within the movement has also taken on a new, much more critical dimension. Overall, it is fair to say that the trajectory of the movement of the unemployed in Argentina parallels the experience of many social movements and their rather limited horizon when their practices are connected only weakly to broader political demands or political actors.

The 2007 election of Cristina Kirchner, the wife of Néstor Kirchner and a consummate politician in her own right, has cemented many of these trends. Her ability to capture 45 per cent of the vote provides a good indication of the success of the Peronist party during the presidency of her husband. However, this support has evaporated rapidly. Notwithstanding Cristina Kirchner's progressive discourse regarding redistribution, her policies have not altered the pattern Argentina has followed since the 1990s in any significant way. Moreover, changes of the magnitude required to redress the socioeconomic inequality generated by neoliberalism will be slow in coming, given the depth of the structural transformation Argentina has experienced.

Sustaining economic growth while controlling inflation has been of primary importance for both Néstor and Cristina Kirchner. The revival of corporatist ties with the CGT has been central as part of the strategy of both governments. Thus, the CGT under the leadership of Moyano has repositioned itself effectively in the negotiation of salaries, a place that has given it a new opportunity to strengthen its position as the hegemonic labor sector in the country. While the conditions under which corporatism might still be effective have changed (Collier and Etchemendy 2007), the trajectory of the relationship between the government and the CGT since 2003 indicates that corporatism is still a relevant aspect of the connection between state and labor. In terms of salaries, more concretely, this has meant that wages have registered some improvements since 2002, when they declined by 24 per cent. However, it was only in the second semester of 2006 that they reached a level previously held in 2001, and that year was the lowest since the 1970s. Moreover, salaries in 2006 were still 13 per cent below the level in 1994, the best year for salaries during the 1990s (*Página 12*, April 13, 2009).

The question is whether Cristina Kirchner's intention to address the most pressing socioeconomic inequality inherited from the past can be accomplished without a major redirection of the economy or an important political transformation. The negative response of the agricultural sector, both large and small producers alike, to her intention to increase export taxes might serve as a sobering reminder of the changes in the power structures in Argentina. While democracy might not be at risk, it might only provide, given the existing distribution of power, a very narrow passage to obtaining a more socially just society.

CONCLUSION

Democracy is not a new experience for Argentina. On the contrary, the country can be taken as both a good example and a cautionary tale regarding the perils that can obstruct the full exercise of democratic rights and the use of democracy to respond to the most pressing demands of the population. Democracy has been instrumental in consolidating a pattern of accumulation and distribution of the gains from economic growth that eluded even brutal dictatorships. Since Argentina's transition to democracy post-1983, democratic rights have been strongly influenced by neoliberal economic policies. The growing fragmentation of key political players, labor in particular, explains part of the transformation. However, the transformation of the Peronist party was also fundamental in consolidating a neoliberal democratic state. Argentina's democracy, then, is inextricably linked to the ability of the Peronist party to remain in control, even when to do so has meant reinventing itself in ways that appeared improbable to many.

In turn, this transformation is strongly correlated to the ability of the party to assimilate as clients the population marginalized by the nature of economic growth. The lesson, in terms of the tension between democracy and growing inequality, is that poverty makes people considerably more vulnerable to undemocratic practices and political manipulation. In short, Argentina emphasizes the point raised in chapter 1 that democratic rights can only be exercised in a limited way in societies where economic and social rights are not effective.

There are positive transformations, however, that need to be underlined. Fundamental among them is the growing commitment to the maintenance of democracy. While one can remain doubtful about the ability of democracy, in the limited sense in which it has popularly come to be understood today, to resolve the larger question of equality in society, it is clear that the democratic process is one of the central ingredients in the search for alternatives. This might be the lesson taken by most political forces in Argentina, and it is certainly not a lesson to be dismissed.

NOTES

1 Neka Jara, a member of MTD Solano, interview with author, La Fogata, 2004.
2 Between 1868 and 1914 (at the outbreak of World War I), Argentina grew at an annual average rate of 6.5 per cent. Per capita income was equal to that of Germany and the Low Countries, and was in fact higher than that of Spain, Italy, Sweden, and Switzerland. Buenos Aires was by then the second largest city in the hemisphere, after New York (Rock 1987, 172). By World War II, wages for unskilled urban workers as a measure of their purchasing power were higher in Argentina than in Germany, although they were lower than in the United States and Britain (Waisman 1987, 72).
3 The new Argentine peso replaced the previous currency, the austral, introduced by Alfonsín in 1987. The exchange rate between them was 10,000 australes per $1 peso.

REFERENCES

Ale, Ana. 2001. "Argentina, paraíso bancario." *Le Monde Diplomatique, Southern Cone Edition,* May 23. *El Dipló Julio 1999/Junio 2001.* CD-ROM.

Alonso, Paula. 2000. *Between the Revolution and the Ballot Box: The Origins of the Argentina Radical Party.* Cambridge: Cambridge University Press.

Altamirano, Carlos. 2001. *Bajo el signo de las masas (1943–1973).* Buenos Aires: Ariel.

Beccaria, Luis. 2001. *Empleo e integración social.* Buenos Aires: Fondo de Cultura Económica.

Buchanan, Paul G. 1995. *State, Labor, Capital: Democratizing Class Relations in the Southern Cone.* Pittsburgh: University of Pittsburgh Press.

Calcagno, Alfredo E., and Eric Calcagno. 2000. "La deuda externa, un proyecto politico." *Le Monde Diplomatique, Southern Cone Edition,* June 12. *El Dipló Julio 1999/Junio 2001.* CD-ROM.

Canitrot, Rodolfo. 1981. "Teoría y práctica del liberalismo. Política inflacionaria y apertura económica en la Argentina, 1976–1981." *Desarrollo Económico* 21(82): 131–89.

Castorina, Emilia. 2009. "The Contradictions of Democratic Capitalism in Neo-Liberal Argentina. A New Politics from 'Below?'" Ph.D. dissertation, York University.

Collier, Ruth Berins, and Sebastián Etchemendy. 2007. "Down but Not Out: Union Resurgence and Segmented Neocorporatism in Argentina (2003–2007)." *Politics & Society* 35(3): 363–401.

Damill, Mario, and Roberto Frenkel. 1992. "Malos tiempos: la economía argentina en la década de los ochenta." *Argentina: evolución macroeconómica, financiación externa y cambio político en la década de los 80.* Ed. Roberto Frenkel et al. Madrid: CEDEAL. 1–24.

ECLAC. 2000. *Statistical Yearbook for Latin America and the Caribbean.* Santiago: ECLAC.

———. 2008. *Statistical Yearbook for Latin America and the Caribbean.* Santiago: ECLAC.

Epstein, Edward. 2003. "The Piquetero Movement of Greater Buenos Aires: Working Class Protest During the Current Argentine Crisis." *Canadian Journal of Latin American and Caribbean Studies* 28(55–56): 11–36.

Gutierrez, Ricardo. 2001. "La desindicalización del Peronismo." *Política y Gestión* 2: 93–112.

La Fogata. 2004. "Reportaje A Neka Jara Militante del Movimiento de Desocupados de Solano." January. April 17, 2009. www.solidaridadesrebeldes. kolgados.com.ar/spip.php?article47.

Laclau, Ernesto. 2008. "Demandas sociales e identidades políticas." *Revista de Trabajo* 4(5): 171–79.

Levitsky, Steven. 2005. "Crisis and Renovation: Institutional Weakness and the Transformation of Argentine Peronism, 1983–2003." *Argentine Democracy: The Politics of Institutional Weakness*. Ed. Steven Levitsky and María Victoria Murillo. University Park: Pennsylvania State University Press.

Lozano, Claudio. 2002. *Catástrofe social en Argentina*. Buenos Aires: Instituto de Estudios y Formación de la CTA.

———. 2005. *Los problemas de la distribución en la Argentina actual*. Buenos Aires: Instituto de Estudio y Formación de la CTA.

Lozano, Claudio, A. Rameri, and T. Raffo. 2006. *Seguirá elinando la desocupación? Una mirada sobre la última información del mercado laboral*. Buenos Aires: Instituto de Estudios y Formación de la CTA.

McGuire, James W. 1997. *Peronism without Perón: Unions, Parties and Democracy in Argentina*. Stanford: Stanford University Press.

Murmis, Miguel, and Juan Carlos Portantiero. 1971. *Estudios sobre los orígenes del Peronismo*. Buenos Aires: Siglo Veintiuno.

O'Donnell, Guillermo. 1978. "State and Alliances in Argentina, 1956–1976." *Journal of Development Studies* 15(1): 3–33.

Página 12. 2001. "La Desocupación Alcanzó un Nivel Histórico." Buenos Aires, December 14: 6–7.

———. 2009. "La pobreza del índice de pobreza." Buenos Aires, March 21. April 28, 2010. www.pagina12.com.ar/diario/economia/2-121899-2009-03-21.html.

———. 2009. "Sindicatos Flacos." Buenos Aires, April 13. April 28, 2010. www. pagina12.com.ar/diario/economia/2-123112-2009-04-13.html.

Palermo, Vicente, and Marcos Novaro. 1996. *Política y poder en el gobierno de Menem*. Buenos Aires: Norma.

Rock, David. 1987. *Argentina 1516–1987. From Spanish Colonization to Alfonsín*. Berkeley: University of California Press.

Smith, William C. 1991. *Authoritarianism and the Crisis of the Argentine Political Economy*. Stanford: Stanford University Press.

Svampa, Maristella. 2008. "The End of Kirchnerism." *New Left Review* 53: 79–95.

Svampa, Maristella, and Sebastián Pereyra. 2003. *Entre la ruta y el barrio: La experiencia de las organizaciones piqueteras*. Buenos Aires: Editorial Biblos.

Torre, Juan Carlos. 1990. *La vieja guardia sindical y Perón. Sobre los orígenes del Peronismo*. Buenos Aires: Sudamericana.

Torres, Pablo. 2002. *Votos, chapas y fideos: Clientelismo político y ayuda social*. La Plata: de la Campana.

Waisman, Carlos. 1987. *Reversal of Development in Argentina: Postwar Counterrevolutionary Policies and Their Structural Consequences*. Princeton: Princeton University Press.

E-RESOURCES

Buenos Aires *Herald* (English) (www.buenosairesherald.com). This is a good source of information about current events in Argentina in English.

Central of Argentine Workers (www.agenciacta.org.ar/). An excellent source of information about labor issues in Argentina.

Centre of Legal and Social Studies (CELS) (www.cels.org.ar/home/index.php). A comprehensive source of excellent information about key issues in human rights.

Institute of Social and Economic Development (www.ides.org.ar/index.jsp). A prestigious research institution in Argentina. The site also provides a link to its excellent publication, *Desarrollo Económico*.

Mothers of the Plaza de Mayo (Linea Fundadora) (www.madresfundadoras.org.ar). The website of one of the most important human rights organizations in Argentina. A very good source of information on the subject of the disappeared, with links to other key organizations working in this area.

Movimiento Nacional de Empresas Recuperadas (www.nodo50.org/derechosparatodos/EmpRecu/cont_emp.htm). News and information for those interested in one of the most important alternative movements to emerge out of contemporary Argentina.

Página 12 (www.pagina12.com.ar/diario/ultimas/index.html). One of the major Spanish newspapers in Argentina, with an efficient and easy-to-use archive.

CONCLUSION
What Works and Why

KATHERINE ISBESTER

Democracy has different meanings for different people. For some, it is little more than ticking a box once every few years. For others, it is a means to achieve a morally correct mode of development. Others still think that democracy is a superior mechanism for achieving economic growth because it reduces social conflict, it is cheaper than authoritarianism, and it promotes economic openness. Those with an institutional bent, define democracy as a form of good governance. The electoral success of the Pink Tide movement in Latin America suggests that Latin Americans see democratic governance as growth with equity. In this book, democracy has been defined as an organization of power dispersed through both formal and informal institutions, the state, and civil society. The distribution of power interacts in a mutually reinforcing dynamic with social norms such as (mis)trust and (in)equality that reside in civil society, which can be powerful or weak, autonomous or captured, and with economic structures (local, national, and international). As a result, each nation's democracy is complex, shifting, and unique. While this definition might appear broad, it is useful for analyzing democratic strengths and deficiencies and determining what needs to be done.

With some notable exceptions, the transition to democracy in Latin America has produced minimum democracies within a weak state. Power has not been dispersed through legitimate and legal state institutions, leaving governmental structures unbalanced and inefficient. Civil society remains insufficiently organized and relations between state and civil society are poorly connected. To a degree, power still operates through informal, non-democratic institutions. Partially due to neoliberalism, the state has been unable to achieve autonomy from its economic elite who has become more entrenched in policy-making as well as continuing to dominate the economic sector. As a result, the state lacks capacity, and certain segments of the population suffer accordingly. In addition to not experiencing improvements in their daily living, some citizens are unable to overcome inequalities and the legacy of authoritarianism, and therefore remain almost entirely excluded from the democratic process. Latin America's transition to democracy has not greatly benefited them. This is reflected in a low level of support for democracy in Latin America.

Latin American nations must build on factors that promote democracy: cooperative social norms, social and economic equality, and state capacity. Under the best of circumstances, this challenge would be daunting. Nonetheless, many Latin American nations are meeting it. Participatory democracy, increased use of referenda, and decentralization have brought democracy closer to citizens and created new political actors, parties, and alliances. Social welfare has been extended through state services, and conditional cash transfers (CCTs) have raised the minimum standard of living for the extremely poor. This has narrowed the Gini coefficient, in as much as the floor has been raised. The recognition of ethnicity has produced new political parties and alliances, and new modes of engaging in politics. Constitutional reforms, strengthened state institutions, strengthened legislatures, strengthened human rights, strengthened rule of law, tax reform, and the exposure of corruption have all reinforced democratic processes. The role of a mobilized civil society has been crucial to reforming the mechanisms of deliberative democracy. Globalization and neoliberalism have challenged diverse social sectors, which have responded by mobilizing through new technologies and spaces, both domestically and internationally. These social movements tend to organize themselves horizontally, transparently, and autonomously, with an identity based on an ethos of social justice. Even so, they are capable of focusing on obtaining a specific public policy, a change in government operations, or a state resource. These actions affect governance, mostly for the better.

The country studies in this book show the considerable range of reforms to governance as well as diverse forms of economic, social, and political development. In addition, they illustrate that Latin America is in substantial flux, sometimes to the point of confusion. Are Latin America's democracies deepening or regressing, or both? Or rather, is democracy deepening at the local level while national politics become increasingly authoritarian? It is difficult for most people to draw definitive conclusions. Thus, it would be helpful to determine which states have the greatest capacity, enjoy the most prosperity, and have the highest level of citizen support. Because politics, economics, and society mutually interact, these measurements would then

TABLE 14.1 GROSS NATIONAL INCOME PER CAPITA, 2008 PURCHASING POWER PARITIES

Country	
Chile	13,250.00
Mexico	14,340.00
Argentina	14,000.00
Venezuela	12,850.00
Uruguay	12,550.00
Costa Rica	10,960.00
Brazil	10,080.00
Ecuador	7,780.00
Peru	7,950.00
Colombia	8,430.00
El Salvador	6,630.00
Guatemala	4,690.00
Paraguay	4,660.00
Bolivia	4,140.00
Honduras	3,830.00
Nicaragua	2,620.00
United States	43,967.80
Canada	36,687.00
Sweden	34,056.00

Source: Adapted from World Bank. 2010. *World Development Indicators*. http://siteresources. worldbank.org/DATASTATISTICS/RESOURCES/GNIPC.pdf.

indicate which democracies are the strongest, and which societies are the most sustainable. With that knowledge, policymakers and students would be better placed to judge the validity of each nation's democratized, neo-liberal state. Unsurprisingly, it is almost impossible to measure the quality of a democracy. However, its very complexity allows us to measure related factors, such as levels of violence, trust in public institutions, and economic inequality. In effect, it is possible to measure the symptoms of a democracy's health. Each factor by itself is insufficient to establish meaning, but accumulated, these data point to some truths about a nation's viability. In the tables, the data have been presented to show the best performing nations in descending order.[1]

A strong economy increases political stability and allows the state to direct the benefits of growth to the disenfranchised. Alleviating poverty is not merely a moral good, it is good politics. Democracies with low levels of

TABLE 14.2 HUMAN POVERTY INDEX: PER CENT OF PERSONS LIVING IN POVERTY AND EXTREME POVERTY, 2000-2007

Country	Year	Poverty	Indigence	Year	Poverty	Indigence
Uruguay	2002	15.4	2.5	2007	18.1	3.1
Chile	2000	20.2	5.6	2006	13.7	3.2
Costa Rica	2002	20.3	8.2	2007	18.6	5.3
Brazil	2001	37.5	13.2	2007	30.0	8.5
Mexico	2002	39.4	12.6	2006	31.7	8.7
Argentina	2002	45.4	20.9	2006	21.0	7.2
Venezuela	2002	48.6	22.2	2007	28.5	8.5
El Salvador	2001	48.9	22.1	2004	47.5	19.0
Ecuador	2002	49.0	19.4	2007	38.8	12.4
Colombia	2002	51.5	24.8	2005	46.8	20.2
Peru	2001	54.7	24.4	2007	39.3	13.7
Guatemala	2002	60.2	30.9	2006	54.8	29.1
Paraguay	2001	61.0	33.2	2007	60.5	31.6
Bolivia	2002	62.4	37.1	2007	30.0	8.5
Nicaragua	2001	69.4	42.5	2005	61.9	31.9
Honduras	2002	77.3	54.4	2007	68.9	45.6

Source: Adapted from ECLAC. 2008. *Report: Social Panorama of Latin America*, 2008. www. eclac.org/publications/xml/3/34733/PST_2008-SintesisLanzamiento.pdf.

per capita income are susceptible to violence, coups, military interventions, organized crime, corruption, and authoritarian practices (Collier 2009). The gross domestic product per capita (GDP pc) reflects the ability of a nation's citizens to produce capital. The more restrictions there are on a person to be economically productive and to participate in the marketplace, the lower the GDP pc will be. These restrictions can be overt and even legally sanctioned, such as racism, sexism, and ageism. Restrictions on economic activity can also operate subtly, such as insufficient education and healthcare, inadequate access to credit or public transportation to get to work, or insufficient reward for honest labor. The single most common form of discrimination in Latin America is against the poor (Latinobarómetro 2008). While poverty had been decreasing in Latin America, the number of people living in extreme poverty remains high. As a result of the global economic crisis of 2009, poverty in the region is estimated to have increased from 2008 by 1.1 per cent to 189 million people, and extreme poverty increased 0.8 per cent to 71 million people (ECLAC 2009a). The global recession of 2009 led to Latin America's exports falling by 24 per cent, its economies contracting

TABLE 14.3 PER CENT OF GDP USED FOR SOCIAL EXPENDITURE, 2004–2005

Country	%
Uruguay	22.0
Argentina	19.4
Brazil	18.6
Costa Rica	17.7
Chile	17.5
Bolivia	13.4
Colombia	13.1
Honduras	11.7
Venezuela	11.6
Mexico	10.8
Paraguay	10.2
Nicaragua	8.9
Peru	7.9
El Salvador	6.3
Guatemala	6.3
Ecuador	5.6

Source: Adapted from ECLAC. 2007. *Social Panorama 2007*. www.eclac.org/publicaciones/ xml/9/30309/PSI2007_Sintesis_Lanzamiento.pdf.

1.8 per cent, and GDP pc shrinking by 2.9 per cent. The drop was not as pronounced as had been predicted, because Latin American states acted decisively to counteract the recession by reducing interest rates, increasing state expenditure, and increasing state-owned bank loans. Combined with its macroeconomic stability and better regulated banking systems, it has been predicted Latin America will have a quick recovery, with real GDP increasing 3 per cent in 2010 (ELAC 2009b; ECLAC 2009c; IMF 2009, 85).

Nonetheless, the global crisis continues to affect Latin America in three ways: reduced credit, liquidity, and direct foreign investment (DFI); declining prices and volumes of export commodities both agricultural and manufactured; and declining amounts of remittances. These reductions will almost inevitably reduce the GDP and raise poverty levels in both absolute and relative terms. High-quality, well-paying jobs are not predicted to return quickly to Latin America, making its growth dependent on China's consumption of its raw resources, and low-skill exports. It is likely violence and social distrust of government will rise. This unfortunate reality is the context within which Latin American nations struggle to safeguard and deepen their democracies.

TABLE 14.4 TOTAL TAX BURDEN AS PER CENT OF GDP, 2007

Country	%
Brazil	25.4
Uruguay	24.2
Nicaragua	21.9
Chile	20.2
Bolivia	19.2
Honduras	17.7
Peru	17.2
Argentina	17.2
Venezuela	17.0
Colombia	16.0
Costa Rica	15.3
El Salvador	15.0
Ecuador	14.9
Paraguay	12.9
Guatemala	12.5
Mexico	11.7
Sweden	48.2
Canada	33.3
United States	28.3

Source: Adapted from ECLAC. 2007b. *Social Expenditure Database*. http://website.eclac.d/sisgen/consultaintegrada.asp; and OECD. 2008. *Revenue Statistics 1965–2007*. www.oecd.org/dataoecd/48/27/41498733.pdf.

When the economy is performing well, social services are usually extended to the poor, improving their chances of participating in the marketplace. This assistance tends to strengthen state institutions and, in the long run, increases productivity, lowers social inequality, and increases support for democracy. As Latin America's economies grew, public social spending as a percentage of GDP increased from a regional average of 12.8 per cent in 1990–91 to 15.9 per cent in 2004–05 (ECLAC 2007c). However, the state can only extend social services if it is capable of raising revenue. Tax revenue is too low in Latin America, with only Chile reaching levels that permit the state to meet its objectives. Tax collection is hindered by corruption, inefficiencies, and irregularities. Furthermore, neoliberal ideologies have shifted the tax burden to a consumption tax, which is a regressive approach, and in poor nations it is unlikely to produce amounts

TABLE 14.5 GINI INDEX, 2007

Country	
1 Nicaragua	41
2 Uruguay	43
3 Mexico	45
4 Venezuela	46
5 Peru	48
6 Costa Rica	48
7 Argentina	48
8 El Salvador	52
9 Ecuador	52
10 Honduras	53
11 Chile	53
12 Guatemala	55
13 Brazil	55
14 Paraguay	57
15 Colombia	59
16 Bolivia	60
Sweden	25
Canada	33
United States	41

Note: 2007 Gini Index: A value of 0 represents absolute equality, and a value of 100 represents absolute inequality.
Source: Adapted from CIA, *World Factbook: Distribution of Family Income–Gini Index.* www.cia.gov/library/publications/the-world-factbook/rankorder/2172rank.html.

adequate for the necessary social programs. This is the classic conundrum of development: the state is too poor to invest in developing human capital, leaving people too poor to pay taxes. In Latin America, the regional average of total tax burden as a percentage of the GDP in 2005 was 17 per cent. In comparison, the total tax burden in the US was 28.3 per cent, and in the EU 15, 39.8 per cent (OECD 2008).

It is interesting to note that Brazil, despite its high levels of social spending and taxation, has not performed as well as less developed nations. One of the reasons is Brazil's continuing high level of social and economic inequality, as can be seen in table 14.5. Social and economic inequality reduces economic productivity because it acts as an inhibitor in the marketplace. High levels of social and economic inequality mean that there can

TABLE 14.6 ESTIMATED NUMBER OF HOMICIDES PER 100,000 INHABITANTS, 2005

Country	
Argentina	5.2
Chile	5.8
Costa Rica	7.7
Mexico	10.5
Nicaragua	17.5
Paraguay	17.6
Ecuador	18.4
Brazil	29.2
Venezuela	31.9
Colombia	52.5
Guatemala	58.7
El Salvador	61.3
Bolivia	...
Honduras	...
Peru	...
Uruguay	...
Sweden	1.4
Canada	2.1
United States	6.0

Source: Adapted from Pan American Health Organization, Health Analysis and Statistics Unit. 2007. Regional Core Health Data Initiative; Technical Health Information System. www.paho.org/English/SHA/coredata/tabulator/newsq/Tabulator.asp; and Pan American Health Organization, Health Surveillance and Disease Management Area. Health Statistics and Analysis Unit. PAHO Regional Mortality Database. Rates based on World Population Prospects 2006 Revision 2008.

be widespread poverty despite strong economic growth. The poor have less ability and incentive to participate in the marketplace, reducing the GDP. Furthermore, high levels of inequality erode social norms such as trust and tolerance, which are conducive to democracy. Finally, inequality offers the elite undue access to the corridors of power, hollowing out democratic institutions. The political and economic elite merge, and cronyism trumps transparency. The result is a state that lacks autonomy from its elite, seriously weakening state capacity. Latin America's Gini Index ranges between 41 and 60, with an average of 51. Anything over 40 is considered to be high enough to act as a drag on the economy, with anything over 50 acting as a political destabilizer.

TABLE 14.7 CORRUPTION PERCEPTIONS INDEX, 2008

Country	Rank
Chile	23
Uruguay	23
Costa Rica	47
El Salvador	67
Colombia	70
Peru	72
Mexico	72
Brazil	80
Guatemala	96
Bolivia	102
Argentina	109
Honduras	126
Nicaragua	134
Paraguay	138
Ecuador	151
Venezuela	158
Sweden	1
Canada	9
United States	18

Source: Adapted from Transparency International. 2008. www.transparency.org/
policy_research/surveys_indices/cpi/2008.

With high levels of inequality, there is a greater incentive to participate in the illegal economy. Crimes such as burglary, assault, and rape are
generally not well reported because the justice system is slow, expensive,
and often corrupt, and the rule of law is weak. However, murder tends
to be better reported. The murder rate in Latin America is worryingly
high. It has the highest regional levels of violence in the world, with five
times more violence than anywhere else on the planet. By 2007, concerns
about crime overtook unemployment as the most important problem
for Latin Americans, superseding both inflation and unemployment
(Latinobarómetro 2008).[2] The strength of organized crime in Latin America
reflects the high Gini coefficient, weak state institutions, accepted practices
of corruption, and the neoliberal ideology of deregulation. High levels of
violence erode trust in institutions such as the police and judiciary, and
in democracy itself. The populace of Latin America is seeking order and

TABLE 14.8 HUMAN DEVELOPMENT INDEX (HDI), 2006

Country	Rank
Chile	40
Argentina	46
Uruguay	47
Costa Rica	50
Mexico	51
Venezuela	61
Brazil	70
Ecuador	72
Peru	79
Colombia	80
Paraguay	98
El Salvador	101
Bolivia	111
Honduras	117
Nicaragua	120
Guatemala	121
Canada	3
Sweden	7
United States	15

Source: Adapted from UNDP. 2006. *Human Development Report*. http://hdr.undp.org/en/reports/global/hdr2006.

security, and might be willing to exchange democracy for authoritarianism if it proves more effective at providing them (Seligson 2005). Law and order have been key campaign issues throughout Latin America since approximately 2000.

Clearly, poverty, inequality, and violence are a toxic mixture for democracy and economic development. Despite reforms, their continuing high levels reflect the inability of the state to overcome its historically weak institutions and engrained practices of clientelism, bureaucratic patrimonialism, and corruption. This is shown in table 14.7, which measures perceived levels of public sector corruption based on business and expert surveys. The higher the number, the greater the perceived corruption is. Chile is the best performing nation in Latin America on this index, but Sweden outperforms all other nations in the world. High corruption levels erode

TABLE 14.9 BERTELSMANN TRANSFORMATION INDEX (BTI), 2008

Country	
Chile	8
Uruguay	9
Costa Rica	12
Brazil	20
Argentina	26
Mexico	28
El Salvador	34
Peru	38
Colombia	46
Paraguay	52
Honduras	53
Nicaragua	54
Bolivia	64
Ecuador	64
Guatemala	71
Venezuela	79

Source: Adapted from Bertelsmann Transformation Index. 2008. bertelsmann-transformation-index.de/fileadmin/pdf/Anlagen_BTI_2008/BTI_2008_Ranking_EN.pdf.

the caliber of state institutions, democratic norms and processes, economic productivity, and equality. This erosion further undermines democracy.

Two databases collect key indicators to create a composite picture of development. The Human Development Index attempts to show how economic development and state policy interact to expand possibilities for citizens to lead more fulfilling and productive lives. One of the most ambitious and influential databases, it integrates gender equity, literacy, health, and GDP pc to indicate general levels of well-being. The Bertelsmann Transformation Index ranks the polity's ability to solve social and economic problems and thereby produce good governance. The lower the number, the better the governance. So Chile's government and its political leaders, for example, performed better than Uruguay's. Because Latin Americans link democracy to improvements in the daily lives of citizens (Camp 2001), these final two indices are linked to citizens' support for democracy.

TABLE 14.10 PER CENT OF THE POPULATION THAT SUPPORTS DEMOCRACY, 2008

Country	%
Venezuela	82
Uruguay	79
Bolivia	68
Costa Rica	67
Colombia	62
Argentina	60
Nicaragua	58
Ecuador	56
Paraguay	53
Chile	51
El Salvador	50
Brazil	47
Peru	45
Honduras	44
Mexico	43
Guatemala	34

Question: With which of the following statements do you agree with most? Democracy is preferable to any other kind of government; an authoritarian government can be preferable to a democratic one; for people like me, it doesn't matter whether we have a democratic or non-democratic regime.

Source: Adapted from Latinobarómetro. 2008. www.latinobarometro.org/informe_LATINOBAROMETRO_2008.pdf.

WHAT WORKS WELL

There are four countries that are consistently at or near the top of these (and many other) databases. The democracies of Chile, Costa Rica, Venezuela, and Uruguay outperform other Latin American nations time and time again, with higher levels of economic growth and social spending, lower levels of poverty and inequality, better respected and more transparent public institutions, and more opportunities for human development. Unsurprisingly, these countries all enjoy considerable domestic support for their democracies. Internationally, only one country is celebrated for this achievement (Chile), one country has been vilified for its public policies (Venezuela), and the other two have been almost completely ignored (Costa Rica and Uruguay).

These four countries share some common factors. All of them are middle income countries, with even Costa Rica (the poorest of the four) having a GDP pc of almost $11,000 per annum. All the countries have achieved a strong state. Centano (2002) examined the histories of Latin American states in the nineteenth century and concluded that Chile uniquely developed a strong state with professional institutions. Costa Rica developed a strong state with the capacity to negotiate between relatively balanced class interests. Uruguay translated its traditional feudal values of corporatism into a strong state, and then instituted democratic processes in the nineteenth century. Uruguay also had an autonomous and well-organized union movement that pushed for the extension of social services and the development of human capital through state expenditure. This further strengthened the state. Venezuela developed a strong state to exploit its natural resource of petroleum, and then centralized power through the 1958 Punto Fijo Pact. These strong states developed human capital, intervened in the economy to redistribute wealth, and negotiated with the forces of globalization to offset the risks associated with a liberalized economy. This can be seen in the social indices of these countries.

As the Bertelsmann Transformation Index shows, Costa Rica, Uruguay, and Chile all have states with competent and embedded bureaucracies. They have strong party systems that facilitate democratic governance, an executive that must work with the legislative assembly, and the rule of law. In other words, the mechanisms that facilitate deliberative democracy, economic efficiency, transparency, and accountability all work to a large degree.

Both Uruguay and Costa Rica had visionary leaders who were able to create the initial momentum for a strong state based on democracy and social justice. The vision of these men, José Batille y Ordóñez (1903–07; 1911–15) of Uruguay and José Figueres (1953–58) of Costa Rica are still evoked today as powerful national myths.[3] Chile's center-left coalition, which was in power after Pinochet's departure in 1990 until early 2010, explicitly uses the language of social justice, as does its recently elected conservative president, Sebastián Piñera. Venezuela's powerful Social Democratic Party came to power in 1945, and shaped mass expectations for socioeconomic justice. Hugo Chávez's redistributive policies are merely the most recent version of this twentieth-century long demand. These democracies have an ethical content that shapes the creation of public policies, and legitimizes critiques of injustice. This ethical content can be seen in the broad social consensus to improve equality and justice through high levels of education, healthcare, and pensions. Costa Rica in particular is the only Latin American country to have a universalist approach to social spending, while Chile is approaching it with pensions (Filgueira 2007).

These four countries also share some factors that are seemingly irrelevant on the surface but which in fact assist in deepening a democracy. Comparatively speaking, they are small. Uruguay is the smallest nation in South America, while Costa Rica and Chile are not much larger. They have relatively homogenous ethnic populations sharing the same faith. Despite the prevalence of neoliberalism, there is a surprisingly high degree of continuity in social care programs. They have long and proud traditions of democracy, despite past interruptions caused by dictatorships. These factors typically facilitate democracy, that is, dense civil society, social norms of trust and equality, and a political culture of social justice. It is more challenging for larger federalized nations with diverse ethnic populations and entrenched informal authoritarianism to create the same underlying social and political practices.

These four countries call into question neoliberalism as a development strategy. All of them are enthusiastic exporters. But they use a range of approaches to neoliberalism. Uruguay implemented mild neoliberalism, but rejected key measures in plebiscites. Venezuela emphatically and bombastically rejected it. Chile embraced it. And Costa Rica performed a complicated dance to engage with it on terms beneficial to its own people. Chile and Costa Rica have strong economic sectors that required market innovation brokered by state intervention. Chile exported its service industry to other Southern Cone countries and developed medium-sized producers in its agricultural sector to absorb surplus labor, while Costa Rica created ecotourism and high-tech industry as its primary exports, predominantly meant for the American market. Thus, economic strategy is not what these countries have in common. What they do have in common is an important export sector in their economies, a strong state able to act with capacity, quality institutions, human capital, democratic norms, and an ethos of social justice. These four countries offer a lesson in the importance of political institutions, political culture, and political economy.

Nonetheless, these nations have their own challenges. As the chapter by Teichman in this book shows, Chile's high Gini coefficient has proved to be politically destablizing, as the Concertación was unable to decide how to deal with the unequal distribution of wealth. Chile's former leftish governing coalition split over policies that would have facilitated the redistribution of income and encouraged civil society participation in policy-making. Social expenditure cannot be expanded unless there is an increase in government revenue, which the business class and the elite vigorously opposed. Furthermore, labor claims that unless laws regarding its "flexibility" are changed, equity cannot be achieved, a demand which both business and the government again resisted. However, as the coalition weakened and redistribution threatened the status quo, civil society participation also increased protests and social unrest. It is possible that the fragile agreement that has allowed Chile to reestablish and deepen its democracy may not thrive due to the inherent contradictions of democracy and inequality.

The drawback of being a country as small as Costa Rica is the prevalence of the same families leading the nation over decades, or even generations. Inevitably, this small political and economic elite has fed cronyism and corruption, alienating citizens from their government. Neoliberalism in general and DR-CAFTA in particular were supported by all the major political parties, including the reformist parties, highlighting how limited democratic options were. This was again evident in its February 2010 election. Costa Ricans elected Laura Chinchilla from the National Liberation Party (PLN) as president. Chinchilla was handpicked by the outgoing president, Oscar Arias, and had served as his minister of justice and vice president. She campaigned on the issues of law and order, export-based free trade (especially with China), and honesty, with a heavy emphasis on fighting crime and corruption. Her opposition was the right-wing newcomer Otto Guevara, who had a remarkably similar campaign but whose major attraction was his lack of political experience. He won 21 per cent of the vote. On the left was Ottón Solís, whose qualified support for DR-CAFTA hardened during the election campaign. He won 25 per cent of the popular vote. Solís may have missed his opportunity to make a powerful political impact. He has been in politics long enough to be tainted by the status quo, but offers nothing new to attract disaffected PLN voters (Malkin 2010; Inside Costa Rica 2010). Furthermore, after a three-year study of nations' compliance with DR-CAFTA's labor and environmental rights, Costa Rica emerged as the only country within DR-CAFTA meeting its agreements. Under the PLN, Costa Rica has increased its labor standards, improved gender training, reduced child labor, created a new small claims labor court, trained labor justice agents, and offered new positions for judges and judicial assistants (WOLA 2009).[4] These reforms have softened the organizing impetus of the anti-DR-CAFTA movement. Nonetheless, with widening economic inequality and an alienated citizenry, the elite must engage with the increasingly organized and confrontational civil society, and broaden political inclusiveness in order to maintain Costa Rica's democracy.

WHAT BARELY WORKS

Most of the rest of the countries in Latin America are middle income, with democracies that more or less function in recognizable structures. The exceptions are discussed below. Performing better than the majority are the big countries of Brazil, Argentina, and Mexico, which are sometimes at or near the top of the data tables. Justifiably, other Latin American nations and foreign governments, institutions, and business sectors watch them more carefully than the smaller nations of Latin America. These "giants" of Latin America have federal governments, ethnic divisions (with the exception of Argentina), and rural poverty. They all have substantial natural resources, excellent track records for niche economic development, and for improving economic infrastructure. These countries have all produced powerful Pink Tide reform movements that captured power in Brazil and Argentina, and came close to doing so in Mexico. Yet their rankings in the databases are unpredictable, a hodgepodge of successes, mediocrities, and failures. Brazil, Argentina, and Mexico have all reduced poverty, and are close to the top performing Latin American nations on the Bertelsmann Index of successful polity organization. Yet they do not perform well on Transparency International's corruption index. They have lower levels of support for their democracies, lower levels of annual increases in GDP, and lower levels on the Human Development Index than the best four performing nations in Latin America. If these giants of Latin America can reform their weaknesses to improve their rankings, then the ability of smaller nations to reform themselves should be greatly enhanced.

Brazil is the single best advertisement for Pink Tide reforms. Consequently, it is advisable to look closely at Brazil to understand the limits of the movement. As Phillips pointed out in chapter 10, almost uniquely in Latin America, Brazil has been able to lower its Gini coefficient, maintain its macroeconomic stability during the global recession, and innovate politically to deepen democracy. As a result, President Luiz Inácio Lula da Silva (2003–10) has been able to maintain his credentials as a reformer while not alienating the elite. However, Lula's successes must be understood in context. The Worker's Party of Brazil is better disciplined than most Latin American political parties, Lula is a charismatic leader able to maintain a broad alliance, and he inherited a stable, well-functioning economy. Brazil's economic stability has been partially due to the reality that, even in a global recession, China has maintained high production levels and needed Brazil's abundant natural resources. As a result, Brazil has had only one fiscal quarter of recession. That meant that Brazilians (both citizens and elected representatives) never had to make hard decisions about how to distribute resources if the economy had continued to shrink from one fiscal quarter to the next. Redistribution by definition means that some will gain and others will lose. In Brazil, everyone has gained and no one has lost. This situation is possible only in a growing economy. It suggests that there is no consensus about the reality of redistribution; the societal commitment to equity is shallow. So if the country experiences a prolonged economic downturn, the gains the poor have made could easily be erased.

Furthermore, Lula's success at deepening democracy was in the sectors of the polity where there were no entrenched economic or political interests. Therefore, his reforms did not alter the existing organization of power in Brazil. Instead, Lula has been repetitively unsuccessful in reforming the constitution or confronting the Brazilian elite. As a result, the Brazilian state still lacks the capacity to overcome its divisions. But its successes outweigh the limitations on its reforms. Unsurprisingly, other countries wish to emulate it. However, the possibility that other countries can achieve reform the way Brazil has is unlikely. For example, the newly elected president of El Salvador, Mauricio Funes, explicitly seeks to emulate Lula's successes, but El Salvador lacks the resource base to produce such a vibrant and diversified economy. Its economic growth is based on the *maquilas* exports to the United States, which have a declining share of the US market. To get elected, Funes distanced himself from the left coalition opposition, splitting the party. In addition to lacking a disciplined political party base, Funes himself lacks the experienced leadership of Lula. El Salvador also has high levels of social distrust and violence, which undermine civil society, and it is much poorer, which weakens the viability of its democracy. This does not mean that Funes cannot achieve some reforms, but rather that the likelihood of success similar to Brazil's is low.

To resolve the demands for social justice, Latin American states have embraced conditional cash transfer (CCT) programs. CCT programs do not redistribute wealth from the rich to the poor, nor were they intended to do so, which is why they enjoy such broad domestic and international support. These programs have been paid for in part by removing subsidies from public transportation, basic foodstuffs, and utilities that have kept the working class from sliding into poverty. So the redistribution of wealth has been from the working poor to the extreme poor. CCT programs have been criticized for offering unequal access to social services or social protection like labor rights, for shifting governmental priorities from reform to elevating the living standards of the extremely poor, and for removing civil society participation in top-down policy-making (Teichman 2008). Another strategy to resolve conflict over the distribution of wealth is to renovate clientelistic practices, analyzed most clearly in Patroni's chapter above. At their most sophisticated, these non-democratic practices operate through civil society organizations (Argentina), government-sponsored social movements (Mexico), fiscal and political decentralization (Brazil), or participatory state agencies (Nicaragua). More crudely, they operate through *caudillismo*. Regardless of the mechanism, clientelism has become embedded within democratic governance.

Compromises to improve democratic governance and promote economic growth are an attempt to resolve one of democracy's contradictions:

a political system based on equality and freedom, with an economic system based on inequality. To genuinely improve democratic governance and improve economic growth, there has to be a new societal consensus to extend the state, combined with a redistributive tax policy, and increased wages (Teichman 2008). However, a societal redistributive consensus must be mediated and implemented by transparent, efficient, and accountable state institutions, and it must be supported by strong economic growth. A societal redistributive consensus under these circumstances might well reduce socioeconomic inequality, build human capital, and develop a political culture of trust and tolerance. These would strengthen civil society and state capacity, and deepen democracy, producing greater economic growth. However, such an extensive societal redistributive consensus seems unlikely at the moment.

A more likely "best case scenario" for the Pink Tide nations is Chile or Costa Rica. Gradualism, accommodation, a social justice ethos, and a strong state have combined to create something of a societal redistributive consensus, or more accurately, a series of hard-fought, heavily negotiated, short-term, modest redistributive compromises. The possibility of Brazil joining that list is high. However, this book's analyses of the weaknesses of Latin America's success stories suggest that this "best case scenario" may have been oversold. Instead, citizens of some Latin American nations have opted for a profound reworking of the state, the economy, and the polity.

WHAT MIGHT WORK

If any countries in Latin America could be said to have a societal redistributive consensus to increase taxation on those most able to pay, to extend state services, increase wages, restructure the organization of the polity to better represent the disenfranchised, negotiate strongly with the forces of globalization to benefit their own citizens, and build a more active civil society, it is the two Andean countries of Bolivia and Venezuela.[5] The governments of both nations also make explicit their intents to rupture with the past, and base their new mode of governance on an identity of ethnicity and social justice. They are probably the most unstable countries in Latin America at the moment. As a result, it is difficult to make persuasive assessments of their development trajectories, although Rice attempts to in her chapters in this book.

Hugo Chávez (1999–), the head of the Bolivarian Revolution Party of Venezuela, has been in power longer than Evo Morales (2006–) of the Movement for Socialism (MAS) in Bolivia. Both leaders came to power riding a wave of mass mobilization. In weak states with minimum democracies, mass mobilization around a single issue becomes a powerful political force. Without strong political parties grounded in the grassroots, mobilization has been organized through identity-based, autonomous social movements. The political might of mass social movements is obvious in Bolivia's Cochabamba water wars where a broad alliance of interests organized through social movements stopped the privatization of water distribution. Now, political parties align themselves with social movements in order to win elections. Social movements also align themselves temporarily with a political party or leader to publicize their causes or influence public policy (Stahler-Sholk, Vanden, and Kuecker 2007, 8–11). On the one hand this is an excellent approach because these movements are based in civil society, are autonomous from the clientelistic practices of the state, typically involve the disenfranchised, and insist on deep reforms. On the other hand, these mass mobilizations are less capable of forging new public policies. This is because it is easier to unite to halt change than to develop an agreement on how, in policy detail, the country should move forward. Furthermore, state institutions are weak and cannot adequately respond to increased public participation. Deliberative democracy is based on compromise and competition in which losers are those who do not win as much, and power is dispersed through institutions. Mass mobilization is extremely difficult to integrate into a deliberative democracy, because mass mobilization is prone to black-or-white, winners-or-losers attitudes. Mass mobilization is so powerful that it overrides any dispersion of power and concentrates it in the phenomenon of the uprising. As a result, it is difficult to mediate conflict through institutionalized negotiation and accommodation. In the long run, mass mobilization can erode democratic norms and procedures, as well as democratic institutions.

In Bolivia, for example, Morales, the head of a political party cum social movement, gained support on a congruence of factors: ethnic identity, resistance to neoliberalism (inequality of wealth and power, and privatization), and Bolivia's minimum democracy with its ineffectual institutions, captured state, and fragmented political parties. The first two factors had produced substantial social movement mobilizations. Now, Morales must reorganize relations of power at a fundamental level to meet the expectations of those who elected him. If he depends too much on powerful discourses like neoliberalism, or negotiates with the US and bends to their hostility to coca production, then he loses the support of his social movements and he will fall from power. But if he transforms too many accepted economic practices too quickly, then he loses political stability, direct foreign investment, and international competitiveness. If he reorganizes political structures to benefit the ethnically disenfranchised, then the white elite can resist on the basis of discrimination. In fact, during the 2007 constitutional rewriting to improve representation of Bolivia's ethnic majority, the right was able to capitalize on just that emotive point, while exploiting divisions within social movements and boycotting legislative sessions. Doing democratic politics with powerful social movements and a non-democratic opposition means that his own people could mistake compromise for co-optation, and the opposition could mistake necessary reforms for radicalism. This is zero-sum politics, and it is inherently unsustainable for a democracy.

A common solution for resolving this problem, in the short term, is populism. Populism is resurfacing in Venezuela as well as among other political systems dependent on mass mobilization to secure power and reforms, such as in Nicaragua. By aligning themselves with "the people" and creating a generalized sense of injustice which the leader then promises to rectify, populism and mass movements are overriding democratic institutions and processes. It is ironic that those countries with powerful social movements shaping reformist political initiatives (normally integral to a democracy) are now tilting the political dynamic toward non-democratic processes. It is a measure of the kind of leader that Morales is that he has so far resisted populism and instead has attempted to deepen democracy.

Initially, Chávez also resisted populism. From the beginning, he opposed efforts by the elite to include him in existing and new business contracts and political systems. Whereas Venezuela's Punto Fijo pact created a corporatist state that balanced the interests of organized labor and businesses through subsidies and clientelism, Chávez's state initially focused on the informal workers and the poor, who were not well-organized and did not participate in mass mobilizations. However, his actions did create broad popular support. Through utilizing this support and the military, Chávez has been able to confront the elite and strip them of their economic and political power base. Clientelistic relationships with corrupt trade unions and political parties were broken. Taxes and royalties on the petroleum industry have risen from 15 per cent to 33 per cent. State ownership of the oil reserves and state majority ownership of any joint public–private partnership effectively nationalized control over core industries, utilities, and telecommunications. This improved Venezuela's budgetary resources—along with the rise in global oil prices—strengthening Chávez's reforms. Rural infrastructure, such as transportation networks, has been built. Agrarian reform programs redistributed land in an effort to increase food production, and stop urban sprawl and food importation. The poverty rate has gone down dramatically in Venezuela, falling 18.5 per cent between 2002 and 2006, with extreme poverty dropping 12.3 per cent (ECLAC 2007a). Citizen participation has risen equally dramatically. There is a strong commitment to social justice within the bureaucracy, which shapes government policy. By pushing for referenda and demanding democratic accountability, the right have inadvertently legitimated Chávez's governance. By 2005, supporters of Chávez controlled the legislature, 20 out of 24 regional governors, and the majority of local governments (Buxton 2009).

Nonetheless, serious problems remain with Chávez's alternative approach to economic and political organizing. First, despite the rhetoric, Chávez has not fundamentally transformed Venezuela's macroeconomics. It remains dependent on commodity exports, with an increasing reliance on oil. Yet Chávez has underinvested in the petroleum industry, reducing its productive capacity. This leaves Venezuela vulnerable to global downturns and fluctuations in commodity prices. With the startling drop in the price of oil in 2008–09, it is unclear if Chávez can continue to meet his social and economic promises, and thereby maintain his popular bases of support. Between 2008 and 2009, Venezuela reduced its foreign expenditures from $79 billion to $6 billion (Romero 2009), presumably to safeguard its domestic programs.

Second, the great success of Chávez has been the improvement of social indices. But the quality of Venezuelan missions (social programs) is low and uneven. The administration may be well-meaning but its employees lack professional expertise, there is little continuity as staff turnover is high, and institutional support remains weak. As a result, there is minimal development of a genuine embedded bureaucracy with institutional excellence. Although missions are increasingly politicized, they lack a theoretical explanation of what constitutes Bolivarianism or *chavismo*. Some community mobilizations verge on self-government, while others impose programs from the top down. There are greater and lesser degrees of participatory democracy. In theory, this range is not a problem; different communities organize and mobilize themselves in different ways. In reality however, it creates confusion, competition, and inefficiencies in supplying government resources. This is the moral content of Chávez's attempt to create a different democracy. A strong understanding of what constitutes the new order would integrate fragmented social justice efforts and disparate community mobilizations. Without a good understanding of why and how *chavismo* operates, and without *chavismo* being better implemented through high-quality state institutions, it becomes easier to erase social justice policies, and indeed democracy itself.

Third, Chávez's democratic governance has increasingly bypassed or politicized democratic institutions and processes, and cultivated the president as a supreme leader. Those critical of Chávez or his policies are almost always removed from legitimate positions of authority, including judges, lawyers, military leaders, bureaucrats, businessmen within the state-owned petroleum company, and community leaders involved with missions. Since winning the 2007 election, Chávez has increasingly ruled by decree and has attempted to extend his term in office semi-indefinitely through constitutional reform, although that effort was narrowly defeated at a referendum in December 2007. Chávez's increasing authoritarianism has alienated moderate members of his own party and raised the profile of extremist members. This has given the opposition more ammunition to criticize Chávez. The dynamic has heightened Venezuela's political polarization and its zero-sum approach to democracy. Chávez has replaced a restricted corporatist democracy with adversarial populism. Democratic politics in Venezuela has become more than competitive; it has slid instead into zero-sum combativeness. That ensures that every win is a triumph wholly for one side and a complete loss for the other; compromises to secure political stability, build economic productivity, and deepen democracy are understood only as a loss to both sides. No democracy can sustain a zero-sum organization of power.

Compounding Chávez's tendency toward autocracy is the Venezuelan opposition. Normally, this is the political and economic elite. However, Chávez has polarized so many sectors of Venezuela that it also includes the Catholic Church, organized labor unions, and the media.[6] These groups along with the business sector and the Socialist Democratic Party had benefited from the Punto Fijo Pact and are now a powerful alliance spanning socioeconomic classes. Nonetheless, this opposition has demonstrated its lack of commitment to democracy by endorsing coups, subversion, and other anti-democratic practices. As a result, the right has lost its legitimacy as a democratic alternative to Chávez. The 1979 Nicaraguan Revolution and the following 11 years of revolutionary government demonstrated the difficulty of accommodating a hostile elite. In Nicaragua, the elite was already split, the economy was mixed (for a socialist party in the 1970s), and the revolutionary government negotiated generous, if secretive, deals with individual families to entice them to participate in the new order. These efforts were only partially successful. Given that in Venezuela the elite has already attempted a coup (2002), and in Bolivia the elite is threatening to secede from the state, neither country can claim even the success of the revolutionary government of Nicaragua in the 1980s. The elites in these countries are receiving financial and logistical support from the US, both from the National Endowment for Democracy (NED) and USAID. It would be naïve to assume that assistance is limited to NED and USAID, as the history of US support for opposition to governments it considers hostile includes private funding, both legal and illegal. Counterproductively, the extent of US hostility to the Bolivarian Revolution and the range of support it has extended to the opposition has legitimated Chávez's increasing control over the polity.

The best hope for the populace of both Venezuela and Bolivia is that the US will remain preoccupied with other global issues. US President George

W. Bush's (2000–08) aggressive policy, "either you're for us or against us" granted Chávez a regional legitimacy he might not have otherwise been able to garner. Fortunately, Bush was focused on two wars and an economic crisis, permitting Chávez to operate with minimal foreign interference, comparatively speaking. However, the new American President Barack Obama (2008–) promises to change his nation's foreign policy to one of inclusion, which would undermine Chávez's legitimacy and his confrontational stance. But unless the global economic crisis is rapidly resolved, failed states reworked, and the two wars are ended, Obama's focus will likely not extend to Chávez. Instead, it is possible that the Venezuelan right will then be forced to mobilize politically and will insist on being included in the democratic political process. Through using democratic mechanisms, the opposition can deepen accountability and transparency, improve bureaucratic efficiency, and offer real alternatives (which it does not have at the moment). Some of the social justice missions are so popular that Venezuela's right are now promising to continue them if elected. If *chavismo* can be clearly articulated, if Venezuela's governments can be democratically elected, and if social justice policies can be maintained through the economic downturn regardless of who is in power, then Chávez will have created a genuine alternative to Latin America's neoliberal democracies. Like the success of Lula in Brazil, Venezuela's path will then be more persuasive to other countries seeking an alternative means to development.

WHAT DOES NOT WORK

While Latin America and the rest of the world have been distracted by the politics in the Andean countries or the Middle East, democratization in other countries has regressed without notice. The Central American nations of El Salvador, Guatemala, Honduras, and Nicaragua perform the worst in most databases most of the time. Some have called this narrow strip of land that joins the Americas "the blood-soaked isthmus" because of its history of near continuous oppression, bloodshed, and civil strife. This has engendered social relations of mistrust and hostility, as well as social polarization, normalizing questions such as "What did you do during the war?" These nations are among the poorest in Latin America, with high levels of extreme poverty.

Guatemala, El Salvador, and Honduras (along with Nicaragua to a lesser extent) have a problem with powerful youth gangs that seriously erode public trust, public safety, and the rule of law. El Salvador has the dubious distinction of being the country with the highest murder rate in Latin America. This widespread violence, entwined with poverty and weak democratic governance, has led to low levels of support for democracy in these nations, with Guatemala having the lowest support for democracy in Latin America at 34 per cent of the population. In Honduras, Nicaragua, El Salvador, and Guatemala, between 59 and 63 per cent of the population preferred an authoritarian government if it solved economic problems. Only Paraguay had a higher percentage of its population (69 per cent) agreeing with that statement. In comparison, Uruguay had 31 per cent (Latinobarómetro 2008).

El Salvador, Nicaragua, and Guatemala all had high levels of foreign intervention to achieve domestic peace. Honduras had such high levels of American support during the 1980s and 1990s that it might be said foreign intervention maintained its peace. Foreign intervention by the UN was celebrated in the case of Guatemala, criticized when it was led by the US in El Salvador, ignored in Honduras, and drew a surprisingly large number of countries and institutions into Nicaragua, including the US, Norway, and the OAS. The result of extensive foreign intervention was the formation of elite pacts that did not offer any of the advantages of elite pacts. These pacts usually reduce political uncertainty by making the role of political actors clear, such as the military and organized labor. They reduce competition by creating governmental structures that narrow access to the corridors of power. Therefore, elite pacts create political stability and mechanisms for resolving conflicts and tensions, even if they do not create an inclusive and deliberative democracy. In Central America, however, the extent of foreign intervention created elite pacts contingent on their continued presence. Once the diplomats returned home, the elite pacts were once again open to debate. This has produced ongoing uncertainty about the role of the state and other political actors, and the basic organization of the polity. Civil society has augmented that dynamic through ongoing civil strife and social unrest. This lack of social and political stability has hindered economic development, which also contributed to political instability. As a result, democratization has become an unresolved intra-elite battle for the control of the state. Those who capture it use it for their own purposes. Through corruption, clientelism, and bureaucratic patrimonialism, the neoliberal democratized states in Central America have enhanced the personal fortunes of the elite, and substantially weakened democratic processes, norms, and institutions.

The clearest example of the extent to which democracy has regressed in Central America was the June 28, 2009, military coup d'état of the democratically elected government of Honduras. The coup demonstrated, in rather stark terms, the failures of democratized neoliberalism in Latin America. José Manuel Zelaya of the Liberal Party was elected in 2006, carrying 62 of the 128 congressional seats, just short of a majority. It is important to note that only 55 per cent of eligible voters cast a ballot, suggesting that the populace saw elections as having little relevance. Zelaya, a wealthy member of the Honduran elite, ran a more progressive campaign than his competitor but was not considered to be a Pink Tide reformer. However by 2008, Zelaya began to make progressive changes to public policy. He reinstated benefits to teachers that had been cut by the previous administration. He increased the labor ministry's budget and trained inspectors to ensure the *maquilas* were abiding by labor standards. He increased the minimum wage by 60 per cent and made connections with peasant groups and organized labor. He used fiery rhetoric to call for social justice and deep reforms in favor of the poor. To overcome the conservative-controlled media, he created his own media sources and manipulated them to serve his needs. In 2008, he signed onto ALBA, the Chávez-initiated alternative banking and trade group, in addition to making supportive statements about Chávez. In exchange, Venezuela sent oil at a discounted price to Honduras, helping to resolve the country's energy needs. Yet in 2008 Zelaya refused to submit the budget to the congress for approval, saying that it was impossible given the global financial crisis. Ironically, he doubled the military's budget, presumably on the assumption that this would buy their loyalty. In 2009, Zelaya insisted that the Honduran constitution needed to be reformed to improve governance. Few would disagree. However, some articles in the constitution cannot be legally reformed, since they exist in perpetuity. Other clauses need two-thirds of the congress to agree to the changes. The assumption was that Zelaya would reform presidential term limits so that he could be reelected. It was so widely broadcast that the notion became a publicly held truth. In fact, Zelaya made no statement of that intent, although it would require considerable naivety to discount that possibility.[7] Nonetheless, the Honduran congress refused to open the negotiations to reform the constitution. In response, Zelaya organized a public non-binding plebiscite about whether or not the constitution should be reformed, with negotiations held in a specially convened constituent assembly. The supreme court upheld a lower court injunction against the referendum, which Zelaya ignored. On the same day the referendum was to be held, the supreme court issued a warrant for his arrest. The military invaded the presidential palace, arrested Zelaya, and flew him out of the country. Speaker of the congress, Roberto Micheletti, was appointed as acting president.

The US and most nations of Latin America said that they would not recognize Micheletti's government. The US cut its aid, and suspended visas for coup leaders. The OAS suspended Honduras. The UN General Assembly condemned the coup. The World Bank said it would "pause" its lending program to the nation. Other countries in Central America suspended trading with Honduras for 48 hours. Extensive international diplomacy to reinstate Zelaya failed. However, no trade blockade was placed on Honduras, and the US did not recall its ambassador. Meanwhile, the government of Micheletti issued a decree establishing a 45-day state of emergency, suspending guarantees of freedom of expression, freedom of movement, and freedom of assembly. According to the September 2009 Inter-American Commission on Human Rights, during this state of emergency, the military and police systemically violated human rights, used excessive force, including sexual violence and arbitrary detention, and committed several murders and "disappearances." The real number of casualties is currently impossible to obtain. This was a futile effort to stop the sustained mass public protests against the coup.

Negotiations finally obtained the agreement that Zelaya would remain in exile for the rest of his life, and that the November 2009 presidential and congressional election would go forward. It was deemed by international adjudicators to be clean. Less than half of the populace voted. Porfirio Lobo of the conservative National Party was elected with a clear majority over the Liberal Party candidate. While the US, EU, and the Latin American nations of Colombia, Costa Rica, Peru, and Panama have recognized the new government, MERCOSUR nations have not.

The coup in Honduras demonstrates some truths about the democratization of Latin America. First, Honduras was not much of a democracy. There was institutional weakness within the government so that the system could not legally reform itself. The institutional framework could not mediate conflict, reach compromises, or accommodate reformist measures. As a result, Zelaya went outside the system for the political legitimacy to enact change. This violated the rule of law, such as it was. The Honduras elite then acted non-democratically to reinstate its democracy, such as it was. The military, which had voluntarily retreated to the barracks with democratization, reemerged as the decisive political decider. The caliber of Honduras's democracy and the implications of its failure suggest that the popular understanding of what constitutes a democracy needs to be more rigorous.

Second, there is no such thing as a consolidated democracy. Zelaya was the fifth democratically elected leader of Honduras after its transition to democracy, suggesting that democratic changes of governments should have been normalized. But the sustainability of a democracy usually depends on its economy. Honduras is one of the poorest nations in the hemisphere, with a purchasing power parity per capita income of $3,830 in 2008 (World Bank 2010). Przeworski et al. (2000) showed that democracy can be all but ensured once per capita income hits $6,500. Due to its poverty, Honduras's democracy was always vulnerable. The only mechanism through which a poor democratic country can escape the destabilizing stress of poverty is through institutionalizing socioeconomic equality in a strong state, as Costa

Rica did. So it is most accurate to say that the viability of a democracy is dependent on whether its equality is shallow or deep, and whether it is well-institutionalized or simply a reward for winning an intra-elite electoral competition.

Third, to be a Pink Tide reformer is tricky. With the exception of Chávez, who has managed to maintain power despite alienating the elite, the rest of the Pink Tide governments have been more cautious about overturning entrenched power interests. In more idealized terms, Pink Tide governments attempt to create a democracy that is inclusive, and that means both the poor and the rich have a stake in the system. Zelaya created a zero-sum dynamic in which the poor gained at the expense of the wealthy. He attempted to redistribute resources and power downwards but, he lacked both a societal redistributive consensus to do so and a strong state with the capacity to implement his ideas.

Fourth, the international community was united in its opposition to the coup. Yet the small, poor, illegal government of Micheletti was able to resist international pressure to reinstate Zelaya. This raises a question: How genuine was that pressure? It was hardly robust. This is partly because the Honduran elite lobbied the US government, hiring law firms and public relations agencies to tell their side of the story. The campaign drew the support of several cold war veterans and Republicans, who blocked two state department appointments until President Obama lifted sanctions against Micheletti (Thompson and Nixon 2009). The crowning success of all that international pressure was an election in which the same two elite-dominated parties, with their narrow mandates, competed for power and were legally elected with a minority of the population legitimating the process. And even that took five months. Throughout these negotiations, the world did not decisively intervene to ensure that human rights abuses in Honduras were halted. This is an empowering message to the disaffected right as Latin America reforms its governance.

The neoliberal democracies of Central America are unacknowledged failures. With international support, they democratized and neoliberalized. Yet this restructuring has served to hide ongoing deprivation and oppression. An attempt to alter that reality resulted in a violent return to the status quo. The failure of these neoliberalized democracies brings to the fore a rarely recognized truth: democracy is more than elections, even if those elections are fair, contested, and regular, and operate to a degree within civil liberties and democratic procedures. Those factors are necessary but insufficient to produce a well-functioning democracy. Democracy must also be embedded in a densely organized civil society, social and economic equality, and a strong autonomous state. Democracy must have a supporting political culture, political structures, and political economy. If that occurs, then democracy becomes a development of the individual and the community, the political and the economic.

NOTES

1 There are a host of databases outlining the rural/urban divide, compliance with international treaties, national income accounts, forms of employment, maternal mortality, environmental resources, and so on. The lacuna is an accurate and sophisticated measurement of civil society organizations and citizen participation, so that analysts might have an idea of the density of civil society. However, given the sheer size of civil society and its inchoate nature, accurate data are almost impossible to find. The best that can be achieved is a counting of the NGOs and their constituents. Since NGOs are strongly shaped by international actors and the middle class, this approach is too inaccurate. Even for the data tables listed here, it would be unwise to rely too much on their statistics and the original database and methodology should be consulted for more information.

2 These statistics do not reflect the increase in murders in Mexico as a result of the war between the Mexican state and drug traffickers, which has killed over 6,000 people per annum since it began in 2006.

3 Seligson (2001, 106) compares national myths, juxtaposing Costa Rica's commitment to democracy to Chile's celebration of its armed forces and Mexico's celebration of its revolution.

4 As those protesting DR-CAFTA predicted, WOLA (2009) found that with the exception of Costa Rica, the rest of the signatory nations had declining labor practices. "Rather than improving labor conditions as a result of the trade agreements, as proponents argued, governments have violated the trade agreements by failing to guarantee internationally recognized workers rights and introducing legislation that reduces labor rights" (20). It also quoted the ILO statement that Central America is now the most dangerous place in the world to be a labor organizer (12).

5 An analysis of Ecuador's reforms is beyond the scope of this book.

6 Buxton (2009) notes that since Chávez lost the 2007 referendum, he has been cultivating labor union support to bolster his popularity. This strategy is consistent with populism.

7 Two-term presidents exist in Colombia, Costa Rica, Venezuela, Nicaragua, and Ecuador, and assist in promoting good governance.

REFERENCES

Bertelsmann Transformation Index. 2008. *Bertelsmann Transformation Index 2008: Political Management in International Comparison*. June 10, 2010. bertelsmann-transformation-index.de/fileadmin/pdf/Anlagen_BTI_2008/ BTI_2008_Ranking_EN.pdf.

Buxton, Julia. 2009. "Venezuela: The Political Evolution of Bolivarianism." *Reclaiming Latin America: Experiments in Radical Social Democracy*. Ed. Geraldine Lievesley and Steve Ludlam. London: Zed Books. 57–74.

Camp, Roderic Ai. 2001. *Citizen Views of Democracy in Latin America*. Pittsburgh: University of Pittsburgh Press.

Centano, Miguel Angel. 2002. *Blood and Debt: War and the Nation-State in Latin America*. University Park: Pennsylvania State University Press.

Central Intelligence Bureau (CIA). 2009. *CIA World Factbook: Distribution of Family Income–Gini Index*. June 18, 2010. www.cia.gov/library/publications/the-world-factbook/fields/2172.html.

Collier, Paul. 2009. *Wars, Guns and Votes: Democracy in Dangerous Places*. London: The Botley Head.

ECLAC. 2007a. *Statistical Yearbook for Latin America and the Caribbean 2007*. Washington, DC: ECLAC.

———. 2007b. *Social Expenditure Database*. June 10, 2010. website.eclac.cl/sisgen/consultaintegrada.asp date.

———. 2007c. *ECLAC Information Services Press Release: Public Social Expenditure Shows Per Capita Growth of 10% Between 2002 and 2005*. June 10, 2010. www.eclac.org/cgibin/getProd.asp?xml=/prensa/noticias/comunicados/2/30362/P30362.xml&xsl=/prensa/tpl-i/p6f.xsl&base=/uruguay/tpl/top-bottom.xslt.

———. 2008. *Report: Social Panorama of Latin America 2008*. June 10, 2010. www.eclac.org/publications/xml/3/34733/PST_2008-SintesisLanzamiento.pdf.

———. 2009a. *Report: Social Panorama of Latin America 2009*. Washington, DC: ECLAC.

———. 2009b. *Preliminary Overview of the Economies of Latin America and the Caribbean 2009*. Washington, DC: ECLAC.

———. 2009c. *International Trade in Latin America and the Caribbean 2009: Crisis and Recovery*. Washington, DC. ECLAC.

Filgueira, Fernando. 2007. "The Latin American Social States: Critical Junctures and Critical Choices." *Democracy and Social Policy*. Ed. Yusef Bangura. New York: Palgrave MacMillan. 136–63.

Inside Costa Rica. 2010. "Solís and Guevara Concede Defeat Early." February 8. February 8, 2010. www.insidecostarica.com/dailynews/2010/february/08/costa-rica-10020803.htm.

International Monetary Fund. 2009. *World Economic Outlook: Sustaining the Recovery*. October 2009. June 18, 2010. www.imf.org/external/pubs/ft/weo/2009/02/index.htm.

Latinobarómetro. 2008. *Informe 2008: Opinion Pública Latinoamericana*. November 14, 2008. June 18, 2010. www.latinobarometro.org/docs/INFORME_LATINOBAROMETRO_2008.pdf.

Malkin, Elisabeth. 2010. "Costa Rica: Female Leader Elected." *New York Times*. February 8: A11.

Organization of Economic Cooperation and Development (OECD). 2008. *Revenue Statistics 1965–2007*. June 18, 2010. www.oecd.org./dataoecd/48/27/41498733.pdf.

Pan American Health Organization, Health Analysis and Statistics Unit. 2007. *Core Health Data Initiative; Technical Health Information System*. Washington, DC: PAHO. June 18, 2010. www.paho.org/English/SHA/coredata/tabulator/newsq/Tabulator.asp.

Przeworski, Adam, Michael E. Alvarez, Jose Antonio Cheibub, and Fernando Limongi. 2000. *Democracy and Development*. Cambridge: Cambridge University Press.

Romero, Simon. 2009. "Chávez's Influence Wanes Along with Oil Revenues." *International Herald Tribune*. May 20: 15.

Seligson, Mitchel A. 2001. "Costa Rican Exceptionalism: Why Ticos are Different." *Citizen Views of Democracy in Latin America.* Ed. Roderic Ai Camp. Pittsburgh: University of Pittsburgh Press. 90–106.

——. 2005. "Democracy on Ice: The Multiple Challenges of Guatemala's Peace Process." *The Third Wave of Democratization in Latin America.* Ed. Frances Hagopian and Scott Mainwaring. Cambridge: Cambridge University Press. 202–31.

Stahler-Sholk, Richard, Harry E. Vanden, and Glen David Kuecker. 2007. "Globalizing Resistance: The New Politics of Social Movements in Latin America." *Latin American Perspectives* 34(5): 5–16.

Teichman, Judith. 2008. "Redistributive Conflict and Social Policy in Latin America." *World Development* 36(3): 446–60.

Thompson, Ginger, and Ron Nixon. 2009. "Leader Ousted, Honduras Hires US Lobbyists." *New York Times.* October 8: A1.

Transparency International. 2008. *Corruption Perceptions Index.* June 18, 2010. www. transparency.org/policy_research/surveys_indices/cpi/2008.

United Nations Development Programme. 2006. *Human Development Report 2006: Beyond Scarcity: Power, Poverty and the Global Water Crisis.* June 18, 2010. hdr. undp.org/en/reports/global/hdr2006.

Washington Office on Latin America. 2009. *DR-CAFTA and Worker's Rights: Moving from Paper to Practice.* Washington, DC: WOLA.

World Bank. 2010. "World Development Indicators database. World Bank Data Catalog: Databases/Tables: Gross National Income per capita Purchasing Power Parities, April 19, 2010." June 18, 2010. http://siteresources.worldbank.org/ DATASTATISTICS/RESOURCES?GNIPC.pdf.

World Bank. 2010. "Honduras: Data Profile." June 18, 2010. http//ddpext.worldbank. org/ext/ddpreports/ViewShareReport?REPORT_ID=9147&REQUEST_TYPE=VIE WADVANCED&DIMENSIONS=100.

NOTES ON CONTRIBUTORS

Katherine Isbester, a former Adjunct Political Science Professor at the University of Toronto, is now an independent scholar in London, England. She is a consultant on development issues and is the author of *Still Fighting: The Nicaraguan Women's Movement 1977–2000* (University of Pittsburgh Press, 2001).

Viviana Patroni is an Associate Professor at York University, Director of the Centre for Research on Latin America and the Caribbean, and Co-director of a Canadian-funded project supporting the development of a Latin American network for human rights. She publishes on Argentina, and her articles have appeared in the journals *Capital and Class* and *Research in Political Economy*. She is also coauthor of *Community Rights and Corporate Responsibility: Canadian Mining and Oil Rights in Latin America* (Between the Lines, 2006).

Lauren Phillips is an Assistant Professor at the London School of Economics and former Research Fellow at the Overseas Development Institute in the International Economic Development Group. She works on comparative political economy and the politics of money in Latin America. She has written many policy-relevant papers for the Overseas Development Institute, the International Monetary Fund's Group of 24, and other European institutions.

Roberta Rice is an Assistant Professor at the University of Toronto, Scarborough. Her work has appeared in the *Latin American Research Review* and the *Canadian Journal of Latin American and Caribbean Studies.* She has carried out extensive fieldwork in Bolivia, Chile, Ecuador, and Peru. Her forthcoming book with University of Arizona Press will focus on indigenous and popular protest in Latin America.

Judith Teichman is a Professor of Political Science at the University of Toronto. She has written extensively on Mexico, Argentina, and Chile. Her publications include *The Politics of Freeing Markets in Latin America: Mexico, Argentina, Chile* (University of North Carolina Press, 2001); *Policy-Making in Mexico: From Boom to Crisis* (Westview Press, 1998); and *Privatization and Change in Mexico* (University of Pittsburgh Press, 1996). She is the coauthor of *Social Democracy in the Global Periphery: Origins, Challenges, Prospects* (Cambridge University Press, 2006).

INDEX